CHALLENGE TO THE COURT

Challenge to the Court

SOCIAL SCIENTISTS
AND THE DEFENSE OF SEGREGATION
1954–1966

I. A. Newby

REVISED EDITION
WITH COMMENTARIES BY

A. James Gregor
Frank C. J. McGurk
R. T. Osborne
Wesley Critz George
R. Gayre
Carleton Putnam
Nathaniel Weyl
Ernest van den Haag

LOUISIANA STATE UNIVERSITY PRESS / BATON ROUGE

To the memory of
my mother

NOMIE BELL FLOYD NEWBY

1899–1965

She would not have agreed with all the views expressed in this study. She would, however, have been proud of my accomplishment in expressing them.

Copyright © 1967 and 1969 by
Louisiana State University Press
Library of Congress Catalog Card Number: 69–17623
SBN 8071–0628–3
Manufactured in the United States of America by
The Colonial Press Inc., Clinton, Massachusetts

A Note from the Publisher

When *Challenge to the Court* was first published in 1967, it was anticipated that some of the persons whose writings were most prominently discussed therein would be heard from. They were. Some simply challenged the author's point of view; others felt they had been misinterpreted and maligned. On the theory that the right of rebuttal is as applicable to book as to magazine publication (if not as practical), the publisher and the author decided to invite Mr. Newby's major antagonists to have their say. Appended to this edition, then, are "letters to the editor" from those who responded and (also in the tradition of the journal) a final word from the author.

PREFACE

The Negro's struggle for equality is one of the heroic episodes in American history. It rightly claims the attention of the American people, and a large measure of their support, too. Americans of both races contribute their resources and energies to this struggle, vote for public officials sympathetic to the Negro's cause, and make heroes of men as diverse as Martin Luther King, John Lewis, and James Baldwin. They debate the civil rights struggle, its strategy and tactics; they read about it, write about it, and make it an object of perpetual concern.

All this is as it should be. The attention heaped upon the civil rights movement has made the American people, or at least the most concerned among them, aware of the Negro's plight and appreciative of his protest. But in their understandable preoccupation with the problems and aspirations of Negroes, Americans too often neglect the other side of the story. They too often ignore segregationists, or, more accurately, too hurriedly dismiss them as nothing more than unreasoning demagogues or cruel and selfish bigots. As a result they misunderstand and underestimate their adversary. Epithets such as "demagogue" and "bigot" may in fact be apt descriptions of many segregationists, but name-calling is an unsatisfactory substitute for thoughtful analysis of the segregationist mind. It is also unconducive to understanding the strength and tenacity of anti-Negro ideas in America. In their zeal to further the Negro's cause, the national press, the communications media, and other molders of mass opinion invariably present segregationists and their ideas in the worst possible light, and more often than not select irrational persons with a Ku Klux mentality to present the anti-Negro point of view. The result is to ridicule segregationists to the amusement and satisfaction of integrationists, but not to help Americans understand the appeal of racist ideas or the tenacity with which white Southerners cling to those ideas. Nor does it induce segregationists to question their own racial views.

This is not to suggest that segregationists be treated with indulgence. After all, they often advocate racial policies of a most callous and exploitative kind, and would deny to Negroes many of the rights and privileges inherent in American citizenship. But this is not the point. Regardless of the offensiveness of the ideas they profess and the policies they advocate, segregationists must be taken more seriously if they are to be understood. Racist ideas are as rational, systematic, and convincing to segregationists as equalitarian ideas are to integrationists. Yet if racial harmony is to be achieved in this country, those racist ideas must be exploded and the racial attitudes of segregationists radically changed. To do this, anti-Negro thought must be understood, which is to say it must be systematically analyzed and subjected unemotionally to tests of logic, reason, history, and science. And the process must be continuous. It is not enough to say that racist ideas are invalid; it is more important to demonstrate their rationale, their logic, their premises, and spell out their implications for American democracy as well as for racial policy. In this way their weaknesses will become apparent and their appeal, hopefully, diminished. Nor is it enough to say that racist ideas have already been refuted or that they fall from their own absurdity, although they have been refuted (or revealed to be value judgments which permit no objective refutation) and many of them are patently absurd. Anti-Negro literature circulates widely among segregationists, who accept much of it at face value and from it derive assurances that their racial policies are correct. One of the integrationists' most pressing tasks is, or should be, to analyze and evaluate that literature, challenge its premises, logic, and data, and point out its real nature to segregationists.

In this spirit I offer this study. Proponents of civil rights and racial integration have, I believe, done their cause a disservice by giving too little attention to anti-Negro ideas and the workings of the segregationist mind. Yet it is those ideas which motivate segregationists and explain their implacable opposition to racial integration. As a practical matter, or so it seems to me, segregationists are segregationists because they are convinced, first, that Negroes are racially inferior to whites, and, second, that this alleged inferiority is genetically fixed and transmitted by heredity. They thus believe that racial intermixture, which they assume is the logical consequence of social integration, will be a racial—and national—catastrophe. Of course, the psychological and sociological dynamics behind Southern racism are profound and complex and are the ultimate source of anti-Negro racism. But the conviction that Negroes are inferior—and the parallel one that whites are superior—is the immediate motive force behind segregation.

Anti-Negro thought is an amalgam of history, religion, and science reinforced by a reactionary social philosophy and a backward-looking view of politics and economics. The relative significance of these factors has differed from time to time, as has the intensity with which segregationists defend their position, but each has endured as an element of racist thinking. In recent years one of the most important and curious features of anti-Negro thought has been a renascence of scientific racism, of the use of science and social science to defend racial segregation. This development, an outgrowth of the Supreme Court's use of psychological and sociological authorities in the decision of *Brown v. Board of Education of Topeka* (1954), is a little-known facet of the racial controversies which now engross this nation, but it is an important element in the South's efforts to prevent racial integration, especially in public schools.

The purpose of this study is to describe the use of science by segregationists since 1954 and to analyze the ideas and the literature which scientific racists now use to defend segregation. To do this, I have focused upon the small group of academic social scientists who are largely responsible for the recent resurgence of scientific racism, and I have discussed their major works in some detail. Since their effort was a direct response to the Brown decision, I felt obliged to discuss the social science evidence presented in the Brown cases. Segregationists use science for two reasons, one of them general—to justify racial segregation—and the other specific—to overturn the Brown decision—and I have emphasized both. I have stressed the *ideas* of scientific racism rather than the uses which segregationists made of those ideas, for my primary objective was to illuminate the segregationist mind and to understand why some Americans so tenaciously defend discriminatory racial policies. Understanding the segregationist mind will not eliminate the necessity for continued Negro protest, nor remove the need for "outside" pressure upon the white South. It will, however, give integrationists a better idea of what it is that they shall overcome.

It seems appropriate at the outset to comment upon the problem of personal bias or "prejudice." In writing this study I found it necessary to play the dual role of historian and commentator. In the former, I sought to relate as straightforwardly as possible the major ideas of scientific racism, and to do so in a factual, objective manner. In the latter, I attempted to discuss and evaluate those ideas (most of which I consider scientifically unsound and socially unwise) within the framework of what seems to me to be sound social science and necessary social policy. In this, I was unable (and, indeed, rather unwilling) to avoid all subjective judgment. In any case, I endeavored to keep the two roles separate and prevent my own convictions from interfering with an accurate presentation of the ideas of scientific racists. The reader must judge for himself the extent to which I succeeded.

In the final analysis, one's attitude toward racial integration, racial equality, interracial marriage, and a multitude of related subjects rests upon basic assumptions and value judgments concerning such debatable issues as human nature, heredity and environment, the nature of democracy, the relationship of the individual to society, and, indeed, the nature and significance of race itself. To say that an individual is "prejudiced" is to say, in part at least, that his assumptions concerning these subjects differ from one's own. Scientific racism, the chief concern of this study, rests largely upon several such assumptions or value judgments—that human nature is fixed by heredity and immune to environment, that behavior characteristics (morality, criminality, ethics) as well as intelligence are genetically determined and directly related to race, that racial differences are relevant to the formulation of public policy, that race, in short, is the basic reality of life.

Given the present state of scientific knowledge and methodology, these assumptions cannot be absolutely disproven, and this, of course, is a major source of strength for those who accept them. Scientific racists are convinced that the assumptions are valid, or probably valid, and base their conviction on what they consider the best available scientific evidence. Most social scientists, however, who are not racists and who reject the major ideas and value judgments of racism, believe those assumptions are false, or largely false, and they, too, base their position on what they accept as "the teachings of modern scientific authority." The disagreement between scientific racists and their critics is thus first of all a disagreement between rival value systems, and the disagreement cannot, unfortunately, be resolved to the satisfaction of everyone by an appeal to objective scientific data. The available data are subject to different interpretations, even by well-meaning men. There is a body of data which *may* be interpreted as evidence of racial inequality, just as there are other data which seem clearly to indicate that races are equal, or potentially equal. Scientific evidence, however, is only one part of a larger whole, and here the logic of the situation seems clearly to favor equalitarians. Scientific racists look to science for guidance in formulating public policy. However, constitutional, legal, and political factors, as well as democracy, justice, and human decency, would seem to be much more important than science in defining the civil rights of Negroes and their proper role in American life. A philosophy of race relations based exclusively upon science is clearly inadequate.

I do not mean to say or imply that the merits of the debate between scientific racists and equalitarians are purely relative, or that the merits depend exclusively upon the validity of the initial assumptions of each side. As this study will show, I believe emphatically that the mass of scientific evidence is such that it is reasonable to assume that races are approximately equal. I recognize, however, that innate racial equality has never been objectively demonstrated by scientists (and neither has innate racial inequality). I am convinced that considerations of racial equality or inequality are of little relevance to the basic issue involved in either the Brown decision or the civil rights struggle. The basic issue is the civil rights which Negroes are entitled to as American citizens, and those rights rest on constitutional guarantees, not scientific data.

Finally, a word about terminology. A major difficulty in writing about race is the problem of "loaded" terms. Segregationists reject as invidious such terms as "racism," "scientific racism," and "racist." As I have used it here, "racism" suggests a belief in innate racial inequality, including the corollaries of Negro inferiority and white superiority. However, most of the individuals discussed in this study insist that they are not racists, that they believe only in racial *differences*, not racial *inequality*. I have therefore applied the term "racist" to anyone who advocates racial policies such as segregation, civil disabilities against Negroes, and prohibition of racial intermarriage—policies which are meaningful only if the races are inherently unequal. A "racist" is thus anyone who believes in racial inequality and/or advocates the above racial policies, and a "scientific racist" is one whose racism rests chiefly upon science or pseudoscience. Virtually all the individuals described in this study as racists or scientific racists object to the descriptions and deny that they are racists.

I wish to express my appreciation to Professors Theodore Saloutos, Roger Daniels, and Ralph Turner of the University of California at Los Angeles, Professor Lawrence B. de Graaf of California State College at Fullerton, and Richard H. Levensky of Hollywood, California, each of whom read all or parts of the manuscript and offered many helpful suggestions for improving it. I alone am responsible for any errors which remain.

I. A. NEWBY

CONTENTS

CHALLENGE TO THE COURT

1

BEFORE THE BROWN DECISION

On May 17, 1954, the Supreme Court of the United States delivered an epochal opinion. On that date the Court issued its long-awaited decision in the series of cases [1] by which the National Association for the Advancement of Colored People had challenged

---

[1] *Briggs v. Elliott*, 95 F. Supp. 529 (E.D. S.C. 1951); *Brown v. Board of Education of Topeka*, 98 F. Supp. 797 (D. Kan. 1951); *Davis v. County Board of Prince Edward County*, 103 F. Supp. 337 (E.D. Va. 1951); *Gebhart v. Belton*, 87 A. 2d 862 (D. Del. 1951); and *Boling v. Sharpe*, 347 U.S. 497 (1954). The Supreme Court decision discussed here is *Brown v. Board of Education of Topeka*, 347 U.S. 483 (1954).

the constitutionality of racial segregation in the public schools of this country.

As Chief Justice Earl Warren read the decision to a hushed, crowded courtroom, its significance became immediately apparent. Flanked by the eight associate justices of the Court, each of whom endorsed the decision he was reading, Warren first surveyed the background of the cases, touching briefly upon the history of racial segregation and the role of public education in American life. He then examined the judicial history of the Fourteenth Amendment, emphasizing its relevance to public education. Finally, he reached the heart of the decision. "Does segregation of children in public schools solely on the basis of race, even though the physical facilities and other 'tangible' factors may be equal, deprive the children of the minority group of equal educational opportunities?" he asked, almost matter-of-factly. His answer was forthright: "We believe that it does." To segregate Negro pupils "from others of similar age and qualifications solely because of their race generates a feeling of inferiority as to their status in the community that may affect their hearts and minds in a way unlikely ever to be undone."

To support this interpretation Warren turned directly to the findings of a lower federal court in one of the cases at hand. "Segregation of white and colored children in public schools," the lower court had held in the case of *Brown v. Board of Education of Topeka,* "has a detrimental effect upon the colored children. The impact is greater when it has the sanction of the law; for the policy of separating the races is usually interpreted as denoting the inferiority of the Negro group. A sense of inferiority affects the motivation of a child to learn. Segregation with the sanction of law, therefore, has a tendency to retard the educational and mental development of Negro children and to deprive them of the benefits they would receive in a racially integrated school system."

This obviously is a statement of sociology or social psychology and not of law, but the Court made no attempt to conceal its reliance upon social science authority. On the contrary, the decision proceeded on a consciously psychological note. "Whatever may have been the extent of psychological knowledge of the time of Plessy v. Ferguson," [2] the Chief Justice continued, "this finding is amply

---

[2] *Plessy v. Ferguson,* 163 U.S. 537 (1896). This decision, which wrote the separate-but-equal concept into American law, was set aside by Brown.

supported by modern authority." To substantiate this sweeping statement, the Court inserted the famous footnote number eleven, around which a long and bitter controversy later swirled. The footnote, a list of references to some of the latest and most authoritative research on the effects of segregation on personality development, was an integral part of the Brown decision, and represented an effort by the Court to buttress its legal case with expert nonlegal authority. Although some supporters of the decision later attempted to play down the footnote and dismiss it as an unimportant aside by the Court, it was clearly intended to supplement the legal basis of the decision, and to blunt the adverse reactions the decision was expected to produce. Enlarged to include complete citations, the footnote read as follows:

Kenneth B. Clark, *Effects of Prejudice and Discrimination on Personality Development* (Midcentury White House Conference on Children and Youth, 1950) ; Helen Leland Witmer and Ruth Kotinsky, *Personality in the Making, The Fact-Finding Report of the Midcentury White House Conference on Youth and Children* (New York: Harper and Brothers, 1952) , Chapter VI, "The Effects of Prejudice and Discrimination," 135–58; Max Deutscher and Isidor Chein, "The Psychological Effects of Enforced Segregation: A Survey of Social Science Opinion," *Journal of Psychology,* XXVI (October 1948) , 259–87; Isidor Chein, "What Are the Psychological Effects of Segregation Under Conditions of Equal Facilities?" *International Journal of Opinion and Attitude Research,* III (Summer 1949) , 229–34; Theodore Brameld, "Educational Costs," in *Discrimination and National Welfare* (New York: Harper and Brothers, 1949) , ed. Robert M. MacIver, 44–48; E. Franklin Frazier, *The Negro in the United States* (New York: Macmillan, 1949) , 647–781. And see generally Gunnar Myrdal, *An American Dilemma* (New York: Harper and Row, 1944) .

On the basis of these authorities and a mass of expert testimony in the lower courts, the Supreme Court concluded that "separate but equal" has no place in the field of public education. "Separate educational facilities," the Justices ruled, "are inherently unequal." [3]

As anticipated, the decision evoked an outcry against the Court. One of a series of "liberal" decisions which have adapted American law and constitutional interpretation to recent socioeconomic and technological changes, the Brown ruling was denounced by a multitude of critics—segregationists, advocates of states rights,

[3] *Brown v. Board of Education,* 347 U.S. 483 (1954) . The text and footnotes of the decision are reproduced in Kenneth Clark, *Prejudice and Your Child* (2nd ed.; Boston, 1963) , 156–65.

strict constitutionalists, and a varied group of social and political conservatives. The decision was a milestone in the Negro's stride toward equality, and as such was especially offensive to segregationists and white supremacists. However, the Court's inclusion of social science authority and its implicit endorsement of the testimony of social scientists who testified for the NAACP in the lower courts, introduced a novel element in the response to the decision.

The segregationists' immediate reaction was shock and dismay, but after recovering their composure they began a broad, concerted counterattack. Initially, they stressed legal and constitutional factors, accusing the Court of ignoring the principle of *stare decisis* and resorting to judge-made law. Southern legislatures passed interposition resolutions designed to nullify the Brown decision by 'interposing' the authority of the states between their citizens and the federal government. Lawyers and politicians "exposed" the Fourteenth Amendment and questioned the legality of its inclusion in the Constitution. A multitude of new laws and ordinances appeared upon the statute books in the South, each in some way designed to defy the Court and frustrate the Negro's achievement of equality. "Respectable" segregationists organized State Sovereignty Commissions or Citizens' Councils, seeking thereby to avoid the image of bigotry and violence which attached to the Ku Klux Klan and compromised its effectiveness. The Citizens' Councils, "uptown Klans" in Thurgood Marshall's telling phrase, channeled Southern energies into economic boycotts, thought control, and community pressures for conformity. They watchdogged public leaders, both elected and otherwise, purged school books of unacceptable ideas, and warned the South and the nation that integration would be a calamity. As part of a general educational or propaganda effort, which was by no means confined to Citizens' Councils, though their leadership was important, segregationists attacked the social science—and social scientists—which the Court utilized in the Brown decision.

The attack was multifold. It was in part negative: an effort to undermine the scientific validity and personal integrity of authorities cited by the Court. It was in part positive: an effort to provide an alternative body of scientific data sufficient in quantity and authority to convince the skeptical that there are rational, scientific justifications for racial segregation. To achieve these ends, a small but articulate cadre of social scientists, who were convinced of the desirability of segregation, especially in "delicate" areas of social relations, began soon after 1954 to formulate a scientific defense of segregation. Their effort inevitably provoked a controversy with other social scientists. Though the controversy involved men of science on both sides, it was waged with a vehemence and intensity dismaying to the layman. The displays of public denunciation and name-calling to which both sides on occasion resorted are timely illustrations of the problems involved in the study of man and society, and demonstrate anew the difficulty man has in studying himself objectively. The two groups approached their studies with divergent assumptions about the concept of race and with differing views on the social implications of race. Segregationists and scientific racists stressed its importance; integrationists and equalitarians played it down. As a result, the two groups drew basically different conclusions, not only from their own research but from general scientific knowledge in the field of race. In every case, apparently, researchers on the subject of race reached conclusions which confirmed their initial assumptions. There seems to have been no instance of a segregationist scientist whose research and study led him to alter his views toward race in any fundamental way. Likewise, no equalitarian scientist was ever led to question his basic assumptions as a result of study and experimentation. If the researcher was convinced at the outset that racial differences are so important that social segregation and racial purity are vital to national survival, his research reinforced that conviction. If, on the other hand, he was convinced that racial differences are superficial and irrelevant to public policy, this conviction was reaffirmed by his research.

Social scientists study controversial and troublesome things: the origin and nature of racial characteristics, the workings of the mechanism of inheritance, the relative importance of heredity and environment, the problems of interracial contact and conflict. The very nature of such subjects makes it impossible for social scientists to speak with the assurance of chemists or physicists. The social scientist must frequently qualify even his most important conclusions. "As far as we now know," "the preponderance of scientific opinion holds," "we can not speak on this point with absolute certainty," "on the basis of this experiment"—such statements appear regularly in his writings. He must, if he is honest, admit that the precise nature of racial differences is not always understood, that the workings of inheritance are not precisely known, that in a host of similar vital areas scientific knowledge is incomplete.

And this is the heart of the problem. The areas of limited

knowledge provide an opening for speculators. They enable both racists and integrationists to inject a substantial element of interpretation, of value judgment, into the most rigorous social science experimentation. In the social sciences, data often mean different things to different men, and the racist (or, again, the integrationist) is enabled thereby to utilize valid data in invalid ways. When a racist is also a social scientist who speaks under an academic or scientific mantle, his authority is notably enhanced, not only among designing bigots but among unsophisticated laymen as well. For this reason scientific racists are important spokesmen for racist causes.

To repeat a truism, the twentieth century is an age of science and education, and any theory of social relations which clothes itself in scientific authority and academic respectability is thereby greatly strengthened. The recent outpouring of scientific racism is evidence aplenty of the segregationists' recognition of this fact. Today a significant element among their number relies chiefly upon science instead of states rights or strict constitutionalism in attacking integration. Exploiting a widespread fear of the possible consequences of racial integration, they tell white Americans that "science" has proven that races are unequal, that Negroes are inferior to whites, and that racial inequality is perpetrated by heredity. They tell them also that integrated schools are but a prelude to the Negro's real goal, racial intermarriage, which is itself a preliminary to mongrelizing the American people and destroying American civilization.

Scientific racism is not a new phenomenon. The Negro's "place" in this country, whether in or out of the South, whether slavery or segregation, has always been based, in part at least, upon science or pseudoscience, and, until recently, scientific racism always had wide support among scientists. Before the Civil War, science was a major ingredient in proslavery thinking.[4] Such dissimilar scientists as Josiah Nott of Alabama, Samuel George Norton of Philadelphia, and Louis Agassiz of Harvard were convinced that Negroes are innately inferior to white men, and based their convictions on the most up-to-date scientific authority. Supported by the latest research and most authoritative speculation in anthropology and anthropometry—sciences which study racial origins and compara-

4 William Stanton, *The Leopard's Spots, Scientific Attitudes toward Race in America, 1815–1859* (Chicago, 1960) .

tive racial differences—and even phrenology, egyptology, and biblical criticism, ideas of racial inequality enjoyed complete scientific respectability before the Civil War. What is equally important, George Fitzhugh, Thomas R. Dew, and a host of other proslavery spokesmen took these ideas and upon them erected a social philosophy, a "sociology" resting on the cornerstones of slavery and racial inequality.[5]

Nor were scientific attitudes toward race significantly altered by emancipation of the slaves or by Reconstruction efforts to give equality to the freedmen. As Professor Thomas F. Gossett has recently shown, the mainstream of scientific thought after 1865 continued to accept racial inequality and Negro inferiority as undisputed facts.[6] And Darwin's evolutionary hypothesis brought new authority to racist opinion. To older arguments of racial inequality it added the idea that racial characteristics are adaptations to the environment in which the race evolved. In the Negro's case, this meant adaptations to the hot, steaming jungles of tropical Africa. To protect themselves from the burning sun, so this idea ran, Negroes developed thick, dark skin, a thick skull, woolly, matted hair, and a capacity for perspiring profusely. This hot, humid environment prevented the development of superior racial qualities. Food was plentiful and readily obtainable; shelter and clothing were unnecessary, or virtually so. As a result, life was easy and Negroes were not forced to develop the qualities which a more rigorous environment produced in other races. The white man evolved in the challenging, invigorating climate of the far north, where he was forced to think for himself, to plan for tomorrow, to reason, to organize, to brave the elements, to conquer nature. In his case evolution produced constant improvement and, ultimately, superiority. The Negro, however, stagnated.

In the half century after Reconstruction several new scientific disciplines also added to the growing authority of scientific racism. Psychology and sociology, joined presently by eugenics and genetics,

5 See George Fitzhugh, *Sociology for the South* (Richmond, 1854) and *Cannibals All; or Slaves Without Masters* (Richmond, 1857); Henry Hughes, *A Treatise on Sociology* (Philadelphia, 1859); Thomas R. Dew and others, *Pro-Slavery Arguments as Maintained by the Most Distinguished Writers of the Southern States* (Charleston, 1852).

6 Thomas F. Gossett, *Race, The History of an Idea in America* (Dallas, 1963), 253–86.

opened whole new vistas in the study of race, and soon they too were offering "proof" of racial inequality and Negro inferiority, reinforcing the evidence of anthropology, ethnology, anatomy, and physiology. In all of these disciplines notable scientific advances occurred in the late nineteenth and early twentieth centuries. It is a striking and chastening fact that the remarkable progress made in this period in scientific knowledge and methodology increased rather than destroyed the prestige and authority of racism.[7]

The net effect was that men of science in the early twentieth century found racist ideas generally acceptable. As applied to Negroes, those ideas went something like this: *Race* is not merely a convenient means of grouping members of the human family; it is instead the ultimate fact of life. To speak of individual traits and potentialities is but to speak of racial traits and potentialities. Racial (individual) characteristics are permanent and unchangeable except by the slow, sure workings of evolution. The physical manifestations of race can be isolated, measured, and used to define racial groupings. Head shape, cephalic index, brain size, facial prognathism, skin color, hair texture—such features are racially determined, and individually or collectively reflect the relative quality of different races. The significance of race, however, is not limited to physical features. Indeed, differences of mentality and psychology are greater than physical differences, and far more important. Racial instincts account for the childishness, joviality, irresponsibility, and other traits which are popularly attributed to the Negro.

Whether physical or psychological, however, racial characteristics were products of centuries of evolution during which the races were isolated from each other. This long period of intraracial inbreeding, undisturbed by "foreign" genes from other races, produced genetic harmony, an equilibrium in the genetic characteristics of the individual and the race. Preserved and transmitted by heredity, this equilibrium is upset by the injection of new and alien genes, which occurs when races interbreed. The halfbreed, a mixture of discordant genes, lacks genetic harmony, and is likely to be unstable and malcontented. The mulatto, the offspring of white

[7] These ideas are discussed more completely in I. A. Newby, *Jim Crow's Defense, Anti-Negro Thought in America, 1900–1930* (Baton Rouge, 1965), 19–51.

and Negro intermixture, is usually erratic, high strung, nervous, troublesome—and a leader of "equality" movements.

The racial mongrel, however, is only one result, although a tragic one, of the inexorable workings of genetic laws. Morality, social behavior, physical constitution are also genetically determined, or largely so. The high rates of illegitimacy, broken families, unemployment, murder, rape, crimes of violence, and even tuberculosis, among Negroes are outward manifestations of inborn qualities. Put another way, the Negro's position in American life, whether social, economic, or political, is the logical and inevitable result of his racial inferiority. Because of limitations inherent in his nature, he is unable to appreciate or derive full benefit from Caucasian civilization, the institutions of which are products of the white man's unique racial genius. Political democracy, constitutionalism, Christianity, free enterprise economics, modern technology are beyond the limits of the Negro's racial capacity, and he cannot compete in a society based upon them.

Carried to a logical conclusion, these ideas posit a direct correlation between race and civilization, a thesis which has been central to racist thought since Gobineau.[8] Each race, so the thesis runs, creates its own civilization, a civilization which expresses or reflects its unique racial genius. To the extent that races differ in this innate genius, so will the civilizations they create differ, and to that extent one race will be unable to absorb the civilization of another. Civilization is, in short, a product of race, that is, of genetic inheritance, and no civilization can survive large scale racial intermixture. Indeed, mongrelization will destroy a civilization more thoroughly than conquering armies, as the history of Greece and Rome vividly proves. Such examples are perpetual reminders of an inexorable law: when mixed, racial characteristics, like water, seek the lowest possible level. White-Negro intermixture will thus result in the inundation of superior white genes in a flood of inferior black genes.

The usefulness of these ideas to white supremacists, especially in the South, is apparent. Segregation, subjection, ignorance, and disfranchisement, they assert, are natural states for the Negro.

8 Gobineau, Arthur de, *The Inequality of Human Races,* trans. Adrian Collins (London, 1915); originally published as *Essai sur l'Inegalite des Races Humaines* (4 vols.; Paris, 1853–55).

Abolishing racial distinctions, especially social and political distinctions, only risks destruction of American civilization, at least where Negroes are congregated in large numbers. To provide Negro and white children with the same education programs makes a mockery of the education process. The Negro's intelligence is too low, his brain is too small, too primitive, too generalized to enable him to master an education program adapted to the capacities of a superior race. Public policy, whether it involves education, the right to vote, social relations, or legal status must reflect racial realities, which is to say it must reflect scientific truth. Segregation and attendant policies do this, or so segregationists claimed. In their view segregation is grounded in the authoritative principles of sociology, psychology, anthropology, and genetics and acknowledges the principles of Darwin and Herbert Spencer. And what scientists endorse as good policy, so also do clergymen, educators, historians, political scientists. "Science," insisted segregationists, merely reinforces what the Bible suggests, what history illustrates, what experience makes manifest—that Negroes are inferior to Caucasians and are likely to remain so in the foreseeable future.

Thus read the scientific racism of the early twentieth century. Significantly, every one of the above ideas, though often embellished by new authority or restated in more plausible and sophisticated language, has reappeared in racist literature since 1954.

Such ideas do not exist in a vacuum. On the contrary, they graphically illustrate the social philosophy of those who accept them, a social philosophy based almost exclusively on racial determinism. One cannot accept the "fact" that Negroes are racially inferior without also accepting social, educational, and political policies which reflect that "fact." As a matter of course, the architects of Southern race policies have always based their racial ideas to one degree or another upon "science," and have assiduously cultivated "authorities" to serve this purpose. It was the fashion among opponents of the Brown decision to decry the Court's use of social science, and to look upon "sociological jurisprudence" as another example of the modern tendency to discard time-honored and proven principles. It all began, they declared, when Louis Brandeis introduced extraneous evidence in his "sociological brief" in *Muller v. Oregon* (1908), and the Supreme Court used his brief, which detailed the harmful effects of long hours on working women, as one justification for upholding the constitutionality of an Oregon law limiting the work day of women to ten hours.

"Sociological jurisprudence," however, goes back much further than 1954 or 1908. The use of sociological evidence has always been implicit, if not explicit, in the South's (and the nation's) treatment of Negroes, whether in or out of the courts. Certainly the Dred Scott decision conformed to pro-slavery "sociology," as did the long list of Supreme Court decisions which defined the Negro's place in this country after the Civil War. In ruling that racial discrimination in public accommodations is not a violation of the Fourteenth Amendment, the Supreme Court in 1883 rejected the Negroes' contention that such discrimination implies a condition of servitude or inferiority for members of their race. "Can the act of a mere individual," asked the Court in the *Civil Rights Cases* of that year, "the owner of the inn, the public conveyance, or place of amusement, refusing the accommodation, be justly regarded as imposing any badge of slavery or servitude upon the applicant?" Certainly not, was the answer. Free Negroes before the Civil War had suffered a multitude of legal, social, and political restrictions, yet nobody had considered such restrictions a mark of servitude or slavery. "No one," the Court said, "thought that it was any invasion of his personal status as a freeman because he was not admitted to all the privileges enjoyed by white citizens, or because he was subjected to discriminations in the enjoyment of accommodations in inns, public conveyances and places of amusement. Mere discriminations on account of race or color were not regarded as badges of slavery." [9] Nor could they be so regarded in 1883. Whatever the legal and constitutional merits of this decision, it conformed nicely to the sociology of white supremacists.

Even more revealing was the decision in *Plessy v. Ferguson* (1896), a decision which segregationists repeatedly praised while denouncing the use of social science in the Brown ruling. As a recent study points out, "sociological and psychological theories controlled the Court's decision" in the Plessy case. That decision, writes Barton J. Bernstein, in the *Journal of Negro History*, "wrote conservative theory and the prevailing social science 'truths' into law. The court explained that the standard of reasonableness is determined 'with reference to the established usages, customs, and traditions of the people. . . . Law is reasonable when it follows custom." [10]

9 *Civil Rights Cases,* 109 U.S. 3; 3 S. Ct. 18.
10 Barton J. Bernstein, "Plessy v. Ferguson: Conservative Sociological Jurisprudence," *Journal of Negro History,* XLVIII (July, 1963), 196–205.

The issues in Plessy were similar to those in the Brown cases fifty-eight years later: Does enforced separation of the races stamp Negroes with a badge of inferiority? Are segregated facilities inherently unequal? Are they in the final analysis intended to remind the Negro in a degrading and humiliating way that his is a race apart, that associating with him even in public places is repulsive and demeaning to whites? The Court answered these questions with an emphatic "No," and incorporated in its answer a generous sprinkling of sociological theory. The Plessy decision thus merits quoting at length:

> The case reduced itself to the question whether the statute of Louisiana [requiring segregated railroad cars] is a reasonable regulation, and with respect to this there must necessarily be a large discretion on the part of the legislature. In determining the question of reasonableness it is at liberty to act with reference to the estimated usages, customs and traditions of the people, and with a view to the promotion of their comfort, and the preservation of the public peace and good order. Gauged by this standard, we cannot say that a law which authorizes or even requires the separation of the two races in public conveyances is unreasonable, or more obnoxious to the Fourteenth Amendment than the acts of Congress requiring separate schools for colored children in the District of Columbia. . . .
>
> We consider the underlying fallacy of the plaintiff's argument to consist in the assumption that the enforced separation of the two races stamps the colored race with a badge of inferiority. If this be so, it is not by reason of anything found in the act, but solely because the colored race chooses to put that construction upon it. . . . The argument . . . assumes that social prejudices may be overcome by legislation, and that equal rights cannot be secured to the Negro except by an enforced commingling of the two races. We cannot accept this proposition. If the two races are to meet upon terms of social equality, it must be the result of natural affinities, a mutual appreciation of each other's merits and a voluntary consent of individuals. . . . Legislation is powerless to eradicate racial instincts or to abolish distinctions based upon physical differences, and the attempt to do so can only result in accentuating the difficulties of the present situation. If the civil and political rights of both races be equal one cannot be inferior to the other civilly or politically. If one race be inferior to the other socially, the Constitution of the United States cannot put them upon the same plane.[11]

This is replete with the ideas of late-nineteenth-century social science. Law, it says, must follow established customs and usages, for as William Graham Sumner was then insisting, social mores are

11 *Plessy v. Ferguson,* 163 U.S. 537 (1896) .

immune to the tamperings of social theorists and reformers. There is, it also says, no assumption of inferiority inherent in segregation laws and customs. If any inferiority is involved, it exists in the minds of Negroes and not in the law itself. Besides, questions of racial inferiority and superiority are beyond the reach of law. Inferiority and superiority are earned; they can not be decreed by legislative enactment or judicial fiat. Nor can law eradicate racial instincts, a term which, incidentally, smacks more of psychology than of law. Nowhere was the Court's acceptance of late-nineteenth-century social science more explicit. Racial instincts, it said, are just that—instincts. They cannot be ignored or altered, and to attempt to do so is to invite trouble. The object of law, however, is to avoid trouble, even though this must sometimes be achieved over the objections of one part of the citizenry. This view of the law was quite narrow, and concerned form rather than substance. The law of Louisiana required segregation but did not, in the Court's opinion, permit discrimination or servitude or fix upon Negroes a badge of inferiority. The law, or so the Court interpreted it, prescribed legal equality. That was all it could do. Social relations and feelings of inferiority were beyond the law's concern.

The Plessy decision in particular and Southern race policies in general, then, reflected the social science of segregationists. For this reason their attack upon the use of expert testimony in the Brown decision appears paradoxical at first sight. Certainly everyone agrees that the law must be reasonable, that it must reflect the accumulating knowledge of mankind. Yet knowledge is just that—accumulating, growing, progressing—and to keep pace with it the law must evolve. Law, as even segregationists admit, is not static. Its meaning and uses change as society evolves. Certainly it must reflect scientific truth, for to deny such a principle is, presumably, to say that truth is irrelevant to law.[12]

The socio-legal views of segregationists who attacked the use of social science in the Brown decision were unambiguous. Segregationists admit that the law changes through evolution, that is, through interpretation and custom, but they insist that it can properly change only in specified ways and within exceedingly narrow limits. Since they are a minority in the nation and oppose the major trends of scientific opinion on the subjects of race and race

12 See the discussion on this point in Clark, *Prejudice and Your Child,* 206–35.

relations, they insist upon a strict interpretation of the Constitution, at least of those sections which serve their ends, and a rigid adherence to legal precedent. These, of course, are the methods best suited to preserve the constitutionality of policies which conform to their sociology. Their position is approximately this: Law must reflect scientific truth, but the social sciences are inexact, and the truth on racial topics is difficult to ascertain. In these areas the courts must use social science with the utmost caution, and recognize only those principles and data which are universally accepted. In cases in which there is any significant disagreement, legal precedent and strict constitutionalism must prevail. This will result in perpetuating racial policies which rest upon old (and, to integrationists, outmoded) social science data and theory. The old data and theory, however, are already incorporated into legal precedent and constitutional law, and need not be subjected to the careful scrutiny which newer data and theory must withstand. The burden of proof rests upon those who espouse the newer findings. The Supreme Court said in 1896 that segregation does not impose a mark of inferiority upon Negroes, and that segregated facilities are not inherently unequal. By virtue of this decision, segregationist sociology was the law of the land, and the law of the land cannot be changed for light and transient causes. The Plessy verdict can be set aside only when integrationists have proven their case so conclusively that the effects of segregation are no longer a matter of debate; that is, when they have proven to the satisfaction of segregationists that segregation is per se inequality, that its purpose is to mark Negroes with an inferior status, and that it violates the equal protection clause of the Fourteenth Amendment.

Segregationists eventually came to understand, once they reflected upon their position, that their objection to the use per se of expert social science testimony in the Brown decision was invalid. Within a few years after 1954 they shifted their ground, and today they object not so much to the use per se of social science testimony as to the use of what they feel is false and invalid social science testimony.

It would seem that everyone must accept as facts certain assumptions about segregation—that Jim Crow laws reflect a belief in Negro inferiority, that social segregation is based on an assumption by whites that racial equality is undesirable, that disfranchisement and civil inequality indicate an assumption that Negroes are incapable of discharging the responsibilities of citizenship, that Negroes are, in other words, a degraded and inferior race. If such assumptions are not valid, segregation would seem to have no *raison d'etre.* But such, it seems, is not the case at all, for the Negro's status under American law before 1954 rested on the premise that those assumptions are false. The law, in other words, was based on a fiction, the fiction that segregation implies no discrimination against Negroes and no assumption of Negro inferiority.

The widespread acceptance of this fiction indicates the magnitude of the task which the NAACP undertook in the Brown cases. Attorneys for the Association had to prove an obvious truth, but a truth which was unrecognized by the law and thus irrelevant to it, namely, that racial segregation is inherently discriminatory and marks the Negro with an inescapable badge of inferiority. Yet how can such a truth be proven, especially in a way which meets the rigid requirements of evidence in a court of law? Since the Brown cases involved public school segregation, would it be necessary to prove the detrimental effects of the single factor of school segregation? Would it be possible to do so? Can one facet of racial segregation be isolated from all others and measured objectively? Can the effects of school segregation be separated from the effects of economic discrimination, housing discrimination, or any one of the thousand ways in which society tells the Negro he is inferior? And must the effects of school segregation be demonstrated in the case of each individual Negro child involved in a suit?

Such were the questions facing the NAACP when it instituted the Brown cases. The Association's position, however, was not without hope. In a series of decisions going back to the 1930's the Supreme Court, though upholding the separate-but-equal principle, insisted upon an increasingly rigorous definition of "equal facilities," and made serious inroads on racial segregation in graduate and professional schools. As early as 1938 the Court held [13] that "equal facilities" must be within one's own state, thus relieving Negroes of the obligation of accepting out-of-state tuition grants at the discretion of the states. A decade later the Court held that facilities for Negroes must be available as soon as those for whites—constitutional rights, in other words, are here and now.[14] In 1950 the Court

[13] *Gaines v. Canada,* 305 U.S. 337 (1938).
[14] *Sipuel v. Board of Regents,* 332 U.S. 631 (1948).

went further in two important decisions. In *McLaurin v. Oklahoma State Regents*,[15] the court ruled that once a Negro student is admitted to a public institution he is entitled to use all facilities of the institution on the same basis as white students. The state of Oklahoma had assigned McLaurin, a Negro who was admitted to the University of Oklahoma by court order, a designated place in the classroom, library, and dining room. This, said the Court, deprived McLaurin of equal protection of the laws, even though his facilities were in the same room as those of whites. Such restrictions, it held, artificially inhibited his ability to study, to exchange views with other students, and to learn his profession. The state could not deprive an individual of the opportunity to gain acceptance on his own merits.

Also in 1950 the Court issued its most significant decision affecting school segregation before 1954. In *Sweatt v. Painter* [16] the Court ruled that a law school built especially for Negroes by the state of Texas was not equal to the University of Texas Law School, and ordered the admission of Sweatt to the University's law school. The Court based its decision not only on tangible factors such as quality and reputation of the faculty, size and quality of library holdings, and variety of courses offered, but also upon intangibles such as the school's reputation in the state, its traditions, the influence of its alumni, and the quality of educational experiences it offered. On this basis the Court found the University's law school superior to the one provided for Negroes. The Court was insisting that graduate and professional schools meet such rigid standards of equality that segregated facilities for Negroes would virtually always be found unequal.

To be sure, none of the decisions before 1954 applied specifically to the public schools, but they did indicate that the Supreme Court was increasingly willing to listen to evidence concerning the effects of segregation upon the individual and the quality of his education. Accordingly, in 1951 the NAACP in cooperation with a group of psychologists, sociologists, and educators undertook to prove in the courts that racial segregation in the public schools is per se discriminatory and that the effects of discrimination are manifested on all educational levels.

15 *McLaurin v. Oklahoma State Regents,* 339 U.S. 637 (1950).
16 *Sweatt v. Painter,* 339 U.S. 629 (1950).

2

THE BRIGGS CASE

An assault upon the legal and constitutional bases of the separate-but-equal principle was a natural outgrowth of the Sweatt and McLaurin decisions. In those decisions the Supreme Court took cognizance of expert social science testimony and looked beyond mere physical facilities in applying the separate-but-equal doctrine. That doctrine, after all, did not *require* segregation; it *permitted* segregation when the facilities available to the two races were equal. Nor had the Supreme Court defined the term "equal," at least not definitively. In fact, the Court had studiously avoided a direct review of the separate-but-equal principle, though it had applied the term "equal" in such a way that eleven of the seventeen states permitting racial segregation in public education had been ordered to admit Negro students to previously all-white graduate and/or professional schools. On these levels, at least, separate facilities had become almost by definition unequal. The Court was gradually shifting the grounds upon which segregation cases were being decided, and the shift was in the direction of arguments offered by NAACP lawyers and endorsed by social scientists who testified in the Sweatt and McLaurin cases.

In 1951, however, the process was incomplete. The separate-but-equal principle remained the law of the land, and the increasingly rigorous definition of "equal" facilities had not been applied to public schools, where the vast majority of Negro students were found. Integration on the graduate and professional levels affected only a handful of Negroes. To be at all meaningful, educational integration had to be extended to the public schools. Moreover, most social scientists who had studied the problem were convinced that the worst effects of school segregation occurred during the earliest years of the child's education.

In the years following World War II social scientists gave ever-increasing attention to the study of racial segregation in this country, especially to its effects upon the motivation, self-respect, and personality development of Negroes. A voluminous literature on these subjects had appeared by 1950,[1] and most social scientists agreed that segregation was harmful to individual Negroes and to society as a whole.[2] In utilizing expert social science testimony to challenge the separate-but-equal doctrine, the NAACP was merely bringing to the attention of the federal courts a body of knowledge and a set of principles which those social scientists already endorsed.

The story of the social science testimony in the Brown cases begins with a report which psychologist Kenneth B. Clark prepared in

[1] For a brief summary of the legal implications of this literature see "Grade School Segregation: The Latest Attack on Racial Discrimination," *Yale Law Journal*, VI (May, 1952), 730–44.

[2] See Max Deutscher and Isidor Chein, "The Psychological Effects of Enforced Segregation: A Survey of Social Science Opinion," *Journal of Psychology*, XXVI (October, 1948), 259–87.

1950 for the Midcentury White House Conference on Children and Youth.[3] This report, the first item cited in footnote eleven of the Brown decision, discusses such subjects as the manner in which small children become aware of race and prejudice, the impact of this awareness upon them, and the reactions, especially among minority group children, to exposure to prejudice and discrimination. In preparing this study Clark utilized not only his own extensive research on the subject but that of such authorities as Gunnar Myrdal, Gordon Allport, Max Deutscher and Isidor Chein, Otto Klineberg, Allison Davis, Mary Ellen Goodman, Ruth Horowitz, and others. In his brief, succinct report is found many of the basic ideas which social scientists later presented in testimony in the Briggs, Davis, Brown, and Gebhart cases.

Clark was first concerned with determining the extent to which children between the ages of three and seven are aware of differences in skin color. This he accomplished by two ingenious tests, his famous doll test and a coloring test. In the doll test, the results of which he described several times in testimony in the Brown cases, Clark presented to a group of children four dolls exactly alike except that two were white and two were brown. He told the children: "Give me the white doll." "Give me the colored doll." "Give me the Negro doll." Among three-year-old Negro children more than 75 percent were aware of the difference between white and colored, and Clark concluded that racial awareness was already developing among Negro children by the age of three. Similar experiments among older children indicated that the extent of racial awareness increased until all Negro children are aware of race by age seven.

Having established this fact, Clark carried his experiment a step further, asking each of the children to point out the doll "which is most like you." Thirty-seven percent of the three-year-olds and 87 percent of the seven-year-olds answered correctly, though light-skinned Negroes had more difficulty than dark-skinned ones. Clark then requested of the children: "Give me the doll that you like to play with." "Give me the doll that is the nice doll." "Give me

3 Kenneth B. Clark, *Effect of Prejudice and Discrimination on Personality Development* (Midcentury White House Conference on Children and Youth, 1951). The report is reprinted as Parts I and II of Clark, *Prejudice and Your Child*. In the discussion which follows, the quotations from the report are from *Prejudice and Your Child*, 17–65.

the doll that looks bad." "Give me the doll that is a nice color."
His purpose here was to determine the extent to which the children associated "white" with "nice" and "Negro" with "bad." He
found that a majority of Negro children at each age indicated an
unmistakable preference for the white dolls and a corresponding
rejection of the brown. The majority was greatest among three-
year-olds, but even seven-year-olds still preferred the dolls with
white skin, thus evidencing in Clark's opinion a desire to identify
themselves with the white dolls. "The fact that young Negro children would prefer to be white," he stated, "reflects their knowledge that society prefers white people. White children are generally
found to prefer their white skin—an indication that they too know
that society likes whites better. It is clear, therefore, that the self-
acceptance or self-rejection found so early in a child's developing
complex of racial ideas reflects the awareness and acceptance of the
prevailing racial attitudes in his community."

To Clark, "prevailing racial attitudes in his community" was
the heart of the matter, the taproot to which he traced all the ill
effects of segregation and discrimination. Children, he wrote, get
their attitudes toward Negroes "not by contact with Negroes but
by contacts with the prevailing attitudes toward Negroes," from
parents, friends, and neighbors, from religious and educational institutions, from the communications media, from social mores in the
community. As the child becomes aware of racial differences he is
made to see racial symbols throughout society. He sees Negroes living in ghettoes, attending dilapidated schools, assigned to segregated sections of public facilities or excluded altogether. He sees
them shunted into the lowliest occupations, working as domestics,
janitors, and menials. He sees them in movies, on television, in
newspapers and comic strips often cast in the role of menial, syco-
phant, or comic. The entire social milieu forces him toward the
conclusion that Negroes *are* inferior and their proper place in society is lowly and dependent. So effective is the process that
Negro children themselves are adversely affected; they, too, often
display negative attitudes toward themselves, their race, and other
Negroes.

According to Clark's findings the warping, stultifying effects of
segregation are already apparent when the five- or six-year-old Negro
child enters a segregated school. By assigning the child to such a

school, society tells him that race is an important factor in education, and this just as he is beginning to comprehend the significance society attaches to race. It is impossible, therefore, or virtually so, for the Negro child to appraise himself except in terms of
racial identity. He is made to understand that his school is segregated because he is a Negro, and he sees for himself that Negro
schools are inferior to those reserved for whites. He thus comes
to understand that society views him and his race with disdain, even
to the extent that whites quarantine their children from him. This
awareness, at so early and impressionable an age, is likely to do
permanent damage to his ego. The standards of society become
"reality" to him, even though "reality" makes him a pariah. His
sense of reality is distorted and his self-respect destroyed. The
seeds of personality damage and emotional disturbance are sown.

Clark supplemented the results of his doll test with a coloring
test designed to further measure the impact of racial awareness
upon young children. After determining that a group of 160 five-to
seven-year-old Negro children understood the color of things (by
having them color a leaf, an apple, an orange, and a mouse), he
gave them the following assignment: "See this [outline drawing of
a] little boy? Let's make believe he is you. Color this little boy the
color that you are." (The wording was appropriately changed for
girls taking the test.) The results were instructive. All the very
light-skinned children colored the figure representing themselves
white or yellow, which Clark interpreted as accurate. However, 15
percent of the children with medium-brown skin and 14 percent of
those with dark brown skin also colored the figures representing
themselves white or yellow or some bizarre color such as red or
green, and this despite the fact that they had correctly colored a
leaf, an apple, an orange, and a mouse. "Their refusal to choose
an appropriate color for themselves," Clark remarked, "was an indication of emotional anxiety and conflict in terms of their own
skin color. Because they wanted to be white, they pretended to be."

Results of the second half of the test were even more striking.
Clark asked the children, "Now this is a little girl [or boy]. Color
her [or him] the color you like little girls [or boys] to be." Forty-
eight percent of the children chose brown as the preferable color,
37 percent white, and 15 percent a bizarre or irrelevant color. Thus
52 percent rejected brown or black as the preferable color, a fig-

ure which Clark interpreted as supporting his findings in the dolls test that 60 percent of the children tested preferred the white doll or rejected the brown one.

In his experiments Clark discovered significant differences in the responses of Northern and Southern Negro children. The differences were quite large and later became the basis of some of the most effective criticism of his tests and of the data he presented in the Brown cases. His interpretation of the differences is therefore important. "Nearly 80 percent of the southern children," he found, "colored their preferences brown, whereas only 36 percent of the northern children did. Furthermore, over 20 percent of the northern children colored their preferences in a bizarre color, while only 5 percent of the southern children did." The two groups also differed in their reactions during the course of the tests. "A record of the spontaneous remarks of the children," wrote Clark, "showed that 82 percent of the southern children spoke as they worked, but only 20 percent of the northern children did so." The latter sometimes reacted with "open demonstrations of intense emotions" when confronted with the choices which the experiment forced upon them, though none of the Southern children showed such reactions. "The Southern children when confronted with this personal dilemma [of making choices based on color] were much more matter-of-fact in their ability to identify themselves with the brown doll" even after they had selected a white doll as the "nice" one or the one they would like most to play with. Some of the Southern children laughed or giggled self-consciously as they identified themselves with the brown doll. "Others merely stated flatly: 'This one. It's a nigger. I'm a nigger.' "

The conclusions Clark drew from these reactions were the focal point of much of the criticism later directed against him.

On the surface, [he wrote] these findings might suggest that northern Negro children suffer more personality damage from racial prejudice and discrimination than southern Negro children. However, this interpretation would seem to be not only superficial but incorrect. The apparent emotional stability of the southern Negro child may be indicative only of the fact that through rigid racial segregation and isolation he has accepted as normal the fact of his inferior social status. Such an acceptance is not symptomatic of a healthy personality. The emotional turmoil revealed by some of the northern children may be interpreted as an attempt on their part to assert some positive aspect of the self.

This conclusion pointedly reveals the dependence of Clark upon his initial assumptions. He was convinced that racial segregation has detrimental psychological effects upon Negroes, effects which manifest themselves as soon as the Negro child becomes aware of racial differences. From the perspective of this conviction, his conclusions regarding the reactions of Northern and Southern Negro children is not only plausible but eminently reasonable. To anyone who rejects his initial assumptions, however, an entirely different conclusion—"that northern Negro children suffer more personality damage from racial prejudice and discrimination than southern Negro children"—is just as reasonable. The value of Clark's findings is due not to the fact that they substantiate the conclusion quoted above—this they do not do in any conclusive, objective way—but to the fact that they corroborate what common sense suggests and experience makes manifest: that the practice of racial segregation in this country is demeaning to Negroes, and an organized means of exploiting and suppressing the race. And as a practical matter, this is what Clark concluded.

Clark's testimony in the Brown cases relied heavily upon his doll and drawing tests. The tests were not designed to determine the specific effects of school segregation as distinct from other forms of segregation; he intended them to show how Negro children are affected by life in a society which is generally prejudiced and segregated. The authority of his report to the Midcentury White House Conference rested upon these tests and upon the scholarship of other authorities, of which he made substantial use. In general, his conclusions may be said to represent the most advanced scholarship on the psychological effects of racial segregation, and his report helped crystallize social science opinion on that subject. Minority group children react to segregation "with deep feelings of inferiority and with a sense of personal humiliation," Clark wrote. "Many of them become confused about their own personal worth" and "develop conflicts with regard to their feelings about themselves. and about the value of the group with which they are identified." As a result they rationalize their internal conflicts in order to accommodate the discrimination and rejection they receive from society with their imperative need for racial and personal respect. The results of their effort vary greatly among individual Negroes, ranging all the way from withdrawal or resignation to hostility and violence. The reactions of an individual depend upon a myriad of personal and environmental factors; in almost every instance, however, it produces damage to the personality and ego.[4]

Clark's stature as a pre-eminent authority on the psychological effects of prejudice and discrimination,[5] his dedication to the principle of racial equality, and the fact that he is himself a Negro [6] made him the logical choice to direct the social science aspects of the Brown cases. In February, 1951, Robert L. Carter of the legal staff of the NAACP asked Clark "whether psychologists had any findings which were relevant to the effects of racial segregation on the personality development of Negro children." [7] The NAACP, Carter explained, "had decided to challenge the constitutionality of

[4] Clark's testimony on the psychological effects of discrimination upon small children is fully supported by the research on the subject since 1951. See Mary Ellen Goodman, *Race Awareness in Young Children* (New York, 1964), 248–68.

[5] See for example the following works by Kenneth B. Clark: "Group Violence: A Preliminary Study of the 1943 Harlem Riot," *Journal of Social Psychology,* XIX (May, 1944), 319–37; "Racial Prejudices among American Minorities," *International Social Science Bulletin,* II (Winter, 1950), 506–13; "Social Science and Social Tensions," *Mental Hygiene,* XXXII (January, 1948), 15–26; Clark and Mamie P. Clark, "The Development of Consciousness of Self and the Emergence of Racial Identification in Negro Pre-school Children," *Journal of Social Psychology,* X (November, 1939), 591–99; Clark and Clark, "Emotional Factors in Racial Identification and Preference in Negro Children," *Journal of Negro Education,* XIX Summer, 1950), 341–50; Clark and Clark, "Racial Identification and Preference in Negro Children," in T. M. Newcomb and E. L. Hartley, (eds.), *Readings in Social Psychology,* (New York, 1947); Clark and Clark, "Segregation as a Factor in the Racial Identification of Negro Pre-School Children," *Journal of Experimental Education,* VIII (1939), 161–63; and Clark and Clark, "Skin Color as a Factor in the Racial Identification of Negro Pre-school Children," *Journal of Social Psychology,* XI (February, 1940), 159–69. See also Clark, *Dark Ghetto, Dilemmas of Social Power* (New York, 1965), a distillation of the report Clark and others prepared for the President's Committee on Juvenile Delinquency and for Harlem Youth Opportunities Unlimited (HARYOU).

[6] Clark was born in the Panama Canal Zone, where his father was employed by the United Fruit Company. At the age of four he moved with his parents, who were West Indians, to New York City. He was educated at Howard and Columbia universities, receiving his Ph.D. in psychology from the latter in 1940. In 1960 he was president of the Society for the Psychological Study of Social Issues, a branch of the American Psychological Association.

[7] This author's account is taken from Kenneth Clark, "Desegregation: An Appraisal of the Evidence," *Journal of Social Issues,* IX (No. 4, 1953), 1–76; Clark, "The Role of the Social Sciences in Desegregation," Appendix V of *Prejudice and Your Child,* 207–15; and Clark, "The Social Scientist as an Expert Witness in Civil Rights Litigation," *Social Problems,* I (June, 1953), 5–10.

state laws which required or permitted racial segregation in the public schools." Specifically, the Association would challenge the Plessy decision and the separate-but-equal doctrine on grounds that segregated facilities are inherently unequal, that social scientists have empirically demonstrated the detrimental effects of racial segregation, and that the concensus of social science opinion is that racial segregation is unjustifiable. Carter invited Clark to collaborate with the NAACP legal staff "in planning for the most effective use of social psychologists and other social scientists in the courts of first instance and appeal." His effort was fourfold: to marshal all relevant social science data and opinion, to assist in making the best use of those data and that opinion, to collect information on previous instances of racial integration in order to determine whether and under what conditions integration can be accomplished peacefully and without lowering educational standards, and to arrange for expert testimony by appropriate authorities in the several cases.

Clark was assisted in his tasks by some of the nation's foremost social scientists. Among those who testified in one or more of the cases were Clark's wife Mamie, a psychologist in her own right; psychologists David Krech of the University of California, Helen Trager and Brewster Smith of Vassar, Alfred McClung Lee of Brooklyn College, Isidor Chein of New York University and the American Jewish Conference, and Otto Klineberg of Columbia; sociologists John J. Kane of Notre Dame University, Frederick B. Parker of the University of Delaware, and Kenneth Morland of William and Mary College; and psychiatrist Frederick Wertham. Other expert witnesses included Horace B. English of Ohio State University, Wilbur B. Brookover of Michigan State University, Louisa Holt of the University of Kansas and the Menninger Clinic, Bettie Belk of the Workshop in Human Relations at the University of Kansas City, Jerome S. Brunner of Harvard, and George Gorham Lane of the University of Delaware.

In each of the cases covered by the Brown decision, there was lengthy testimony by social scientists and educators, so that given in one case necessarily overlaps or repeats that in the others. The most comprehensive presentation of evidence was made in the Briggs and Davis cases, and a brief review of those cases will indicate the nature and scope of the testimony as a whole.

The case of *Briggs v. Elliott* [8] grew out of the efforts of Negroes in Clarendon County, South Carolina, to improve the educational facilities available to their children. Located in the heart of the South Carolina low country, Clarendon County is typical of those areas of the deep South where Negroes are most heavily concentrated. By attacking school segregation in this black belt country, the NAACP was challenging the Southern way of life at its very roots. In one respect the Briggs case was an assault upon school segregation in its most vulnerable area, for the Negro schools of Clarendon County met none of the standards which the Supreme Court had enunciated in the Sweatt and McLaurin decisions, nor indeed of the standards implicit in the separate-but-equal principle itself. In other respects, however, the institutions and customs of segregation were nowhere stronger or better protected than in Clarendon County or in School District No. 22, the district directly involved in the Briggs suit. The people of Clarendon County, or the white minority at least, were united to a man in their determination to protect racial segregation, which they rightly regarded as the cornerstone of their way of life. To outsiders, they presented the appearance of a monolith determined to resist anything which might alter the pattern of race relations in their community. In 1955 *The Nation* described the county as a place where whites "talk of Citizens' Councils and the 'economic squeeze,' where the Ku Klux Klan met with Bryant Bowles, head of the National Association for the Advancement of White People, as a featured speaker, where integration is freely referred to as a 'Communist-Catholic-Jewish plot,' where a place of business displays the latest newspaper clippings showing crimes of Negro against white, where private citizens discuss the hated Ford Foundation along with the price of tobacco, where the NAACP has only a small chapter and where you hunt long and hard for a defender of the Negro." [9] A measure of the determination— and success—of Clarendon County whites is the fact that their schools, including those of District No. 22, remained segregated until 1965, ten years after the District was enjoined by the federal courts from discriminating against Negro pupils on the basis of

[8] 98 F. Supp. 529 (E.D. S.C. 1951).

[9] Quoted in Howard H. Quint, *Profile in Black and White* (Washington, 1958), 12–13.

race. In the fall of 1965 six Negro children finally "integrated" the white schools of District 22. [10]

In 1951 when the Briggs case began its long journey through the federal courts, the population of Clarendon County was approximately 31,000, of which perhaps 23,000 were Negroes. Public school enrollment totaled 6,531 Negroes and 2,375 whites, though expenditures for the last school year had been $395,329 for white schools and $282,950 for Negro schools,[11] which amounted to approximately $166 for each white student and $43 for each Negro. In District No. 22, 298 white and 2,259 Negro students were enrolled in 1951. The inferiority of Negro schools in the district was glaring, and the first objective of the Briggs suit—to demonstrate the physical inequality of Negro schools—was easily achieved. The point, in fact, was not contested by attorneys for South Carolina and District No. 22. Instead, they admitted the inequality and based their defense upon the fact that the state and district had already undertaken an emergency construction program to bring Negro schools up to white standards.

The NAACP, however, had a more fundamental objective, which was to show that racial segregation in public education is in and of itself psychologically damaging to Negro children and segregated Negro schools are thus per se inferior to white schools. This, attorneys for the state and school district would not concede.

The chief object of the social science testimony in the case was to prove this contention. Kenneth Clark testified first and at greater length than any other expert witness in the Briggs case.[12] He introduced the most significant of the social science arguments against school segregation, and presented the data he had discussed in his report to the Midcentury White House Conference on Children and Youth. "I have reached the conclusion," he testified, "that discrimination, prejudice and segregation have definitely detrimental effects on the personality development of the Negro child. The essence of this detrimental effect is a confusion in the child's concept of his own self-esteem—basic feelings of inferiority, conflict, confusion in

10 James Leeson, "Desegregation," *Southern Education Report,* I (September-October, 1965) , 32.

11 Quint, *Profile in Black and White,* 12.

12 For Clark's testimony see *Briggs v. Elliott,* 98 F. Supp. 529 (E.D. S.C. 1951) , transcript of record, in transcript of *Brown v. Board of Education,* 347 U.S. 483 (1954) .

the self-image, resentment, hostility towards himself, hostility towards whites, . . [or] a desire to resolve his basic conflict by sometimes escaping or withdrawing."

Clark was careful to point out that this and his other observations were not his alone. Anticipating later charges that he was a special pleader who allowed personal prejudices to interfere with his scientific detachment, he showed convincingly that an overwhelming majority of social scientists in this country believe that educational segregation is psychologically harmful to Negro children. In 1948 a survey of the attitudes of social scientists on this point was made by psychologists Max Deutscher and Isidor Chein.[13] Their survey, which the Supreme Court cited in footnote eleven to the Brown decision, was based upon responses of 517 anthropologists, sociologists, and psychologists to questionnaires designed to determine their attitudes toward racial discrimination. They were asked whether in their opinion "enforced segregation" even with equal facilities had "detrimental psychological effects" upon Negroes and/or whites. Ninety percent replied that in their opinion enforced segregation was harmful to Negroes, and 83 percent thought it also was harmful to whites. The results were remarkably consistent for sociologist, psychologists, and anthropologists—Southerners and non-Southerners. "Substantial majorities of social scientists who may be said to have competence with regard to the matters under inquiry," Deutscher and Chein wrote, "agree that enforced segregation is psychologically detrimental to both the segregated and enforcing groups even when equal facilities are provided." [14]

Clark also had responsibility for answering specific objections to the social science testimony in the Brown cases. One of the most plausible arguments which segregationists made against the testimony was that witnesses spoke in such general terms that their testimony failed to meet minimum standards of relevancy and admissibility. The witnesses spoke of the ill effects of segregation upon Negroes in general or upon "the Negro" in abstract, but did

[13] Deutscher and Chein, "The Psychological Effects of Enforced Segregation"; and Chein, "What Are the Psychological Effects of Segregation Under Conditions of Equal Facilities?" *International Journal of Opinion and Attitude Research*, III (Summer, 1949) , 229–34.

[14] Deutscher and Chein, "The Psychological Effects of Enforced Segregation," 268.

not, charged segregationists, prove that individual plaintiffs had suffered specific, demonstrable damage from *de jure* school segregation. In making this charge, segregationists were insisting that social science evidence be narrowly construed by the courts and that it be required to meet the same tests of relevancy and admissibility as evidence in a criminal prosecution. In this manner they sought to have it thrown out altogether or, failing this, to have its usefulness to the NAACP severely restricted. The latter could be achieved by having the court reject all social science testimony not directly relating to specific injuries to individual plaintiffs. Under such a procedure an order admitting individual Negro plaintiffs to white schools would not apply to other Negroes. It would instead require each Negro who sought admission to a white or integrated school to demonstrate in court specific injuries which he had personally suffered from segregated education. Such a ruling would be virtually worthless to Negroes and would neutralize almost all the testimony of the social scientists.

To answer the segregationists on this point, Clark insisted repeatedly that the particular effects of school segregation could not be isolated from the effects of other forms of segregation. The personality of a segregated child, he pointed out, is molded not by his educational experiences alone, but by the totality of his environment, by all the varied influences touching his life. A child's earliest experiences are his most important insofar as lasting impressions are concerned, and the Negro child suffers the ill effects of segregation long before he enters a segregated school. Segregated education is only one facet of life in a segregated society. The major evil is the general system of segregation, not the specific practice of segregated schools. This emphasis upon the ill effects of the broader issue rather than the narrower one was characteristic of much of the social science testimony of the Brown cases, and it suggests the NAACP was fighting segregation itself and not just segregation in public schools. But surely, countered segregationists, local school boards cannot be held responsible for the effects of community customs and practices, even though those customs and practices might adversely affect the child's personality development and his ability to learn in school.

Attorneys for the NAACP rejected the arguments of segregationists on these points, and insisted instead that the relevancy and admissibility of social science testimony be construed in the broadest possible way. But they also attempted to show that the ill effects of segregation, including segregated education, are particular and individual as well as general. A few days before he testified in the Briggs case, Clark conducted one of his doll and coloring experiments upon the Negro children involved in the case. He asked sixteen children between the ages of six and nine the same questions he had asked in earlier experiments. Each of the children correctly identified the white and Negro dolls, and their reactions to the dolls were similar to those of other children Clark had tested. Ten of the sixteen chose the white doll as preferable to the colored; eleven selected the brown doll as "bad" and only one chose the white doll as "bad." (The others made no choice.) The experiment indicated, or was so interpreted by Clark, that segregation had produced in the children "basic confusion" about themselves and conflict in their self-images. When asked to color a figure representing herself, one of the darkest of the children colored it flesh colored, and seven of the sixteen children picked the white doll as the doll most like themselves. "This must be seen," said Clark, "as a concrete illustration of the degree to which the pleasures which these children sensed against being brown forced them to evade reality—to escape the reality which seems too over-burdening or too threatening to them." He added later, "The conclusion which I was forced to reach was that these children in Clarendon County, like other human beings who are subjected to an obviously inferior status . . . have been definitely harmed in the development of their personalities; that the signs of instability . . . are clear, and . . . that every psychologist would accept and interpret these signs as such." [15]

The significance of Clark's testimony in the Briggs case is apparent in the Brown decision. The Supreme Court incorporated many of his views in the decision, and cited his works and those of other authorities to whom he referred in his testimony. For this reason it is significant that the attorneys for South Carolina and School District No. 22 made no effort to rebut his testimony through witnesses of their own. Their only rebuttal witness was E. R. Crow, superintendent of schools in Sumter County, South Carolina, and chairman of the State Education Finance Commission, an agency recently created to equalize the educational facilities of the two

[15] *Briggs v. Elliott*, transcript of testimony, 86, 127.

races. Crow was not a psychologist but he did have considerable experience as a public school administrator. He was obviously intended to be a "practical" spokesman who recognized the impossibility of integrating the schools of South Carolina and who therefore contrasted sharply with the "academic" and inexperienced, and thus impractical, Clark.

This illustrated one of the major devices of defense attorneys in the Brown cases—to attempt to discredit the social science testimony on grounds that the witnesses had no experience in the public schools of the South and could not therefore understand the practical problems of school administration and policy formulation. Tolerance, equality, and brotherhood might be praiseworthy principles, argued the attorneys, but they present insurmountable problems to Southern school officials if they can be achieved only through racial integration. The public schools depend upon public support, they continued, and the arbitrary imposition of racial integration without regard to popular feelings would undermine that support and might even destroy the school system. "The existence of the feeling of separateness between the races of this state," Crow testified, "would make it such that it would be impossible to have peaceable association with each other in the public schools." [16]

Clark's testimony was supplemented by that of David Krech, who testified concerning the psychological consequences of legalized segregation. Through legalized segregation, Krech declared, society defines the individual Negro and his legal rights in racial terms and tells him thereby that race is a factor of overriding significance in life. The message, however, is not restricted to Negroes. It is made equally clear to whites that theirs is the preferred race, the superior race which must be protected from the contamination which comes from associating with Negroes. Both races are made to consider racial factors pre-eminent, and whites especially are inculcated with feelings of racial prejudice. In fact, Krech suggested, legalized segregation is the single most important source of racial prejudice and of the belief among whites in racial inequality. "No one," he declared, "unless he is mentally diseased . . . can maintain any attitude or belief unless there are some objective supports for that belief. . . . Legal segregation, because it is legal, because it is

16 *Briggs v. Elliott*, transcript of testimony, 113.

obvious to everyone, gives . . . environmental support for the belief that Negroes are in some way different from and inferior to white people, and that in turn . . . supports and strengthens beliefs of racial difference [and] racial inferiority." Segregation in the public schools is an especially important facet of legal segregation for it separates white and Negro children at a critical point in their psychological development. Just as they begin to form views of the world and of the people in it, they are placed in an artificial situation. They come to look upon themselves as a people apart, and to view persons of the other race not as individuals but as members of a strange and alien group. The result is distortion—and prejudice. Psychologists have long since given up the notion that IQ is independent of education and experience, said Krech in illustrating his point. Inadequate education, which is implicit in segregation, especially for Negroes, results in a lower (or less well developed) IQ and in lesser ability to cope with the problems of life. Through segregated education "we build into the Negro the very characteristics, not only intellectual, but also personality characteristics, which we then use to justify prejudice." [17]

These ideas were further developed by Helen Trager of Vassar College.[18] Mrs. Trager, an educational psychologist, had conducted extensive tests and interviews in Philadelphia with white and Negro children between the ages of five and eight, and her testimony was a discussion of her research. She had found children of both races aware of racial differences by age five, but she noted that this awareness produced different reactions among whites and Negroes. White children talked freely about race and race differences; Negro children on the other hand showed "obvious discomfort" discussing these subjects, and accordingly sought to avoid them. Both groups, however, "saw being Negro as a disadvantage." White children recognized that theirs is the preferred group in American society, and they answered "yes" when asked if they thought Negroes would prefer to be white. Negro children displayed unmistakable signs of conflict and tension on this point, and answered Mrs. Trager's query by stating "that Negro children

[17] *Briggs v. Elliott*, transcript of testimony, 133–34.
[18] *Briggs v. Elliott*, transcript of testimony, 138–47. For more detailed discussion of her research see Helen G. Trager and M. R. Yarrow, *They Learn What They Live: Prejudice in Young Children* (New York, 1952).

liked to be Negro but that Negro children would [also] like to be white." To Mrs. Trager this contradiction seemed "terribly important," representing as it did "a conflict and an inability to accept one's own group and yet [manifesting] the psychological need to accept what one is."

Interestingly enough, as Mrs. Trager pointed out, both white and Negro children understood "Negro" as meaning the same thing: "that you are not liked by people, that you won't be asked to play, that you won't be allowed to do things that other children can do." Both groups had fears and misconceptions about each other, and gave "the weirdest, and most frightening and inaccurate explanations" of the meaning of "race." But unlike the white children, the Negro children "showed a tendency to expect rejection," and the expectation increased sharply between ages five and eight. "At 5 a Negro child would indicate that he expected Negroes not to be accepted and would give as the reason 'Because he isn't white,' or 'Because he is black,' or using the vernacular 'Because he is a nigger.' " At eight, however, explanations were "evasive, avoidant," and accompanied by definite feelings of discomfort. Now the explanations were: "Because he can't play the way they can"; "because he doesn't live near them"; but not "because he is colored." Mrs. Trager concluded that segregation and discrimination frustrated the Negro child's basic emotional need for self-respect. "A child who expects to be rejected," she declared, "who sees his group held in low esteem, is not going to function well[.] He is not going to be a fully developed child[.] He will be withdrawn, or aggressive in order to win the acceptance he doesn't get."

The testimony in the Briggs case had little effect upon the three federal judges who heard it. Chief Judge John J. Parker of North Carolina, whom Herbert Hoover once nominated for the Supreme Court only to have the nomination rejected by the Senate in part because of NAACP opposition, and Judge George Bell Timmerman of South Carolina, whose son was later governor of that state, rejected the plea of Negro plaintiffs. They ruled that segregation in the public schools of Clarendon County did not violate the Fourteenth Amendment, now that efforts were underway to bring the physical facilities of Negro schools up to the standards of those available to whites. The third member of the Court, J.

Waties Waring, also a South Carolinian, but one who had a record of decisions favorable to Negroes, dissented vigorously.[19]

Although the social science testimony made little impression upon the court, attorneys for both the NAACP and South Carolina dealt with the testimony at length in their briefs to the Supreme Court, to which the NAACP promptly appealed the lower court's decision. The appellees' brief,[20] which the South Carolinians submitted to the high court, is perhaps the earliest statement of the ideas of scientific racism which the Brown decision helped to crystallize. Despite their failure to call expert witnesses of their own, the South Carolina attorneys now challenged the social science testimony, and did so vigorously. This in itself was noteworthy, for it indicated they now considered the testimony important and feared its impact upon the Supreme Court. Their challenge centered largely around the contentions that (1) the witnesses had no responsibility for decisions in educational policies and no experience in the public schools of South Carolina or the South, (2) the empirical data offered to the court did not prove that public school segregation was psychologically and educationally detrimental to Negro children, and (3) spokesmen who understand racial mores in the South recognize that large-scale integration of the public schools is impossible, even undesirable, and a court order to integrate would likely destroy the public school system there.

The South Carolina attorneys drew a distinction between the general effects of racial segregation and the specific effects of *de jure* school segregation, and asked the Court to concern itself only with the latter. They argued, for example, that the testimony of Mrs. Trager, which was based upon studies made in Philadelphia, was thus irrelevant to the issues in the Briggs case, for the public schools of Philadelphia were by law integrated.

---

[19] "From their testimony," Waring wrote in his dissent in reference to the NAACP witnesses, "it was clearly apparent, as it should be to any thoughtful person, irrespective of having such expert testimony, that segregation in education can never produce equality and that it is an evil that must be eradicated. This case presents the matter clearly for adjudication and I am of the opinion that all the legal guideposts, expert testimony, common sense, and reason point unerringly to the conclusion that the system of segregation in education adopted and practiced in the State of South Carolina must go and must go now."

"*Segregation is per se inequality.*" *Briggs v. Elliott*, transcript of record, 206–08.

[20] Brief for Appellees, No. 2 *(Briggs v. Elliott)*, transcript of *Brown v. Board of Education* 347 U.S. 483 (1954).

They dealt with the testimony of Kenneth Clark at greater length. The crucial point of Clark's testimony was his contention that the "symptoms" which his doll tests and interviews revealed among Negro children demonstrated the ill effects of segregation. Here the appellees challenged Clark by quoting one of his own studies against him.[21] In analyzing the results of a study he and his wife had made a few years previously, Clark had offered a detailed comparison of the reactions of Northern and Southern Negro children to his tests, and here as elsewhere had found some differences. In this instance 69 percent of the Southern children identified themselves with the colored doll, compared to 61 percent of the Northern children. Seventy-two percent of the Northerners chose the white doll as "nice," compared to 52 percent of the Southerners. Seventy-one percent of the Northerners likewise chose the colored doll as "bad," compared to 49 percent of the Southerners, and 63 percent of the former chose white as the "nice" color, compared to 57 percent of the latter. To the South Carolinians these figures indicated "that Negro children in the South are healthier psychologically speaking than those of the North."

Moreover, the "conflicts" which Clark found in Negro children in Clarendon County, continued appellees, were unrelated, except in an indirect and tangential way, to school segregation. "Negro children are already aware of race and accompanying value judgments at the preschool age," and the possibility "that the schools play an initiating role in creating psychological conflicts" is thus eliminated. Nevertheless, they continued, "the age of starting school is a crucial one in the development of the child's ego structure." At this time the child "is especially sensitive to the accepted social values of his larger environment, because he seeks group identification and personal self-esteem," and it is questionable whether a Negro child, at such a tender age, should be forced into the tense and uncertain atmosphere of an integrated school, there to compete with white children whom he more likely than not regards as his superiors. Such an issue, the South Carolinians suggested, is "fraught with difficulty" and requires "the most careful and painstaking consideration, necessarily involving study of the accumulated data which the most thorough, impartial and scientific research can supply." It must be resolved in the child's best

21 Clark and Clark, "Racial Identification and Preferences in Negro Children."

interest and without regard for impractical theorists or outside
pressure groups. It is an issue "for the legislative and educational
authorities of the state to decide and not for the courts."

On these points the South Carolina attorneys made their most
effective criticisms of the social science testimony. They did not
prove the testimony false nor demonstrate empirically that their
own position was valid, and in discussing the problems of race
relations they treated the symptoms rather than the malady itself.
They did, however, point out some of the limitations of the testimony. They based their arguments largely upon two contentions,
each of which is partially valid: that empirical data on the
psychological effects of segregation are piecemeal and inconclusive,
and that scientific research on the subject is still experimental and
likely to be influenced by the researcher's prejudices. In other
words, after attacking the social science testimony as internally
contradictory, they suggested it was not what it appeared on the
surface to be. The implication was that the witnesses, each of
whom was committed to the principle of racial integration, had
allowed this commitment to influence their research and prejudice
their conclusions. The issue, they suggested, is still open; the conclusions of expert witnesses are only their opinions and entitled to
consideration on that basis alone. The witnesses might have acted
from the loftiest of motives and might be convinced that their
testimony is valid, but this is not reason enough to overturn the
legal basis of the South's racial policies.

To support their position the attorneys summoned "the opinion
and judgment of leading sociologists and educators who, unlike the
witnesses for appellants, have . . . years of research, observation,
and practical experience in states where the two races live in the
same area in great numbers." This seemed to promise that they
would cite authorities of their own, matching in stature and reputation those who testified for the NAACP, but such was not the
case—with one notable exception. The "leading sociologists and
educators" turned out to be (other than E. R. Crow, who was
mentioned previously, and Howard Odum, who was indeed a leading sociologist and is discussed below) Frank P. Graham, then
president of the University of North Carolina; Colgate W. Darden,
former governor of Virginia and in 1951 president of the University

of Virginia; Hodding Carter, the Mississippi author and newspaper editor; and, surprisingly, W. E. B. Du Bois and Gunnar Myrdal.[22]

Graham, Darden, and Carter, especially Graham and Carter, were well known throughout the nation as Southern liberals on racial matters and as representatives of the best elements in public life in the South. As such, their opinions carried weight among liberals and moderates outside the South, and to quote them was an effective move on the part of appellees, even though none of the three was a scientist or social scientist. According to a statement by Graham, race relations in the South are expressed in social mores which reflect history, the large number of Negroes in the section, racial differences, a "universal consciousness of kind," and "the economic competition of the low income groups." These mores, he admitted, sometimes produce discrimination against Negroes, a fact he deplored, but improvement can be effected only by "a new emphasis on the influence of religion, education, personal kindness, decent respect for the human dignity of persons, and voluntary cooperation of people of good will for better relations in the local communities, in the long haul of the generations for justice on this earth." Hodding Carter added in a similar vein, "It will be tragic for the South, for the Negro and the nation itself if the government should enact and attempt to enforce any laws or Supreme Court decisions that would open the South's public schools and public gathering places to the Negro. The one saving factor would be the Southern Negro's own common sense refusal to implement the law." The Southern Negro, Carter continued, "by and large, does not want an end to segregation in itself any more than does the Southern white man."

The comments reflect the viewpoint of many Southern white liberals in 1951 and pointedly illustrate the dilemma in which men of liberal views have often found themselves in the South. Graham and Carter and thousands of other Southern whites like them were (and are) men of good will with a sincere interest in improving

22 The appellees quoted a statement by Myrdal that Negroes were divided among themselves on questions of school integration, and cited an article in which Du Bois had suggested that Negro children might suffer more from the hostile atmosphere of integrated schools than from inferior facilities in Jim Crow schools. See Gunnar Myrdal, *An American Dilemma* (New York, 1944), 901–02; and W. E. B. Du Bois, "Does the Negro Need Separate Schools?" *Journal of Negro Education,* IV (July, 1935), 325–35.

race relations and bettering the condition of Negroes in their region. Historically, however, the liberal Southerner has been particularly vulnerable to attack from segregationists. In proposing any change in race relations or the status of Negroes, he runs the risk of losing whatever influence in public life he might have. He has therefore been forced to speak the language of moderation and endorse the larger policy of segregation in order to achieve the lesser goal of improving the Negro's status. The expediency might well have been necessary, and Negroes would certainly have benefited had the views of Graham and Carter become public policy in the South. It is nevertheless significant that neither man criticized segregation per se, and the result was that the segregationist attorneys were able to quote such relatively enlightened men as Graham and Carter in defending racial segregation.

The facility with which segregationists could use the rhetoric of Southern moderates was strikingly illustrated by an address which Howard W. Odum delivered to the Southern Sociological Congress in April, 1951, and from which appellees quoted at length. Dr. Odum, who was Kenan Professor of Sociology at the University of North Carolina and one of the nation's most renowned and respected social scientists, was widely recognized as one of the South's most enlightened spokesmen on racial matters.

He had for a long time promoted interracial cooperation and had actively sought to improve the status and opportunities of Negroes in the South. But for whatever reason, either from expediency or conviction, Odum defended racial segregation in much the same tone as Graham and Carter had done. The appellees' attorneys were much impressed not only with Odum's academic and professional stature but with his racial views as well. They referred to his "acknowledged freedom from anything which could even remotely be suggested as prejudice or preconceived approach to racial questions," and described him as "the best informed authority in the country on southern racial matters."

In the address from which the attorneys quoted, Odum urged a four-point program concerning education and race relations in the South: (1) "remedy the inexcusable situation with reference to brutalities, injustices, inequalities and discrimination"; (2) adopt "Operation Equal Opportunity" to equalize white and Negro schools; (3) "provide immediately for non-segregation in all university education on the graduate and professional level"; and

(4) "move judiciously but speedily toward agenda for negotiations and specifications for future achievement on the total front." But lest Negroes and integrationists read too much into his program, Odum cautioned them to recognize the South's "cumulative racial and conflict heritage," and remember Nehru's admonition that "no solution which is not acceptable to the large masses of the people can have any possible enduring quality." It was such passages as these which segregationists found most appealing in Odum's address. To those who urged militancy upon Southern Negroes or demanded that the Supreme Court outlaw racial segregation, Odum addressed this warning:

If there are those who hold that the South, having too many people of both races, would profit by a certain amount of violent revolution and slaughter of the people, as I have heard prominent metropolitan leaders say, that might be a democratic prerequisite; but to urge the Supreme Court to set the incidence of such a conflict is something else. . . .

Anyone who is not naive enough to try to repeal the laws of individuation, of personality, of freedom, of opportunity, of classification, knows that the major construct [in Southern race policy] is not segregation *or* non-segregation but non-segregation *and* segregation, developed through total processes of interaction and growth, of means and ends, of moral imperatives and administrative reality.

But despite its strong roots in the past, the South, Odum continued, is undergoing a profound though gradual change, and the Southerner's task is to accommodate himself and his section to the change with the least difficulty. The "Southern compound bi-racial culture," he said, is slowly giving way to the "American complex integrated multicultured society," but this is being accomplished without a radical upheaval and does not prevent Southerners from salvaging the best elements in their traditional way of life. "Such a conversion," Odum declared, "brings with it no more compulsion or specifications for negating the facets of race and ethnic minorities, supreme in whatever personality and cultural loyalties they may wish. Such a conversion automatically, as in any organic structure or process, carries with it the inevitable continuity of separateness, autonomy, and segregation inherent in not only the American ideal but in all the differential-groups to have a say in how they shall integrate themselves in the new world society." In plain language this means that racial segregation and white supremacy will continue in the South, even though modifications in traditional practices will occur.

As this résumé indicates, the appellees' effort to refute the social science testimony in the Briggs case was uneven and incomplete. Whatever the limitations of the testimony of Clark and his collaborators, it was vastly more authoritative than the effort made by segregationists to refute it. In fact, the appellees' attorneys made poor use of the social science materials which favored their own position. At the time of the Briggs hearing there were a number of academic social scientists who believed racial segregation preferable to integration and who perhaps would have testified in behalf of this belief. The failure to call them was a gross error of judgment and can be explained in only one way—the state and local officials who handled the case considered the social science testimony less important than legal precedents. They proceeded on the assumption that the law narrowly construed was on their side. They miscalculated, and the eventual disposition of the case by the Supreme Court illustrates the magnitude of their miscalculation. (But perhaps the Supreme Court also miscalculated, for the public schools of Clarendon County are for all practical purposes still segregated today.)

3

THE DAVIS CASE AND THE APPEAL

The case of *Davis v. County School Board of Prince Edward County, Virginia*,[1] illustrates other features of the assault upon school segregation through the use of social science. Like Clarendon County, Prince Edward County was a part of the black belt, and the racial attitudes there were those of the deep South. In Prince Edward and surrounding counties "massive resistance" to racial integration was always more than a slogan; it was a way of life and

[1] *Davis v. Country School Board of Prince Edward County*, 103 F. Supp. 337 (E.D. Va. 1951).

a policy literally employed. According to the census of 1950, 45 percent of the population of Prince Edward County were Negroes, and the percentage of Negro children in the public schools was even higher. Like everything else in the county, the schools were rigidly segregated, and Negroes were relegated to an inferior status. Negro schools were grossly inferior to those of whites, and interracial tensions had recently increased because of white intransigence in the face of Negro demands for better schools. On one occasion Negro students had undertaken a short-lived boycott of their schools, and the immediate occasion for filing the Davis suit was the decision not to construct a new Negro high school in the county.

There were, however, important differences between the Briggs and Davis cases. The former involved segregation in elementary school, whereas the latter concerned segregation at the secondary level. More important for present purposes, attorneys for Virginia and Prince Edward County took the social science testimony much more seriously than had the South Carolinians. From the beginning they seem to have sensed that the NAACP was mounting a meaningful assault upon the legal and constitutional bases of segregation, and not the least of the reasons for their concern was the social science testimony in the case. As a result, they made a much greater effort to refute the testimony, first by rigorous cross-examination of each of the witnesses, and then by calling witnesses of their own. To a greater extent than any of the other cases covered by the Brown decision, the Davis case involved a systematic presentation of social science evidence by both sides. After the Brown decision was issued, segregationists charged repeatedly that the Supreme Court decided the cases without considering the evidence supporting segregation. The charge is only partially true. It is true that the segregationists' case was not presented as carefully or as thoroughly as was the integrationists', but their case was presented in the Davis testimony, and by witnesses of their own choosing.

Brewster Smith, chairman of the psychology department at Vassar, was one of the principal NAACP witnesses in the Davis case. He testified concerning racial intelligence and the relationship between race and learning ability.[2] This relationship was especially im-

2 *Davis v. County School Board of Prince Edward County*, transcript of testimony, 180ff.

portant to segregationists because of their conviction that Negroes are inferior to whites in intelligence and have less ability to learn in school. Smith disputed the idea, declaring that race and color are irrelevant to learning ability. He pointed out that there is complete overlap in the distribution of intelligence and aptitude among races and emphasized that individual differences within each race are vastly larger than differences in racial averages. Nevertheless, racial differences as measured by intelligence tests do exist, but Smith accounted for them by the "environmental handicap to which the Negro group has been subjected as a result of segregation, discrimination, and prejudice." This handicap, he suggested, comes not from school segregation alone, but from the total social environment, which impairs the Negro's intellectual and educational development. "The society in which we live, with its values, with its sources of recognition and prestige, is predominantly a white society," Smith explained. "Any pattern of human relationships that involves cutting off a segment of the group, the Negro, from full participation in this predominantly white culture that we live in, with its historical continuity of values, is, in itself bound to be impoverishing as far as the intellectual and educational development of the individual is concerned." As a result of the isolation of the Negro child from the general community, his cultural horizons are restricted, and his incentive to learn and his intellectual curiosity are less well developed than those of the white child. He has less reason to discipline himself, to sacrifice today for rewards tomorrow. He concludes that the rewards go to the white man, and in so doing surrenders to the system and becomes the kind of individual described in the racist stereotype—"stupid, illiterate, apathetic, [and] happy-go-lucky."

Smith was cross-examined at length. Attorneys for the state made much of the fact that IQ tests almost invariably show significant average differences between whites and Negroes. They also attempted to invert Smith's statement that segregation results in personality distortions among Negroes and use it for their own purposes. Forced integration, they suggested, might be just as much an insult to the integrity and self-respect of white children as forced segregation is to Negroes. This suggestion, which Smith rejected, was raised on many occasions by segregationists, but they offered no evidence other than personal surmises to substantiate it. (It would probably be even more difficult to prove objectively than the contention that segregation is psychologically harmful to Negroes.) It was a point segregationists reached by deduction, but through faulty logic, for they ignored the fact that segregation means one thing to whites and something entirely different to Negroes. Ironically, the point was premised upon a fact which Smith had gone to great lengths to prove—that segregation is an expression of the white man's contempt for Negroes. More significantly, it indicated that segregationists and integrationists had basically different views of the issues in the Davis case. The NAACP obviously considered the case as part of a general attack upon racial segregation in American society and upon the legal props which support it. The state of Virginia, however, like the state of South Carolina in the Briggs case, regarded the issue as no more than whether racial segregation should continue in the public schools of one school district in the state. The NAACP expected that victory in the Brown cases would signal the beginning of the end of segregation as a way of life; attorneys for Virginia and South Carolina clearly expected segregation to continue as the general policy in the South regardless of the outcome of the Davis and Briggs cases. This difference explains, in part at least, why the issues which the social scientists raised were not discussed or debated more effectively, why no real dialogue ever developed between the two sides in either of the cases. There was no agreement on fundamental issues, and, without this, attorneys for the two sides could do no more than argue at each other. The statement that enforced segregation would be injurious to the personalities of white children was meaningless from the integrationists' view of the issues in the case, but it was full of meaning for segregationists.

In cross-examining Smith, the attorneys raised another of the segregationists' major arguments, that court-ordered integration would be no more effective than national prohibition had been in the 1920's. They declared that an overwhelming majority of the people of Virginia were opposed to integrating the public schools, and would simply but massively refuse to obey a court order to that effect. And this, they warned, would bring the courts and the law itself into disrepute. Smith was unimpressed by this reasoning. The research of social scientists upon this point, he said, tends to show that peaceful integration can be accomplished, and in fact has been accomplished, even where a high degree of prejudice exists, provided there is a willingness on the part of state and local authorities to enforce the law firmly and impartially.[3] Even among prejudiced persons, there "is a tendency to accept directions of authority, to accept the convictions imposed by those who are regarded as superior." If, therefore, "with full authority of the court, with full and sincere backing of the state authorities, segregation were ruled . . . unconstitutional," Smith concluded, "I would say that the more highly prejudiced individual would be likely to fall in line and comply." [4]

Isidor Chein of the American Jewish Congress and co-author with Max Deutscher of the major study of the attitudes of social scientists toward racial segregation, followed Smith to the witness stand. Dr. Chein (a Ph.D. in psychology from Columbia) testified concerning the study he and Max Deutscher had made of the attitudes of social scientists toward racial segregation.[5] He discussed the ill effects of segregation upon personality, emphasizing its effects upon whites as well as Negroes. In his view segregation inflicted as much personality damage upon whites as upon Negroes, though of a different sort. The treatment accorded Negroes in a segregated society, he suggested, generates in many whites an exaggerated, unreal feeling of their own superiority and makes then contemptuous of Negroes. At the same time, it produces in them a sense of guilt and uneasiness. The result is a "dissociation of moral values," a compartmentalization of values which enables an individual committed to the democratic, egalitarian rhetoric of American life and the humanitarianism of New Testament Christianity to act and feel toward Negroes as a segregated society demands. This weakens the moral system not merely in an ethical sense but "in terms of the control which the individual has which sustains his relationship to

[3] The most convenient of these studies is by Kenneth Clark and others and is Part III of "Desegregation: An Appraisal of the Evidence," 13–68.

[4] It is perhaps appropriate to note here that events since 1954 have generally borne Smith out. The processes of integration have almost invariably worked smoothly where there has been a determination by state and local officials to uphold law and order, as in Louisville, Atlanta, Charlotte, and Miami. Violence has tended to develop only where officials themselves overtly or covertly condoned defiance, as in Little Rock, New Orleans, Oxford, and Birmingham. The analogy between prohibition and integration, which seemed at first so valid, has proven less and less accurate in recent years. Integration as the law of the land is today winning increasing acceptance among the American people, including white Southerners. Time and events are proving Smith's assessment more valid than that of the Virginia attorneys.

[5] *Davis v. County School Board of Prince Edward County*, transcript of testimony, 209ff.

authority." As a child he is told by the authority of the state that segregation is desirable and necessary, and therefore morally right, and if he has a basic respect for and loyalty to the state he must incorporate this "fact" into his value system. At this point the distortion of moral and ethical values crystallizes.

The last NAACP witness was Kenneth Clark who repeated much of his testimony from the Briggs case, but he also discussed interviews which he had with fourteen of the plaintiffs' children.[6] The purpose of his interviews was to assess the effects of segregation upon the Negro children of Prince Edward County, especially in terms of attitudes toward their schools. He found that the children had negative, critical attitudes toward their own schools, which contrasted sharply with their positive impressions of white schools in the county. "Not one of these children seemed to have thought of the possibility that the white school could have something wrong with it," Clark stated, and he concluded that school segregation creates conditions "which leads to completely distorted concepts of reality." He noted among all the children "an excessive preoccupation with matters of race [and] racial struggle." Their experiences had oriented them to consider themselves, their schools, family, and society primarily in racial terms, and invidious racial terms at that. "The most important thing to them," Clark observed, "is racial."

The attorneys for Virginia and Prince Edward County presented their rebuttal through a series of witnesses which included political and civic leaders of the state, educators, and social scientists. One of the most significant of their witnesses was Dr. Lindley Stiles, dean of education at the University of Virginia. A native of New Mexico and educated (doctorate in education) at the University of Colorado, Dean Stiles testified on a wide range of subjects, and his testimony is one of the most instructive statements of the segregationist position in the voluminous transcript of the Brown cases.[7] This is itself remarkable, for Stiles had a curiously ambivalent attitude toward segregation. He was convinced that public school segregation had many advantages for Negroes, which he enumerated at the beginning of his testimony. Segregated schools provide employ-

---

[6] *Davis v. County School Board of Prince Edward County,* transcript of testimony, 254ff.

[7] *Davis v. County School Board of Prince Edward County,* transcript of testimony, 493ff.

ment for educated Negroes, he declared, employment which they could not hope for in integrated schools, and give the race a voice in running its own school system. They shield Negro children from the taunts of white children, remove them from competition with children of a more advanced race, and protect them from the indifference or even hostility of white teachers. "Those of us who study this question," Stiles testified, "are convinced that the relationship between the teacher and the child, and between the child and the group in school, is of utmost importance in terms of how much and how well he learns in school. The teacher's acceptance of a child, her understanding of him and his background . . . her ability to teach him, or the child's being accepted in a group, or being emotionally a part of a group, is [sic] a vital factor in how well he learns."

To illustrate his point Stiles related the case of two Negro children who, he said, had enrolled in an otherwise all-white school in New Jersey. In the new school, they encountered so much difficulty that within "a very short time, the doctor ordered that [they] be taken out of the white school, because the emotional and psychological impact on their personalities was so great that they simply could not make the adjustment." Such incidents, Stiles continued, are products of race prejudice and can be prevented only by segregated schools, for prejudice exists without regard to law. In fact, he said, segregation laws tend to restrain the growth of prejudice. "Where segregation prevails by law, people seem to depend upon the law and certain customs to maintain a division between the races that is acceptable, to the white people particularly. Where the law does not exist, prejudice is substituted for the law, and many people depend much more heavily upon developing prejudices in order to defend the kind of segregation they want, than they do here in Virginia." The effects of integration might therefore be the opposite of what integrationists anticipate.

Stiles then turned his attention to the immediate issue in the Davis case, the specific problems relating to integration in secondary schools. Curiously, he thought the problems of integrating elementary schools were not insurmountable, and he foresaw "very little problem" in admitting Negroes to white graduate and professional schools. "I have seen Negro children and white children go to school . . . at the early elementary stages with very little difficulty," he testified. "But as they approach adolescence . . . where Negro and white children attend the same schools, resistance develops because of home teaching on the part of both races." And the schools, despite Stiles's faith in them as instruments of social reform, were unable to overcome this "resistance."

Stiles's testimony on this point indicates one of the most significant anomalies in the segregationists' testimony—a tendency to interpret evidence to meet an immediate need. Integration at the high school level was the immediate issue in the Davis case, and Stiles testified in effect that this was the level at which integration was most likely to prove unworkable. One wonders what the South Carolinians, who were simultaneously involved in the Briggs case which sought to integrate the elementary schools of Clarendon County, thought of Stiles's statement that integration at the elementary level could be achieved "with very little difficulty." Such inconsistencies in the segregationists' case resulted from the equivocal nature of the convictions of moderates like Stiles, and illustrated the difficulties in reconciling the moderate and more extreme defenses of segregation.

This difficulty was further reflected in other parts of Stiles's testimony. Like other moderate segregationists, Stiles was committed in his own mind to the principles of democracy and New Testament Christianity, and he felt impelled to speak in terms compatible with those principles. "In theory," he said, "I feel that Negroes are entitled to every opportunity that anyone else has, that they show the potentiality of earning." But he added, "I do not think that we have rights that come automatically"; rather, "we earn certain benefits in a society by the way we develop as a race or as individuals." Such statements are both internally contradictory (does one "earn" benefits as an individual or as a member of a race?) and implicitly discriminatory (they would require individual Negroes to "earn" rights which all whites receive automatically), but no one who accepts them can defend segregation unless he is convinced that segregation is not discriminatory.

Yet Stiles was apparently unconvinced on this point. "Obviously, a person in education who holds my convictions is deeply concerned about how we move and feel toward the abolition of segregation," he stated, "and in terms of my theory of democracy and belief in Christianity, I simply don't accept segregation as a social practice." So, immediately after testifying that segregation was beneficial to Negroes and compatible with equality of opportunity, he declared that he himself was not a segregationist. He overcame this apparent contradiction by embracing a view widely held by Southern moderates: that integration, though theoretically desirable, is impossible in the South at this time because the mores and prejudices of Southern whites will not tolerate it. Like other racial moderates, Stiles was optimistic. "It seems to me," he told the court, "that education is the intellectual and moral penicillin by which the bacteria of segregation [a curious phrase for a witness *for* segregation] are being destroyed, and the degree that Negro children are given equal opportunities to learn, and to the extent that all children in Virginia are provided better schools, segregation, in my opinion, is in fact in the process of being abolished."

Here then is the final paradox. The segregation system contains the seeds of its own destruction. The ultimate product of segregated schools in the South will be an integrated society. The process by which this is to be achieved is slow and difficult, and Stiles's argument with the NAACP witnesses was due to their desire to speed it up artificially. "The debate that goes on in this court," he declared, "is not over whether or not this patient (our society) can or should be cured of the ailment of segregation, but rather, it is a debate as to how to treat the disease; and I favor the administration of the antidote education in ever increasing dosages, rather than surgery at a time when the patient may not yet have strength enough to withstand the shock, or when the risk of spreading the infection would be too great." [8]

Stiles's equivocation stemmed from the perennial dilemma of racial moderates in the South—how best to reconcile the reality of segregation with their hopes for interracial progress and Negro improvement. Here was a man, a democrat and a Christian, who admitted that segregation violated the precepts of democracy and Christianity, and yet he testified in court in favor of an indefinite

[8] The transcript of the Davis testimony does not record that the attorneys for Virginia and Prince Edward County were discomforted or chagrined by Stiles's endorsement of integration, or by his statement that the educational system of the state was really a gigantic effort to achieve an integrated society. Stiles's optimism, though superficially plausible, was naive and contrary to the South's racial experience. There is nothing in the history of that section to indicate that integration or any improvement in the status of Negroes comes voluntarily or spontaneously; on the contrary, every advancement in the past has been a direct result of "outside" pressure and Negro protest.

continuation of segregation. By reading his testimony carefully one sees clearly that he was aware of the inequities in the dual school system of Virginia and was troubled by the injustices the system perpetrated. Moreover, his faith in the efficacy of education as a social cathartic indicated a belief in environmentalism and a view of social progress which are anomalous in a segregationist. He had, however, no corresponding faith in law and public policy as instruments of social change, and he was blind to the fact that changes in race relations in the past, whether emancipation, disfranchisement, segregation, or even various instances of integration, had invariably been forced upon the Negro or the Southern white or both. It would be possible, perhaps, to dismiss Stiles as a naive idealist or even an unctuous hypocrite, but to do so would be to miss an important point. By his ability to compartmentalize his ideas and values, he avoided conscious hypocrisy, and, more than that, had the best of both worlds: an intellectual conviction in favor of integration (and thus presumably an easy conscience) and at the same time a willingness to condone (even support) segregation as necessary and desirable for the time being.

Dr. William H. Kelley, a neurologist and psychiatrist of wide experience, followed Stiles to the witness stand. Dr. Kelley was director of the Memorial Foundation and Memorial Guidance Clinic of Richmond, a treatment center for children with behavior problems. Some form of segregation, he declared, was an integral part of all societies and cultures; and without saying so outrightly, he implied it was an inherent part of human nature.[9] Racial integration always produces racial problems, he explained, but at the secondary school level the difficulties are expecially great, for there "sex problems begin to come into the picture." The truth is that integration and not segregation is the problem, Kelley insisted, because the incessant propaganda of integrationists has an unsettling effect upon Negro children. They are told repeatedly that segregation is an evil, that they are victims of racial discrimination, and as a result they become dissatisfied with themselves and their lot in life and express their dissatisfaction in antisocial behavior.

The most significant phases of Kelley's testimony dealt with Kenneth Clark's doll tests and the relevancy of those tests to Prince

[9] *Davis v. County School Board of Prince Edward County,* transcript of testimony, 519ff.

Edward County. The tests, Kelley thought, were interesting but of dubious value. They were projective tests, that is, tests in which psychologists attempt to externalize or objectify feelings which are internal and subjective. The results of such tests are too variable and too easily manipulated to be relied upon completely, Kelley stated. The sex or race or skin color of the person administering them, to say nothing of his attitudes and prejudices, might significantly influence the results. In addition, Clark's tests were not sufficiently standardized. Before their value can be determined, they should be administered by whites to Negroes, by Negroes to whites, and to other minority groups, and the results of the various combinations compared. In any case, Kelley warned, all such experiments should be used cautiously. The social sciences are still young, their techniques imperfect, their data inexact and subject to conflicting interpretations. Clark's interpretations are nothing more than his own conclusions from his particular point of view, and acceptable only to those who share his point of view. His interviews with Prince Edward County school children are similarly suspect, for more often than not such interviews only confirm the prejudices of the interviewer. The interviews and doll tests are ingenious but questionable devices through which Clark collected ostensibly objective data to buttress his personal prejudices, but they are hardly sufficient authority for a court order upsetting the Southern way of life.

Under cross-examination Kelley admitted that his observations were not based on his own professional experience, that he had in fact never conducted integrated therapy groups and had himself never studied the effects of integration on personality development or behavior patterns. These admissions, of course, reflected seriously upon his stature as an authority on the effects of integration, and undermined the effectiveness of his testimony. His views on the limited value of projective tests, however, are widely shared by psychologists.

The state climaxed its case by calling Professor Henry E. Garrett, then chairman of the psychology department at Columbia University, and a past president of the American Psychological Association. Garrett was one of the nation's most prominent psychologists, and his appearance was a major *coup* by the Virginia attorneys. Born in Virginia in 1894, he received his undergraduate education at Richmond University, and after a brief interlude as a high school teacher in Virginia, entered Columbia as a graduate student in psychology. This Southern background is quite important to an understanding of Garrett's racial views. In spite of his education at Columbia and his distinguished career as a psychologist, he never overcame many of the racial attitudes which his early life in the black belt ingrained in him. On the subjects of race, Negroes, and segregation, he is even today a proponent of ideas which an earlier generation of Americans imbibed from such books as Madison Grant's *The Passing of the Great Race* (1916) and Earnest Sevier Cox's *White America* (1923). His views are essentially the same as those of the Mississippi Citizens' Councils and other outspoken segregationists of the deep South.

In 1923 Garrett completed his graduate studies, received his Ph.D., and with it an appointment in the psychology department at Columbia, where he remained until retiring in 1956. Among his students at Columbia were Kenneth Clark, Mamie Clark, and Isidor Chein, and his attitude toward them in the Davis case was that of a learned mentor, wise with years and experience, chiding his students for their naivete and overenthusiasm. Garrett's career has been distinguished and full of recognition. During his last fifteen years at Columbia he was chairman of the psychology department. His fellow psychologists elected him president of the Psychometric Society in 1943, the Eastern Psychological Association in 1944, and the American Psychological Association in 1946. He is the author of a number of authoritative works, among them *Statistics in Psychology and Education* (1926), now in its fifth edition, *General Psychology* (1955), now in its second edition, and *Great Experiments in Psychology* (1957), a history of significant experiments in differential experimental psychology. He has, in addition, written dozens of articles and reports, and is a general editor of the *American Psychological Series*. Since his retirement from Columbia he has been visiting professor of psychology at the University of Virginia.

With this distinguished background, Garrett spoke with considerable authority on psychological subjects, especially testing and psychometrics. And inasmuch as he accepted in its entirety the segregationist position in civil rights controversies, he was a godsend for segregationists in the Davis case; he was especially useful to the Virginia attorneys, a man whose credentials matched those of any witness for the NAACP. Garrett's attitude toward segregation bore little resemblance to that of Dean Stiles. He showed none of Stiles's ambivalence, repeated none of Stiles's homilies about the future of interracial progress in the South. He endorsed segregation openly and directly, and his testimony in the Davis case was only the first of a long list of services he has performed for segregationists and scientific racists. Since 1954 he has played a leading role in the history of scientific racism, and his name will appear frequently in the course of this study.

Wasting no time on preliminaries, the Virginia attorneys at once asked Garrett if psychologists had yet reached the point "where true measurement can be made by objective tests, or any other tests, as to the impact on personality of such a factor as segregation." [10] Garrett replied simply, "I think it is very doubtful," and he proceeded to challenge the major points made by NAACP witnesses. Racially segregated schools, he declared, are no more discriminatory than parochial schools for Catholics or Jews. "Provided you have equal facilities," he stated, "it seems to me that in the State of Virginia today, taking into account the temper of its people, its mores and its customs and background, that the Negro student at the high school level will get a better education in a separate school than he will in mixed schools."

If a Negro child goes to a school as well equipped as that of his white neighbor, [he added later] if he had teachers of his own race and friends of his own race, it seems to me that he is much less likely to develop tensions, animosities, and hostilities, than if you put him into a mixed school where, in Virginia, inevitably he will be a minority group. . . . They are marked off, immediately, and I think, as I have said before, that at the adolescent level, children, being what they are, are stratifying themselves with respect to social and economic status, reflect the opinions of their parents, and the Negro would be much more likely to develop tensions, animosities, and hostilities. . . .

I think, in the high schools of Virginia, if the Negro child had equal facilities, his own teachers, his own friends, and a good feeling, he would be more likely to develop pride in himself as a Negro, which I think we would all like to see him do—to develop his own potentialities, his sense of duty, his sense of art, his sense of histrionics; and my prediction would be that if you conducted separate schools at the high school level for Negroes and whites, one of two things might happen: that the Negroes might develop their schools up to the level where they would not mix,

10 *Davis v. County School Board of Prince Edward County,* transcript of testimony, 548ff.

themselves; and I would like to see it happen. I think it would be poetic justice. They would develop their sense of domestic art, and music, which they seem to have a talent for—athletics—and they would say, "We prefer to remain as a Negro group." The other would be in a mixed school where, as I said, a great many animosities, disturbances, resentments, and hostilities, and inferiorities would develop.

Here are the contrasts between Garrett and Stiles. Garrett's attitude toward the Negro is that of the Southern white traditionalist and paternalist. He assumes, implicitly, that Negroes are intellectually inferior to whites, and that their genius lies in areas which require little intelligence. His static, hereditarian view of society was much more characteristic of segregationists than was Stiles's view.

Garrett attempted to rebut the major facets of the testimony presented by the NAACP witnesses, but he did this by speaking as a learned and experienced psychologist instead of offering specific empirical data. Asked about Brewster Smith's statement that racial segregation is an insult to the integrity of the individual, he replied, "The term 'insult' to an individual's personality . . . is fairly strong language. . . . I think an idealistic person, who is likely to let his sympathies go beyond his judgment may be so strongly prejudiced on the side of abstract goodness that he does not temper the application of the general principle with a certain amount of what might be called common sense." In similar fashion he dismissed the study of social science opinion by Isidor Chein and Max Deutscher. Their questionnaire, he said, consisted of "shotgun" or "blunderbuss" questions which are subject to varying interpretations. "I would not like to make a bet," he added, "but I would wager that I could send a questionnaire and phrase it rightly and get almost any answer I wanted."

The testimony by Garrett was doubly effective because of his professional stature. His appearance marked a significant break in academic opinion concerning integration. Moreover, he emphasized what was probably the segregationists' most effective argument— that psychology and the social sciences are infant disciplines, inexact and easily manipulated. To the data, experiments, and opinions offered by NAACP witnesses, he replied that the issues are still unresolved, that sufficient data have not yet been collected to enable one to speak with assurance. From a psychologist of Garrett's reputation, such statements were not without authority. Interestingly, much of his effectiveness came from the restraint with which he asserted the authority of psychology and the social sciences, and from the respect he paid to open-mindedness. His restraint and open-mindedness here, however, are in marked contrast to his later pronouncements on the subject. In his writings since 1954 he has often stated that the social science evidence concerning segregation and racial differences *is* conclusive, and that it demonstrates both the inferiority of Negroes and the necessity for racial segregation.

The social scientists who testified for the NAACP made virtually no impression upon the special three-judge court which heard the Davis case. In their unanimous decision the three judges, Albert V. Bryan, Armistead M. Dobie, and Sterling Hutcheson, endorsed the segregationist position in its entirety.[11] "Maintenance of the separated [school] systems in Virginia," they wrote, "has not been social despotism. . . . Whatever its demerits in theory, in practice it has gotten greater opportunity for the Negro. . . . We have found no hurt or harm to either race."

The task of Clark and his associates did not end with their appearance as expert witnesses in the Briggs, Davis, and other cases. The NAACP appealed each of the cases to the Supreme Court, and sought the assistance of social scientists in making the appeal. The NAACP attorneys asked Clark and his associates to prepare a social science appendix to their brief to the Supreme Court and in other ways assist them in making the most effective presentation of social science material to the high tribunal. Prepared by Gerhart Saenger, Isidor Chein, Stuart Cook, and Clark, the appendix to appellants' brief was a succinct and forceful statement of psychological, sociological, and educational arguments against racial discrimination, and was endorsed by thirty-five leading social scientists, among them Gordon Allport, Allison Davis, Otto Klineberg, Alfred McClung Lee, Robert M. MacIver, Gardner Murphy, Robert Redfield, Ira De A. Reid, Arnold Rose, Brewster Smith, and others of similar stature.[12]

The appendix consisted of two parts, the most important of

11 Opinion of the Court, No. 4 (*Davis v. County School Board of Prince Edward County*), 621, in transcript of *Brown v. Board of Education*, 347 U.S. 483 (1954).

12 The appendix is reprinted in "The Effects of Segregation and the Consequences of Desegregation: A Social Science Statement," *Minnesota Law Review*, XXXVII (May, 1953), 427–38; and also as Appendix III in Clark, *Prejudice and Your Child*, 166–84.

which summarized the kind of material presented in the Briggs and Davis testimony, and need not be repeated here. The appendix, however, went much further than the testimony, especially in dealing with two questions frequently raised by segregationists and likely to be of concern to the Supreme Court: (1) Will widespread integration of schools adversely affect educational standards? and (2) Is school integration in the South likely to be accompanied by violence? The first question rests heavily upon the assumption that Negroes as a race are intellectually inferior, and the authors of the appendix answered it with an emphatic "no." Relying upon the pioneering works of Otto Klineberg, they noted that "the available scientific evidence indicates that much, perhaps all, of the observable differences among various racial and national groups may be adequately explained in terms of environmental differences." It had been found, they continued, that "the differences between the average intelligence test scores of Negro and white children decrease, and the overlap of the distribution increases proportionately to the number of years that the Negro children have lived in the North." Other studies, also by Klineberg, had shown that this change could not be explained by the hypothesis of selective migration. "It seems clear," they concluded, "that fears based on the assumption of innate racial differences in intelligence are not well founded." Arguments concerning the intellectual abilities of Negroes and whites are, therefore, arguments for homogeneous or ability groupings, not racial segregation.

The question whether school integration would be accompanied by violence was a vitally important one, not only for segregationists who raised it repeatedly but for social scientists trying to make a case for integration. In stressing the possibility, indeed the likelihood, of violence, segregationists insisted that laws cannot alter fundamental human convictions, and warned that the average Southern white man was so thoroughly committed to school segregation that he would use violence to prevent integration. Attorneys for South Carolina and Virginia freely predicted violence would accompany any effort to desegregate the public schools of their states, and if their predictions were accurate, a court order outlawing school segregation would indeed be unwise.

To answer such predictions the authors of the appendix studied the history of specific instances of racial integration and found numerous examples of successful integration in areas where violence had been commonly predicted. Integration in the armed forces, already virtually complete, had occurred without major incident despite the involvement of Southern men and installations on a substantial scale. Successful integration had also occurred in such sensitive areas as housing, employment, recreation facilities, and general community life. Under the right circumstances, the appendix stated, "desegregation not only proceeds without major difficulties, but has been observed to lead to the emergence of more favorable attitudes and friendlier relations between races."

The social scientists' final task was to assist NAACP attorneys in answering a series of questions which the Supreme Court asked appellants and appellees to discuss in a reargument of the Brown cases. Their assistance was especially important in answering question IV: "Assuming it is decided that segregation in public schools violates the Fourteenth Amendment, (a) Would a decree necessarily follow providing that, within the limits set by normal geographic school districting, Negro children should forthwith be admitted to schools of their choice, or (b) May this court, in the exercise of its equity powers, permit an effective gradual adjustment to be brought about from existing segregated systems to a system not based on color distinctions?"

The significance of the question is apparent, for it suggests that the justices were already considering a decision permitting gradual integration, or, in their own words, integration "with all deliberate speed." The question reflected the Court's concern that a ruling directing immediate massive integration might disrupt the public school system in the South and lead to widespread disorder and violence. It also indicated that the justices thought gradual integration would be less likely to provoke violent reactions among segregationists. The implications of the question were profound, and Clark and his associates at once set about studying those implications in light of available social science data.[13]

What they did was greatly to expand their study of the history of actual instances of integration. They studied integration in Northern, Southern, and Border states, examining each episode in as much detail as the evidence permitted. They found a surprisingly large number of instances of successful integration in such diverse areas as churches, the armed forces, housing, interstate

13 For the results of their efforts see Clark, "Desegregation: An Appraisal of the Evidence."

transportation, public accommodations, organized sports, employment, voting, government service, higher education, and even in public elementary and secondary schools. In some cases integration had been voluntary; in others the result of court orders, political pressure, administrative action, population changes, threats of adverse publicity, interracial negotiation, or a combination of these. Sometimes it had been gradual and piecemeal, at other times immediate and largescale. Rarely, however, had there been "overt violent resistance." The most significant and perhaps the most surprising result of the study was the evidence that immediate desegregation was no more likely to produce violence than was gradual desegregation. Indeed, wrote Clark summarizing the study, "there is some suggestive evidence that the larger the scale of the desegregation the greater the likelihood of general acceptance or the lack of overt resistance."

On the basis of this study Clark and his colleagues asked the Supreme Court for a decision ordering substantial desegregation of public schools within a brief period of time. The Court, of course, rejected this advice, a point which is never mentioned by segregationists who allege that the Court was "duped" by the social scientists, and chose instead to permit school integration to be dragged out interminably. On two crucial points—the speed with which integration must be achieved and the amount of integration necessary to satisfy the letter of the law—the Court ignored the best available social science data and followed instead a course which the social scientists warned against.[14]

[14] When viewed from the hindsight afforded by the history of integration over the last dozen years, the evidence offered by the social scientists on these points seems astonishingly valid. Despite some conspicuous exceptions, e.g., abandonment of the public school system in Prince Edward County, the evidence has stood the test of time well. If the Supreme Court had not been so lenient in interpreting the phrase "with all deliberate speed," and had not so readily accepted pupil placement laws, which from the beginning were transparent devices to limit school integration to tokenism, the transition from a segregated to a desegregated society in the South might have been more rapid and less agonizing. Despite vehement denunciations from Southern segregationists, the Brown decision as modified by "all deliberate speed" and pupil placement laws is a tokenism decision rather than an integration decision. Its effectiveness depends almost completely upon the willingness of local officials to abide by it, and there has accordingly been much school integration in border areas and very little in the deep South. Moreover, most of the integration in the deep South since 1954 has occurred in areas outside the classroom and has come from sit-ins, picketing, and voter registration

Despite the limitations which the Court has accepted in implementing the Brown decision, the decision was itself substantially influenced by the work of Clark and his collaborators. They did an impressive job summarizing a massive amount of scientific evidence and presenting it to the courts. The measure of their performance is the Brown decision itself which recognized as a fact that racial segregation in the public schools is psychologically damaging to Negroes and that this fact "is amply supported by modern [social science] authority."

drives rather than the Brown decision itself. Even the speed-up in school integration since 1964 has been a result of the Civil Rights Act of 1964 and, in turn, of the Birmingham riots of 1963 and only indirectly from the decision.

4

SCIENTIFIC RACISM AND PSYCHOLOGY

The Brown decision caught segregationists by surprise. They expected the Court to uphold the separate-but-equal principle on condition that the facilities and curricula of Negro schools be brought up to white standards at once. Such a decision would be acceptable to them for it would follow the recommendations of Professor Garrett and others who testified for segregation in the Davis case. The Court, however, rejected both Garrett's testimony and the separate-but-equal doctrine, and to whatever extent the Brown decision rested upon science it was the science of equalitarians and environmentalists. To segregationists, however, "equalitarian" science was pseudoscience, a nefarious mixture of calculated misrepresentation, artful pleading, and wishful thinking—and patently invalid. It is not surprising, then, that in attempting to discredit the Brown decision they turned to science. They sought not only to refute the social science incorporated in the decision, but more importantly, they endeavored to develop a systematic scientific defense of segregation, especially segregation in the public schools of the South.

The success of this endeavor would depend upon their ability to enlist the services of at least a few reputable social scientists, whose task would be to systematize the ideas of scientific racism and marshal scientific data in the manner most useful to segregationists. Nor were they entirely unsuccessful. They attracted to their ranks a small cadre of academic social scientists, who over the last decade have produced a substantial body of ostensibly scientific literature, some of which has achieved a wide circulation and a certain notoriety. In concert with these social scientists, segregationists have sponsored an effort, informally coordinated, to "educate" the American people on the subject of race and challenge the Brown decision in the federal courts on grounds that it rests upon false science. The result has been not to reverse the decision—this the courts have refused to do—but to stimulate a series of bitter controversies between racists and hereditarians on one side and equalitarians and environmentalists on the other. Another result has been the publication of a large body of literature which many racists today accept as scientific proof of Negro inferiority, and which they often cite as justification for segregation. The purpose of this and succeeding chapters is to discuss the major works and ideas of these social scientists who have served the cause of segregation and to demonstrate the close ties between them and Southern segregationists.

The immediate objective of segregationists has been to prevent the integration of public schools in the South. As a result, the most pressing task of scientific racists has been to formulate a scientific defense for segregated education, and no social science discipline has been more important in that task than psychology. Scientific racists are especially concerned with comparative racial intelligence, psychological test results, and the relative educational capacity of whites and Negroes. They are similarly concerned with the psychic traits and personality characteristics of both races, especially Negroes, and the extent to which these are transmitted by heredity and influenced by environment. To psychologists who serve their cause, segregationists posed several crucial questions: Are Negroes inferior to whites in intelligence? Do psychological test results prove this inferiority? Will integration lower educational standards in "white" schools? Are Negroes by nature more immoral and socially irresponsible than whites? Are such traits transmitted by heredity? Will racial amalgamation lower the quality of the American people? Racists answer these questions in the affirmative, but they seek from psychologists a scientific basis for their answer.

In exploiting psychology racists enjoyed several advantages. Negroes *do,* on the average, make consistently lower scores than whites on intelligence, aptitude, and achievement tests. Negro schools *are,* on the whole, inferior to white schools. The level of achievement of Negro students *is,* in general, significantly below that of whites, especially in the South and the ghettoes of Northern cities. Negroes *do,* on the average, commit more crimes of violence and have higher rates of illegitimacy and venereal disease. They *do* have more broken homes and more rundown neighborhoods. They *do* deviate further from middle class standards of conduct.[1] The point of controversy between racists and equalitarians is not whether these conditions exist, but rather the cause and cure of them. To blame them on race is easy and convenient, and, to racists at least, obviously correct. That explanation suits their purposes and they find it easy to defend. One need only look around, they insist, to see the importance of race and the differences it produces between whites and Negroes. These differences, whether of physical features, intelligence test scores, or personal and moral traits, are, in the eyes of racists, the meaning and manifestation of race.

The exploitation of psychology by racists had no specific beginning. Among psychologists in this country there has always been a group, of varying numbers and influence, committed to the idea of innate racial inequality. After World War I, however, as investigative techniques improved and social scientists became more careful and objective in studying race, psychologists found the idea of

[1] For a brilliant summary of these facts see Daniel Patrick Moynihan, *The Negro Family: The Case for National Action* (U.S. Department of Labor, 1965).

innate inequality less and less acceptable. By the 1930's and 1940's they had discarded it altogether, or virtually so. But it left a legacy, in the form of a voluminous literature ostensibly proving racial inequality and Negro inferiority, which latter-day racists have searched out, dusted off, and used liberally.

Other psychologists who have contributed substantially to the literature of scientific racism in recent years, in addition to Henry E. Garrett, are Frank C. J. McGurk, Audrey Shuey, and Robert T. Osborne.[2] Professor McGurk, in an article published in *U.S. News and World Report* in 1956, made what was apparently the first systematic effort by a social scientist to dispute the social science incorporated in the Brown decision.[3] Born in Philadelphia in 1910, McGurk received his undergraduate education at the Catholic University of America, where he also earned a Ph.D. in psychology in 1951. He has had several teaching appointments, at the University of Pennsylvania, the Catholic University, Lehigh, and from 1956 to 1964 at Villanova University, where he was an associate professor of psychology. He is now a professor of psychology at Alabama College. He has had several years' experience as a staff psychologist, including two years at the United States Military Academy. An academic, a psychologist, and an apologist for racial segregation, McGurk has been sometimes rebuked and often challenged by his fellow psychologists, few of whom find much merit in his work on comparative racial intelligence. Because of their criticisms he and other scientific racists have come to look upon himself as a martyr to academic freedom.[4]

As a social scientist, McGurk is chiefly interested in psychological testing, especially comparative testing of white and Negro intelligence and the influence of socioeconomic factors on test results,

2 Since Professor Garrett's contributions easily outweigh those of the others, and since his services as a protagonist for segregation transcend psychology, he is treated in a later chapter.

3 Frank C. J. McGurk, "A Scientist's Report on Race Differences," *U.S. News and World Report,* September 21, 1956, pp. 92–96.

4 McGurk has been especially concerned by the fact that most of his fellow social scientists are "liberals." He feels that this has resulted in the creation of an orthodoxy in the social sciences which is intolerant of dissenting opinion and has virtually destroyed academic freedom. For one of his discussions of this subject see his paper, "The Law, Social Science, and Academic Freedom," *Villanova Law Review,* V (Winter, 1959–60), 247–54. This paper was read at a symposium on law and social science at the annual meeting in 1959 of the American Psychological Association.

and his interest long antedated the Brown decision.[5] His research had convinced him well before 1954 that whites and Negroes are so different in intelligence or scholastic aptitude that they cannot be effectively educated together. In 1951 he offered as his doctoral thesis a study entitled "Comparison of the Performance of Negro and White High School Seniors on Cultural and Non-cultural Test Questions," [6] the purpose of which was to determine whether socio-economic factors account for the consistently lower scores of Negroes on intelligence tests. In accomplishing this study, which is frequently cited by scientific racists, McGurk administered tests consisting of 103 "least cultural" and 81 "most cultural" questions to 213 white and 213 Negro high school students in New Jersey and Pennsylvania. Matching the two groups in age, sex, educational background, socioeconomic status, and other environmental factors which affect test results, he believed that he was enabled thereby to eliminate or neutralize environmental factors and thus measure innate racial intelligence. His results, however, were substantially the same as those obtained by other psychologists in studies in which environmental factors were not controlled. Negroes made significantly lower scores than whites, overlapping the white average by approximately 28 percent.[7] But, surprisingly, they did better on the "most cultural" than on the "least cultural" items, a fact which McGurk took as additional evidence that the low scores of Negroes cannot be explained by environment. As a further check, he divided the students into groups according to socioeconomic status and compared the results of each status group by race. He found "high-status" Negroes well below "high-status" whites, though Negroes did relatively much better in lower status groups. In fact, the higher the status of the groups the poorer the Negroes' relative performance. "There is no evidence," McGurk wrote in a later study, "that as the socioeconomic status of the Negro increases, racial test-score differences decrease." [8]

---

[5] Frank C. J. McGurk, "Comparative Test Scores of Negro and White School Children in Richmond, Virginia," *Journal of Educational Psychology,* XXXIV (November, 1943), 473–84.

[6] (Washington: Catholic University of America Press, 1951, microcard).

[7] "Overlap" refers to the percentage of Negroes who equal or exceed the average score made by whites. An overlap of 50 percent represents equality.

[8] Frank C. J. McGurk, "On White and Negro Test Performance and Socio-economic Factors," *Journal of Abnormal and Social Psychology,* XLVIII (July, 1953), 450.

It was from this background that McGurk published his article in *U.S. News and World Report* in September, 1956. In that article he refined and reiterated the basic ideas of his 1951 study. "Are Negroes really equal to whites in their capacity for education?" he asked again. Can they compete on even terms in mixed schools, or do they drag down educational levels? His answers were substantially the same as they had been in his earlier study: Negroes are significantly below whites in educational capacity, and their incapacity is not removed by improving their socioeconomic conditions.

To substantiate these answers, McGurk examined the results of several experimental studies in comparative racial intelligence. Specifically, he compared the results of tests given to Army inductees in World War I with those of several studies made between 1935 and 1950, in which the examiners attempted to control environmental variables. The technique was ingenious. McGurk reasoned that the socioeconomic status of Negroes had improved markedly since World War I, and, if the environmental hypothesis were valid, Negroes should score significantly higher in 1935–50 than they had in 1917–18. The first of these assumptions is no doubt valid, but to transpose it into the conclusion that Negroes should therefore score higher on psychological tests is fallacious. The transpositions ignores environmental improvements which whites have also undergone, as well as changes in the test themselves. Though Negroes did not improve their scores relative to whites, there is evidence that both races had substantially improved their performance on psychological tests since World War I. In one study, for example, in which a group of white enlisted men in World War II were given the much simpler tests used in World War I, 83 percent exceeded the average score made by enlisted men in the earlier war.[9]

In addition to these weaknesses, McGurk also failed to specify the environmental improvements among Negroes which he thought should improve their relative test scores. In 1935 and 1950 Negroes were still generally segregated, still discriminated against, still told by society that theirs was a second-class race and they were second-rate human beings. In a thousand subtle and unsubtle ways they were still made to feel inferior and despised. Despite such factors as

---

9 See Thomas F. Pettigrew, *A Profile of the Negro American* (Princeton, 1964), 121–22.

these, McGurk found that the Negroes' performance had not significantly changed between 1917–18 and 1935–50, and their overlap of white averages was only 20 to 30 percent in each period. The significant improvement in socioeconomic status, he concluded, had not materially affected their performance on psychological tests.

Delving further into the relationship between environment, socioeconomic status, and intelligence, McGurk reported the results of a study of his own in which he had attempted to control environmental factors. He found that high-status Negroes overlapped high-status whites by only 18 percent, while low-status Negroes overlapped low-status whites by 41 percent. "What we have found is, again, a strange kind of reversal of what most writers say about the efficacy of socio-economic factors," he wrote. "If social and economic factors were so important, there should have been no differences between Negroes and whites in any of these comparisons." However, the reverse was the case. "An improvement in the socioeconomic positions of the Negro made him *less* able to compete with whites on psychological tests." He concluded therefore that "the factual evidence *completely* denies the theory that improveing the social and economic status of the Negro improves his capacity for education." [10]

Having drawn this conclusion McGurk related his findings to the integration controversy. But he did so indirectly, for he always insisted that he was a disinterested scientist following wherever his research led. "As far as psychological differences between Negroes and whites are concerned, we have wished—and dreamed—that there were no such differences," he declared. "We have identified this wish with reality, and on it we have established a race relations policy that was so clearly a failure that we had to appeal to distorting propaganda for support. When that, too, failed, we appealed to the legal machinery to do what nature was not content to do." Clearly the Brown decision was unwise, for school integration placed whites and Negroes in an unnatural relationship. The social order, McGurk wrote elsewhere, must recognize that "biogenetic factors play a major role in causing psychic differences between races." [11]

[10] McGurk, "A Scientist's Report on Race Difference," 96, 95. Emphasis added.
[11] Frank C. J. McGurk, "Introduction" to Nathaniel Weyl, *The Negro in American Civilization* (Washington, 1960), v. See also Frank C. J. McGurk, "Fact and Prejudice," *Contemporary Psychology*, III (September, 1958), 280.

The significance of McGurk's article in *U.S. News and World Report* in the developing controversy between racists and equalitarians is indicated by the response it evoked from both groups. Segregationists hailed it as definitive proof that school integration violates the laws of science and nature, and cited it repeatedly in their controversy with integrationists. *The Citizens' Council* described it as a "severe jolt" to integrationists, and another outspoken segregationist considered it "thorough and well-documented" proof "that the White race has a greater innate capacity to respond to favorable environment." [12]

Social scientists were less impressed. Eighteen of them issued a statement challenging McGurk's premises and method and denying the validity of his conclusions.[13] Citing the 1950 UNESCO "Statement on Race," a 1952 statement by physical anthropologists and geneticists, and the appendix to appellants' brief in the Brown cases, they dismissed McGurk's article as misleading to laymen and a misuse of science. "The scientific material available to us," they wrote, quoting the 1952 statement of physical anthropologists and geneticists, "does not justify the conclusion that inherited genetic differences are a major factor in producing the differences between the cultures and cultural achievements of different people." And they added, "we know of no new research which would reverse [this 1952 conclusion]."

In more specific terms they rejected McGurk's claim that he (or anyone else) had adequately controlled or neutralized environmental factors which affect the results of psychological tests. They insisted that such a task was impossible, at least at present, and that anyone who presumed otherwise was deceiving himself and, more

---

12 *The Citizens' Council*, II (October, 1956), 4; and Richard W. Edmonds, *Segregation, Is It Justified?* (Columbus, Georgia, 1957), 29, 34.

13 "Does Race Really Make a Difference in Intelligence?" *U.S. News and World Report*, October 26, 1956, pp. 74–76. The signers of the statement were Otto Klineberg of Columbia University; Theodore Newcomb and Daniel Katz of the University of Michigan; Gardner Murphy of the Menninger Foundation; David Krech of the University of California; Allison Davis of the University of Chicago; Anne Anastasi of Fordham University; Stuart Cook, Isidor Chein, and Marie Jahoda of New York University; Kenneth Clark of City College of New York; Nevitt Sanford of Vassar; Robin Williams, Jr., of Cornell University; Jerome Brunner of Harvard University; Bingham Dai of Duke University; Irving Lorge of Teachers College, Columbia; Solomon Asch of Swarthmore College; and David Rapaport of the Austen Riggs Foundation. The statement is also printed in "No Scientific Evidence of Race Differences," *Science News Letter*, October 27, 1956, p. 265.

importantly in McGurk's case, was misleading laymen. Segregation and discrimination, which exist in some form or another throughout this nation, make it impossible to equate environmental factors for whites and Negroes, or to devise a valid "non-cultural" test as McGurk claimed he had done. As two of his critics pointed out, the indices of socioeconomic status which McGurk used in formulating "noncultural" tests were designed to measure the differences between social *classes,* but the differences between social *castes* cannot be reduced to a neat index. "Not only in the South but [in the] North as well," wrote psychologists Ralph M. Dreger and Kent S. Miller, "whites and Negroes comprise separate castes; they are not merely representative of different classes." [14]

According to McGurk's critics, then, both his methodology and his conclusions were unscientific. His tests did not do what he claimed for them. He read far too much into his data, while at the same time ignoring evidence of his own which pointed to a direct relationship between environment and intelligence. His high-status subjects, whether whites or Negroes, scored substantially above his low-status subjects, but he apparently saw no significance in this. In his considerable research on racial intelligence, McGurk found that Negroes as a group score significantly below whites as a group, a fact which is universally acknowledged. But that, substantially, was all he found. He *inferred* that the lower Negro performance was due to factors connected with race, and not environment, but it was only an inference. He gave it the appearance of an empirically demonstrated fact by discussing several other studies which made, but did not prove, the same inference. In his writings, however, he gave the inference the coloration of fact, and it thereby became the basis for his views on social and educational policy.

McGurk's critics insisted that "any decision to use differences in average achievement of the two racial groups for classifying in advance *any individual child,* Negro or white, is scientifically unjustified." [15] And therein lies a major difference between equalitarians and scientific racists. Racists categorize people as members of a race, and define their civil rights and social status in racial

14 See Ralph M. Dreger and Kent S. Miller, "Comparative Psychological Studies of Negroes and Whites in the United States," *Psychological Bulletin,* LVII (No. 5, 1960) , 361–402.
15 "Does Race Really Make a Difference in Intelligence?" 76.

terms. Equalitarians, on the other hand, insist that innate differences in intelligence have not been proved and cannot be assumed, and that in any event racial intelligence is irrelevant to political and social policy. Constitutional and civil rights are rights of the individual as a citizen and are his without regard to race or intelligence, they assert. A citizen is an individual, not a racial abstraction, and must be treated as such by his government. If Negroes score *on the average* below whites on intelligence tests, racists accept this as sufficient cause to segregate public schools. Equalitarians draw no such conclusion, reasoning instead that if IQ is an appropriate criterion for assigning children to a particular school, it should be applied without regard to race. To them, McGurk's evidence, insofar as it was relevant to educational policy, argued not for racial segregation but for segregation by ability or intelligence. Racists reject this reasoning, and their rejection indicates that their real concern is not educational standards but racial segregation.

In a reply to two of his critics McGurk contended that he had no interest in trying to prove that Negroes are less intelligent than whites.[16] He was not even sure, he said, that IQ tests measure innate intelligence, though he was convinced that they accurately predict scholastic achievement. In integrated schools, he reasoned, whites will be held back by Negroes, and in the process the nation's intellectual resources will be wasted. The same objection, however, applies to Negro schools. Slow students impede bright ones without regard to race. If, as scientific racists insisted repeatedly, intelligence is the best guarantee of the survival of America and of Western civilization, it behooves the nation not to squander its intellectual resources, whether those resources are white or Negro.

Scientific racists do not claim that *all* Negroes make lower test scores than *all* whites. There is always an overlap, but this, they insist, should not obscure the more significant differences in racial averages. Typically, Negroes overlap whites by 20 to 30 percent. In his 1951 study, for example, McGurk found an overlap of 28

---

16 Frank C. J. McGurk, "Negro vs. White Intelligence—An Answer," *Harvard Educational Review*, XXIX (Winter, 1959), 54–62. He was answering William M. McCord and Nicholas J. Demerath III, "Negro Versus White Intelligence: A Continuing Controversy," *ibid.*, XXVII (Spring, 1958), 120–35. McCord and Demerath offered evidence from a study of their own that IQ test scores are closely related to environmental factors.

percent. Such figures, however, are sometimes deceiving, especially
to laymen. Technically, "overlap" means the percentage of Negroes who score higher than the *average* score made by whites.
Thus, an overlap of 50 percent, not 100 percent, means equality.
Perhaps a more meaningful way to express test results to laymen
is to point out the *range* of scores made by each racial group. In
the tests in which McGurk found a 28-percent overlap, *91 percent*
of the Negroes scored between the highest and lowest scores
made by whites who took the test.[17] By expressing results in this
fashion it becomes apparent that the differences *within* each race
are much larger than the differences *between* the races. But here
as elsewhere racists insist that racial *differences,* however minute,
are the crucial factor.

McGurk's study is not the racists' most important work on Negro
intelligence. That distinction belongs to a lengthy and detailed
study, *The Testing of Negro Intelligence,* published in 1958 and
reissued in a second edition in 1966, by Professor Audrey M.
Shuey, chairman of the department of psychology at Randolph-
Macon Woman's College, Lynchburg, Virginia. Dr. Shuey was born
in 1900 in Illinois, and received her undergraduate education at
the University of Illinois. She earned graduate degrees at Wellesley
and Columbia, receiving a Ph.D. in psychology from the latter in
1931. At Columbia she studied under Professor Henry E. Garrett,
and he contributed a laudatory foreword to both editions of her
study of Negro intelligence. She has held various academic appointments, at Barnard, Washington Square College of New York
University, and since 1943 at Randolph-Macon. In *American
Men of Science* she lists her specializations as "after images; learning behavior of kittens; [and] race differences."

The Testing of Negro Intelligence is, in briefest terms, a catalog-
ing of the statistical results of some 240 studies of the performance
of Negroes (and, in some instances, of whites) on psychological
and intelligence tests from 1913 to 1958. The studies included results from approximately sixty different tests and 80,000 Negro subjects, not including those who took the armed forces psychological
tests in the two world wars. Professor Shuey's intention was to collect the results of all the studies of Negro intelligence ever made in

[17] See Howard Hale Long, "The Relative Learning Capacities of Negroes
and Whites," *Journal of Negro Education,* XXVI (Spring, 1957), 121–34.

this country and to understand the meaning of the accumulated results. This was a worthy objective, and also a colossal task. It involved not only a prodigious amount of research but also a detachment which only the most careful students possess, and a full awareness of the limitations and pitfalls of psychological testing. Miss Shuey's research was remarkable despite the fact that she omitted "numerous and important publications . . . which run counter to [her] conclusion." [18] Her lack of detachment, however, led her to make questionable use of the data she had so painstakingly collected.

She divided the studies into seven groups, according to the age or condition of the Negro subjects: preschool children, elementary school children, high school and college students, armed forces inductees in the two world wars, "deviates" of exceptionally high or low intelligence, delinquents and criminals, and "racial hybrids." In virtually every study she used in each of the categories, Negroes scored on the average significantly below whites. Several of her findings are noteworthy:

1. Among preschool children the average IQ for Negroes is 96.3, for whites 105.9. This was the highest average reported for any age group of Negroes and the best relative performance. After this age Negro IQ scores *decrease* both relatively and absolutely.

2. Among elementary school children, Southern urban Negroes score four to six points higher than Southern rural Negroes, and six to nine points below Northern and border state urban Negroes. The average IQ of Southern Negro children is 79, of Northern Negro children 87.

3. Among high school students the average IQ of Southern Negroes is approximately 82, of Northern Negroes 91. In both groups the Negro averages are significantly below those of whites, despite the fact that Negroes in high school are much more highly selected than whites in high school. "About half or possibly two-thirds" of the difference between the test scores of Northern and Southern Negroes, Miss Shuey concluded, are due to environmental factores, the remainder to selective migration of superior Negroes from South to North.

4. Negro college students, who are still more highly selected than whites, do poorest of all in relation to whites. The explana-

[18] Pettigrew, *A Profile of the Negro American,* 102.

tion for this "may lie in the abstract nature of the test material used on the college group," for Negroes do consistently better on tests of "common-sense concrete material than on tests involving abstract concepts." The results of the college tests left "serious doubt" in Miss Shuey's mind "that the obtained differences are completely or primarily due to the cumulative effect of an inferior environment." [19]

5. Negro soldiers in World War II did as poorly as those of World War I, and in both wars Negroes scored well below whites. "This holds true in comparisons between the northern Negro and the southern white draft, although the difference between these groups is less marked than between the northern Negro and the northern white or between the southern Negro and the southern white." [20] This was Miss Shuey's description of what were for racists the most embarrassing results of the World War I tests, namely, that Negroes in four Northern states made higher scores than whites in four Southern states. Otto Klineberg reported these results as follows:[21]

Whites	Median Score	Negroes	Median Score
Mississippi	41.25	Pennsylvania	42.00
Kentucky	41.50	New York	45.02
Arkansas	41.55	Illinois	47.35
Georgia	42.12	Ohio	49.50

Racists countered Klineberg's listing by pointing out that whites in Pennsylvania, New York, Illinois, and Ohio scored much higher than Negroes in those states, just as whites in Mississippi, Kentucky, Arkansas, and Georgia scored substantially above Negroes in those states.

6. In most instances there is a direct correlation between the skin color of "racial hybrids" and their performance on the tests: the lighter the skin color, the higher the score. Professor Shuey, however, did not place great weight upon this.[22]

---

[19] Audrey Shuey, *The Testing of Negro Intelligence* (Lynchburg, Va., 1958), 177–78. The second edition of this work was published in 1966 by the Social Science Press of New York.

[20] Shuey, *The Testing of Negro Intelligence*, 219.

[21] Otto Klineberg, *Race Differences* (New York, 1935), 182.

[22] Cf. the statement of Harvard psychologist Thomas F. Pettigrew: "A further embarrassment to racist theories is created by the fact that the degree of white ancestry does not relate to Negro I.Q. scores." Pettigrew, *A Profile of the Negro American*, 130.

On the basis of such findings Miss Shuey reached the following general conclusion:

The remarkable consistency in test results . . . the fact that the colored-white differences are present not only in the rural South and urban South, but in the border and northern areas; the fact that relatively small average differences are found between the IQ's of northern-born and southern-born Negro children in northern cities; the evidence that the tested differences appear to be greater for abstract than for practical or concrete problems; the evidence that the differences obtained are not due primarily to a lack of language skills, the colored averaging no better on non-verbal tests than on verbal tests; the fact that differences are reported in all studies in which the cultural environment of the whites appeared to be no more complex, rich, or stimulating than the environment of the Negroes; the fact that in many comparisons (including those in which the colored appeared to best advantage) the Negro subjects have been either more representative of their racial group, or more highly selected than have the comparable white subjects; all point to the presence of some native differences between Negroes and whites as determined by intelligence tests.[23]

This conclusion is remarkably cautious in view of the massive evidence Miss Shuey offered to substantiate it. In fact, if her evidence is as valid as she claims it is, she understated her conclusion. In her compilation of test results, she heaped study upon study in which Negroes scored significantly below whites, but in drawing her general conclusion, she backed away from the obvious implications of her evidence—assuming the evidence is valid. If it is valid and her handling of it sound, if the tests she summarized do measure innate intelligence, and if psychologists are able to control or neutralize environmental factors as she believed, then she has proven that Negroes are innately inferior to whites. She has also proven that their inferiority is sufficiently large to justify public school segregation. Ironically, her restrained conclusion and dispassionate language have enhanced the book's usefulness to scientific racists, for they are enabled thereby to point to it as cautious and restrained and to Miss Shuey as a disinterested scientist who refused to read more into her data than was actually there. *The Testing of Negro Intelligence* is not written in the impassioned tones characteristic of most of the literature of scientific racism. It is not full of loaded phrases, nor does it take the usual side swipes at integrationists. It is scientific racism in its most effective form.

23 Shuey, *The Testing of Negro Intelligence*, 318.

"The scientist, to be of any value to society, must avoid wishful thinking and report the truth as far as he has discovered it, without pretending to know more than he actually does," wrote Miss Shuey in her Introduction, and in this spirit, ostensibly, she offered her study. In his Foreword, Professor Garrett remarked that the *"honest* psychologist, like any true scientist, has no preconceived racial bias," and he welcomed "every *honest* effort to aid Negroes in improving their status as American citizens." [24] Miss Shuey, however, sometimes ignored Garrett's admonition, just as she sometimes forgot her own stated principles. Invariably, she interpreted her data in the manner most favorable to Negro inferiority and white superiority. She accepted at face value all studies which indicated Negro inferiority, but sought to explain away the results of those in any way favorable to Negroes. On the point in which the evidence supporting environmentalism was strongest, the effects of selective migration upon the performance of Northern Negroes, she included an entire chapter, though she did this for no other such topic. Northern Negroes made significantly higher test scores than Southern Negroes (some investigators have even found a positive correlation between IQ and length of time individual Negroes had lived outside the South), and equalitarians accepted this as an indication of the influence of environment upon IQ.

Miss Shuey's method is suspect in several important instances. She was interested only in the statistical results of the studies she cited, which she lumped together without regard to the limitations of individual studies or the comments or warnings of the authors. She accepted all the studies as equally valid, whether made in 1913 or 1957. In quantifying the results, she failed to distinguish adequately between studies which made no effort to control environmental factors, and those which, with varying degrees of success, did make such an effort. Even more seriously, she was uncritical of the tests themselves. She made insufficient allowance for such questions as whether the tests had been standardized upon

24 "We are forced to conclude that the regularity and consistency of [psychological] test results strongly suggest a genetic basis for the differences [between test scores of whites and Negroes]," Garrett wrote in his Foreword to the second edition. "I believe that the weight of evidence (biological, historical, and social) supports this judgment." *Ibid.*, 2nd ed., vii. Emphasis added.

white, middle-class Americans; whether or to what extent Negroes in various parts of the United States are handicapped by socio-economic status, caste, motivation, educational discrimination, and a multitude of other factors; and whether the rapport between examiner and subject was satisfactory. The doubts she might have had about such questions she overcame by noting the "remarkable consistency" in the test results, which indicates that she thought the questions were of limited significance. What she did, then, was to lump together an odd assortment of experiments, the sum of which she took to be proof of "some native differences" between the races. But the sum depended upon the validity of its parts, and Professor Shuey totaled up not only the statistical results of the tests but also their limitations, biases, and other deficiencies.

Consider, for example, her treatment of a 1913 study in which Howard Odum compared the results of tests he administered to white and Negro school children in Philadelphia. Odum reported that white children scored substantially higher than the Negroes, but concluded that "environment alone seems sufficient to account for [the] majority of results." Miss Shuey duly noted this comment, but then added Odum's results to her totals, where they became part of the evidence for "some native differences" between the races. Or consider her treatment of Carl C. Brigham's study of the tests administered to Army inductees in World War I. Brigham found marked Negro inferiority and concluded that "the average negro child cannot advance through an educational curriculum adapted to the Anglo-Saxon child in step with that child." [25] A few years later, however, Brigham had second thoughts about the matter and repudiated his earlier findings on the grounds that environmental factors were such that the tests were not true indicators of racial intelligence.[26] Miss Shuey used Brigham's results as part of her evidence, but dismissed his repudiation of his own study as unimportant. Her authority for doing so was a statement by Professor Garrett that the repudiation was of no merit.[27]

The use of Garrett in this manner indicates a significant charac-

[25] Carl C. Brigham, *A Study of American Intelligence* (Princeton, 1923), 194.

[26] See Carl C. Brigham, "Intelligence Tests of Immigrant Groups," *Psychological Review*, CXXXVII (1930), 158–65.

[27] Shuey, *The Testing of Negro Intelligence*, 196–97, 206–07.

teristic of the literature of scientific racism: it is heavily inbred. Since there are few social scientists who lend their authority to racism, those who do must cite each other frequently. In this instance Miss Shuey cited Garrett, who wrote the Foreword to her study, to prove an important point. On another occasion she cited McGurk to explain the decline in Negro test scores from elementary school through college, declaring that "there remains the possibility that we have here a real and normal decline in the IQ's which may be expected of children of dull-normal intelligence." [28] These examples are typical, and if a scientific work depends in part upon the strength of its authorities, they are germane to an evaluation of the literature of scientific racism.

It is obvious, then, that Miss Shuey did not approach her study completely free of the "preconceived racial bias" Garrett warned against.[29] Her study was widely applauded by segregationists and racists of various persuasions. *The Citizens' Council* printed a highly favorable review, quoting a statement by Garrett that the study "should be a standard scientific reference work in every well-informed person's library." Nathaniel Weyl, himself a disseminator of ultraconservative and racist views, likewise accepted it as "a definitive summary." [30]

Social scientists, however, are generally less impressed, and are in fact almost invariably critical of Miss Shuey's assumptions, methods, and conclusions. A reviewer in *Eugenics Review*, journal of the British Eugenics Society, did describe her work as "a valuable and scholarly survey," "as impartial a study as any that have been made in the racial field, [and] an important corrective to extremist views on both sides." [31] But this was an exceptional view. More typical were the responses to a questionnaire conducted by Princeton sociologist Melvin M. Tumin under sponsorship of the

28 *Ibid.*, 156.

29 Long before 1958 she published a study in which she reached conclusions similar to those of *The Testing of Negro Intelligence*. See Shuey, "A Comparison of Negro and White College Students by Means of the American Council Psychological Examination," *Journal of Psychology*, XIV (July, 1942), 35–52.

30 *The Citizens' Council*, III (May, 1958), 4; and Weyl, *The Negro in American Civilization*, 181.

31 P. E. Vernon, "Negro Intelligence," *Eugenics Review*, LII (October, 1960), 174. For a favorable review by Italian sociologist Corrado Gini, see "The Testing of Negro Intelligence: A Review," *Mankind Quarterly*, I (October, 1961), 120–25.

Anti-Defamation League of B'nai B'rith. Tumin asked four social scientists, each a student of race or psychological testing, the following question: "In your judgment, is there sufficient evidence in the Shuey volume to justify Dr. Shuey's conclusion regarding the presence of native differences between Negroes and whites . . .?" He posed the question to Henry C. Dyer, vice-president of the Educational Testing Service and an authority on intelligence and ability testing; psychologist Silvan S. Tomkins of Princeton, an authority on personality testing; sociologist Ralph H. Turner of UCLA, an authority on social and cultural patterns among Negroes; and anthropologist Sherwood L. Washburn of the University of California, formerly president of the American Anthropological Association, and one of the country's most distinguished anthropologists.

These authorities dismissed Dr. Shuey's conclusions as unfounded and unsubstantiated by her evidence. The studies she used did not measure native or innate racial intelligence, they stated. The tests used in the studies were not "adequate tests of native intelligence and other mental and psychological capacities, with proven reliability and validity." Such tests, they added, are impossible to devise, at least at present, and racial intelligence cannot therefore be measured with any degree of accuracy. "Even the most avid defender of intelligence tests today will acknowledge that the tests measure the effects of opportunity to learn the kinds of items included in the tests, motivation, and meaningfulness of the items to the test-takers as well as innate capacity," stated Professor Turner. Dr. Dyer was equally emphatic. "The nature of intelligence tests," he added, "is such that they are incapable of identifying *native* (i.e. genetic) differences between any two groups." [32]

Racists were not impressed by such criticisms.[33] *The Testing of Negro Intelligence,* they insisted, dealt with facts. It offered empirical data to substantiate its conclusions, and it could not be refuted by questionnaires or by resolutions adopted by equalitarian-dominated social science associations. Only factual data, they declared, only the results of tests in which Negroes equal or exceed white averages, will suffice.

These responses to critics of Dr. Shuey are good illustrations of

[32] Melvin M. Tumin (ed.), *Race and Intelligence* (New York, 1963), 14, 15.
[33] See for example Ernest van den Haag, "Intelligence or Prejudice?" *National Review,* December 1, 1964, pp. 1059–63.

PERFORMANCE OF SOUTHERN WHITES ON INTELLIGENCE TESTS COMPARED TO PERFORMANCE OF NORTHERN WHITES

(From Shuey, *The Testing of Negro Intelligence*)

Test Used in Study	Reference (Shuey's page)	Location Of Study North	Location Of Study South	Number Tested North	Number Tested South	(Score or I.Q.) North	(Score or I.Q.) South
Stanford Binet, Forms L & M	10–11	Minneapolis (1944) Philadelphia (1945)	Arlington, Va. (1954)	341 113	49	107.1 (IQ) 103.9 (IQ)	95.8 (IQ)
Stanford Binet, 1916 Form	32–33 28–29 30–31	Lawrence, Kansas (1920)	New Orleans (1925) Nashville, Tenn (1933)	58	947 30	103.9 (IQ)	91.2 (IQ) 96.4 (IQ)
Pintner-Patterson Scale of Performance Test	34–35	Kent Co., Ont.	West Virginia (1928)	211	100	109.59 (IQ)	99.0 (IQ)
Arthur Point Scale	36–37	*Nat'l Norms*	Rural Co. in Virginia (1940)		25	100.0 (IQ)	94.2 (IQ)
Haggerty Delta I	62–63	*Nat'l Norms* Median Scores Age 7–59 Age 8–68	Elizabeth City, N. Ca. (1923)		71	59.0 (Score) 68.0 (Score)	42.0 (Score) 30.0 (Score)
Otis Quick Scoring Mental Ability, Alpha	68–69	*Nat'l Norms* 100.00	Rural Co. in Va. (1952)		53	100.0 (IQ)	90.0 (IQ)

TABLE II

PERFORMANCE OF SOUTHERN WHITES ON INTELLIGENCE TESTS COMPARED TO PERFORMANCE OF NORTHERN WHITES

(From Shuey, The Testing of Negro Intelligence)

Test Used in Study	Reference (Shuey's Page)	Location Of Study North	Location Of Study South	Number Tested North	Number Tested South	(Score or I.Q.) North	(Score or I.Q.) South
Kuhlman-Anderson	90–91	Nat'l Norms 100.0	N. Ca. Co. (1923)		438	100.00 (IQ)	93.0 (IQ)
	90–91		Nashville, Tenn. (1939)		112		98.5 (IQ)
							96.6 (IQ)
	90–91		Rural Co. in Va. (1940)		521		88.1 (IQ)
	90–91		Williamson Co., Tenn. (1945)		3,501		86.6 (IQ)
National Intelligence Test	94–95	Los Angeles (1923)		4,326		106.0 (IQ)	
	96–97	New York City (1924)		194		102.0 (IQ)	
	96–97	New York City (1937)		5,007		97.8 (IQ)	
	96–97	Kent Co., Ont.		386		103.59 (IQ)	
	94–95		Mississippi 1926; 3rd and 4th Grades		9,500		89.64 (IQ) 95.98 (IQ)
Pintner General Ability Verbal Series	108–109	Nat'l Norms 100.0 (IQ)	County in N. Ca. (1947)		1,980		91.4 (IQ)
California Test of Mental Ability	110–111	Nat'l Norms 100.0 (IQ)	Rural Co., Va. (1952)		53		Lang.—87.0 (IQ) Non-L.—95.2 (IQ)
Detroit Primary Test	112–113	Nat'l Norms 100.0 (IQ)	West Va. (1928)		3,567		3rd Gr.—88.0 (IQ) 4th Gr.—84.0 (IQ)
Army Tests—World War I	190–191 196–197	Draftees from North (1918)	Draftees from 300,000 South (1918)		100,000	Ohio —66.7 Ill. —63.0 Penna. —64.6 N. Y. —64.0	*Sample of State Scores* Miss. —41.25 Ky. —41.50 Ark. —41.55 Ga. —42.12

the racist mind at work. In their controversy with equalitarians, racists invariably do one of two things. They assume racial inequality and Negro inferiority as first premises, or accept studies such as Miss Shuey's as proof of such inequality and inferiority. They take as proof of their case all evidence from which it is possible to infer that Negroes are inferior, and concede to equalitarians only the evidence from which it is impossible to infer Negro inferiority.

Among the criticisms of Miss Shuey's study none was more telling than that of educator Horace Mann Bond, himself the author of one of the studies she used in proving "some native differences" between whites and Negroes. Reviewing *The Testing of Negro Intelligence* for the *Journal of Negro Education,* Bond took her method and with it sought to determine the relative intelligence of Southern and Northern whites. Extracting from her charts all the information on that subject, he constructed a chart of his own (see Tables I and II), and found a "remarkable consistency" in the test results. On the basis of Miss Shuey's own evidence, he concluded, with tongue in cheek, that there are "some native differences" between the intelligence of the two groups, and that the differences all indicate that Southern whites are inferior. If her charts are valid, so also are Bond's, for his rest upon the same logic and data as hers.[34]

Robert Travis Osborne, professor of psychology and director of the student guidance center at the University of Georgia is a third academic psychologist who has made significant contributions to the literature of scientific racism. Born in Florida in 1913, Professor Osborne was educated in Florida and Georgia and received his Ph.D. from the University of Georgia. Since 1937 he has been on the faculty at Georgia.

Osborne is especially valuable to scientific racists because his work complements that of McGurk and Miss Shuey. McGurk and Miss Shuey have not themselves tested the intelligence or educational achievement of significant numbers of Negroes in the deep South, those Negroes, that is, who would attend integrated schools if the Brown decision were fully implemented. Osborne has made such a study.

[34] Horace Mann Bond, "Cat on a Hot Tin Roof," *Journal of Negro Education,* XXVII (Fall, 1958) , 519–23.

In Savannah and Chatham County, Georgia, between 1954 and 1960 Osborne conducted "a comprehensive longitudinal study of ethnic differences in mental growth in school achievement," during which he studied the comparative mental maturation of more than eight hundred white and Negro students as they progressed from the sixth through the twelfth grades. The students were tested four times, in the sixth, eighth, tenth, and twelfth grades, and Osborne compared the progress of white and Negro pupils in school achievement and mental maturity. He hoped in this way to be able "to point out some of the practical problems for educators who are forced to balance their schools in terms of factors other than knowledge of and skills in the fundamental subjects." [35] As this indicates, Osborne is avowedly a segregationist. He is convinced that psychological test scores prove that segregated schools are necessary for quality education.

Osborne reported the results of his study in the form of comparative abilities of whites and Negroes in basic school subjects. In the sixth grade, he found, the reading level of white pupils is two full years above that of Negroes, and by the twelfth grade more than three years. In arithmetic skills the differences are even more pronounced. The white advantage is only one year in the sixth grade, but increases to almost four years by the twelfth grade. He found, in fact, that white eighth graders do slightly better in arithmetic skills than Negro twelfth graders. Concerning the comparative rates of mental growth, he found that both races improve at first, but Negroes improve more slowly than whites and their rate of improvement "appears to slow down and level off in the 14 to 16 year age range." Thus, the mental age of Negroes is about two years below that of whites in the sixth grade and about three years below in the tenth, after which their mental growth ceases altogether.

Osborne was careful to point out that these results could not be explained by environment. In his opinion the fact that Negro pupils did relatively better in arithmetic than reading corroborated "the careful work of McGurk and others who consistently report that it is not the cultural but the non-cultural items which are

[35] Robert T. Osborne, "Racial Differences in School Achievement," *Mankind Monographs*, III (November, 1962), 3. See also Osborne, "Racial Differences in Mental Growth and School Achievement: A Longitudinal Study," *Psychological Reports*, VII (October, 1960), 233–39.

[most] difficult for Negro pupils to learn." [36] Nor, he added, could the sorry performance of Negroes be blamed upon poor teaching, for Negro teachers in Savannah and Chatham County have more years of college training and more master's degrees from "the better" Northern and Eastern universities than white teachers, and they receive higher average salaries. He apparently intended these facts to mean that the Negro schools of Savannah and Chatham County are equal to those of whites.

Osborne's study was valuable to segregationists because of its implications for school policy. "What the [public school] administrator needs to know is how to assimilate into white school systems Negro children who in spite of better-trained and higher paid teachers still learn at a rate only one-half to three-fourths that of the white children in the same school district," he wrote. In integrated schools administrators can do one of three things. They can lower academic standards to the Negro's level, thereby reducing white pupils to boredom; maintain standards at white levels, thereby inviting a failure rate among Negro pupils of 40 to 60 percent in intermediate grades and 80 to 90 percent in high school; or group children according to ability, thereby restoring *de facto* segregation, especially in upper grades. "An education system artificially balanced in terms of some factor other than academic performance," Osborne wrote elsewhere, "can do nothing more than polish a dull mediocrity." [37] This is not the place to go into the effects which ability grouping would have upon racial balance in the classroom, or whether such groupings are educationally desirable. It should be noted, however, that nothing in the Brown decision prevents the schools from segregating pupils on the basis of their ability.

Osborne concluded from his study that the schools must be segregated, for only in this way can the schools meet the needs and develop the potentialities of every student. By the twelfth grade, Negro performance is so poor that virtually all white stu-

36 On this point see Osborne, "Cultural Bias of Psychological Test Items," *Mankind Quarterly,* IV (January–March, 1964) , 134–37.

37 Osborne, "School Achievement of White and Negro Children of the Same Mental and Chronological Ages," *Mankind Quarterly,* II (July–September, 1961) , 29.

dents perform at a higher level than the best Negroes. Even those Negroes who equalled or exceeded the performance of some white students in the sixth grade were one or two years behind the same white student by the twelfth grade. Regardless of the perspective from which he viewed his study, Osborne reached the same conclusion: Negroes are so inferior to whites in mental growth and educational capacity that for their own good, and the good of society as well, they must be educated in segregated schools.

Despite Osborne's confidence in his study, the conclusions he drew from it are as questionable as those reached by Shuey and McGurk. Their validity rests almost entirely upon the implicit though unstated assumption that Negro schools in Savannah are equal to white schools and are therefore sufficient to neutralize the environmental disadvantages which Negroes experience in the deep South. Osborne's statement that Negro teachers have more years of college and more masters degrees from non-Southern universities and receive more pay than white teachers is insufficient evidence for so sweeping an assumption. To validate his study he must demonstrate, not merely assume, that the schools of the two races were equal. This, of course, would be a difficult if not impossible task. Perhaps nowhere in the South were Negro schools in 1954 equal to those of whites, and, though in many instances remarkable improvements were made after that date, it is questionable whether equal physical facilities could in a few years overcome the effects of earlier inequalities. In virtually every relevant category of measurement, whether expenditure per pupil, physical facilities, teacher-pupil ratio, or number of library·books per pupil, to say nothing of intangibles such as the Supreme Court took cognizance of in the Brown decision, Negro schools were inferior to white schools in 1954, and more often than not continued to be of inferior quality in 1960.

Osborne's case would have been stronger had he admitted that the inferiority of Negro schools accounted for a substantial part of the poor performance of Negroes in his tests. In explaining his test results, however, he gave no weight to environment. It is a striking fact, however, that students in the best school system in Savannah—the white system—achieved the best scores on Osborne's tests, and the longer they attended the superior schools the better their relative performance. And the opposite is true of Negroes. The longer they attended the inferior schools, the poorer their performance.

In fairness to Osborne it should be remarked that he never discussed the subject of innate racial inequality or claimed that Negroes are genetically inferior to whites in intelligence. That he believed this was the case, however, is indicated in his writings. He referred to his Savannah study as a "genetic longitudinal approach" to racial intelligence, and his failure to give weight to environmental factors suggests that he believed the results of his tests were genetically determined. Finally, his endorsement of segregated schools indicates that to him racial differences are permanent and largely immune to environmental influences.

Osborne, McGurk, and Shuey have each made major contributions to scientific racism since 1954. Their works are vitally important to segregationists who seek to reverse the Brown decision or prevent school integration in the South. But despite their appeal among racists and segregationists, they and their works are not widely accepted among psychologists. A few older psychologists endorse the racist position in varying degrees, but such exceptions only prove the generalization. Henry E. Garrett and Clairette P. Armstrong accept the views of Osborne, McGurk, and Shuey, and Stanley D. Porteus accepts portions of it, but their acceptance is atypical. Best known for the Porteus Maze Test, which he developed in 1914, Porteus is an emeritus professor of clinical psychology at the University of Hawaii. Born in Australia in 1883, he is chiefly interested in the psychology of primitive peoples, and it was this interest which led him to develop his maze test. He does not agree with racists that innate racial inequalities have been demonstrated, and he insists that his only interest is the study of racial and ethnic differences. Some of his views, however, are appealing to racists. He has, for example, criticized "missionaries, educators, social workers, reformers and extreme environmentalists" for creating the "beautifully consoling illusion" that all men are "born with equal individual potentialities." [38] He has also served as advisory editor of *Mankind Quarterly*, the chief publication outlet for scientific racists in recent years, and his article, "Ethnic Group Differences," is circulated by the Mississippi Citizens' Councils.

Dr. Clairette P. Armstrong of New York City is even more pronounced than McGurk, Osborne, and Shuey in her views concerning racial inequality. Born in Memphis, Tennessee, and educated at Columbia and New York University, she holds a Ph.D. in psychology from the latter. She has had wide experience as a clinical psychologist and is chiefly interested in the psychology of juvenile delinquents. For a time in the mid-1920's, she was a staff psychologist at Bellevue Hospital in New York City, and later served in a similar capacity in Boston Psychopathic Hospital and in the Childrens' Court and Domestic Relations Court in New York City.

In a critique of the social science testimony in the Brown cases [39] Miss Armstrong went much further than McGurk, Osborne, or Shuey in attacking school integration on the basis of psychological evidence. The idea that segregation is a basic cause of personality disturbance among Negroes is completely false, she stated. In fact the opposite is more likely the case. "Mass integration," she declared, "will create many unhappy misfit Negro school children—today's incipient truants and juvenile court cases, and often tomorrow's criminals." Therefore, the integration movement is "an extremely cruel, inhuman hoax." It instills exaggerated hopes in Negroes, only to shatter those hopes abruptly when "over-age, dull Negroes" find themselves in class with "younger, brighter White classmates." The Negroes are "embarrassed and chagrined by their scholastic disabilities and all that accompanies low mental age," and the result is rage, resentment, frustration. Integration thus denies the Negro child an opportunity for success. Yet, she warned, everything psychologists know about personality adjustment indicates that reasonable prospects for success in life are vital to men-

[38] Stanley D. Porteus, "Ethnic Group Differences," *Mankind Quarterly*, I (January, 1961).

[39] Clairette P. Armstrong, "Psychodiagnosis, Prognosis, School Desegregation and Delinquency," *Mankind Quarterly*, V (October–December, 1964), 63–80.

tal health. For their own mental well-being, Negroes should be segregated and offered "more manual training and trade schools" and other educational experiences suited to their capabilities. "There is no evidence of 'pathogenicity' to Negro children from segregated schools," Dr. Armstrong concluded, "but rather of 'pathogenicity' from desegregated schools as shown by truancy, nervous habits, home deserting and juvenile delinquency." Integrated schools "worsen the plight of most Negro children causing maladjustment, lasting trauma, unhappiness, and delinquency."

Miss Armstrong was convinced that much of the integrationists' concern about the emotional stresses of Negro children is misplaced. "Self-control under stress is one differential between stability and instability, between normal and abnormal," she declared, and everyone, including Negro children, must accept this fact. "Resistance to the temptation to lament unpleasant realities builds good mental health. Restraint of the segregated southern Negro, if under strain, does credit to parents, perhaps to teachers too. Children can be toughened psychologically as well as physically. Character is built by discipline. Repressions in many ways make for good mental health."

The failure of racists to impress more than a handful of American psychologists is explained by the fact that they have been unable to prove their case scientifically. They have therefore failed to convince psychologists that racial segregation is in the public interest. Psychologist Thomas F. Pettigrew of Harvard has demonstrated with great effectiveness the limitations and fallacies in the studies of a number of scientific racists, and has amassed an impressive collection of evidence from a multitude of sources which point to nonracist conclusions.[40]

In *A Profile of the Negro American* Pettigrew summarized much of the recent research of psychologists on the subject of intelligence, and reported the results of dozens of recent studies which seem to indicate that the influence of environment upon intelligence is

[40] Pettigrew, "Negro American Intelligence: A New Look at an Old Controversy," *Journal of Negro Education*, XXXIII (Winter, 1964), 6–25; and Pettigrew, *A Profile of the Negro American*, 100–35.

much greater than racists believe. Intelligence, Pettigrew suggested, is influenced by both heredity and environment. Heredity sets the generally wide limits of individual, but not racial, capacity, and environment determines the extent to which that capacity is realized. According to studies he cited, intelligence is affected by such diverse environmental factors as the diet of the mother during pregnancy, home life, cultural opportunities, especially during early childhood, personality, personal ambition, racial discrimination, and "role-playing" by Negroes. Other scholars have offered similar evidence, equally damaging to the racists' case.[41] It must be admitted that the evidence of the equalitarians is not yet definitive, that is, they have not been able to prove that the races are equal in intelligence or educational capacity. They have, however, clearly demonstrated that environment plays a major role in both IQ test results and intellectual achievement.

The extent to which social scientists reject racist ideas is indicated by a series of resolutions adopted in recent years by several professional groups. The Society for the Psychological Study of Social Issues, a division of the American Psychological Association, and the Society for the Study of Social Problems, a division of the American Sociological Association, have both denounced scientific racism. The latter group declared in 1961 that "the great preponderance of scientific opinion has favored the conclusion that there is little or no ground on which to assume that [whites and Negroes] are innately different in any important human capacity. . . . The conclusion of scientists is that the differences in test performance by members of so-called racial groups are due not to racial but to environmental factors. This is the operating assumption today of the vast majority of the competent scientists in the field." [42] Similarly, the American Anthropological Association, also in 1961, repudiated "statements now appearing in the United

41 See for example Otto Klineberg, "Negro-White Differences in Intelligence Test Performance: A New Look at an Old Problem," *American Psychologist*, XVIII (April, 1963), 198–203; and Dreger and Miller, "Comparative Psychological Studies of Negroes and Whites in the United States." See also such important works as Otto Klineberg, *Race Differences*; J. McV. Hunt, *Intelligence and Experience* (New York, 1961), and Anne Anastasi, *Differential Psychology* (New York, 1958.)

42 Quoted in Pettigrew, *A Profile of the Negro American*, 133.

States that Negroes are biologically and in innate mental ability inferior to whites, and reaffirm[ed] the fact that there is no scientifically established evidence to justify the exclusion of any race from the rights guaranteed by the Constitution of the United States. . . . All races possess the abilities needed to participate fully in the democratic way of life and in modern technological civilization." [43]

[43] Quoted in "Science and Segregation: The American Anthropological Association Dips into Politics," *Science*, CXXXIV, December 8, 1961, p. 1869.

5

THE FIELD MARSHALS
OF SCIENTIFIC RACISM

Despite the significance of Osborne, McGurk, and Shuey, theirs was not the most important role in the racists' exploitation of psychology. Individually and collectively their contributions were overshadowed by those of Professor Henry E. Garrett, one of the nation's leading authorities on psychometrics and psychological testing.[1] Because he is the most distinguished social scientist who joined the racists, Garrett's significance transcends that of other psychologists. By and large, McGurk, Osborne, and Shuey did little

1 See above p. 53–57.

more than undertake individual studies and publish their findings. Garrett, however, has alternately played the role of oracle and field marshal for scientific racists of all sorts, whether academic social scientists or outspoken white supremacists. He challenges the data and conclusions of anyone who questions the racist-hereditarian point of view; acts as a general propagandist for racial inequality, and school segregation; issues jeremiads against social integration and racial amalgamation; and cooperates with such zealous segregationists as those who join the Citizens' Councils of America. In each of these tasks he assumes the stance of a purveyor of ideas from the scientific community to the general public, and many laymen accept him as just that.

Garrett's role in the story of scientific racism is best approached within the framework of his social and racial philosophy. He endorses the major ideas of McGurk, Osborne, and Shuey,[2] though he is even readier than they are to translate those ideas into propaganda for racial segregation and political and social reaction. Perhaps the most instructive statement of his social and racial views is his article, "The Equalitarian Dogma," which first appeared in *Perspectives in Biology and Medicine,* was reprinted in *U.S. News and World Report,* and reissued in revised form as a pamphlet, *The South and the Second Reconstruction.*[3] In its various forms the article illustrates the facility with which Garrett combines science and racism, and the extent to which he uses science to buttress reactionary social and political convictions.

"The equalitarian dogma" of which Garrett wrote is nothing more than the ideas of racial equality and environmentalism, ideas which he accused equalitaritarians of accepting on faith and in the face of absolutely convincing data to the contrary.[4] The dogma

[2] See for example Henry E. Garrett's "Foreword" to Shuey, *The Testing of Negro Intelligence,* vii–viii; Garrett, "Genetics and Intelligence," *Mankind Quarterly,* IV (April-June, 1964), 202–04; Garrett, "Klineberg's 'Negro-White Differences in Intelligence Test Performance,'" *ibid.,* 221–22; and *Race, 11 Questions and 11 Answers* (Washington, n. d.), 3–12.

[3] Henry E. Garrett, "The Equalitarian Dogma," *Perspectives in Biology and Medicine,* IV (Summer, 1961), 480–84; Garrett, "One Psychologist's View of 'Equality of the Races,'" *U.S. News and World Report,* August 14, 1961, pp. 72–74; and Garrett, *The South and the Second Reconstruction* (no imprint).

[4] My summary of Garrett's ideas about "the equalitarian dogma" follow his pamphlet *The South and the Second Reconstruction.* Garrett recently repeated many of these same ideas in his *Desegregation: Fact and Hokum* (Richmond, 1965), published and distributed by "the Patrick Henry Group."

appeals to intellectuals, humanitarians, social reformers, crusaders, sentimentalists, politicians, ministers, liberals and communists, he declared, and has infiltrated the social sciences, the education establishment, the press, and other communications media. This situation is the reverse of what it was two generations ago—when Garrett grew up and was educated and the racist-hereditarian viewpoint dominated American social science—and one of his major concerns was to explain the change.

It all began with "modern" anthropology, which he traced to the influences of his one-time colleague at Columbia, Franz Boas. Through Boas, Garrett charged, equalitarianism infiltrated the social science departments of colleges and universities, and eventually became a major premise of most social scientists. On another occasion, Garrett described his personal observation of this process. At Columbia, "[I] was able to observe the influence of Boas as founder of the so-called subject of cultural anthropology in America," he wrote in a letter to the New York *Times*,[5] "and to witness the extent to which Boas' socialistic ideology dominated his thinking and permeated the teaching of his disciples, first at Columbia and later at other universities fed from the Boas cult." As a result of Boas' influence, equalitarian orthodoxy replaced freedom of inquiry in the social sciences. College classes became indoctrination sessions in which students were taught to "parrot the equalitarian arguments without competent familiarity with the evidence" and to shift "from the scientific to the moral position as the occasion requires." The "evidence" to which Garrett referred was Professor Shuey's study of Negro intelligence, and it does not, he declared emphatically, favor the equalitarian dogma; in fact, it discredits that dogma.

A second factor which contributed to the success of equalitarianism in social science circles was the racist excesses of Hitler and the Nazis. "Hitler was a true 'racist,' " declared Garrett, "as is anyone who believes in the general superiority in intelligence and character of some group (usually his own). Racism uses such terms as 'nordic supremacy' and 'Chosen People.' " Hitler's extremism was unfortunate in many ways. It made the study of race suspect at best and odious at worst, and subjected anyone who speaks of

---

[5] Garrett and Wesley C. George to editor, New York *Times*, October 24, 1962, p. 38.

racial differences to charges of racism and fascism. It made many Americans, including Jews, overly sensitive to "anything that smacks of racial exclusion." As a result, many well-meaning people have lost all perspective concerning race, and in overcompensating for Hitlerism they indiscriminately support any movement, however radical or irresponsible, which claims to foster brotherhood, racial integration, or civil rights. "Ironically enough," Garrett added, "the Jews who usually draw the racial line at the marriage altar stand to lose very little by so-called integration."

A third reason for the triumph of equalitarianism was the rise of African nationalism and the emergence of independent pseudonations in Negro Africa. Equalitarians blame colonialism for the backwardness and savagery of black Africans, Garrett charged, but it is the Africans themselves who are to blame. The white colonial powers rescued the continent from witch doctors, cannibals, and slave traders, and in their stead brought civilization, Christianity, and the rule of law. Expelling white colonialists is thus an effectual example of misdirected do-goodism and an illustration of the blind faith equalitarians have in their dogma. There is little evidence that Africans can govern themselves, Garrett declared, but overwhelming evidence, as events in the Congo recently demonstrated, that without the supervision of white men they turn naturally to murder, mutilation, slavery, and cannibalism.

The fourth factor which Garrett offered to explain the success of equalitarianism was the Brown decision, a decision which not only rested upon false social science but was patently unconstitutional. He also pointed out that Barry Goldwater had ably demonstrated this weakness in *The Conscience of a Conservative*. As a matter of fact, Garrett charged, it was the absence of valid constitutional precedents which led the Court to turn to social science. The justices, however, knew even less about psychology and sociology than they did about law, and allowed themselves to be deceived by equalitarian witnesses. Of the eight social scientists they cited in footnote eleven, "none had a national reputation; one had 18 citations of membership in communist front organizations, [and] another 10. Two were Negroes. Obviously the Court's authorities did not come before the American people without bias and with clean hands." [6]

[6] Garrett's reference to the fact that two of the authorities were Negroes

A final reason for the spread of equalitarianism was the influence of communism. "It is certain that the Communists have aided in the acceptance and spread of equalitarianism," Garrett wrote, "although the extent and method of their help is difficult to assess. Equalitarianism is good Marxist doctrine not likely to change with gyrations of the Kremlin 'line.' Moreover, the forceful application of the dogma foments tensions and bitterness on which the Communists thrive."

According to Garrett, these five factors account for the spread of the equalitarian virus and explain the success of environmentalists in deceiving the American people and leading them away from truths which an earlier generation knew and accepted. The truth had not changed, only the willingness to accept it and use it in formulating social policies. "The weight of the evidence strongly favors the view that racial differences in mental ability are real and are probably genetic," Garrett wrote, and the nation can ignore this fact only at great peril. This does not mean that Negroes must be exploited and deprived of their basic rights, as has sometimes happened in the past. "No effort should be spared to give the Negro better training, to upgrade him in his job, to provide technical and professional education," continued Garrett. "But unless the equalitarian dogma is discredited and abandoned, it will lead inevitably to social integration, inter-marriage, amalgamation of white and Negro, and to a general deterioration in American standards of culture and intelligence."

These remarks, from *The South and the Second Reconstruction,* are typical of the views which Garrett expressed, somewhat more circumspectly, in an article in *Perspectives in Biology and Medicine,* a journal published chiefly for physiologists and medical researchers. "The equalitarian dogma, at best, represents a sincere if misguided effort to help the Negro by ignoring or even suppressing evidence of his mental and social immaturity," he wrote

---

is typical of an inference frequently made by segregationists. He rejected Negroes as authorities on racial matters because of their obvious grounds for bias, though it apparently never occurred to him that a white man might have a bias of his own. Perhaps he agreed with the traditional view of Southern segregationists: living among Negroes in the South does not make the white man biased or prejudiced; on the contrary, it is the only way a white man can ever understand and appreciate Negroes.

in the scientific journal. "At worst, the equalitarian dogma is the scientific hoax of the century."

For a scientific journal to print such an article is unusual, and its appearance brought down a torrent of criticism upon the journal and its editor, physiologist Dwight J. Ingle of the University of Chicago, himself no racist. At its annual meeting in September, 1961, the Society for the Psychological Study of Social Issues (SPSSI), a division of the American Psychological Association, adopted a resolution describing Garrett's article as unscientific and denouncing it as a misuse of science for undemocratic purposes. There is "no evidence" that racial differences in intelligence test scores are innate, the psychologists declared. "Quite to the contrary, the evidence points overwhemingly to the fact that when one compares Negroes and whites of comparable cultural and educational background, differences in intelligence diminish markedly; the more comparable the background, the less the difference." [7] In fact, they pointed out Garrett was himself unwilling to state flatly that innate differences in intelligence have been proved. He only suggested that such differences as exist may be or appear to be innate. For purposes of social and educational policy, however, he assumes—and this is the crucial point—that the differences are innate. He thus made a major unproven assumption in translating "scientific" data into social policy.

Garrett did not take the SPSSI resolution in silence. In a reply published in *American Psychologist*,[8] he took vigorous exception to it. To the statement that there is no evidence that racial differences in intelligence are innate, he replied that psychologists have clearly demonstrated that such differences exist and that they persist even when environmental factors are neutralized. As proof he cited the studies of McGurk, Shuey, H. A. Tanser,[9] and others. He noted

[7] "Statement on Race and Intelligence from the Society for the Psychological Study of Social Issues," *Perspectives in Biology and Medicine,* V (Autumn, 1961) , 129.

[8] Henry E. Garrett, "The SPSSI and Racial Differences," *American Psychologist,* XVII (May, 1962) , 260–63.

[9] H. A. Tanser, *The Settlement of Negroes in Kent County, Ontario, and A Study of the Mental Capacity of Their Descendants* (Chatham, Ontario, 1939) . The premise of Tanser's study was that Negroes in Kent County, located opposite Detroit, were not discriminated against and had all the advantages enjoyed by white Canadians. Tanser thus reasoned that they offered an opportunity for the study of innate racial differences. He found significant differences between the races in favor of whites. For criticism of this study see Pettigrew, *A Profile of the Negro American,* 102–03.

the results of several studies which tended to support the view that the performance of Negroes improves when environmental factors are controlled, and found the results "dubious at best." He concluded: "Instead of the evidence for diminished differences between Negroes and whites of comparable status being 'over-whelming' as the SPSSI statement asserts, it is, in fact, nonexistent."

Like other racists Garrett accepts the plot theory of history. In his writings in recent years there is an implicit assumption that the civil rights movement, like "the equalitarian dogma," is in part the result of a gigantic conspiracy to stifle scientific inquiry and conceal the truth from the American people. Convinced that equalitarians are engaged in a concerted effort to abuse, ridicule, censure, and impugn the motives of nonequalitarians, he came to regard any social scientist who questioned equalitarian orthodoxy as a hero in the perennial struggle for academic freedom and the pursuit of truth. Following the appearance of McGurk's article in *U.S. News and World Report* in 1956, Garrett declared, McGurk "was castigated by rabid equalitarians, resolutions were passed condemning his study, the newspapers were bombarded with denunciatory letters . . . he and his wife were beseiged with anonymous telephone calls, he was 'silenced' by his university for a year, and it was demanded that he be expelled from the American Psychological Association." [10] And this because "he had published what he found." Similarly, several major publishers turned down Professor Shuey's study of Negro intelligence solely because they objected to its point of view and its conclusions.

To Garrett and Dr. Wesley C. George, who expressed these views in a letter to the editor of *Science,* this censorship was a real threat to academic freedom. "Frequently we have been told by young scientists that they would not dare to 'come out' for hereditary differences between Negroes and whites," wrote Garrett and George, for "their promotions, even their jobs would be in jeopardy. Even in the South, young scientists find that school officials have the attitude that it is better to keep quiet and play it safe; reprisals are not unknown." It was these convictions which led Garrett (and George) to conclude that equalitarians had organized a cabal against freedom of inquiry. "Attacks on those who support racial differences are too persistent, too regular, and too

10 Henry E. Garrett and Wesley C. George, letter to the editor, *Science,* February 28, 1964, p. 913.

emotional to be unplanned and accidental. And so is the name calling."

Garrett is influential among scientific racists because he embodies so many of their opinions. His criticisms of intellectuals are representative of the anti-intellectualism endemic in scientific racism. His denunciations of Jewish integrationists and the new African nations are typical too, as are his endorsement of right-wing political and constitutional views and his prophecies of gloom and doom. He insists that the integration movement is no mere effort to secure rights for Negroes. It is instead an assault upon the American way of life and the United States Constitution, and a threat to the fabric of western civilization. The South, he believes, is fighting to preserve America, to uphold the Constitution, to perpetuate the grandest civilization in man's history. This explains "why the South is refusing again to be reconstructed," and why the agitation for "so-called integration" will not induce Southerners to abandon social segregation. "Like most white Americans whose contact with the Negro is direct and personal," he wrote, white Southerners "realize . . . the great gulf between the two races. They know intuitively that we can ill afford any retrogression in the world today. And racial amalgamation might just be the difference between survival and destruction." [11] This is the great concern of segregationists, of Citizens' Councils, of Southern politicians. Their motive is not callous self-interest, not prejudice and bigotry. They are selfless fighters for freedom, for law and order, for human progress. And their efforts are rooted in scientific truth.

Unfortunately, Garrett and other racists never systematically developed the political implications of these claims. Scientific racists, or at least those in academic circles, seek to avoid the appearance of overt racial bigotry, and they disclaim any intention or desire to deprive the Negro of his civil rights, including the right to vote and equality before the law. But this involves a paradox, which scientific racists have never satisfactorily resolved. "Civil rights as legally defined, include the right to vote, to hold public office, and to have free access to the courts," wrote Garrett and George in their letter to the editor of *Science*. Upon occasion, they admitted, these rights have been denied to Negroes, as well as to other underprivileged Americans. "But no responsible scientist

[11] Garrett, *The South and the Second Reconstruction*, 9th page. (This pamphlet has no pagination.)

who believes in native differences between Negroes and whites has advocated the withdrawal of civil rights for *anyone*." Of course, they added, "the *facts* of racial differences must be faced by those in power," who must recognize that "the demand for social privileges and associations, based on the no-difference assumption, will lead to continuing strife and could lead to national disaster." There are "no moral imperatives which demand social acceptance of Negroes by whites, and the Constitution does not guarantee social 'rights' to anyone—Negro or white." Despite this, "extreme champions of 'rights' for Negroes often include in their demands forms of legal compulsion which cannot be tolerated in a free society."

These generalities are, of course, open to interpretation and are therefore too imprecise to serve as a practical guide for public affairs. If Negroes can vote freely, for example, there is the possibility, indeed the likelihood, that they will vote for integrated schools. But integrated schools violate Garrett's scientific and constitutional principles as well as his admonitions against social integration. May, then, Negroes vote freely for everything—except integrated schools? In recent years Negroes and their political allies have demanded the integration of public accommodations, and their voting strength and political pressure have been sufficient to accomplish their objective. This, too, however, violates Garrett's scientific and constitutional principles, but is a logical consequence of Negro voting. Would Garrett again interpose his scientific principles to prevent integration of public accommodations? To do so would circumscribe the Negro's right to vote in a way in which the white man's is not circumscribed. Garrett would allow the white man to use government, which rests upon the right to vote, to preserve segregation, but he would deny Negroes the use of government to achieve integration.

The truth is that Garrett's distinction between political and social rights is, as a practical matter, an artificial one. If Negroes vote they will be courted—no pun intended—by white politicians. More importantly they will be wooed by Negro politicians, and might, as Garrett himself foresees, elect Negroes to office. When this occurs can social integration be avoided? Elected officials have social as well as official responsibilities, and so also do appointed officials and party politicians. Apparently Garrett would permit Negroes to be elected to public office but would require them to preserve social segregation when dealing with their white colleagues and constituents. The success of the civil rights movement is due to the Negro's ability to bring democratic political pressure. It is a direct result of the right to vote. Anyone who endorses the Negro's unconditional right to vote must, it would seem, reconcile himself to the "so-called" integration movement.

Garrett's political philosophy, like that of other segregationists, is intensely conservative, not to say reactionary. To him racial integration, when forced by the federal government, is a form of "legal compulsion which cannot be tolerated in a free society." Yet it might just as easily be maintained that segregation is itself a form of legal compulsion which is incompatible with free society. To Garrett compulsory segregation is tolerable for Negroes, but compulsory integration is intolerable for whites. Whenever any part of the citizenry objects to integration or segregation there is of course an element of compulsion in each, but there are meaningful distinctions between the two forms of compulsion that would seem to have constitutional significance. Compulsory segregation of Negroes implies a stigma of inferiority and a denial of equality before the law, whereas compulsory integration carries no similar implications. In his preoccupation with compulsions which produce social and educational integration and in his solicitude for the white man, Garrett forgot those compulsions which inhere in segregation.

His oversight, however, is consistent with the attitude he has toward Negroes. "Observers here and abroad generally agree that the Negro is usually cheerful, frequently childish, often slovenly and irresponsible," Garrett wrote in one instance. "Many Negroes, of course, do not possess these traits to a greater degree than does the White man. But the conviction that most Negroes do is widespread and strong and it holds more than a kernel of truth." On other occasions, he described Negroes as equal or superior to white men in physical strength and agility, in sports, and in "certain forms of entertainment and music," but inferior in "abstract intelligence" and "the sort of ability that creates a modern technical society," including the ability "to think in terms of symbols—words, numbers, formulas, diagrams." [12] Perversely, Garrett's de-

---

[12] See Garrett, *Race, 11 Questions and 11 Answers*, 10; Garrett, "The Scientific Racism of Juan Comas," *Mankind Quarterly*, II (October–December, 1961), 100–06; and Garrett, "Race Mixing Could be Catastrophic," *U.S. News and World Report*, November 18, 1963, pp. 92–93.

scriptions do have a certain accuracy. He acknowledged, perhaps unwittingly, the fact that Negroes excel in those areas where they meet the least amount of prejudice and discrimination, in sports, entertainment and hard physical labor. But even this needs further refining. In certain sports, for example, boxing, football, and baseball, Negroes encounter little or no discrimination outside the South, and in these their accomplishments equal or perhaps exceed those of whites. In socially oriented sports, however, such as tennis and golf, racial discriminations are more meaningful and the accomplishments of Negroes much less impressive. Racists usually recognize certain activities as appropriate for Negroes and acknowledge—and applaud—their accomplishments in those areas. Elsewhere, however, they belittle Negro achievement while failing to take sufficient account of the prejudice and discrimination which handicap the race in those areas.

Garrett's conviction that the racial traits and capacities of Negroes are inferior to those of whites is the basis of his opposition to racial amalgamation, for he believes that those traits and capacities are perpetuated by heredity. But though he spoke as a scientist on this point, his opposition seems largely social. "When you come to a race mixture, I don't see that there would be any evil effects as far as the physical structure of the hybrid is concerned," he told an interviewer in *U.S. News and World Report.* "The difficulty, it seems to me, comes in mass mixing, which is the goal of the Negro pressure groups." Apparently he never discussed the specific genetic factors which make mixing undesirable. He seems to believe something like this: first, Negroes are inferior to whites in important capabilities which are necessary to preserve and expand the complex, technological civilization of today; second, inferior racial characteristics tend to predominate over superior ones in inheritance; and third, mass racial intermixture will therefore lower the quality of the American people.

To substantiate these views, Garrett pointed not to scientific studies of race crossings but to history. "I don't believe that, historically, amalgamation with the Negro has ever done anything except lower the general level of the national life of those people who have been willing to mix," he declared, and as proof cited the history of Latin America. Latin Americans, he believed, had failed to match the achievements of North Americans because the Europeans who settled in South America failed to keep their race pure, and he saw in the failure an object lesson for the United States. "My concern was—and is—that American whites, under the prodding of equalitarians and moralistic social reformers will become convinced that it is their duty to absorb the eighteen million or so Negroes and Negroids in this country," he wrote, warning that nothing has ever so imperiled the nation. "No matter how low (in a socioeconomic sense) an American white may be," Garrett stated, "his ancestors built the civilizations of Europe; and no matter how high (again in a socioeconomic sense) a Negro may be, his ancestors were (and his kinsmen still are) savages in an African jungle." The mass mixture of races of such uneven accomplishments is "not only dysgenic but socially disastrous." [13]

Garrett's views on this subject help explain his attitudes toward civil rights and voting. Here as elsewhere he tended to look upon Negroes as members of a stereotyped racial group. He sometimes gives the impression that individual Negroes, whatever their personal merit, are to be judged by the worst features of their racial past, and he gives each a share of guilt for the misdeeds and failures of every other Negro. Individual whites, on the other hand, he judges by the best accomplishments of their race. To give a specific example, Garrett believes that the recent atrocities in the Congo are to be explained by the racial shortcomings of Negroes, but he sees no racial significance in the atrocities committed by Germans in World War II.

"It is idle," Garrett once stated, "to argue that all members of *homo sapiens* should be treated as individuals regardless of race." [14] Yet to judge an individual on his personal merits is an elemental feature of democracy. Democracy, however, was another subject Garrett never discussed. His writings imply that he views democracy in terms of a nineteenth-century *laissez faire* liberal, which is to say he has a fear of centralized government and is in mid-twentieth century terms a political reactionary. To him, the best way to preserve American democracy is to interpret the Constitution as strictly as possible and to limit government to the fewest possible responsibilities (at least in the realm of race relations and social welfare). In this way he reconciled his endorsement of

13 Henry E. Garrett, "Racial Differences and Witch Hunting," *Science*, March 16, 1962, pp. 982–84.
14 Garrett, "The Scientific Racism of Juan Comas," 106.

Negro suffrage with his support of legalized segregation. Negroes should be able to vote, he felt, but the value of their vote will be circumscribed by rigid limits placed on the powers of government, especially the federal government. The latter, he insisted, must not be used to serve the whims of pressure groups or special interest blocs. It must not, in other words, promote the civil rights movement. It could be argued, however, that the government's *failure* to act might serve the interests of one pressure group (segregationists) just as its actions might serve another (Negroes). Historically, segregation has been perpetuated by the widespread use of government power, including the power of the federal government. Since this is the case, Garrett is vulnerable to the charge that he is not so much fearful of governmental power per se as he is of the use of power for ends he disapproves.

Garrett is convinced that segregation and democracy are compatible. Public policy, he insists, must benefit the maximum number of people, and segregation does just that. It benefits Negroes as well as whites. "Maintain separate schools," he advised equalitarians who sought ways to improve Negro education. "Set up the Negro curriculum to accommodate their [sic] lesser degree of abstract intelligence, stop excusing the Negro's lag as being wholly 'environmental,' and stop misleading him by urging goals he cannot attain." [15] The "alleged horrors" of segregated schools exist only in the minds of adult white do-gooders, who feel that the Negro child *should be* frustrated by segregation because they would themselves be frustrated. Actually, wrote Garrett, integrated schools benefit no one, least of all the Negro child, who suffers "real emotional harm" when forced into a hostile white school by court order.[16]

Thus it was that Henry E. Garrett, after a long and distinguished career as a psychologist, emerged as the most significant exponent of racism in social science circles. Even his contributions to the journal of the Citizens' Councils of America[17] and his active co-

[15] Garrett's review of Wallace A. Kennedy, et al, *A Normative Sample of Intelligence. . . ,* in *Mankind Quarterly,* V (July–September 1964), 58–59.

[16] Henry E. Garrett, " 'Benefits' of Integrated Schools Are a Myth!" *The Citizen,* XI (January, 1965), 4–6.

[17] See for example Henry E. Garrett, "Facts vs. Opinions on 'Race and Reason,' " *The Citizen,* VII (February, 1963), 7–12; Garrett, "Professor Cites Fallacies of Integration Arguments," *The Citizens' Council,* II (October, 1956), 1, 4; and Garrett, " 'Benefits' of Integrated Schools Are a Myth!"

operation with the Councils did not lessen his appeal among social scientists who are also racists. Not even his favorable reviews of unscientific work by racists, white supremacists, or political reactionaries dim their ardor for him.[18] Garrett has not accomplished what he set out to accomplish—to provide a scientifically valid rationale for racial segregation—but he has reinforced the impression among laymen that there are valid scientific reasons for segregation and white supremacy.

Scientific racists needed a broader base for their ideology than psychology alone could provide. With the assistance of such cooperative psychologists as McGurk and Osborne, they demonstrated, to their own satisfaction, that racial differences in intelligence and educability are so great as to justify school segregation. But this was only one facet of a larger task. They needed also to demonstrate that white-Negro differences in IQ test scores are matched by equally significant differences in physiology and morphology, and that all racial differences, whether psychological or physiological, are perpetuated by an unerring process of heredity. Thus, biology, physiology, and genetics are also important to racists, and from these disciplines they seek evidence to buttress their case against school integration and racial amalgamation. Their success in these disciplines, however, has been less substantial than in psychology. A miniscule number of racists have appeared in these disciplines, but they have exerted no influence among the generality of their colleagues. They have, however, significantly enhanced the appeal of scientific racism among segregationists.

The most notable result of their efforts and perhaps the most important item in the literature of scientific racism is Wesley Critz George's *The Biology of the Race Problem* (1962). George is one of not more than three or four biological scientists who have endorsed the ideas of scientific racism. His value to racists therefore far exceeds the scientific merits of anything he has written. Born in North Carolina in 1888 and educated in his native state

18 See for example his review of James J. Kilpatrick, *The Southern Case for School Segregation, Mankind Quarterly*, III (April–June 1963), 264–65; his comments on Carleton Putnam's *Race and Reason, The Citizen*, VII (February 1963), 7–12; and his castigation of liberals in his laudatory review of James Burnham's *Suicide of the West, Mankind Quarterly*, V (July–September 1964), 53–54.

(he received a Ph.D. in zoology from the University of North Carolina in 1918), he has held teaching positions at several Southern universities in zoology, biology, histology, embryology, and anatomy. From 1924 until his retirement a few years ago he was professor of anatomy at the University of North Carolina Medical School, serving as chairman of the department from 1940 to 1949.

George's contributions to the literature of scientific racism are not as voluminous as Professor Garrett's, but he shares with Garrett the role of field marshal of scientific racists. His writings and public utterances are as authoritative among racists as Garrett's, and the contributions of the two men admirably complement each other. Garrett's special preserve is racial psychology, George's the physiology of race, and both would use "science" as the basis for formulating social, educational, and racial policies.

In 1961 Governor John Patterson of Alabama invited George to undertake a brief study of science and race, in which he would spell out the scientific facts about race and explain their implications for race relations and school integration. The governor gave George $3,000 of state funds to finance the study. The product of his endeavor was *The Biology of the Race Problem,* an 87-page booklet published by commission of Governor Patterson and now in its fifth printing. Since its publication in 1962, it has been cited and endorsed by racists of all shades of opinion, and is today distributed by such groups as the Citizens' Councils, the National Putnam Letters Committee, and the American Eugenics Party, the last a tiny fringe group which urges, among other things, such "eugenic reforms" as absolute prohibition of interracial marriage, sterilization of defectives, and immediate "return" of all Negroes and mulattoes to Africa. An official of the Citizens' Council praised George's work as "a major scientific report" which "shattered the equalitarian myth" and deserves "careful study by all serious students of racial problems." Garrett described it as "the best single reference" on the physiology of the Negro brain.[19]

Because of its authority among scientific racists, *The Biology of the Race Problem* deserves examination in detail. Written in sim-

[19] W. J. Simmons, "The Truth About Racial Differences!" *The Citizen,* VII (October, 1962), 7–8; and Garrett, "Facts vs. Opinions on 'Race and Reason,' " 12.

ple, straightforward language, it was obviously aimed at laymen, who are perhaps overawed by the paraphernalia of scholarship and the multitude of scientific authorities quoted, footnoted, or otherwise alluded to. It is filled with citations of and quotations from many of the nation's most respected scientists and social scientists. At first glance it is an impressive work, especially to laymen seeking scientific justification for racial segregation.

George had several purposes in writing *The Biology of the Race Problem*. He sought to prove that whites and Negroes are psychologically as well as physiologically different, that psychological differences between whites and Negroes are of such a nature and magnitude as to constitute white superiority and Negro inferiority. He hoped also to demonstrate that racial amalgamation would destroy the small but vital margin of white superiority, a margin which, in his opinion, is the genetic basis of American civilization. On the basis of his evidence on these points, he warned the American people that integration of the public schools will inevitably lead to social equality, racial amalgamation—and national deterioration.

George devoted the first four pages of his work to listing and identifying most of the scientists he later cited, and an impression results that his study rests upon massive scientific authority. Though uneven, the list is imposing. It includes several prominent scientific racists, Garrett, McGurk, Shuey, and the late British geneticist R. Ruggles Gates; several anti-equalitarian scientists whom racists are fond of quoting, among them Roger J. Williams of the University of Texas, author of *Free and Unequal* (1953), a denunciation of environmentalism;[20] and a number of older scientists who accepted in varying degrees the ideas of racial inequality and Negro inferiority, such as Sir Francis Galton, Robert M. Yerkes, Henry Pratt Fairchild, and Robert Bennett Bean. More significantly, George's list also contains a number of contemporary authorities on race and related subjects, including Ward C. Hal-

[20] "The uniformity doctrine is in accord with Communistic thinking and is basically completely out of line with liberty-loving democracy and its emphasis on individual worth," wrote Williams in a typical passage. "The acceptance of the uniformity idea, which has often been done vaguely without facing the implications, has undoubtedly much to do with the fear mentioned earlier, namely that to understand Communism might lead to its acceptance." *Free and Unequal* (Austin, Texas, 1953), 142.

stead, professor of experimental psychology, Department of Medicine, University of Chicago; Charles J. Herrick, late professor of neurology, University of Chicago and editor of the *Journal of Comparative Neurology*; Wilder Penfield, professor of neurology and neurosurgery at McGill University and director of the Montreal Neurological Institute; Curt Stern, professor of genetics, University of California, Berkeley; anthropologist Carleton S. Coon, and others of similar stature. Altogether George listed forty-one authorities and in addition cited perhaps two dozen others in the body of his work.

The list gives the impression that *The Biology of the Race Problem* rests upon the authority of the scientists in the list. Now, if the research of those scientists did in fact support George's conclusions, his work would indeed be authoritative. This, however, is not the case, as George himself indirectly admits. "The views of these and other scientists will follow," he wrote at the end of the list. But then he added, *"I do not ascribe any particular opinion to any of these people regarding the school integration problem*, but as to the specific points on which they are cited, their testimony is authoritative." [21] The whole purpose of *The Biology of the Race Problem* was to prove the necessity for public school segregation, and for George to disassociate his authorities from his purpose is a revealing confession. The disclaimer was his way of saying that most of the scientists in the list disagreed with his use of their works and the conclusions he reached.

There are numerous indications that *The Biology of the Race Problem* is more concerned with racist propaganda than scientific truth. "One of the most important problems facing Americans today," wrote George in the introduction, "is, Shall we pursue programs that would result in mixing the genes of the Negro race with those of the White race and so convert the population of the United States into a mixed-blooded people?" This question is really George's chief concern. "Before saying yes to that question, before making any revolutionary decisions relative to so important and irreversible a matter, the information we have that bears on the issue should be carefully and critically evaluated." A mixed-blooded people, he warned, will be the logical result of educa-

21 Emphasis added.

tional (and thus social) integration. *The Biology of the Race Problem* was his effort to demonstrate the folly of such a policy.

The appeal of George's work is enhanced by his failure to inform his readers on two critical points: the relative stature of the scientists he quotes and their attitudes toward Negroes, segregation, and racial equality. He treated each of his authorities as equally valid and ignored their racial views altogether. He thus told only a part of the story, and as a result created the erroneous impression that his conclusions are supported by massive scientific authority.

To illustrate the magnitude of the deception, consider, for example, the first entry in George's list of authorities: "Robert Bennett Bean, M.D.; anthropologist; Professor of Anatomy, University of Virginia." Bean's usefulness to George rested upon a study of the size and morphology of Negro brains made in 1906 and which few authorities today consider of any value whatever.[22] George accepts Bean's study at face value and treats Bean himself as a scientist whose studies are as valid as those of the most recent and disinterested scholars. He fails to mention that Bean was a racist of the most patronizing sort whose racial attitudes were typical of Southern segregationists of the post-Reconstruction era. Bean's racial views pervade everything he wrote about race, including the 1906 study which George cited. One of the tasks Bean set for himself in that study was to explain the social and psychological implications of his findings that the Negro brain is inferior to the white brain. "The Caucasian—more particularly the Anglo-Saxon, which was derived from the Primitives of Europe, is dominant and domineering, and possessed primarily with determination, will power, self-control, self-government, and all the attributes of the subjective self, with a high development of the ethical and aesthetic faculties," Bean wrote. "The Negro [on the other hand] is primarily affectionate, immensely emotional, then sensual and under stimulation passionate. There is [among Negroes] love of ostentation, of outward show, of approbation; there is love of music, and capacity for melodious articulation; there is undeveloped artistic power and taste—Negroes make good artisans, handicraftsmen—and there is instability of character incident to lack of self-control,

---

[22] See for example the review of Bean's study in Dwight J. Ingle, "Comments on the Teachings of Carleton Putnam," *Mankind Quarterly*, IV (1963), 30–36.

especially in connection with the sexual relation." [23] These qualities, Bean explained, are due to the differences in size and morphology of the brains of the two races. Despite such pseudoscience
as this, George offered Bean as one of his authorities, and few
laymen feel able to challenge the work of a man identified only
as an M.D., an anthropologist, and a professor of anatomy at the
University of Virginia.

Numerous other instances, involving contemporary authorities,
are equally damaging to George's case. On two occasions he cited
geneticist Curt Stern, once to summarize the contributions of
Gregor Mendel (p. 8), and again to state that *men* (Stern does
not say or imply *races*) differ and are genetically unequal (p.
54). On this basis George lists Stern as one of the authorities
whose "views . . . will follow." Again, however, he omits vital parts
of the story. He fails to note that Stern is an outspoken equalitarian who on at least one occasion predicted the complete amalgamation of whites and Negroes in America and foresaw no ill
consequences as a result. In Stern's view, neither Negroes nor
mulattoes have any biological or mental deficiencies which make
them, as a group, inferior to Caucasians.[24] Stern's view, then, was
the opposite of what George was trying to prove, namely, that
racial amalgamation is scientifically unwise and will bring genetic
deterioration and national disaster. Stern is one of the nation's
foremost geneticists, and George, himself a member of the American Society of Human Geneticists, presumably felt Stern's name
would add luster to his work, even though Stern's research adds
nothing to the case he was attempting to prove.

Several of the men George included in his list have themelves
denounced his misuse of their works. He quoted statements by
biopsychologist Ward C. Halstead to the effect that frontal lobes
of the human brain control the higher forms of intelligence, and
underdevelopment of the frontal lobes adversely affects intelligence.
Halstead did indeed say these things, but in no wise implied that
they had any racial significance. Instead, he has disavowed the

[23] Robert Bennett Bean, "Some Racial Peculiarities of the Negro Brain,"
American Journal of Anatomy, V (September, 1906), 379. For similar views
see Bean, "The Training of the Negro," *Century Magazine*, LXXII (October,
1906), 947–53.

[24] Curt Stern, "The Biology of the Negro," *Scientific American*, CXCI (October, 1954), 81–85.

use of his works by racists such as George and Carleton Putnam. "Both authors quote my work . . . indicating that the frontal lobes of the brain are of particular significance to the advance of civilization," Halstead has written. "This is my view, and I am quoted correctly by both of them—but I am quoted in a context which has in some, if not many readers, generated the impression that I subscribe to the views on racism set forth by George and Putnam. I wish to make it clear that this is not the case. It is probably a sound perspective in biology to be extremely wary of the *non-sequitur* involved in generalizing from our limited science of *human-organisms* to value judgments about people. . . . In my opinion the ghost of racist dogma must be laid to rest before any comprehensive investigation of the important scientific problem posed by race can be undertaken." [25]

Neurologist Wilder Penfield, whose research on the morphology of the human brain George cited, similarly repudiated the abuse of his work by racists. "In my clinical and pathological work I know of no good evidence of superiority in structure or function of the brain of White or Black, either way," Penfield declared. "Variations in human capacity have not been directly correlated to differences in brain structure by any clear scientific work as yet. . . . My own belief is that the innate intellectual capacity of White, Mulatto and Negro is probably the same." [26] Another of George's authorities, geographer George F. Carter of Johns Hopkins, wrote of *The Biology of the Race Problem* that its "arguments . . . are Swiss cheese—full of holes." [27]

It seems fair to say that an overwhelming majority of the scientists cited by George, at least of those whose major works were published within the last generation, regard his use of their works as spurious, and consider *The Biology of the Race Problem* pseudoscience. But in spite of his shortcomings as a scientist, George is an effective propagandist, and the fact that most of the authorities he cites are equalitarians has worked to his advantage. He and the racists to whom he appeals are enabled thereby to present his study to unsuspecting laymen as a genuine work of science and scholarship.

George begins his study by first erecting and then demolishing

[25] Quoted in Ingle, "Comments on the Teachings of Carleton Putnam," 38.
[26] Quoted in *ibid.*, 38–39.
[27] Quoted in Carleton Putnam, "These Are the Guilty," *The Citizen*, VII (March, 1963) , 40.

an equalitarian straw man. He will prove, he states at the outset, that equalitarians (who are unnamed) are incorrect in contending that "all babies [are] approximately uniform and equal in endowments when they are born." These nameless equalitarians, he continues, have foisted upon the American public the erroneous idea that "all men are equal biologically"; and as a result the "doctrine of the essential uniformity of human infants" is now "held by a great body of social psychologists, sociologists, social anthropologists and many men in public life." This is a misrepresentation of environmentalist views concerning the significance of individual differences. No reputable scientist or social scientist has ever accepted such notions as the biological equality of all men or the "essential uniformity of human infants." [28] But by alleging that equalitarians, i.e., integrationists, do accept such ideas, and then refuting those ideas, George perhaps enhanced the plausibility of his own views, at least to uncritical readers.

The first significant issue George dealt with was "non-morphological racial differences." His purpose was to describe the psychological and personality traits of Negroes and, more significantly, to relate them to the physiology of the race. To a considerable extent the validity of his entire work depended upon his ability to accomplish the latter task.

To illustrate the psychological and personality traits of Negroes, George cited four authorities, the first of them Sir Francis Galton, who in discussing African Negroes in 1869 had referred to them as "savages" and spoken of their "incapacity . . . for civilization" and their unwillingness to work steadily for a sustained period of time. The second authority was Francis B. Stevens, an American diplomat whose knowledge of the characteristics of Negroes came from his diplomatic services in Africa. African Negroes, Stevens remarked in an interview in *U.S. News and World Report,* are "highly emotional," "readily goaded by irresponsible leaders into violence against blacks or whites alike," and "normally content if they have the security of food, shelter and police protection." Dr. J. C. Carothers, an Englishman who spent much of his adult life in Africa and for a time was a medical officer in the British colonial government in Kenya, was George's third authority on the characteristics of Negroes. In 1953, under auspices of

28 See for example Theodosius Dobzhansky, *The Biological Basis of Human Freedom* (New York, 1956) .

the World Health Organization for which he was then a consultant, Carothers published *The African Mind in Health and Disease,* a work which racists are fond of quoting. To a considerable extent, Carothers' view of the African reflected his experiences as a colonial official, though he was rather cautious in most of his conclusions. He did, however, describe Africans as typically lacking in foresight, perseverance, and power of concentration, as "governed more by emotion than by intellect," as dominated by "momentary and explosive thinking," and so enamored of their own conversation and discussion that they lose sight of "the essential triviality, inconsequence, or even falsity of [their] themes." George's final authority was Dr. Simon Biesheuvel, Director of the South African National Institute for Personnel Research in Johannesburg, who described Negroes in much the same language as Carothers, Stevens, and Galton.

None of George's authorities offered any empirical evidence to substantiate his description of Negroes. Each reported his personal observations, and each described African Negroes, though George was elsewhere preoccupied with American Negroes. The apparent reason for this sudden shift to African Negroes is twofold. First, American Negroes do not always conform to the stereotyped description he sought to convey, and Africans are too far away for his readers to observe personally; and second, American Negroes are so racially mixed that, as racists frequently point out, they are no longer "pure." In making the shift George was assuming that there are behavioral and personality characteristics which "pure" Negroes everywhere have, whether in Africa or America.

Having decided that Negroes behave substantially as Galton and the other authorities indicated, George turned his attention to more specific aspects of racial behavior such as IQ test scores and crime rates, but this time of American Negroes. His authorities here are McGurk, Garrett, H. A. Tanser, H. M. Roland (a county school superintendent in North Carolina), a statement made in 1929 by sociologist Pitirim Sorokin, FBI crime reports, and the United States census bureau. Noting the high crime rates among Negroes as reflected in FBI crime statistics, he concluded that the race has a special propensity for crime.[29] Throughout his discussion

---

[29] George ignored the vast literature which disputes his conclusions on this point. See for example Marvin E. Wolfgang, *Crime and Race, Conceptions and Misconceptions* (New York, 1964). Wolfgang is a sociologist at the University of Pennsylvania.

of this and related subjects, George's lack of scientific detatchment is especially obvious. He had a double standard in discussing whites and Negroes, always interpreting his material in the most derogatory manner possible for Negroes.

The lack of objectivity is especially apparent in George's effort to prove that personality traits, IQ test scores, and crime rates are "attributable to inherent morphological rather than environmental causes." Are there, he asked, "hereditary structural and other biological differences between individuals and races that might serve to explain the observed differences in intelligence and in behavior in those areas of activity that make western civilization?" His answer was an emphatic "yes." The cerebral cortex and frontal lobes of the brain, he explained, control the higher mental processes, and cited Wilder Penfield, Theodore Rasmussen, Ward C. Halstead, and C. Judson Herrick to substantiate the point.[30]

Having demonstrated the significance of the cerebral cortex and frontal lobes of the brain, George then pointed to several studies concerning the morphological differences between white and Negro brains, emphasizing their conclusions that the frontal lobes and cerebral cortex in Negro brains are underdeveloped. He cited four studies, by Robert Bennett Bean in 1906, Franklin P. Mall in 1909, F. W. Vint in 1934, and C. J. Connolly in 1950. George considered the study by Vint, who in 1934 was director of the Medical Research Laboratory in Kenya, especially valuable because of the various differences Vint reported in his measurement of white and Negro brains. He had found, for example, that the supragranular layer of the cortex of the average Negro brain was about 14 percent thinner than that of the average Caucasian brain, and on the basis of this and other differences equally significant, had concluded that the brain of an average Negro is morphologically inferior to that of an average Caucasian.

Endorsing Vint's conclusion, George now linked the studies of Penfield, Rasmussen, Halstead, and Herrick—who said that the frontal lobes of the brain control the higher mental processes—with those of Vint, Bean, Mall, and Connolly—who said the frontal lobes in the Negro brain are underdeveloped—and claimed the authority of all eight men for his statement that the behavioral

30 These men were eminent authorities on this subject, but unfortunately for George's case, three of them have publicly repudiated the implications he drew from their studies, and the fourth, Herrick, is dead. See Ingle, "Comments on the Teachings of Carleton Putnam," 38–39.

and personality traits of Negroes are explained by the morphology of the Negro brain. Penfield, Rasmussen, Halstead, and Herrick, however, had made no such claim, and as for the studies of Vint, Bean, Mall, and Connolly, there is little of scientific value in them. According to physiologist Dwight J. Ingle of the University of Chicago, who has carefully reviewed and compared these four latter studies, none of them has any real scientific merit. There is no scientific evidence, Ingle declared, that the Negro brain is in any respect inferior to that of the Caucasian. On this point, the most vital in his study, George's authorities failed him. They simply did not substantiate the conclusions he based upon them.

But he was not yet ready to leave the subject. To further buttress his conclusion he offered statements from J. C. Carothers, Audrey Shuey, and psychologist Robert M. Yerkes [31] that Negroes do well enough on tests which measure lower forms of mental ability but quite poorly on those which measure higher forms, those forms, that is, which are controlled by the frontal lobes. Again George links the works of bona fide scientists with those of scientific racists. The line that separates the works of Penfield, Halstead, Rasmussen, and Herrick from those of Bean and Vint, Shuey and Yerkes is the line that separates science from pseudoscience and scientism. The similarity between the two groups of authorities consists largely of the fact that both were interested in brains and intelligence.

George's next important task was to demonstrate that the physiological basis of the Negro's intelligence, social behavior, and personality traits is inherited. Again he quoted Sir Francis Galton, this time citing Galton's observation that a few families in Britain had in the last few generations contributed a disproportionate number of British leaders in public service, religion, society, and the arts. Galton concluded from this fact, and George did, too, that superior ability runs in certain families, and both men accepted it as evidence that heredity predominates over environment. Neither Galton nor George felt it necessary to inquire into the extent to which equality of opportunity actually existed in Victorian Britain or the degree to which "establishment" families offered their members built-in advantages. George was convinced

31 Yerkes, a Yale psychologist, was director of psychological testing for the United States Army in World War I. After the war he published several studies drawing racist conclusions from the test results he obtained during the war.

that ability rises to the top regardless of environmental conditions.

It was the latter fact which led him to place so much weight upon several studies of criminality and mental abnormality among identical twins. The studies showed unmistakably that if one twin is a criminal or is mentally abnormal the incidence of the same thing in the second twin is higher than in the population as a whole. The studies, however, deal with individual, not racial, inheritance, and their implications for race are unclear—rather the implications depend upon one's concept of race and the extent to which individual traits are racially determined. George concludes from the studies that the Negro's alleged propensity to crime is inherited. His reasoning here is best illustrated syllogistically: Studies of identical twins indicate that "genetical influences are probably important in criminal behavior"; crime rates are higher among Negroes than whites; therefore, Negroes inherit a greater propensity to crime than do whites. "When one sees at one end of the scale that genius runs in families," George wrote, "and at the other end of the scale that microcephaly and amaurotic idiocy run in families, and remembers that crime does also, one can hardly avoid the conclusion that heredity is an important factor in determining the character of a population." The validity of this conclusion would seem to depend in large part upon whether it refers to individual or to racial inheritance. Leaving aside altogether the question of its validity, the evidence which George presents suggests only that some *individuals* inherit a propensity toward certain behavior traits. He does not prove that the inheritance is related to the individual's race.

Like other scientific racists, George readily made the transition from scientist to social critic. He warned that racial amalgamation would produce a nation of mulattoes intermediate in ability between whites and Negroes and would thus destroy that vital margin of difference between whites and Negroes, the margin which represents the white man's capacity to create and advance civilization and the Negro's incapacity for either. To George, this margin explained the difference between European and African civilizations. Civilization is dependent upon "the presence or absence in the population of the pool of genes necessary to produce the minds and the personalities that will find and make use of . . . ideas," he wrote. It was their "pool of genes" which made Europeans a creative people, and they retained their creativity wherever they preserved their genetic purity, in North America, Australia, New Zealand, South Africa. In Latin America, however, where they amalgamated with Indians or Negroes, they stagnated. "The facts of history throughout the world provide no justification for any faith that a mulatto population would advance our civilization in this country or would even maintain it," George declared. "No where in the world have [mulattoes] demonstrated that they have the creative capacities (the intelligence, the industry, the drive, and the persistence) to make a civilization; nor is there an advanced civilization in any area where there has been a high degree of absorption of Negro genes into a white population." [32]

The supreme danger, then, was racial amalgamation, and George urged the American people to look upon "civil rights" and school integration from the vantage point of genetics. Americans must "avoid those actions and programs that seem destined to bring about deterioration in the quality of [their] genetic pool," he warned. They must shun "compulsory programs that would tend to bring about the mating of well-endowed, potentially creative people with poorly endowed, uncreative people." They must "adopt programs that have good promise of raising the quality of [their] pool of genes." White Americans might "assist Negroes in providing as good an environment for their children as they are capable of creating; but for the federal government to compel White parents to send their children to school in as bad an environment as Negroes can and do create is neither social justice nor wise national policy." [33]

This means, of course, that the individual is less important than the race, and here as elsewhere George's views paralleled those of Garrett. "During recent months we have often heard the appealing argument that we should treat every one according to his worth as an individual regardless of his race," he observed. "To be sure, we should value every man according to his merit—within his own race. It does not follow that virtue would be served by admitting every man or woman that we value, regardless of his race, into those areas of Caucasian social life where mates are chosen. If we open those doors to select Negroes of high merit, we also open them in the end to millions of inferior individuals." [34]

Except for a handful of racists, scientists have either condemned

32 George, *The Biology of the Race Problem*, 73–74.
33 *Ibid.*, 75–76.
34 *Ibid.*, 78.

or ignored *The Biology of the Race Problem*. A writer in *Science* described it as "hokum," [35] and that term seems aptly to summarize the attitudes of most scientists. Scientific journals did not review it, for which George blamed the alleged conspiracy of equalitarians to suppress everything which challenged their prejudices. It is more likely, however, that scientific journals ignored *The Biology of the Race Problem* because their editors did not consider it a work of science. One might as well condemn astronomers for ignoring the latest work of astrology or horoscope reading as criticize scientists for ignoring George's work.

Many scientists, in fact, did not ignore it, though their interest in it was due solely to their determination to prevent racists from misusing science. A committee of the American Association for the Advancement of Science denounced George's study, along with other items of scientific racism, as reactionary racist propaganda and scientifically worthless.[36] The committee repudiated George's contention that science is a proper basis for determining the civil rights and constitutional rights of Negro citizens. "To criticize a judicial decision by means of scientific evidence which is wholly irrelevant to the issue is to conceal a fallacy in the cloak of scientific precision," the committee stated. There is no evidence, they continued, that Negroes are in any way racially inferior to whites, nor is there any valid evidence to support the assertion that scientists have "conspired to mislead the public about the scientific evidence regarding racial differences." On the contrary, the committee concluded, George and his fellow racists have no real understanding of race or, indeed, of the scientific process itself.[37]

---

[35] "Science and Segregation: The American Anthropological Association Dips into Politics," 1868.

[36] "Science and the Race Problem: A Report of the AAAS Committee on Science in the Promotion of Human Welfare," *Science*, November 1, 1963, pp. 558–61.

[37] George is author of several other items in the literature of scientific racism, among them, "Brains, Intelligence, and Race," in Garrett, *Race, 11 Questions and 11 Answers*, 21–34, which he prepared to present to a Senate committee hearing testimony on the Civil Rights Act of 1964; and a booklet, *Race, Heredity, and Civilization* (New York, 1963), the introduction to which was by Archibald Roosevelt of the Veritas Foundation, a prominent spokesman for some of the ultraconservative elements in American politics. Roosevelt's letter of introduction is printed in "Why Won't They Teach the Truth About Race?," *The Citizen*, VII (July–August 1963), 4–6.

6

SCIENTIFIC RACISTS ORGANIZE

The history of scientific racism since 1954 is not exclusively a story of individual scientists. The role of certain individuals was vital to the development of scientific racism, especially in the cases of Garrett, who was already an established authority in his discipline, and George, who proved to be an effective propagandist. A propaganda or "educational" movement, however, needs organization and central direction, and for scientific racists this was especially true. For maximum effectiveness, it was essential that they have an organization to oversee and coordinate their efforts, a central agency to encourage and publish their research, circulate their

118

literature, act as a clearing house for their ideas, and serve as a liaison between social scientists and Southern segregationists. To a considerable extent, their achievements in recent years were due to their success in organizing such an agency.

The agency is a little-known organization with an imposing title, the International Association for the Advancement of Ethnology and Eugenics (IAAEE). Chartered in 1959 in Baltimore, the IAAEE is a nonprofit educational corporation "dedicated to the further-ance of the sciences of ethnology and eugenics, including the re-lated disciplines of physical and cultural anthropology, sociology, psychology, raciology, archaeology, linguistics, physiology, genetics, ecology, and demography." According to a statement appended to all its publications, it is also interested in "encouraging a free flow of information between scholars in the above disciplines in the United States and in the other countries of the Western World and in restoring freedom of inquiry to those areas (particularly the study of race and race relations) where extraneous political and philosophical predispositions have frequently terminated dis-cussions to the general detriment of the social and biological sciences."

The key to this statement and to the real objectives of the or-ganization is the reference to *restoring* freedom of inquiry to the study of race and race relations and to eliminating "extraneous political and philosophical predispositions" which allegedly in-terfere with that freedom. The Association promises to study racial topics unfettered by the biases and prejudices which so often in-trude therein and make those topics touchy and controversial. Un-fortunately, however, the Association has consistently ignored its own admonitions. Far from promoting the unbiased and unpreju-diced study of race, it has done more than any other "scientific" body in the country to facilitate the use of science and scientific literature by segregationists and anti-Negro racists. This fact is made abundantly clear by an examination of the racial views of the officers and governing body of the Association and of the litera-ture it endorses and circulates.

The president of the IAAEE is Robert Kuttner, a biologist at Creighton University Medical School, Omaha, Nebraska. Dr. Kutt-ner, who holds a Ph.D. in zoology from the University of Con-necticut, detailed his racial views before a congressional committee hearing testimony on the civil rights legislation President Kennedy submitted to Congress in the aftermath of the race riots in Birmingham, Alabama, in 1963.[1] He appeared before the committee not as an official representative of the IAAEE but as spokesman for the ultraconservative Liberty Lobby.

Kuttner opposed the pending legislation (it eventually became the Civil Rights Act of 1964) on several grounds, not all of them scientific. He objected to the coercive features of the legislation, which he thought would intensify rather than ameliorate racial antipathies, infringe upon property rights, and violate the basic precepts of free enterprise. The increasing regulation of private property by the federal government, he told the committee, encourages emerging nations in Africa and Asia to believe that capitalism and free enterprise have inherent limitations in coping with the complexities of the twentieth century. "And this," he added, "encourages Marxism."

The purpose of Kuttner's testimony, however, was not to repeat the reactionary economic and political views of the Liberty Lobby, but to provide a scientific rationale for the Lobby's opposition to the civil rights bill. Kuttner warned the congressmen that the pending legislation would encourage racial intermixture, a consequence which he thought even more abhorrent than violating the Constitution or threatening free enterprise. "Doubtless, this is merely the first of a series of cumulative measures aimed at complete social blending," he testified. "This bill caters to the motivations underlying much of the drive for social blending. Association with whites has become for some segments of the Negro population a sort of status symbol. This is abnormal and destructive of the development of a mature and stable Negro society."

Kuttner had other objections to the legislation on scientific grounds. "Psychological, biological, sociological facts cannot be ignored in making good laws," he reminded the congressmen, and the "facts" indicate that the proposed bill is unwise. The "facts," which he then brought to the committee's attention, consisted largely of the high rates of immorality and illegitimacy among Negroes and the poor performance of the race on intelligence tests, which are not, he suggested, due to environment alone. "I would seriously question whether or not the element of heredity

[1] U.S. House of Representatives, Committee on the Judiciary. *Hearings on Civil Rights*, May 8 to August 2, 1963, pp. 1963–80.

does not enter into some areas of performance in society," he said ambiguously. "I do not believe in a doctrine of race superiority, but I do recognize race differences, and this might mean that one race might perform better in one task than another." He did not believe, he added later, "that there is [racial] equality on the great majority of items one could measure."

But aside from this, Kuttner continued, civil rights legislation "often loses sight of existing psychological, biological, and sociological realities." In some instances the white majority suffers from integration. "Integrationists believe that [it is good] educational experience for white children to attend school with illegitimate Negro children. Yet few white parents would regard this as a desired broadening for the purpose of schools."

Kuttner's remarks sometimes went far beyond the legislation then pending before the committee. He repeatedly criticized the civil rights and school integration movements, charging that both are products of a "dangerous idealism" and are led by "misguided individuals who have misjudged the extent of damage that some of their actions may produce." He also hinted that the two movements have been substantially influenced by communists. "I recognize," he said, "that [communists] are very strong environmentalists."

There was nothing distinctive in Kuttner's views. Nor was he an effective spokesman even for his own point of view. In testifying before the committee he had great difficulty articulating his views. He frequently rambled off the subject and made vague, ambiguous statements which members of the committee often challenged. It is for this reason, perhaps, that Kuttner is not the most important spokesman for the IAAEE. That distinction belongs to A. James Gregor, secretary of the Association. Gregor, who was born in New York City in 1929, is the youngest and in many respects most distinctive of the prominent scientific racists. Perhaps it is accurate to say that he is unique among them. Certainly his intellectual orientation is vastly different from that of other social scientists whose names have appeared in this study. Educated at Purdue and Columbia, he earned a B.A. (history), M.A. (philosophy), and Ph.D. (social and political philosophy) from the latter institution. He has held several academic appointments, in the philosophy departments of Washington College in Maryland, the University of Hawaii, and, since 1964, the University of Kentucky.

Gregor's distinctiveness is the result of several factors. He is younger than other prominent scientific racists by a generation or more—Garrett, Miss Armstrong, Miss Shuey, McGurk, Osborne, van den Haag, and Kuttner were each born between 1888 and 1914—and he does not have the intimate ties with the South which some of them have. The intellectual orientation of these older scholars was originally molded, directly or indirectly, by the intellectual and racial milieu in this country between 1890 and 1925. During those years most social scientists were hereditarians, and they accepted the ideas of racial inequality and Negro inferiority. But they also shared the patronizing and paternal attitude toward Negroes which was typical of that generation and which was also, in a perverse way, not unsympathetic to individual members of the race. Those attitudes, often reshaped and reinforced by life among Negroes in the South, are the source of the racial views of George, Garrett, and many other scientific racists today. The Southern white man, with orthodox segregationist views, especially of George and Garrett's generation, *knows* the Negro and is oblivious to anyone who questions his racial convictions. It is important to remember, however, that this attitude incorporates an element of paternalism and patronizing good will which prevents Southern segregationists from "disliking" Negroes— at least those Negroes who remain in their "place." One result of this is that the most extreme ideas of anti-Negro racism (e.g., deportation of Negroes to Africa) have never appealed to such men as George and Garrett. Another is that they regard themselves as men of goodwill who "like" Negroes and who use science as merely one more prop for traditional Southern race policies.

Gregor's racism is of an entirely different sort. He has read widely in older authorities; indeed, he is perhaps more knowledgeable in the literature of scientific racism than any other social scientist previously discussed in this study. But he has none of the paternalism of the older generation. His writings give the impression that he is a racist not because he *knows* Negroes as do Southern paternalists or European colonialists, or because of the influence of an older scholar such as Garrett or George, but because of sheer intellectual conviction, a conviction that is at once austere, scientific, and logical and immune to emotion or humaneness. Where George and Garrett are racists by emotional commitment and, one might say by force of circumstance, Gregor is a racist because his intellect has propelled him to that conclusion. The difference is illustrated by the fact that George and Garrett are concerned only with immediate issues—race relations and school integration in this country—whereas Gregor has given much more attention to formulating a scientific concept of race applicable to the entire spectrum of interracial and interethnic relations.

Gregor developed his racial views in a series of articles published during the last several years. A primary ingredient of his views is the conviction that "race prejudice," as equalitarians call it, is really a deep-rooted, instinctive preference for one's own kind. This "instinctive" explanation of race prejudice, which most racists accept without bothering to articulate, is especially important to Gregor. He uses it to elevate his racial views from the level of bigotry and intolerance to the more satisfying one of human instinct. In the process he transforms "consciousness of kind" into an objective phenomenon which he thinks can be studied rationally and demonstrated scientifically. Race prejudice, Gregor wrote in an article circulated by the IAAEE,[2] is the surface manifestation of "a consciousness of kind, an identification of like members" which disposes the individual "to identify with an ideal physical type" of his own race, and in turn is "the psycho-social basis for *race* prejudice." In simplest terms, this means that human beings prefer the familiar and are repelled by the alien and unfamiliar. Physical differences set races and ethnic groups apart, and the extent to which their differences are obvious to the eye is the extent to which the instinct for exclusiveness operates. This is always true wherever races and ethnic groups meet, and Gregor predicted it will remain so in the future. Racial prejudices (or preferences) are therefore instinctive, and are immune to environmental influences, whether civil rights laws, Supreme Court decisions, or brotherhood weeks.

If such a view is correct, racial accommodation can at best consist of nothing more than mutually agreeable segregation. In fact, if Gregor were correct one would expect segregation to be voluntary and spontaneous. His "consciousness of kind," however, seems to work only among whites, and not even among all whites. Many Southerners have it in excess while most Northerners and Westerners apparently have less than their share. Mulattoes present a curious problem. Their "consciousness of kind" might

2 A. James Gregor, "On the Nature of Prejudice," *Eugenics Review*, LII (January, 1961).

lead them to prefer association with either of the two races, or perhaps only with other mulattoes, thus creating a third element in the race problem. Should it lead them to prefer association with whites and whites to reject that association, it could be the source of an unresolvable racial dilemma.

Gregor never developed these aspects of his theories. In 1961, however, he did pursue his ideas concerning consciousness of kind at greater length in an article which demonstrated his intellectual debt to sociologists Franklin Henry Giddings and E. A. Ross, to Josiah Nott (whose *Types of Mankind,* 1855, was the foremost work of scientific racism published in the United States before the Civil War) and to the contemporary Italian sociologist, Corrado Gini.[3] In this article Gregor takes Giddings' concept of the consciousness of kind and makes it the central factor in the formation of races. Consciousness of kind, he explained, is not only a source of racial preference, it is also "a behavioral 'syndrome' having positive selective value in the process of race formation." Thus, racism or racist thinking should not be thought of as "an excrescence of capitalism or the rationale for an economy of exploitation," as equalitarians and communists suppose, but as a basic human instinct. As Gregor defined it, Giddings' concept of consciousness of kind goes far beyond race in its implications. He understood it to include a "self-regarding tendency to associate with [one's] own kind (religious, political, social, cultural, economic, or racial group)" and "a systematic disposition to limit contact with outgroup members and to regard that which is foreign as at best curious, at worst the target of enmity." But these factors, too, have racial implications, for they lead to genetic isolation, even of groups living side by side, and intensify what Gregor termed "the will to group identification." The relevance of this to race relations in the United States is obvious. "The high social visibility of the Negro," Gregor explained, "acts as a focal point, around which collect all the attitudes that characterize man as a social animal, as a product of microevolution, given to identifying with kind, animated by a natural disposition to conform to prevailing racial as well as cultural norms." Racial prejudice in America will therefore never disappear; racial harmony will come only when whites and Negroes agree to live together—separately.

[3] A. James Gregor, "Corrado Gini and the Theory of Race Formation," *Sociology and Sociological Research,* XLV (January, 1961), 175–81.

The most striking fact about Gregor's racism is its admitted kinship with some of the ideas of fascist race theorists. In 1958 he published an article in *The European,* the journal of British fascist leader Sir Oswald Mosley, surveying the evolution of race theories in Nazi Germany.[4] He distinguished three stages in the evolution. The first, before 1935, was characterized by an absurd Aryanism and hysterical Nordicism which were pure fantasy and of no scientific or historical validity. The second, approximately 1935 to 1940, was a period of transition in which serious Nazi scholars began to formulate sounder racial theories but in which the fantasies of the earlier period still dominated Nazi thinking. The third, from 1940 to 1945, witnessed major changes as the research of responsible Nazi scholars began to appear and to influence Nazi race theorists. This process was never completed, however, because of the military collapse of Germany. In the dislocations accompanying the German defeat and the ensuing military occupation, the scholarship of the war years was scattered or destroyed, and "the tragic-comic image" of the irresponsible Nordicism of the early 1930's remained as "the popular misconception" of Nazi racial theories. Gregor's description of the third phase of Nazi racial thought is worth quoting at length:

Actually the elements of a far more profound theory are to be discerned in a few surviving books that mark the last dynamic phase of development of a concept of race free of the encumberances of an hysterical Nordicism.

Everywhere the talk was no longer of fixed and immutable races, but of races in formation, the components for which arise out of the crucible of the past—races in formation cast over by the ideal of a living heritage—for Germany a Nordic Mythos, for Italy an animating devotion to Romanita. The talk is of races yet to be fashioned by living an ideal, united by a common destiny, nurtured in a common environment, the political expression of which is nationhood.

Here are the germs of a world view which makes of man a creator, a builder of future races; a philosophy which unites history, politics, and race, eugenics and humanism, pride in self and respect for others, a philosophy scientifically sound and emotionally satisfying.[5]

[4] A. James Gregor, "National Socialism and Race," *The European,* XI (July, 1958) , 273–91.

[5] It was in this period, the reader will recall, that the Nazis liquidated millions of Jews and Eastern Europeans in the process of implementing their racial views.

This is the promise of a world-view as yet half-formulated and ill-expressed, with which our time must contend; the Weltanshauung which bears within itself the promise of Nietzsche's Good European.

This description of Nazi race theory is important to the story of the IAAEE and scientific racism in this country because it corresponds to Gregor's own view of what "race" is. In the same year he published this description of Nazi race theories, he wrote another article detailing his own racial views.[6] The similarity between his own views and those he previously attributed to the Nazis is remarkable.

"Race" in any significant natural sense can only signify a given breeding community (a mendelian population) which displays a difference of relative frequency for specific variables. . . . Historic continuity for such a race can be established only tentatively by demonstrating the temporal persistence of an empirically ascertained genetic balance. This must always be qualified by the knowledge that balanced polymorphism is a dynamic constant, that relative frequencies can be altered by a differential birth rate, an accelerated mutation rate, successive changes in breeding practices . . . eugenic or dysgenic practices in the environment.

Such a dynamic conception of race synthesizes natural, cultural, economic, political and biological factors. All influence the evolutionary development of races. All have influenced the racial composition of our planet in the past and will continue to influence it in the future either through intelligent control or happenstance.

The importance of such a mature conception of race cannot escape the intelligent layman. It helps point up the fallacies of "Marxist biology," on the one hand and the narrow "racism" of the recent past which did so much to undermine the cultural and political vitality of Europe.[7]

In 1963 Gregor published a critique of the social science testimony in the Brown cases, in which he not only vigorously denounced that testimony but applied his racial views to the question of public school integration.[8] Like other scientific racists, he believed the Supreme Court had been grossly misled by the social scientists. His chief objection to the testimony was its failure to prove that *de jure* school segregation itself had caused the per-

[6] A. James Gregor, "The Logic of Race Classification," *Genus,* XIV, (1958), 150–61.

[7] The reference to "narrow 'racism' " is to the early racist views of German and Italian fascists, as opposed to those views which began to appear in the late 1930's.

[8] A. James Gregor, "The Law, Social Science, and School Segregation: An Assessment," *Western Reserve Law Review,* XIV (1963), 621–36.

sonality disturbances in Negro children which Clark and other witnesses had described. "No argument [was] offered to indicate that the 'self-hatred' and 'in-group rejection' evinced by Negroes was the consequence of school segregation per se," Gregor wrote; yet this was the issue before the Court. The witnesses should have limited their testimony to the specific effects of *de jure* school segregation upon children in the same age and circumstances as those involved in the suits. He insisted that the witnesses isolate and measure the ill effects of one facet of segregation, and charged that social scientists had been unable to do this because there were in fact no ill effects of school segregation per se. Negro school children do suffer certain "psychodynamic impairments," he admitted, but these inhere in their minority status and are substantially the same in segregated and integrated schools, though the differences which exist favor segregated schools.

As this statement indicates, Gregor assumed that a Negro child attending a technically integrated school was in a bona fide integrated situation. His assumption, however, ignores the fact that such a child almost certainly comes from an environment in which *de facto* segregation and race discrimination are the rule, not the exception. The effects of this environment cannot be put on and taken off like a cloak when the child enters or leaves an "integrated" classroom. The school is not isolated from society; on the contrary, it reflects the society it serves. If the ill effects of segregation are to be eliminated from the classroom they must be simultaneously eliminated from society at large.

Gregor did not merely dispute the testimony in the Brown cases; he asserted positively that the available data indicate that Negro children are psychologically better off in segregated schools. Perhaps the final truth is not yet in, he declared, "but where social science material is available, *it tends to support racial separation in the schools, at least through adolescence under conditions approximating equality of plant and instruction.*" This statement is the key to Gregor's view of school integration. "Minority children of high social visibility," he wrote, "enjoy positive advantages at critical periods of personality formation in a racially insulated environment." To support this view Gregor cited, among other things, Kenneth Clark's study on the comparative responses of Northern and Southern Negro children to the doll and drawings tests, and Mary Ellen Goodman's *Race Awareness in Young Chil-*

dren. The latter he took as evidence that Negro children have psychological problems in schools where "de jure segregation does not obtain and where the incidence of Negroes is considered 'optimum.' " [9]

As further justification for school segregation, Gregor took evidence that white children have "negative attitudes" toward Negroes and used it against Negroes. In integrated schools, Negro children face "systematic and regular rejection" from white classmates, he remarked, and "the result can only be serious personality defects" on the part of Negroes. "Children, *before they enter school,* evince attitudes which would only create an atmosphere of tension for minority children of high social visibility," he wrote. "There is little reason to believe that such attitudes, which antedate school attendance, can be reduced by either education, protracted contact, propaganda, or a combination of these. Minority children of distinctive appearance can only suffer serious personality disabilities as a consequence of congregation." Moreover, these disabilities would be exasercbated by the low academic achievement, for most Negro children, Gregor believed, simply do not have the mental capacity to compete with whites. The Negro child who becomes aware of this fact in an integrated classroom can not fail to conclude that his race is inferior. The result will be "gross feelings of inferiority and a deep sense of personal humiliation."

Why this result should be undesirable to Gregor is puzzling. If his comments on the Negro's intelligence and scholastic ability are correct, Negroes are in fact inferior, and it is unclear why the truth should be hidden from them. Presumably an individual's image of himself and his own racial group should be realistic. If Negroes *are* inferior it would seem to be best for them, and for whites too, if they recognized and accepted that fact and ceased their efforts to enter the white man's schools. Gregor said as much in the last pages of his article. "The Guatemalan Indians seem to suffer no personality impairments as a consequence of their inferior status," he stated. "This is because they are sustained by a

[9] Miss Goodman's study did indicate this, but a more accurate statement would be that her study demonstrates that the ill effects of *de facto* segregation and discrimination outside the schools are apparent in integrated schools. Her study was a persuasive argument for general racial integration, not for segregated public schools.

coherent sense of possessing an integral and significant culture of their own. They do not attempt to identify with the upper caste and consequently do not suffer status frustrations, self-rejection, and its attendant disabilities."

Here at last is Gregor's real view. If Negroes would only accept their assigned place in American society and halt their efforts "to identify with the upper caste" the whole issue of the psychological effects of segregation would be solved. This was to Gregor the real solution to the integration dispute.[10]

The relationship between the IAAEE and the social scientists previously discussed in this study is not limited to the similarity of their ideas concerning race. Members of the Association's executive committee in 1965 included, besides Kuttner and Gregor, Henry E. Garrett, Wesley C. George, Robert T. Osborne, Clairette P. Armstrong, Stanley D. Porteus, Frank C. J. McGurk, and sociologist Ernest van den Haag of New York University. These are, however, only the more significant Americans on the committee. There are several others whose racial views are germane to an evaluation of the IAAEE.

Philosopher Gerrit Daams of Kent State University, Kent, Ohio, is one of the lesser-known members of the IAAEE executive committee. Professor Daams detailed his racial views in an address prepared for delivery to the Portage County, Ohio, Board of Realtors and reprinted by the Mississippi Citizens' Councils.[11] He offered a number of arguments for racial segregation, among them "objective differences between the races that cause white people to prefer freedom of choice and association." These differences include, in Daam's words, "temperamental differences in mode of mental functioning," "electro-encephalogram characteristics which proceed further in the European than in the black native," and

10 Accompanying Gregor's article was a closely reasoned rebuttal by Professor Ovid C. Lewis of the Western Reserve Law School. See Lewis, "Parry and Riposte to Gregor's 'The Law, Social Science, and School Segregation: An Assessment,' " *Western Reserve Law Review*, XIV (1963), 637–82. Lewis emphasized the fact that in concentrating on the relevancy of social science testimony Gregor lost sight of the larger issue–justice for Negroes. In perhaps his most damaging criticisms, Lewis pointed out that Gregor distorted the meaning of several of the authorities he quoted, or quoted them out of context. Many of the authorities Gregor cited in favor of segregation were actually arguing in favor of integration.

11 Gerrit Daams, "Northern Professor Summarizes Reasons for Racial Segregation," *The Citizen*, IX (May, 1965), 12–20.

"differences in comparative anatomy," including indications of "superior development of the white brain." The evidence on all these points "is not perfect," he conceded, "but that cannot be grounds for basing a social revolution on the assumption that the opposite of the best available evidence is true."

Daams warned that school integration will have bitter consequences. "Children are suggestible and readily assimilate the experiences, conceptual beliefs, customs, and morals of others," he stated. "When the child comes into contact with secondary groups that are markedly different . . . the child's value system looses [sic] coherency and his self-conception is undermined. The child either abandons cherished values, or undergoes adjustment to conflicting customs and possibly mutually exclusive values with debilitating psychological consequences for the process of maturation."

Just why the psychological influences of integration is a one-way street Daams did not explain. He seems to say in the above passage that immoral and antisocial Negro children will exercise a pervasive and sinister influence over white children, but that the influence of white children upon Negroes will be negligible. In any event, Daams thus fails to resolve the issue of the relative significance of heredity and environment. He believes that personality and behavioral traits are racially determined and those of Negroes are immune to environment. Those of whites, however, are fragile enough to be destroyed by association with Negroes in the public schools.

Daams' most novel idea was that American Negroes, far from being victims of racial discrimination, in fact receive special benefits solely because of their race. At each socioeconomic level, he pointed out, whites score higher than Negroes on IQ tests, a fact which he took to mean that it is easier for a Negro than a white man of equal ability to advance up the socioeconomic ladder. Given the frequency distribution of intelligence among Negroes and whites, he reasoned, it is easier for a Negro than a white man to enter a profession or white collar employment. "Our society tends, on the average to demand more ability and performance from the whites than the Negroes for the same economic rewards," Daams told the realtors. "This is equivalent to the Negro having had, since a few decades prior to World War II, on the average, a better chance of attaining some desired socio-economic status level than does a white person of equal ability and performance. . . . On the average, the Negro is NOT required to be more able than a white person in order to get the same rewards. . . . White people in general are sympathetic to the underdog. Then, the skin color of the Negro aids in making him visible so as to draw the solicitous attention of white people, whereas the disadvantaged white man is more easily hidden and forgotten."

Charles C. Josey, emeritus professor of psychology at Butler University, is still another member of the IAAEE executive committee. As long ago as 1923 Professor Josey spelled out his racial views in a volume entitled *Race and National Solidarity*. In that work, he had sounded an alarm to the American people, warning them that race was the most important issue then facing the world and urging them to make race instead of nationality the primary element in international relations. In a booklet published in 1965 by the IAAEE, *An Inquiry Concerning Racial Prejudice* Josey updated and repeated many of the ideas he first expressed more than forty years ago.[12] Racial prejudice, he declared is a much misunderstood subject, because equalitarians intentionally seek to obfuscate its true nature. It may very well be that "some of the attitudes and processes lumped under the rubric prejudice are essential to man becoming a free, rational, moral person," Josey suggested. Everyone has a natural preference for others of his own kind, the healthy exercise of which produces a sense of identity and a feeling of belonging and is the basis of group dynamics and the source of much of the inspiration which spurs human progress.

The concept of race preference did not contain, at least for Josey, the pessimistic implications of Gregor's ideas on the same subject. For Josey, race preference was a bedrock upon which harmonious race relations could be made to rest, and his view of racial harmony was that of a Southern paternalist and traditionalist. "That two races can live in the same community with mutual respect and goodwill has been demonstrated by numerous communities in the South," he wrote. "There, in spite of physical proximity, psychological and social distance prevented one [race] from appearing to the other as a threat," and the result was in-

12 Charles C. Josey, *An Inquiry Concerning Racial Prejudice* (New York, 1965). This 32-page booklet is No. 1 in the IAAEE Monograph Series.

terracial harmony.[13] To Josey, the Brown decision was "a step backwards" in race relations because it introduced an unfortunate coercive element in the relations between whites and Negroes. "Might and court decrees cannot engender love, friendship, good-will, and righteousness, or even justice," he declared, "when they ignore the rights, wishes, and ideals of larger segments of the population."

"We live in a morally confused age, one that lacks standards and definite norms," Josey continued. "This can reasonably be at-tributed in part to the mingling of diverse ethnic groups, for in an ethnically homogeneous group the chances are increased of develop-ing common standards" and protecting children "from romantic attachments that can only bring unnecessary difficulties and sor-row." The incompatibility of the latter statement with his previous remarks about natural preferences for one's own kind is instruc-tive. Josey, like other racists, sometimes used contradictory argu-ments, and not the least of his contradictions concerned his state-ment that the Brown decision did violence to the precepts of American democracy. "Democracy can only flourish when men respect the feelings and wishes of each other, and are animated by a refined and delicate sense of self-respect, forebearance, and concern for the common good," he stated. "The democratic way of life is too complex to be imposed or regulated by law. . . . To preserve a democracy, it is important to recognize that it is not always *right* to insist upon 'legal rights.' Otherwise, the law and the courts may smother both freedom and democracy." To apply these statements to segregation in the South is to reveal again the logical difficulties in Josey's position. Racial segregation, which he defended, does violence to every precept he listed as an essential feature of democracy.

George A. Lundberg, emeritus professor of sociology at the Uni-versity of Washington, is another member of the IAAEE executive committee. Professor Lundberg is one of the nation's better known sociologists, having been president of the American Sociological Society and the Sociological Research Association, and from 1941 to 1947 editor of *Sociometry*. Author of a number of significant

---

13 Perhaps no one ever gave a more striking illustration of the tendency of racists to view race relations solely from the white man's perspective. Josey was concerned only with the extent to which Negroes "threatened" whites. It never occurred to him that whites might themselves threaten Negroes.

sociological works, his racial views are not as pronounced as those of most other members of the IAAEE. He specifically disavows the idea of racial superiority or inferiority, but his emphasis upon racial differences, his denunciations of equalitarians, and his implied criticisms of the civil rights movement are appealing to racists.

They find his essay, "Some Neglected Aspects of the 'Minorities' Problem," which the IAAEE has reprinted, especially attractive.[14] It is a résumé of standard criticisms of equalitarians, though with a few distinctions of its own. *"Some* of the hostility complained of by *some* minorities is not based on prejudice at all, but on grounds warranted by community consensus," he remarked in a revealing statement. Moreover, "the right to discriminate and to choose one's primary group associates on whatever discriminatory basis one pleases is among the most generally recognized in our culture by both common and statute law." What equalitarians are fond of calling "inalienable rights" originate in "community consensus and continue only as long as community consensus supports them. It is the privilege of those who disagree with the consensus to attempt to alter it by whatever means the mores allow. In the meantime it is the privilege of others to exercise without apology the rights which by consensus are recognized."

What Lundberg did in "Some Neglected Aspects of the 'Minorities' Problem" was to remove from the discussion of minority rights every element of justice, morality, and humanity. By so doing, he claimed to have achieved the impartiality and disinterestedness which he accused equalitarians of lacking. The question is worth asking, however, why criticizing equalitarians is less biased than criticizing racists, or why justice, morality, and humaneness are irrelevant to "the minorities problem," especially when disregarding them serves the cause of racial and ethnic intolerance. Whether Lundberg intended it or not, the banishment of justice, morality, and humaneness from his discussion of race relations played directly into the hands of racists and segregationists.

Such are the racial views of the American members of the

14 George A. Lundberg, "Some Neglected Aspects of the 'Minorities' Problem," *Mankind Quarterly,* III (April–June, 1963). Lundberg, in collaboration with Lenore Dickson, is also the author of the most recent publication of the IAAEE, *Selective Association of Ethnic Groups in a High School* (New York, 1965), which is IAAEE Monograph No. 2.

executive committee of the IAAEE. Despite their scholarly degrees and their stature in the academic world, these men espouse racist views themselves or are tolerant of racism in others. As a practical matter, their view of the Negro's proper place in American life is not unlike that of many Southern segregationists and white supremacists. Like segregationists and white supremacists, they, too, would make the Negro a segregated citizen, which is to say a second-class citizen whose rights and interests are subordinated to those of white men.[15]

One of the major purposes of the IAAEE is "to publish a series of books, monographs, and articles presenting the results of original research and summarizing the state of contemporary scientific opinion in the areas of its principal interest." Accordingly, the Association encourages research by social scientists with acceptable racial views and facilitates publication and distribution of their works. The effort is threefold: publication of a Monograph Series, sponsorship of a Reprint Series, and promotion of a journal, *Mankind Quarterly*.

[15] In addition to the men listed above, Clarence P. Oliver of the University of Texas, David C. Rife of Ohio State University, Ralph W. Erickson of Mississippi State College, William E. Hoy of the University of South Carolina, and Herbert Sanborn of Vanderbilt University are members of the IAAEE executive committee. Until his death in 1964, historian Charles C. Tansill of Georgetown University was also a member. Tansill is perhaps best known for his criticisms of American foreign policy of the 1930's and 1940's, and for his charge that Franklin Roosevelt maneuvered the United States into World War II by enticing the Japanese to destroy the American fleet at Pearl Harbor. In recent years Tansill had been a regular contributor to the John Birch Society magazine, *American Opinion,* of which he was a contributing editor at the time of his death. On Professor Hoy, who testified for segregationists in *Brown v. School District 20 of Charleston County,* one of several cases in which segregationists have sought to overturn the Brown decision by social science evidence of their own, see *Southern School News,* September, 1963, p. 22.

Non-Americans on the IAAEE executive committee in 1965 were John R. Baker and C. D. Darlington of Oxford University; Robert Gayre of Scotland and the University of Saugor, India; Luigi Gedda, Corrado Gini, and Michele Marotta, University of Rome; J. D. J. Hofmeyr, Pretoria University, South Africa; Bertil Lundman, University of Uppsala, Sweden; Branimiro Males, University of Tucuman, Argentina; Otto Reche, University of Vienna; Dr. Helmut Reuning, National Institute of Personnel Research, South Africa; and Pierre Vassal, University of Paris. This author has made no effort to study the writings of these non-Americans associated with the IAAEE. A cursory reading of a few items by some of them gives the impression that they are not so obviously racists as are some of the Americans associated with the IAAEE. However, if any of the non-Americans have criticized the racism of their American colleagues, it has escaped the notice of this author.

The Monograph Series was launched in 1965 with publication of Charles C. Josey's *An Inquiry Concerning Racial Prejudice*. According to an editorial statement in the Foreword of this work, the purpose of the series is "to expose the fact that the findings of many prominent natural and social scientists do not support the dogmatic assertions on the question of racial differences of the contingent of social scientists who now dominate America's institutions of higher learning." Here, spokesmen for the Association dropped their mask of impartiality and disinterest, and their statement more accurately reflects the Association's real purposes than does the list of aims and objectives appended to its publications. The Association encourages the study of race and related subjects by scientists who reject the premises and conclusions of equalitarians and who therefore, intentionally or not, promote the ideas of racial inequality and the practice of racial segregation and white supremacy. This fact is amply demonstrated by an examination of the Reprint Series, which constitutes the major part of IAAEE literature.

Several of the items in the series have already been discussed in this study,[16] and several others incorporate in varying degrees elements of racist, elitist, or hereditarian thought which racists find attractive.[17] One of them, John M. Radzinski's "The American Melting Pot"[18] merits a brief review since it indicates that the Association's interests are not restricted to Negroes and race relations in the United States. Dr. Radzinski was born in Poland in 1901,

[16] The items in the Reprint Series already discussed are Garrett, "Klineberg's Chapter on Race and Psychology"; Gregor, "On the Nature of Prejudice"; Porteus, "Ethnic Group Differences"; Lundberg, "Some Neglected Aspects of the 'Minorities' Problem"; Garrett, "The SPSSI and Racial Differences"; van den Haag, "Social Science Testimony in the Desegregation Cases—A Reply to Professor Kenneth Clark"; and Armstrong, "Psychodiagnosis, Prognosis, School Desegregation and Delinquency." These are Reprints Nos. 1, 3, 4, 8, 9, 10, and 13, respectively.

[17] E. Raymond Hall, "The Zoological Subspecies of Man," *Mankind Quarterly*, I (October, 1960), 113–19, reprinted from *Journal of Mammalogy*, XXVII (November, 1946), 358–64; R. Ruggles Gates, "The Emergence of Racial Genetics," *Mankind Quarterly*, I (June, 1960); Bertil J. Lundman, "The Racial History of Scandinavia," *ibid.*, III (October–December, 1962); C. D. Darlington, "The Control of Evolution in Man," *Eugenics Review*, L (October, 1958); and Sir Cyril Burt, "The Inheritance of Mental Ability," *American Psychologist*, XIII (January, 1958).

[18] John M. Radzinski, "The American Melting Pot: Its Meaning to Us," *American Journal of Psychiatry*, CXV (April, 1959).

but at the age of twelve migrated to this country with his parents, who settled in Chicago. Educated at the University of Chicago's Rush Medical College, he was a neurologist and psychiatrist. His foreign birth is especially interesting because "The American Melting Pot" is an attack upon American immigration policies and the melting pot concept, which in tone and content resembles the nativist writings of such men as Madison Grant and Lothrop Stoddard. The late Dr. Radzinski (he died in 1963) denounced the immigration policies of this country as too lax because, in his opinion at least, they permit the entrance of too many people whose ethnic makeup is unlike that of older Americans. He dismissed the melting pot concept as a delusion concocted by environmentalists to promote equalitarian social policies which were to him indistinguishable from those of communism.

Endorsing the ideas that civilization is the product of a creative minority of mankind and that genius for civilization is inherited and varies among ethnic groups, Radzinski believed that a too rapid change in the ethnic composition of a nation will inevitably lead to a degeneration of its culture and civilization. The probable cause of the decline of ancient Rome, he suggested by way of illustration, was "a biologic dislocation of the delicately balanced genic constellations required for creative potentialities," which in plain language means that too many prolific non-Romans entered Italy at a time when the birth rate among old Romans was too low. Similarly, the mass immigration of Europeans to this country in the last century brought together "the greatest assortment of ethnic stocks in the world and probably in history," and a serious cultural decline is even now under way. "Symptoms of the decline are already apparent in the deteriorating state of some aspects of our culture, in the irresolution and confusion of our national leaders and in the virulence of frank antisocial behavior among our people far in excess of that encountered in west European countries, Canada, and Australia," Radzinski wrote. "We face the unpalatable truth that the present American society is sick."

But this is only the general picture; the details are even worse. "In the past 40 years, America has produced few political figures comparable in clarity of wisdom and purpose to some of the great names of the preceding century. At the same time, we have suffered an alarming epidemic of traitors in high places compared to whom Benedict Arnold was a rather sympathetic figure. Foreign governments and blocs of poorly assimilated Americans," the Polish immigrant wrote, "have been able to influence and sway the American ship of state causing it to flounder in the mire of conflicting interests and indecision. American 'masses' are clamoring for bonuses, pensions, subsidies and other sinecures. . . . Today no less than 37.8 million Americans are receiving direct monthly checks from the federal government. The Revolutionary maxim that that government is best which governs least has fallen by the board."

Radzinski's article was in reality a racial-genetic explanation for all the things which racists, segregationists, and political reactionaries object to and cite as evidence of national decline. If Radzinski's analysis is correct, however, its implications are terrifying, for nothing fundamental can be done to check national degeneration. The American people today are victims of the genetic folly of their ancestors—how such superior people could commit so gigantic a blunder is puzzling—and they must wait passively upon those "centuries of incubation and biologic fusion" which will eliminate the genetic disharmonies caused by the melting pot. Prolonged breeding between these diverse races and ethnic groups will eventually result in "biologic fusion" and genetic harmony and—hopefully—a new ability to create and sustain an advanced civilization. "Much time will, elapse, measurable in generations, before a biologic fusion among the White elements of our population is attained," Radzinski wrote. "Many more generations, measurable in centuries, will be required to effect a biologic integration with the non-White segments of our people, provided, of course, that the problem is not perpetuated by further infusion of large numbers of immigrants of any race."

In the meantime, the American people must learn from experience. "If there is one practical lesson to be derived from the present status of the American melting pot, it is that we should be extremely circumspect in our immigration policies," Radzinski stated, drawing the moral of his essay. "The U.S.A. can no longer afford to be the foster home for the unfortunates of the world. Biologically, there already are present here so many human types that further additions can hardly enhance the genetic end product. But such additions will tend to postpone indefinitely the salutary fusion necessary for harmonious society. Today, in excessive homicide, treason, juvenile delinquency and other crimes with their tremendous cost in suffering and treasure, we are paying the price for our reckless generosity to peoples of other lands. Politicians, who for reasons of expediency and false humanitarianism press for the relaxation of our too liberal immigration laws, are, in effect, asking for the perpetuation of this high tide of confusion and lawlessness."

Mankind Quarterly, a small journal with an imposing name, is the nearest thing scientific racists have to an official journal. Published in Edinburgh, Scotland, it has, since its first issue in 1960, played a major role in the promotion of scientific racism. In many instances the same men direct the affairs of the *Quarterly* and the IAAEE. Among the Americans who are or have been members of the honorary editorial board of the *Quarterly* are Henry E. Garrett, an honorary associate editor, Frank C. J. McGurk, Stanley D. Porteus, Audrey Shuey, Charles C. Tansill, Herbert Sanborn, Clarence P. Oliver, and anthropologist Harry Turney-High of the University of South Carolina. Robert Kuttner and A. James Gregor, the chief officials of the IAAEE, have served as assistant editors. Robert Gayre, a Scotsman, is editor. R. Ruggles Gates, a British geneticist who generally endorsed the ideas of scientific racism, was, until his death in 1962, an honorary associate editor.

According to the editors, *Mankind Quarterly* is "an international quarterly journal dealing with race and inheritance in the fields of ethnology, ethno- and human genetics, ethno-psychology, racial history, demography, and anthropo-geography." In point of fact, however, it is little more than an outlet for disseminating the ideas of scientific racism which have been discussed in this study. This conclusion is demonstrable in several ways. The journal and its editors espouse racial views which were fashionable among social scientists two generations ago but which have since largely disappeared from scientific circles. The editors regularly print articles of the kind which filled scientific journals two or three generations ago: articles describing anthropometric features of whites and Negroes; articles discussing "natives" and aboriginal peoples in condescending tones; articles attacking environmentalism, "the cultural hypothesis," and Franz Boas; and articles denouncing liberals, reformers, integrationists, intellectuals, and communists.

The editors frequently open their journal to racists, segregationists, and political reactionaries, some of whom are not scientists and make no pretense at scholarship or scientific detachment but who use science as a point of departure for denouncing the civil rights movement and racial integration.[19] A few excerpts from one such author will demonstrate this. A 1963 issue of the *Quarterly* carried William A. Massey's article, "The New Fanatics," an emotional polemic against intellectuals. The following passages typify its tone and content:

Who are the new fanatics? They are the intellectuals: those people whose interests extend beyond the people and problems in their own area. They are writers, commentators, reporters, clergymen, teachers, social scientists, and many other executive and professional groups.

.   .   .   .

The argument that science has shown that all races are equal is not satisfactory. The scientists who claim they have proved that all races are equal are suspect because of their obvious desire that all races should be equal. This may seem strange but it can be verified by a study of the literature in sociology and related fields.

.   .   .   .

The fog of sentimentality generated by those who believe in the brotherhood of men and nations has so befuddled America and Western Europe that we are ashamed of our superiority. And we obviously are superior, for it is the other nations that envy us and not vice versa. . . . This backwardness of certain races would seem to argue that they are not our equal. Treating them as such is, if not stupid, at least neurotic.

.   .   .   .

The uncomfortable fact is that the Negro may never make a good American citizen. Even if he is of adequate intelligence he may be tempermentally unsuited for citizenship in a democracy. It is possible that democracy is not the natural state of mankind, in spite of our fond belief to the contrary.

The real nature of *Mankind Quarterly* is further illustrated in its book review section. Each issue includes several book reviews, a surprisingly large number of which are of works that are not scientific and make no pretense of being scientific. Most such works deal with civil rights and racial integration, though some of them are propaganda tracts by political reactionaries or out-

19 See for example William A. Massey, "The New Fanatics," *Mankind Quarterly*, IV (October–December, 1963), 70–104; Carleton Putnam, "These Are the Guilty," *ibid.*, IV (July–September, 1963), 12–27; Nathaniel Weyl, "Ethnic and National Characteristics of the U.S. Elite," *ibid*, I (January–March 1961), 245; and Armstrong, "Psychodiagnosis, Prognosis, School Desegregation and Delinquency."

spoken anticommunists. Invariably, books with a segregationist, reactionary, or hereditarian slant receive favorable reviews, while those expressing integrationist, liberal, or environmentalist views receive unfavorable treatment. Among the books which have been reviewed favorably are T. Robert Ingram, *Essays on Segregation* (1960), a collection of articles in praise of segregation by several Protestant ministers; Lambert and Patricia Schuyler, *Close That Bedroom Door!* (1957), a polemic against racial amalgamation, the tone of which is indicated by the title; Robert Kendall, *White Teacher in a Black School* (1964), an account of the author's experiences in a Negro school, an account which segregationists and political conservatives have praised highly; and Frank L. Kluchhohn, *Lyndon's Legacy: A Candid Look at the President's Policymakers* (1964), a collection of ultraright-wing charges against President Lyndon Johnson and his administration. Even Fulgencio Batista's *The Growth and Decline of the Cuban Republic* (1964), the ex-dictator's impassioned defense of his regime, received favorable notice from an anonymous reviewer.

Scientists in America and elsewhere have been outspoken in their criticism of *Mankind Quarterly*,[20] and have focused that criticism invariably upon several specific points: the lack of scientific standards, the intrusion of editorial views in supposedly scientific articles and reviews, and the use of science to defend racist ends. No sooner had the first issue appeared than the Yugoslav anthropologist Bozo Skerlj resigned as an honorary associate editor and repudiated the *Quarterly* for "seem[ing] to show such little concern for facts and to be so distorted by racial prejudice." [21]

A torrent of criticism from other scientists soon followed. A. J. Cain, a demonstrator in animal taxonomy at Oxford, reviewed the first two issues of the *Quarterly* for *Race,* the journal of the Institute of Race Relations (London). "It will be difficult for any serious scientist to read without deep misgivings the first two issues of this new journal," Cain wrote. Some of its articles "are written intemperately, and show besides a method of argument that should never be used in a scientific work, and a lack of information that is surprising." In those articles, "confusion follows close on plati-

---

[20] An exception was the British *Eugenics Review,* which favorably reviewed the first two issues. See "The Mankind Quarterly," *Eugenics Review,* LII (October, 1960), 135.

[21] Bozo Skerlj to editor, *Man,* LX (November, 1960), 172–73.

tude" and "overstatement is added to confusion." He concluded, "I can only record that by the publication of this journal, I consider that the scientific study of the races of mankind has not been promoted." [22]

Man, the journal of the Royal Anthropological Institute of London, was equally outspoken in its condemnations. "Few of the contributions have any merit whatsoever," wrote Dr. G. Ainsworth Harrison, who reviewed the first three issues of *Mankind Quarterly*, "and many are no more than incompetent attempts to rationalize irrational opinions." Concerning an article by Editor Robert Gayre, Harrison wrote, "To evaluate the general substance of the paper is impossible unless one is trained in the art of criticizing nonsense." Of the journal as a whole he wrote, "the primary aim of many of the contributions seems to be to elude the facts." Most of the contributions, he thought, are "trivial and third rate. None of the authors rigorously and objectively appraises the limitations of the tests he uses . . . and the few that formulate testable hypotheses appear only to be critical of the evidence which fails to support what they want to demonstrate. The fact that every contribution is concerned with discrediting 'environmentalist' conclusions strongly indicates the editorial policy. What is particularly insidious in a supposedly scientific journal is the use of words with overtones of moral judgment." Harrison concluded his review with an earnest hope "that *The Mankind Quarterly* will succumb before it can further discredit anthropology and do more damage to mankind." [23]

In *Science,* the journal of the American Association for the Advancement of Science, Santiago Genoves of Mexico accused the editors of *Mankind Quarterly* of consciously using "science, or rather pseudoscience, to try to establish postulates of racial superiority or inferiority based on biological differences," and he deplored their efforts. "I have no other purpose," he stated, "than to denounce this attitude of men of science who, with strange antiscientific spirit, distort facts, as Archbishop Wilberforce did a century ago." [24]

Spokesmen for *Mankind Quarterly,* especially the editors and

22 A. J. Cain, "The Mankind Quarterly," *Race,* II (May, 1961) , 78–82.

23 G. Ainsworth Harrison, "The Mankind Quarterly," *Man,* LXI (September, 1961) , 163–64.

24 Santiago Genoves, "Racism and 'The Mankind Quarterly,' " *Science,* December 8, 1961, pp. 1928–32.

several leading contributors, did not take such criticisms in silence. They responded in kind, and the result was a bitter, name-calling controversy which raged for two or three years and smolders even yet. The principle episode in the controversy was sparked by Mexican anthropologist Juan Comas, who published a critique on *Mankind Quarterly* in an American journal, *Current Anthropology*.[25] Comas described the *Quarterly* as "a supposedly scientific journal whose contents are the cause of profound concern to those interested in racial questions in the biological and anthropological fields as well as in the social field." To substantiate his charge he offered not a general review of the *Quarterly* but a systematic critique of Henry E. Garrett's "Klineberg's Chapter on Race and Psychology: A Review," which appeared in the first issue. Comas sought to discredit Garrett and the *Quarterly* by demonstrating the racism of both. As a result of his effort, he and spokesmen for the *Quarterly* became involved in the recurrent controversy between environmentalists and hereditarians, a fact which increased the significance of their dispute, since they waged it within the context of the larger controversy. *Current Anthropology* submitted Comas' critique of Garrett to twenty scientists, including Garrett himself, R. Ruggles Gates, and Robert Gayre, and published their reactions along with Comas' article. Most of the twenty scientists endorsed Comas' position, though several expressed reservations about his tendency to allow his zealous equalitarianism to intrude unduly into his discussion. The controversy continued through 1962 and 1963, generating more emotion and invective than understanding.[26]

Editors Gayre and Gates assumed the chief responsibility for answering critics of their journal. "The attacks on the Mankind Quarterly," wrote Gates in a letter to the editor of *Man,* "are not based on science at all but have a political basis, having been made mainly by Communists or their fellow travellers. That some are willing to allow their science to be submerged and vitiated by

25 Juan Comas, " 'Scientific' Racism Again?" *Current Anthropology,* II (October, 1961).

26 Comas' original article, the comments by the twenty scientists, and several items in the exchange between Comas and his critics, notably A. James Gregor, Robert Gayre, Henry E. Garrett, and Donald A Swan, were printed by *Mankind Quarterly* in "Anatomy of a Controversy," *Mankind Monographs,* VI (3 parts, Edinburgh, 1963–64).

their political views is one of the tragedies of the period of disturbance through which we are passing." [27] As these remarks indicate, communists as well as equalitarian social scientists have attacked *Mankind Quarterly,* and the attacks from communists, especially those in Iron Curtain countries, were welcomed by defenders of the *Quarterly.*

Gayre made the most systematic response to the attacks. He denied that his journal or any of its contributions were racist or endorsed racial inequality, insisting instead that the *Quarterly* merely refused to accept the "non-sensical assertions" of "a-racist egalitarians." In a revealing statement, he explained the editorial views of his journal: [28]

We wish to state categorically what are the views of the editors on the matter of racial equality. While rejecting egalitarianism as having no warranty in honest scientific expositions and investigations, we do not, on the other hand, subscribe to doctrines of racial *superiority or inferiority.* We believe that just as all individuals within a particular racial stock are different, so is one racial group in relation to another. In respect of some characters various stocks will be superior to others, and in other characters inferior, but in many cases no perceptible differences may be apparent. While environment, both physical and social, may influence these characters, we believe that heredity is by far the most important single factor, and the current fashion to eschew the significance of heredity is a definite disservice to the understanding of what makes for differences in the various characters which distinguish one group from another. Furthermore, we do not presume to judge what is desirably superior or not. We think that within the ambit of the type of civilization erected by the White-Brown stocks or the Yellow races, the Black which has shown no natural predilection to that form of organization will be at a disadvantage in any competition—and is *in that sense* inferior. . . .

With such considerations in mind, no one ought to be surprised if intelligence or other tests *designed primarily for the conditions of life which are those of the Caucasoid stock show* when applied to Negroids, that the Black races are inferior *in these respects.* It would be very odd if that were not the case. But if, in contrast, tests were applied which suited the genius of the Black races, such as those which give due credit in the field of humor, music, art, ability to live a communal life and existence (as distinct from the competitive form of civilization which the Caucasoids tend to erect) feeling for emotional religious expression, or physical abil-

27 "A propos 'The Mankind Quarterly,'" *Man,* LXII (January, 1962), 13.
28 [Robert Gayre] "The Mankind Quarterly Under Attack," *Mankind Quarterly,* II (October–December, 1961), 79–84.

ity in boxing, running, and much else, it would be very surprising if the Negroids did not prove themselves superior to the Europeans. Thus we do not believe in *absolute* superiority or inferiority between one stock and another. There are racial differences, and difference implies inferiority or superiority in relation to this or that character involved.

There is, Gayre added, "a middle position between racial equalitarianism and the Nazi doctrines of racial superiority," and in his view it was this middle position which *Mankind Quarterly* occupied.

Gayre's statement reveals the limitations inherent in the views of scientific racists—who did, after all, look upon their racial views as moderate and responsible. It is well enough to speak of racial differences and to deny the existence of absolute racial inequality, but more important are the implications which Gayre and other racists derived from their belief in racial differences and relative racial inequality. It is clear from Gayre's list of things in which Negroes allegedly excel—music, entertainment, athletics, and "communal life"—that his view of the race is not unlike that of paternalists, segregationists, and white supremacists. He states explicitly that Negroes are inferior to whites in ability to meet the challenges of modern western civilization, and the implications of this are clear—Negroes are superior only in qualities that are irrelevant to human progress, which is to say as a practical matter that the race is inferior. And if the purpose of social, political, and economic policies is to preserve civilization and further human progress, it also means that such policies must accept the white man's interests as paramount to the Negro's. Whether Gayre intended it or not, he provided "scientific" justification for racial segregation and exploitation.

Neither the IAAEE nor *Mankind Quarterly* have any influence in scientific circles. Both, however, are well received by racists, segregationists, and political reactionaries. Among the items which the Citizens' Councils list in their official journal as "Citizens' Council Literature" are subscriptions to *Mankind Quarterly*; ten of the thirteen items in the IAAEE Reprint Series; the two items in the IAAEE Monograph Series; volume IV of *Mankind Monographs,* a record of the controversy between Juan Comas and *Mankind Quarterly*; and Ernest van den Haag's "Negroes, Intelligence, and Prejudice," reprinted from *National Review* under an IAAEE imprint.[29] In a recent issue of the John Birch Society magazine *American Opinion*, Dr. Revilo P. Oliver endorsed the IAAEE Reprint Series. "If such reprints are widely distributed," wrote Oliver, a professor of Classics at the University of Illinois, "the 'Liberals,' of course, may have to force the learned and professional journals to exclude articles that do not conform to the Communist line." [30] Professor Oliver recently achieved considerable notoriety by charging that President Kennedy was a communist agent whom the communists themselves assassinated because he procrastinated in his promise to communize the United States.

The endorsements from the Citizens' Councils and Oliver are but two instances of the relationship between segregationists and reactionaries on the one hand, and scientific racists on the other. The efforts of segregationists and reactionaries to apply the ideas of scientific racism to American race policies are themselves an important part of the recent history of scientific racism and are worth discussing in detail.

29 A recent list of Citizens' Council literature is in *The Citizen*, IX (June, 1965) , 27–28.

30 Revilo P. Oliver, "Brainwashing," *American Opinion*, VII (November, 1964) , 32n.

7

POPULARIZERS OF SCIENTIFIC RACISM

The recent history of scientific racism consists of two parallel developments. The first was an accomplishment of academic social scientists who, intentionally or not, provided "scientific" data for racists and a "scientific" rationale for segregation and discrimination. The second was an achievement of nonscientists, of popularizers who explained scientific racism to white supremacists and segregationists who in turn sought to make those explanations the basis for racial policy. Both are important elements in the history of civil rights since 1954. The works and speculations of a few academic scientists were of limited significance in themselves and would remain so unless translated into a philosophy of race relations and a program of racial policies. This was the task of popularizers. The story of their achievement is significant in its own right, because it demonstrates the close relationship between segregationists and the social scientists discussed in this study, and illustrates the extent to which the works of the social scientists served the ends of calculating racists. It also explains the efforts segregationists have recently made to apply "science" to race relations.

The efforts were more difficult than might at first appear. Most segregationists do not think in scientific terms. They find the abstractions of science uncongenial; they are more comfortable discussing legal precedents and constitutional interpretations than ruminating in the world of science. Historically, defenders of Southern race policies have been more remarkable for emotion than intellectuality, and few of them ever felt it necessary to think through their racial ideas and formulate a systematic racial philosophy. Traditionally, they found justification aplenty for segregation in their experiences with Negroes. They *knew* the race, they felt, as no other white men ever had. When provoked into defending the "Southern way of life," the essential element of which was first slavery and then segregation, they turned invariably to legal and constitutional arguments, emphasizing the twin doctrines of states' rights and limited (federal) government. Pressed further, they might add that Negroes are not "ready" for integration, that integration violates basic precepts of human decency, Christianity, or "God's way." In any case, they always believed that Negroes prefer segregation and are satisfied with life in the South.

Southern segregationists have usually accepted these arguments as an adequate defense of their racial policies. In effect, they accepted first slavery and later segregation as "right" and "natural" without bothering to develop a rational defense for either. Of course, scientific arguments were always a minor theme in the defense of both, but never more than a minor theme irregularly employed. Southerners have usually ignored scientific justifications for their race policies during periods of racial quietude, turning to science only when outside pressures necessitated a more careful defense of their policies. The antebellum slaveocracy developed a "scientific" defense of slavery only when the abolitionist attack upon the peculiar institution became effective. After 1890 segregationists again turned to science, this time seeking arguments to blunt Northern criticism of new laws and state constitutions disfranchising Negroes, nullifying the Fourteenth and Fifteenth amendments, and legalizing the most rigid kind of racial discrimination. However, once Northerners and the federal government acquiesced in the new policies the Southerners' interest in science diminished. But again after 1954 Southern whites recognized the seriousness of a new challenge to their race policies, and turned once more to science.

The story of this latest effort to use science to defend discriminatory race policies is in part a story of writers, lecturers, and organizers who bridged the gap between academic social scientists and segregationists and white supremacists. The division between the academics and the popularizers, however, is not absolute. Such scientists as Garrett and George are also popularizers, and nonscientists sometimes speak as though they are scientists. It is the popularizers, the nonscientists, who have the most direct impact upon segregationists and white supremacists.

The most significant of the popularizers is Carleton Putnam, a Yankee by birth and inheritance, a Southerner by choice and persuasion. Born in New York City in 1901, Putnam comes from a distinguished New York and New England family and is descended from the Revolutionary War general, Israel Putnam. Educated at Princeton (B.S. in history and politics, 1924) and Columbia (LL.B., 1932), he has spent most of his adult life as an airlines executive. He has been for some time engaged in writing a multivolume biography of Theodore Roosevelt, and more recently, a defense of racial segregation in the South.[1] Though Thomas R. Waring, the archsegregationist editor of the *Charleston News and Courier* has described Putnam as "a dyed-in-the-wool Northerner" and "a Yankee in the true sense of the word," Putnam has in fact spent much of his adult life in the South and the environs of Washington, D.C.

Putnam's emergence as a major spokesman for scientific racists illustrates many crosscurrents in the recent history of scientific racism, including the close relationship between segregation, scientific racism, and political reaction. Though he and his admirers

[1] For a brief account of Putnam's life see W. D. McCain, "Who Is Carleton Putnam?" *The Citizen*, VII (March, 1963), 52–54.

frequently refer to his "science degree," he is not a scientist; his degree is a bachelor of science in history and politics. These references to Putnam's "science degree" are apparently intended to buttress the authority of his scientific preachments, and are another instance of the tendency of racists sometimes to state things in a way that creates a false impression. The fact that Putnam is not a scientist, however, has not inhibited him in his writings on race, nor has it lessened his appeal among segregationists and white supremacists. It has, in fact, been advantageous to him, for it makes him oblivious to the nature and limitations of the scientific process and relieves him of all doubt about the sufficiency of his logic and his evidence.

When the Supreme Court issued the Brown decision, Putnam was not, he says, much concerned one way or another.[2] Gradually, however, casual reading in the public press and the shock of the Little Rock crisis aroused his interest in both the Brown decision and the larger problem of race relations in general. The more he read the more he was aroused. He found the arguments of segregationists cogent, logical, and well presented; those of integrationists "inept" and "lacking in perception." He wondered if no one else saw this. Driven by a growing sense of outrage at the actions and illogic of integrationists, he decided to speak out, to enter the war of words then raging between segregationists and integrationists. His first step was to express his concern in letters to the editors of *Life* magazine and the Memphis *Commercial Appeal*. *Life* ignored his letter, but the *Commercial Appeal* printed it in full. The experience was significant. It convinced Putnam that the national press had closed its mind on race and race relations and erected a "paper curtain" around those subjects to conceal the truth from the American people. In contrast, the appearance of his letter in the *Commercial Appeal* elicited considerable enthusiasm from Southern readers, a fact which further convinced him of the soundness of his own views and the open-mindedness of Southerners, even on the sensitive issue of race relations.

This was a typical reaction of segregationists in similar situations. So convinced are they of their own reasonableness and truthfulness, indeed of their own righteousness, that they are often unable

[2] This author's narrative follows closely that of Putnam himself in his *Race and Reason, A Yankee View* (Washington, 1961), a work which is among other things a self-adulatory account of Putnam's role in defending segregation and spreading the ideas of scientific racism.

to evaluate rationally the views of other people. Putnam was sure that anyone who agreed with him was reasonable, truthful, and righteous, for he was convinced that those terms aptly described his own views. Nor is the reference to righteousness misplaced. A sense of self-righteousness and moral indignation pervades all his writings on race and leads him to the conclusion that his critics are naive, ignorant, immoral, unpatriotic, or all of these. This fact is in part responsible for his failure to provoke a meaningful debate with integrationists, though the shallowness of his ideas, the inconsequence of his evidence, and the disingenuousness of his logic also contributed to his failure. Putnam blamed his failure on the unwillingness of integrationists to debate an issue in which the evidence is against them. Debate, however, is possible only between open-minded men of good will who are receptive to facts and to points of view which differ from their own. Racial topics by their very nature are difficult to debate, whether the debaters be segregationists or integrationists, but Putnam had more difficulty than most men. As a result, he has had more success exhorting the faithful than persuading the skeptical.

In 1958 in the aftermath of the Little Rock crisis, Putnam decided that a direct appeal to President Eisenhower was the best way to dramatize the segregationists' case. Accordingly, he wrote a letter to the President, hoping to convince him of "the reasonableness behind the Southern position." This was the first of several letters from Putnam to prominent public officials, and such letters have since become the chief device for drawing attention to his ideas.

The letter to Eisenhower [3] is a summary of Putnam's objections to the Brown decision and racial integration. In it, Putnam relied very little upon scientific arguments, a fact which indicates that he had not yet realized their usefulness to segregationists. He objected to the Brown decision because it ignored local customs and racial mores in the South, because it represented court-made law and disregarded "the white man's right to freedom of association," because it violated the lessons of history and sought to give Negroes something they had not earned, because it "set back the cause of the Negro in the South by a generation." He told Eisenhower that the integration movement rested upon a false con-

[3] It is printed in Putnam, *Race and Reason*, 5–9.

struction of the Jeffersonian principle of human equality and a misunderstanding of the Christian doctrine of brotherly love. "The command to love your neighbor," he explained, "is not a command either to consider your neighbor your equal, or yourself his equal."

These are standard criticisms of the integration movement, and Putnam's use of them demonstrated his kinship with traditional segregationists. It was axiomatic to him that race relations are the exclusive concern of whites, and that whatever upsets the Southern white man damages "the cause of the Negro." In Putnam's view, the Negro's "cause" was to stay on good terms with white men, not to go around indiscriminately demanding social and political rights. He assumed that the white man's interests are superior to the Negro's, for he also assumed that the South, like the United States as a whole, is a white man's country in which Negroes are permitted to live although without any real voice in primary social or political decisions.

No objection to integration was more important to Putnam than the idea that Negroes have not "earned" the right to equality. "Social status has to be earned," he declared. "It cannot be achieved by legal fiat. . . . Any man with two eyes in his head can observe a Negro settlement in the Congo, can study the pure-blooded African in his native habitat as he exists when left on his own resources, can compare this settlement with London or Paris, and can draw his own conclusions regarding relative levels of character and intelligence—or that combination of character and intelligence which is civilization." This statement has interesting implications. It raises the question, How can Negroes "earn" equal status? What can "clean," God-fearing, hardworking, patriotic, intelligent, middle class Negroes do to "earn" equality? Putnam seems to answer "nothing"—until the "average" Negro matches the "average" white man in the above qualities, and the civilization of Africa equals that of Europe. As a practical matter, this means that individual Negroes can do nothing—but wait and remain segregated. But other questions also arise. Does the emergence of independent Negro nations in Africa count for anything? Does the integration movement itself count for anything? Through this movement Negroes are overcoming all the obstacles and intimidations which the white man's resourcefulness and ingenuity have devised to keep the race down. Is not this movement, so hateful to segregationists, itself a process of "earning" status? Not to Putnam. To him it is a plot by selfish, power-hungry white politicians to "give" special privileges to Negroes in exchange for votes on election day.

President Eisenhower ignored Putnam's letter, a fact which Putnam took to mean that Eisenhower was a part of the national conspiracy of silence against the South and the segregationist point of view. To overcome this conspiracy and get his views before the American people, Putnam sent a copy of the letter to Virginius Dabney, editor of the Richmond *Times-Dispatch,* who printed it and praised it editorially. Other Southern newspapers picked it up, and Putnam was presently inundated with a flood of favorable replies from across the South. At the urging of columnist John Temple Graves of the Birmingham *Post-Herald,* one of the South's most outspoken defenders of segregation, a group of prominent Alabama politicians, among them Albert Boutwell, now mayor of Birmingham, organized a committee to facilitate the distribution of Putnam's letter outside the South. The favorite device of the Putnam Letters Committee, as the group called itself, was to print Putnam's letters in paid advertisements in major newspapers outside the South.[4] Each advertisement included an appeal for funds, which the Committee used to buy still other advertisements in a continuing assault upon the "paper curtain." The effort had an element of the quixotic about it, but it had a certain appeal to thousands of segregationists who derived from it the satisfaction of having participated in a concerted effort to do something about the threat of racial integration.

The response to the Eisenhower letter, the first to be widely printed in non-Southern newspapers, was, according to Putnam, successful beyond all expectations. Within five months, he states, contributions totaled $37,000, and the advertisements continued sporadically over several years. A more important result of the Committee's efforts was the thousands of letters from Northerners and Westerners which, again according to Putnam, overwhelmingly supported his position. "The man and woman in the street in the North," he wrote, "seemed to be on the side of the South," and here was a vast reservoir of good will which Southerners

---

[4] The letter to Eisenhower appeared in the New York *Times,* January 5, 1959.

could exploit in their crusade against integration, and if properly exploited might enable them to win their fight and reverse the Brown decision.

Reverse the Brown decision! That chimera was and remains Putnam's great objective, the Holy Grail he pursues with the ardor and singlemindedness of a medieval knight. Though he is certain that the American people are basically sympathetic to segregation, he is confronted with the stubborn fact that they sometimes act like integrationists. They allow Negroes to vote and attend integrated schools; they follow political, civic, and religious leaders who endorse integration; they support institutions of higher learning in which their children are taught that men are equal and racial segregation is irrational. To reconcile this paradox, Putnam resorts to a favorite device of racists, the plot theory of history. He, too, believes that intellectuals, social scientists, liberals, socialists, and communists have brainwashed the American people into believing against their better judgment that the races are equal and integration is the only rational system of race relations. He therefore warned Americans to beware of "a movement calling itself, here, Communism, there Marxism, somewhere else Socialism," for whatever its name, its objective is always the same, "the subversion of science as well as governments."

Putnam felt compelled to broadcast his convictions, and in March 1959 he expressed them in another letter, this time to Eisenhower's attorney general, William P. Rogers. It was the preparation of this letter that led Putnam to science. He studied the scientific arguments put forth by segregationists and integrationists, read the testimony in the Brown cases, and traced the integrationists' ideas and, indeed, the origins of the equalitarian "conspiracy" back to Franz Boas and the social anthropologists Boas trained at Columbia. Reading Boas' works, he found, was an astonishing experience. "Here was clever and insidious propaganda posing in the name of science," he wrote, "fruitless efforts at proof of unprovable theories," "slippery techniques in evading the main issue," "prolix diversions," "sound without . . . substance." Boas was not simply a poor scientist, he was ludicrous, and while reading his works Putnam was reduced to "laughing out loud."

He decided to pursue the matter further. If he, a nonscientist, saw through Boas' fabrications and insipidness, surely trained scientists did too. To find out for himself, he approached a num-

ber of leading scientists, soliciting their opinions on the works of
Boas and his disciples in social anthropology. He found "professional scientists aplenty" who agreed with his assessment of Boas,
but he also found something else—they would admit their true
feelings in private but not in public. They were inhibited, he decided, by the stranglehold equalitarians have over the academic
and scientific world. "One prize-winning Northern scientist whom
I visited at his home in a Northern city asked me, after I had
been seated a few minutes in his living room, whether I was sure
I had not been followed," he wrote. "Another disclosed in the
privacy of his study that he had evidence he was being checked by
mulattoes at his lectures."

To Putnam, such incidents confirmed his belief that American
science was in an intimidated state. When he first approached the
scientists they were "hesitant, withdrawn and fearful," even those
with national and international reputations. Gradually, however,
their reserve broke down and many of them talked freely, but—
alas!—confidentially, to Putnam. And being an honorable man, he
refuses to violate their confidence; he will not publicly name the
scientists who privately agree with him. "Any public official who
will guarantee their livelihood," he wrote, "can get their names
from me, on one condition—that the scientists themselves agree."

Such a statement can only be taken as a measure of Putnam's
failure to find reputable scientists who agree with his racial views.
Obviously he cannot produce an impressive list of scientists who
support segregation on scientific grounds (though it would be a
simple matter to produce a list of those who condemn it on those
grounds), so he resorts to an unsubstantiated claim that scientists
are cowered into silence or, even worse, into endorsing equalitarianism against their better judgment. His comments about the scientific and academic communities are in notable contrast to the
usual charge by political reactionaries that academic freedom and
tenure are camouflage for intellectual license. If Putnam is correct,
what exists is not academic freedom at all but a degree of thought
control that would do credit to a police state. However, the reader
need only recall the academic appointments of scientists already
discussed in this study to see that Putnam is not entirely correct.
Despite the existence of an equalitarian consensus in the academic
community, there is still a number of social scientists who publicly
dissent from that consensus. The wonder is not that there are no

hereditarians or scientific racists in the nation's colleges and universities, but that there are so many proponents of racial views which are generally discredited.

Putnam's excursion into scientific racism convinced him that the strength of the civil rights movement lay in the fact that the American people have been misled into believing the false scientific claims of equalitarians and environmentalists. Americans have been convinced, erroneously he believed, that "science" has proven the races equal and that heredity has little influence upon character and intelligence. They have therefore decided, also erroneously, that segregation is unscientific, unnatural, and unjust. This conviction is widespread even in the South, Putnam declared, where it has created guilt feelings in many white Southerners who are made to suspect that segregation might after all do violence to scientific truth and thus to justice and "right." Because of this conviction, most Americans are impervious to the appeals of segregationists, especially when their appeals are based on states' rights and constitutional precedents. If segregationists are to succeed, if they are to reach the American people, they must, Putnam concluded, drop their emphasis upon legal and constitutional arguments and turn instead to science. The South can preserve segregation only by convincing the rest of America that equalitarian science is invalid. False sentimentalism and humanitarianism must not be permitted to interfere with the acceptance of scientific truth or with the application of science to race relations. "Any American worthy of the name feels an obligation of kindness and justice toward his fellow man," Putnam told Attorney General Rogers. "He is willing to give every individual his chance, whatever his race, but in those circumstances where a race must be dealt with as a race, he realizes that the level of the average must be controlling, and that the relatively minor handicap upon the superior individual of the segregated race, if it be a handicap at all, must be accepted until the average has reached the point where desire for association is mutual."

Putnam hoped that his letter to the attorney general [5] might embolden intimidated scientists and relieve the consciences of guilt-stricken segregationists. In this letter his major arguments against integration are scientific in nature. He repeated the usual racist

5 It is printed in Putnam, *Race and Reason*, 21–29.

criticisms of the social science in the Brown decision. A majority of the authorities cited by the Court appear "either to belong to Negro or other minority groups, or to have prepared their studies under the auspices of such groups," he noted. "To expect these groups to present impartial reports on the subject of racial discrimination is like expecting a saloon keeper to prepare an impartial study on prohibition." It was his "considered opinion," he added, "that two generations of Americans have been victimized by a pseudo-scientific hoax in this field, that this hoax is part of an equalitarian propaganda typical of the left-wing overdrift of our times, and that it will not stand an informed judicial test. I do not believe that ever before has science been more warped by a self-serving few to the deception and injury of so many."

To correct the misconceptions in this "hoax," Putnam explained to the attorney general that each race should be measured by its "character-intelligence index." This index he defined as "the combination of intelligence with all of the qualities that go under the name of character, including especially the willingness to resist rather than to appease evil." It "forms the only possible index of the capacity for civilization as Western Europeans know it," he added, "and there is no test for [it] save in observing the native culture in which it results. Such observation does not sustain the doctrine of [racial] equality."

This index, which is central to Putnam's case, is apparently his own contribution to scientific racism. To prove its validity he cited the failure of Negroes in Africa to create a civilization equal to that of modern Europe, a fact which he thought was genetic in origin, though much of his evidence to prove it was historical. Where, he asked rhetorically, is the Negro Shakespeare? The Negro Milton, Edison, Napoleon, Columbus, Lincoln, Beethoven? The Negro city to match London or Paris?

Putnam's discussion of African civilization illustrates the extent to which social darwinism permeates his thinking. "The essential question in this whole [integration] controversy," he wrote, "is whether the Negro, given every conceivable help regardless of cost to the whites, is capable of full adaptation to our white civilization within a matter of a few generations, or whether the record indicates that such adaptation cannot be expected save in terms of many hundreds, if not thousands, of years, and that complete integration of these races, especially in the heavy black belts of the

South, can result only in a parasitic deterioration of white culture, with or without genocide." Negro improvement is a matter of centuries. "Changes in a race occur by mutation and natural selection which involve the gradual elimination of those genes which are unsuited to the surrounding environment," Putnam wrote.[6] "This takes place by mating choices within the race itself and by the dying-off without children of those with a preponderance of unsuitable genes. The process must obviously be a slow one, involving many generations, before the adapting race can hope to achieve equality."

The Putnam Letters Committee printed the letter to Attorney General Rogers in non-Southern newspapers, just as it had the one to Eisenhower, and the response was, says Putnam, overwhelmingly favorable. However, a small minority of those who responded disagreed with Putnam and raised a number of questions which he felt compelled to answer. From their questions he selected those he thought were most significant and prepared answers to them, intending the answers to serve as a general reply to his critics. He decided to publish these answers, hoping thereby to achieve an even wider distribution. The result was *Race and Reason, A Yankee View* (1961), certainly the most widely circulated and probably the most influential defense of segregation written since 1954. It has been especially influential in stimulating among segregationists an interest in scientific racism and awakening them to the possibilities of science as a bulwark for segregation. Published by Public Affairs Press, it reportedly sold more than 100,000 copies within two years. Its circulation has been facilitated by right-wing "patriotic" bookstores as well as segregationist organizations, and some of the latter distribute free copies.

It is a significant book for several reasons. Not only does it detail many standard arguments against integration, but it reflects almost in caricature the intellectual orientation of segregationists. Putnam looks backward nostalgically to the glories of the past, to the days before the American republic was sullied by the New Deal and modern liberalism. In those days, he believes, Americans obeyed the laws of God and nature, lived by moral and ethical absolutes, accepted the inequalities of man, revered the Constitution, and respected legal precedents. There was stability

6 Putnam, *Race and Reason*, 56.

and order, a reverence for principles, a respect for the ideals which had made this a great nation. In the last thirty years, however, or so Putnam thought, all this had eroded away. Change replaced stability and continuity as the natural order of things; the federal government became a bloated tyrant, twisting the Constitution beyond recognition; moral relativism displaced moral absolutes; labor unions became too powerful; racial and ethnic minorities grew restive, challenging the status and middle class ethic of old Americans. All this alarmed Putnam, and his impassioned alarm is a major reason for his appeal among segregationists. Basically, he is neither a scientist nor a pedagogue, but an exhorter. He tells faithful segregationists and white supremacists what they want to hear, and gives them the assurance which comes from having their racial views rationalized and justified.

Race and Reason is a catechism for "true believers," to borrow Eric Hoffer's telling phrase. It consists largely of a series of questions and answers in which Putnam attempted to refute what he thought were the chief arguments against segregation. Despite the ecstatic praise it has elicited from segregationists, it is unusually simplistic, even for a racist work. In fact, Putnam's evaluation of the works of Franz Boas aptly describes his own: "Here [is] clever and insidious propaganda posing in the name of science, fruitless efforts at proof of unprovable theories," "slippery techniques in evading the main issues," "sound without . . . substance," an approach "so saturated with wishful thinking as to be pathetic." There are, however, no "prolix diversions," for Putnam is an effective writer with a fluid style and beguiling presentation.

One of his basic techniques is to avoid troublesome issues by diverting attention from them through the use of *non sequiturs.* The following examples are typical:

Q. You are preaching a doctrine of white supremacy and allying yourself with lynchers and bombers. Worse, don't you realize that this is the doctrine that led to Hitler's barbaric policies?

A. I am advocating a doctrine of white leadership based on proved achievement, not supremacy in any sense of domination, exploitation, or violence.

In this casual manner he glossed over the harsher aspects of white supremacy. White supremacy can be maintained only by denying Negroes the right to vote, which is to say by dominating and exploiting the race, and the recent rise in Negro militancy seems to indicate that white supremacy can be preserved in the future only by a willingness of whites to resort to violence.

But to return to his answer:

As far as the Negro race is concerned, if it is interested in such cultural elements as our white civilization has to offer, it should realize that to destroy or to debilitate the white race would be to kill the goose that lays the golden egg. . . . Regarding Hitler, can we condemn Christianity because of the atrocities of the Spanish Inquisition? . . . (pp. 55–56)

Q. The NAACP maintains that your comparison of the achievement of great white men with those of Negroes is pointless. They say the same comparison could be made between white men and white women, yet no one claims that women are biologically inferior. They also say that the early Irish immigrants to this country were more shabby and lived in poorer shanties than the Negroes. What is your answer?

A. As to the achievements of women, not even in *Alice in Wonderland* do we find an attempt to equate biological inequivalents. Most women, through history, have been in the home, bearing and rearing children, and to see a Negro man hiding behind a white woman's skirts is just a little sickening.

Concerning the Irish, when the NAACP can point to a Negro city the equal of Dublin or Cork or Belfast, it will be time to discuss it. (p. 59)

Q. Isn't it wrong to injure the self-esteem of any man by reflections on his racial background?

A. No man's self-esteem need be injured by the truth concerning his racial background, any more than an acceptance of innate limitations by people in any sphere need affect their pride. Most of us do not hang our heads in shame if we cannot invent like Edison or write like Shakespeare. . . . (p. 64)

Q. Isn't it unfair to discriminate legally against the exceptional Negro on the basis of a racial average?

A. We discriminate legally against exceptional minors by not allowing them to vote, although certain of them may be more intelligent than many adults. Discriminations of this sort are necessary to the practical administration of human affairs. (p. 64)

Putnam has not answered his own questions. He sometimes dismissed the question as unimportant (e.g., his dismissal of the reference to the Irish), sometimes raised extraneous issues (e.g., his reference to Hitler, Christianity, and the Spanish Inquisition), and sometimes introduced false analogies (e.g., between Negroes and minors). He justifies discrimination against Negroes by pointing out that minors are discriminated against. But the discriminations against minors apply to *all* minors and are temporary. In addition, Negro adults are not minors, nor is intelligence the criterion for American citizenship. Elsewhere Putnam is a staunch advocate of strict construction of the Constitution, and his effort to base the rights of citizenship upon intelligence, which is certainly extra-constitutional, indicates that race, not intelligence or the Constitution, is his principal concern.

His performance is no better on questions relating to science:

Q. While there is no positive scientific proof that the Negro is the equal of the white man, neither is there any positive scientific proof that he is not. Under these circumstances, how can the Negro's inferiority be assumed?

A. It is true that anthropology is not an exact science in the sense that mathematics is, and that its propositions cannot be proved or disproved like mathematical formulae. Nevertheless, the evidence is as clear as the nature of the science permits, and it is all that reasonable men can ask. . . .

"The evidence" to which he referred is the studies of Negro intelligence by H. A. Tanser, Audrey Shuey, and Frank McGurk, and the studies of brain morphology by Wilder Penfield, Ward C. Halstead, and C. J. Connolly. As previously noted, however, the studies by Tanser, Shuey, and McGurk prove only that most Negroes make lower scores than most whites on IQ tests; they do not demonstrate that the lower scores result from innate factors.[7] Penfield and Halstead have repudiated Putnam's use of their works, and have specifically stated that they know of no valid evidence which indicates that Negroes are inferior to whites.[8] Connolly's study also has serious limitations for Putnam's purposes, as physiologist Dwight J. Ingle has demonstrated.[9] Reviewing the studies on brain morphology by F. W. Vint, Robert Bennett Bean, and Connolly, Ingle noted that "the three authors' descriptions of differences did not agree, although each concluded that no morphological feature was found to be exclusively characteristic of either the White or the Negro brain. There is no objective evidence that any of the average differences claimed to exist are marks of inferiority or correlate with intelligence and behavior." So, despite Putnam's statement to the contrary, the evidence is *not* "all that reasonable men can ask."

[7] See above, Chapter IV.

[8] Halstead and Penfield's letters to the editor of *Perspectives in Biology and Medicine* are quoted in Ingle, "Comments on the Teachings of Carleton Putnam."

[9] Ingle, "Comments on the Teachings of Carleton Putnam," 30, *et passim*.

Putnam made his most ambitious use of science in replying to this question: "The NAACP asserts that there is virtually unanimity among scientists on the biological equality of the Negro. Is this true?" He phrased the question ingeniously, attributing the belief in "biological equality" to the NAACP, not to scientists, which was itself enough to discredit the question among segregationists. The phrase "biological equality" is itself ingenious. What does it mean? It could mean that there are no valid biological reasons for racial discrimination, but Putnam apparently intended his use of it to suggest that the races are biologically identical. Certainly the manner in which he used it obscured the distinction between racial differences and racial inequality. By confusing racial equality and biological sameness, he undertook to discredit the former by ridiculing the latter.

Putnam's answer to the question was emphatic. "It is not. There is a strong northern clique of equalitarian social anthropologists under the hypnosis of the Boas school which . . . has captured important chairs in many leading northern and western universities. This clique, aided by equalitarians in government, the press, entertainment, and other fields, has dominated public opinion in these areas and has made it almost impossible for those who disagree with it to hold jobs." Those who do disagree "have been forced largely into the universities of the South where they are biding their time." What was his authority for this? "My files," he wrote, "provide ample proof of this."

Unfortunately for his case, this is no proof at all. If he has proof, his obligation to produce it transcends his respect for those timid scientists he claims to protect. For if Putnam's racial views are correct, the integration movement *is* a threat to Western civilization, and the necessities of civilization outweigh the convenience of a few spineless scientists. But apparently for Putnam and many of his readers, the allegations were sufficient in themselves. "In a moral sense," he wrote, "we are confronted with what might almost be called a trilogy of conspiracy, fraud and intimidation: conspiracy to gain control of important citadels of learning and news dissemination, fraud in the teaching of false racial doctrines, and intimidation in suppressing those who would preach the truth." Despite Putnam's assurance on this point, it might be argued that his references to conspiracy, fraud, and intimidation are more applicable to such areas as Mississippi, the state in which Putnam is most influential, than to areas where equalitarian social science is widely accepted. One need only recall the stranglehold of segregationists upon the University of Mississippi, the pressures brought upon Professor James Silver there,[10] the racism that fills the columns of many Mississippi newspapers, and the intimidations against anyone in the state who deviates from orthodoxy on racial matters. Zealous segregationists are at least as insistent upon orthodoxy and conformity as are zealous integrationists. Certainly no area of the country has more zealously guarded its school children from unacceptable racial views than has the deep South.

Putnam has still other scientific authorities to offer. He cited three obscure works in French, G. Lefrou's *Le Noir D'Afrique* (1943), G. A. Heuse's *Biologie du Noir* (1957), and J. Millot's *Biologie des Races Humaines* (1952), which he assured his readers "are considered authoritative by our leading physical anthropologists." From these works he extracted quotations describing Negroes in most unflattering terms. Lefrou, for example, repeated the long-discredited idea that the intellectual development of Negroes ends at puberty. "There are two quite distinct stages in the intellectual life of the Negro," he wrote, quoting another French author. "As a child he is amiable, gentle, gracious, spontaneous and docile. He appears very precocious, more precocious by all odds than the great majority of European children. He understands and easily assimilates many things. At the date of puberty a radical metamorphasis takes place. A sharp arresting of development occurs and even a slight regression. The intellectual progress of the Negro is rapid during the first ten or twelve years, next it slows down, becomes stationary, then proceeds slowly, diminishing during some fifteen years. Finally a rapid enfeeblement occurs." Lefrou's views are based upon the idea that Negroes are more primitive than whites and closer to animals on the evolutionary scale. Like animals, the idea runs, their infancy is brief; they reach physical maturity quite early, but their intellectual development is arrested by the advent of puberty, when the sutures of the brain are said to knit together so firmly that the physical growth of the brain is halted completely. Adult Negroes are thus physically—and sexually—mature but intellectually adolescent, children with the physical and sexual appetites of grown-ups.

10 See James Silver, *Mississippi, The Closed Society* (New York, 1964).

Lefrou, Millot, and Heuse, plus Nathaniel Weyl (who is not a scientist), and biologist Garrett Hardin of the University of California, Santa Barbara,[11] are the "nonequalitarian anthropologists" cited by Putnam. His "science" is therefore much weaker than that of such writers as George, Garrett, Shuey, and McGurk. *Race and Reason* is important to the history of scientific racism not because of the amount of empirical data it offers (which is none at all) or the array of scientific authorities it quotes (which is anything but impressive), but because four important scientific racists wrote a laudatory introduction to it. The four were Henry E. Garrett, Wesley C. George, editor Robert Gayre of *Mankind Quarterly*, and R. Ruggles Gates. They were "in complete accord" with Putnam's science and endorsed "his balanced presentation of genetic and environmental factors in the area of both racial and individual biology." [12]

They also agreed with Putnam's "estimate of the extent to which non-scientific ideological pressures have harrassed scientists in the last thirty years." Like Putnam, they thought this pressure "often [resulted] in the suppression or distortion of truth" and was responsible for the widespread acceptance of equalitarianism. "Man must be guided by science, but scientific thought must not be molded to preconceived political ideas," they declared, molding their own scientific thoughts to preconceived political ideas. "Statesmen and judges today frequently take positions based upon an inadequate knowledge of the facts so far as they relate to the nature of man," they continued. "We do not believe that there is anything to be drawn from the sciences in which we work which supports the view that all races of men, or all ethnic groups are equal and

11 See Garrett Hardin, "The Competitive Exclusion Principle," *Science*, April 29, 1960, pp. 1292–97. It is difficult to see why Putnam cites this article to support his position. There is no racism in it, merely a discussion of the "competitive exclusion principle," an ecological hypothesis which suggests that in nature complete competitors cannot coexist. Hardin suggests that the principle has parallel implications for economics, genetics, and ecology. "As a result of recent findings in the fields of physiological genetics and population genetics, particularly as concerns blood groups, the applicability of both the inequality axiom and the exclusion principle is rapidly becoming accepted," Hardin wrote. He used the word "inequality" to refer to differences which favor survival in nature. He did not give it social and racial significance, or imply that it had any.

12 Putnam had written, for example, that "intelligence is almost entirely a matter of heredity." *Race and Reason*, 58.

alike, or likely to become equal or alike, in anything approaching the foreseeable future. We believe on the contrary that there are vast areas of difference within mankind not only in physical appearance, but in such matters as adaptability to varying environments, and in deep psychological and emotional qualities, as well as in mental ability and capacity for development."

Putnam hoped *Race and Reason* would accomplish two objectives: awaken America to the evil consequences of integration and lead the South to a new and better strategy in defending segregation. Integration is evil, he believed, because it leads inevitably to racial amalgamation, which in turn will be disastrous because Negroes have "no inborn capacity for Western civilization." Furthermore, he wrote, "It is not the South which is committing a moral crime against the Negro in maintaining segregation, but the North which is committing a moral crime against the South in forcing integration."

One test of the cogency of Putnam's logic is to take his admonitions concerning Negroes and apply them to segregationists in Mississippi, among whom *Race and Reason* was well received. "The capacity for a free civilization involves many attributes," Putnam wrote, "self-control (which, among other things, includes resistance to emotionalism), self-reliance, self-responsibility, willingness to bear the burdens of others without casting upon others the burdens one should bear one's self, willingness both to accept the verdict of majorities and to concede the rights of minorities, willingness to obey the law even when it hurts, willingness to support rather than to raid a treasury, emphasis upon the importance of the individual." Judging by the recent history of race relations in Mississippi, most Mississippi segregationists are not notable for "self-control" or "resistance to emotionalism." Nor is "self-reliance, self-responsibility, [and] willingness to bear the burdens of others without casting upon others the burdens one should bear one's self" the best way to describe their exploitation of Negroes. The reference to a "willingness . . . to accept the verdict of majorities and to concede the rights of minorities" is even more to the point. Mississippi segregationists have shown little concern for the rights of the Negro minority in their midst, nor are they willing to accept "the verdict of majorities" in those areas of the state where Negroes outnumber whites. Like John C. Calhoun before him, Putnam forgot that there are several kinds of majorities and minorities, and to be valid a defense of majority rights must be applicable to all majorities and consistent with the rights of all minorities. The admonition to Negroes "to obey the law even when it hurts" is particularly ironic in view of Putnam's defense of Mississippi, a state which has systematically subverted or ignored not only the Brown decision but the Fourteenth and Fifteenth amendments and the civil rights acts of 1957, 1960, 1964, and 1965. Finally, it should be noted (according to the Library of Congress Legislative Reference Service) that for every $218 paid by Mississippians in federal taxes, the federal government spent $327 in the state in 1959–61. And of every $1,000 in Mississippi income, $286 came from the federal government. It would seem that Mississippians do not always live up to Putnam's admonitions to support rather than raid the public treasury.

Segregationists have heaped lavish praise upon both Putnam and *Race and Reason*. An official of the Citizens' Councils described the latter as a "brilliant" work which "filled an aching need." [13] Dr. W. D. McCain, president of the University of Southern Mississippi, who reviewed *Race and Reason* for *The Citizen* reported in the spring of 1963 that the book had been reviewed 658 times, 544 of which were favorable, fourteen noncommittal, and one hundred unfavorable. However, he added, thirty-two of the unfavorable reviews appeared "in Negro newspapers which could scarcely be expected to view the book objectively." [14]

The impact of *Race and Reason* cannot be fully measured by counting favorable reviews, most of which were apparently in Southern (white) newspapers. More significant was the response of political and educational leaders in some areas of the deep South. Governor Ross Barnett of Mississippi was so impressed that he proclaimed October 26, 1961 "Race and Reason Day" in his state.[15] *Race and Reason* is "a significant and valuable new book" which "meets a long-recognized need in improving communications between patriotic Americans, informing responsible Northern citizens of the viewpoint on race relations held by loyal Southerners,

13 W. J. Simmons, "The Reason for 'Race and Reason,'" *The Citizen*, VII (March, 1963) , 5.

14 McCain, "Who is Carleton Putnam?" 53–54. See also Garrett, "Facts vs. Opinions on 'Race and Reason,'" 7–12. For a favorable review by a Virginia attorney see Stuart Campbell's review in *American Bar Association Journal*, XLVIII (June, 1962) , 567.

15 His proclamation is printed in *The Citizen*, VI (November, 1961) , 4.

and the reasons therefor," Barnett proclaimed. It has "made an important contribution towards creating in the North an understanding of the South's problems, attitudes and actions in the matter of race relations, and has brought together in authentic form the pertinent facts in a manner which Southerners have found most helpful." He urged Mississippians to observe "Race and Reason Day" by reading and discussing the book, by calling it "to the attention of friends and relatives in the North, and by participating in appropriate public functions, thereby demonstrating the appreciation of the people in our state for Mr. Carleton Putnam and for his splendid book."

By all accounts "Race and Reason Day" was a notable occasion. A number of civic, political, and business leaders arranged a testimonial banquet to honor Putnam, and more than five hundred guests paid twenty-five dollars a plate for dinner and the privilege of hearing an address by the guest of honor.[16] In a speech entitled "This Is the Problem," Putnam repeated the major ideas in *Race and Reason* and urged white Mississippians to renewed efforts to overcome the "paper curtain" of Northern ignorance and indifference. *"You have a completely indoctrinated society in the North!"* he told the Mississippians, and "on that indoctrination the integration movement rests." In peroration he added, "The *fight* is your affair! Do the best you can! I'll put it in the words of George Washington himself: 'Erect a standard to which the wise and honest can repair. The event is in the hands of God.' "

There is no evidence that God was impressed by Putnam's plea, but much evidence that segregationists were. Shortly before "Race and Reason Day" in Mississippi, the Louisiana State Board of Education adopted the following resolution:

WHEREAS, There is increasing evidence that the science of biology and anthropology are being distorted and perverted to serve the purposes of certain pressure groups whose aims are inimical to the customs, mores, and traditions of this Nation, and

WHEREAS, An eminent American scholar has written a book that exposes the flagrant distortion and perversion of scientific truth by so-called social anthropologists and socialistically oriented sociologists, and

WHEREAS, The State Board of Education has the legal and moral responsibility of prescribing the curricular experience offered in the schools of

16 Carleton Putnam, "This is the Problem," *The Citizen,* VI (November, 1961), 12–23.

the State which, in the judgment of the Board, will best prepare students for their duties and responsibilities as citizens of the United States, and

WHEREAS, It is the consensus of this Board that selected mature students in certain schools would profit from the careful reading and study of the book RACE AND REASON, A YANKEE VIEW, by Carleton Putnam . . .

THEREFORE BE IT RESOLVED by the Louisiana State Board of Education, that the State Department of Education take such steps as may be necessary to bring this book to the attention of Louisiana school administrators and teachers. . . .

The Board also recommended *Race and Reason* to "selected college personnel," including deans, instructors, students enrolled in courses in anthropology, sociology, and psychology, and a mandatory course in communism vs. Americanism, and certain high school students selected on the basis of "maturity, sincerity, and dependability." [17]

Scientists have been less impressed by *Race and Reason*. Not long after the Louisiana Board of Education passed the above resolution, the Committee on Science in the Promotion of Human Welfare, an affiliate of the American Association for the Advancement of Science, condemned *Race and Reason* as scientifically invalid.[18] "We know of no scientific evidence which can challenge [the] axiomatic principle" that "all citizens are to be regarded as equally entitled to the benefits of citizenship," they continued. "The assertion that such evidence exists ignores the rule of relevance and the limitations inherent in our knowledge of the complex interactions among social groups. In addition, by fostering the illusion that the social decisions about interracial relations can be determined by 'objective scientific fact,' it shields the individual's conscience from a confrontation of the grave moral issues which at present confound the relations among racial groups." The available scientific evidence, they concluded, "cannot properly support a challenge to the principle of human equality, which is assured by the Constitution of the United States." Putnam was unimpressed by the committee report. "It is a tissue of fallacies and confusion," he declared, "put forward by men of no special qualification in the pertinent disciplines of anatomy and phys-

---

17 See [Margolis] "Science and Segregation," *Science*, December 8, 1961, pp. 1868–69. For an account of efforts to get the Virginia Legislature to pass a resolution endorsing *Race and Reason*, see New York *Times*, February 18, 1962, p. 62.
18 "Science and the Race Problem," *Science*, November 1, 1963, pp. 558–61.

ical anthropology, who have acted with transparent political motivation." [19]

The American Anthropological Association and the American Association of Physical Anthropologists also condemned Putnam's views as unscientific. "The American Anthropological Association repudiates statements now appearing in the United States that Negroes are biologically and in innate mental ability inferior to whites," read a resolution adopted by the Association in 1961, "and reaffirms the fact that there is no scientifically established evidence to justify the exclusion of any race from the rights guaranteed by the Constitution of the United States." [20] The physical anthropologists were equally emphatic. "We, the members of the American Association of Physical Anthropologists, professionally concerned with differences in man, deplore the misuse of science to advocate racism," read a resolution adopted in 1962. "We condemn such writings as *Race and Reason* that urge the denial of basic rights to human beings." They also expressed sympathy for "those of our fellow teachers who have been forced by misguided officials to teach misguided race concepts that have no scientific foundation," and they affirmed again "that there is nothing in science that justifies the denial of opportunities or rights to any groups by virtue of race." [21] This resolution is especially significant in view of Putnam's charge that equalitarianism had no real support from physical anthropologists, whose discipline was most directly concerned with the physical aspects of race.

Several scientific journals reviewed *Race and Reason,* all unfavorably. Gordon Allen of the Public Health Service reviewed it for *Eugenics Quarterly,* the journal of the American Eugenics Society, and noted that Putnam wrote "with dangerous persuasiveness." But he added, Putnam's "facts and . . . logic are not very sound scientifically," for he "repeatedly violates scientific standards of accuracy." And "alleged scientific justification for dealing with Negroes as a race stems from a mistaken notion of the genetic

[19] Putnam, "Science and the Race Problem," *Science,* December 13, 1963, pp. 1419–20.

[20] "Science and Segregation: The American Anthropological Association Dips into Politics," *Science,* December 8, 1961, pp. 1868–69. For Putnam's response see his letter to the editor, *Science,* March 16, 1962, pp. 966–68; and New York *Times,* December 2, 1961, p. 47.

[21] "American Physical Anthropologists Condemn Racism," *Current Anthropology,* III (October, 1962), 445.

nature of individual and racial differences," wrote Allen. "Putnam evidently regards races as absolute and clearly homogeneous divisions of mankind instead of the arbitrary classification on a continuum that they are. Ignoring the particulate nature of heredity, Putnam infers that each individual carries the genetic qualities of his entire race and that all his genes are, in a sense, marked. The facts indicate that, for the most part, Whites and Negroes share the same genes and differ mainly in the relatively frequency of those genes. Each individual has his own assortment of genes, his own genotype. With respect to the sort of hereditary adaptation to civilization, an individual's manifest traits are the best guide to his genotype. These may be a poor guide, but the traits of preceding generations are even poorer and remote ancestry can add no information at all." [22]

Theodosius Dobzhansky, one of the nation's foremost geneticists, reviewed *Race and Reason* for the *Journal of Heredity*.[23] Noting that Senators Richard Russell of Georgia, Harry Byrd of Virginia, and Strom Thurmond of South Carolina had praised the book, he described it as "a political tract combatting the desegregation decision of the Supreme Court," and not a work of science. "By no stretch of its meaning can Putnam's book be said to be 'scientific,' " Dobzhansky wrote. "Race prejudice arises from emotion not from reasoning, although time and again it has sought to shore itself up with pseudo-science." [24]

The refusal of scientists to accept his premises infuriates Putnam, but does not lead him to re-examine his premises or con-

[22] Gordon Allen, review of *Race and Reason, Eugenics Quarterly,* VIII (June, 1961), 105–07. For a rejoinder to Allen see Henry E. Garrett, "Comment on Gordon Allen's Review of Putnam's Race and Reason," *ibid.,* (December, 1961), 218–20; and Allen, "Reply to Garrett Concerning Putnam's Race and Reason," *ibid.,* 221–22.

[23] Theodosius Dobzhansky, "A Bogus 'Science' of Race Prejudice," *Journal of Heredity,* LII (July-August, 1961), 189–90.

[24] There are numerous other instances of adverse comment on *Race and Reason* by scientists. "The evidence cited by Putnam is without scientific value," writes physiologist Dwight J. Ingle, in "Racial Differences and the Future," *Science,* October 16, 1964, pp. 375–79. See also Julian H. Steward, letter to the editor, *Science,* March 16, 1961, pp. 964–66; Stanley Diamond, "Race and the Ideology of Race," *Current Anthropology,* III (June, 1962), 285–88; Donald C. Simmons, "Scientific Racism," *New Republic* (January 5, 1963), 9–10. See also the symposium edited by Princeton sociologist Melvin M. Tumin, *Race and Intelligence,* in which sociologist Ralph H. Turner of University of California at Los Angeles; anthropologist Sherwood L. Washburn of the University of California, Berkeley; psychologist Silvan S. Tomkins; and testing expert Henry

clusions. He has aroused a great deal of controversy but no debate; he has generated much heat but no light. From his own point of view, nothing constructive has come from his controversies with scientists. He has merely encouraged them to denounce his works and refute his claims. Putnam versus the scientific community in America is no even match. Even David faced smaller odds in battling Goliath, and Putnam is no David.[25]

Putnam is by no means the only significant popularizer of scientific racism. Among the others the most accomplished writer is James Jackson Kilpatrick, whose *The Southern Case for School Segregation* (1962) is the most literate defense of segregation published in recent years. Editor of the Richmond *News Leader* and a nationally syndicated newspaper columnist, Kilpatrick is both less extreme in his views and more effective in expressing them than are most other apologists for segregation.

His use of science [26] parallels Putnam's. He praises *Mankind*

C. Dyer condemn *Race and Reason*. For the most systematic refutation of *Race and Reason* see Ingle, "Comments on the Teachings of Carleton Putnam." See also Putnam, "A Reply to Dwight Ingle," *Mankind Quarterly*, IV (1963), 43–48.

[25] Putnam's career as a dispenser of scientific racism continues even today. The National Putnam Letters Committee is still active, still dispensing his letters and speeches. In 1962 he addressed the Louisiana Attorney General's Conference for District Attorneys, and told an audience that included Louisiana Governor Jimmy Davis and members of the state Supreme Court that equalitarian propaganda has "infiltrated the life sciences since New Deal days." Putnam, "The Road to Reversal," *The Citizen*, VII (March, 1963), 23–34. In 1963 he told the Putnam Letters Club in a Lincoln Day address that "genetic racial differences in intelligence, character and behavior are the basic reality of life." Putnam, "These Are the Guilty," *ibid.*, 36–51. "These Are the Guilty" appeared also in *Mankind Quarterly*, IV (July–September 1963), 12–27. Putnam's most recent letter to a prominent official was to the late President Kennedy following the integration crisis at the University of Mississippi in 1962. See New York *Times*, October 3, 1962, p. 33. See also criticisms of this letter by Columbia University anthropologist Morton H. Fried, *ibid.*, October 10, 1962, p. 46; and the reply to Fried from Henry E. Garrett and Wesley C. George, *ibid.*, October 24, 1962, p. 38. See also Putnam's letters to Dwight Ingle, Margaret Mead, and David W. Kendall, special counsel to President Eisenhower, in *Three Letters on Science and Race* (National Putnam Letters Committee, undated). The latest statement of Putnam's views is his *Framework for Love, A Study of Racial Realities* (National Putnam Letters Committee, 1965).

[26] Kilpatrick, *The Southern Case for School Segregation*, 43–93. See also Kilpatrick, "View from a Southern Exposure," in Robert A. Goldwin (ed.), *100 Years of Emancipation* (Chicago, 1963), 103–28.

Quarterly (it was launched by "a group of distinguished anthropologists, psychologists, and social scientists, rebelling against the obstinate attitude of the [Ruth] Benedict-[Ashley] Montagu school") ; denounces "Liberal social anthropologists" and "the entire school of Franz Boas"; singles out Kenneth Clark, Otto Klineberg, Juan Comas, Gunnar Myrdal, and UNESCO for special villification; and praises the works of Frank McGurk, Wesley C. George, Robert M. Yerkes, H. A. Tanser, and Nathaniel Weyl. He reserves his highest encomiums for Carleton Putnam, who has, he says, "driven the Liberal anthropologists practically to apoplexy by the unfair tactic of reading their works and taking them seriously—something no layman is expected to do. The rule is that non-anthropologists must treat anthropologists respectfully, even when anthropologists write nonsense."

A curious but striking inconsistency runs through Kilpatrick's treatment of scientific racism, and destroys whatever effectiveness his arguments might otherwise have. The ideas of scientific racism would seem to be no more valid than the premises upon which they rest, and their most important premise is that heredity is far more significant than environment in determining the ability and character of an individual and a race. Without this premise scientific racists have virtually no case. It is astonishing, therefore, that after reviewing the controversy between hereditarians and environmentalists, Kilpatrick dismissed it as unimportant. Segregationists "have regularly overestimated the factors of heredity and underestimated the factors of environment," he wrote. "Their position would be improved if they simply acknowledged that the question of the Negro's innate inferiority has not been proved and hence is still open." Later he adds, "In terms of the problem immediately at hand, the question of whether the Negro's shortcomings are 'innate' seems to me largely irrelevant anyhow. The issue is not likely to be proved to the satisfaction of either side any time soon; it may not be susceptible of proof at all. Whether [the characteristics of Negroes] are inherited or acquired, they *are*."

In view of this dismissal of so vital a subject, Kilpatrick's unstinted praise of scientific racists is paradoxical. "The evidence put together by Shuey and McGurk is solid, dispassionate, unbiased, and overwhelming," he wrote in a typical passage. In point of fact, however, if the works of Miss Shuey and McGurk are valid they demonstrate beyond doubt that heredity *is* vastly more important than environment in determining the intelligence of Negroes. It was the intention of those authors to demonstrate the relative significance of heredity and environment upon racial intelligence and the validity of their works rests in part upon whether they achieved that goal. If their works are "solid, dispassionate, unbiased, and overwhelming," they settle the heredity-environment controversy, and if they do not settle the controversy it is difficult to see how they merit such unstinted praise.

His inconsistency on this point is puzzling, but only at first appearance. Kilpatrick is steeped in the lore and mythology by which segregationists have traditionally defended Southern race policies, and that lore and mythology emphasize not science but states' rights and strict construction of the Constitution. In his defense of segregation, Kilpatrick, who had a leading role in resurrecting the doctrine of interposition in the years immediately following the Brown decision, falls into the trap Putnam warned against. He consumes his energies discussing states' rights and constitutionalism because, in the final analysis, he is not convinced of the significance of the scientific arguments he employs. "The ruins of Zimbabwe are a long way from Prince Edward County, Virginia, and the finest analysis of electroencephalic findings among the Zulus is of small importance in teaching a class of Alabama sixth-graders," he writes. "The arguments of anthropology are of interest to the South, and I would not wish to leave any impression that would minimize their importance; the fear of ultimate racial interbreeding, encouraged by prospective generations of desegregated and integrated school systems, is a very real fear in the South and not an imagined one. If these Negro characteristics *are* innate, the white Southerner sees nothing but disaster to his race in risking an accelerated intermingling of blood lines. And even if these Negro characteristics are not innate, the white Southerner wants no intimate association with them anyhow."

Kilpatrick's inconsistency went unnoticed by segregationists and scientific racists. Henry E. Garrett, who spent a vast amount of time and energy attempting to prove the predominance of heredity over environment, favorably reviewed *The Southern Case for School Segregation* for *Mankind Quarterly*. "This book," he wrote, "should be required reading for every young American lawyer and law student." He made no mention of Kilpatrick's ambivalence on the heredity-environment controversy.[27]

Nathaniel Weyl, best known as a spokesman for conservative, anticommunist political causes, is another prominent popularizer of scientific racism. More systematic in his treatment of scientific authorities than either Putnam or Kilpatrick, he is also probably less influential. Three of his works are significant, *The Negro in American Civilization* (1960), *The Geography of Intellect* (1963), which he wrote in collaboration with another prominent political conservative, Professor Stefan Possony of the Hoover Institute on War, Revolution and Peace at Stanford University, and *The Creative Elite in America* (1966), in which he repeats and expands many of the views he expressed in earlier works.

The Negro in American Civilization is broader in scope than *Race and Reason* or *The Southern Case for School Segregation*. It does not, however, introduce any new ideas and need not be reviewed here.[28] *The Geography of Intellect,* however, is not so readily disposed of. It is a remarkable work, and to read it is at once frightening and fascinating. It is many things—a collection of racist and nativist ideas, some of them no longer fashionable even among racists; an anticommunist tract written by two prominent conservatives; a mixture of truths and half-truths, common sense and nonsense, *non sequiturs* and irrelevancies. It is a distillation of several facets of racist thought, and in the words of Martin Mayer in *Commentary,* it provides integrationists and egalitarians with "a relatively complete list of what it is we shall overcome." [29]

Weyl and Possony begin with the plausible assumption that brainpower is the most vital human asset in the twentieth century. They also assume, more questionably, that the brainpower necessary to maintain and advance modern civilization "does not exist, either actually or potentially in the requisite qualities among all nations, peoples and races." North Europeans and Jews, they

[27] Henry E. Garrett, review of *The Southern Case for School Segregation, Mankind Quarterly,* III (April–June, 1963), 264–65.

[28] Psychologist Frank C. J. McGurk wrote an introduction to Weyl's *The Negro in American Civilization,* describing the work as a "refreshing antidote" to the "one-sided environmentalist argumentation" which "could serve as a basic reference text in any scientific consideration of race and race difference."

[29] Martin Mayer, "Race and Ability," *Commentary,* XXXVIII (July, 1964), 61–63.

think, possess it in considerable quantities, other Europeans and Mongoloids in lesser amounts. Latin Americans and Arabs have even less, and Negroes virtually none at all. Christian peoples have more than non-Christians (except Jews, who have most of all), and Protestants have more than Catholics. "The I.Q. distributions of Protestant nations," the authors remark solemnly, "tend to be markedly higher than those of Catholic nations."

The chief purpose of *The Geography of Intellect* was to demonstrate the truth and significance of the ranking of ethnic groups noted above. In doing this, Weyl and Possony give considerable attention to Negroes. To demonstrate the inferiority of the race they cite an odd assortment of authorities, from Sir Francis Galton to anthropologist Carleton Coon, from Thomas Jefferson to David Hume and Montesquieu. Negroes, they write drawing heavily upon the ideas of darwinian racists, lack "personality integration" and "capacity for sustained thought or introspection at any level." Negroes are unable "to reason coherently, to maintain attention or even a consistent emotional reaction"; their most conspicuous characteristics are "imitativeness, lack of originality, passivity and childish self-aggrandisement."

Other groups, especially Latin Americans and Arabs, are not much better. "Negro Africa, the Middle East, Latin America, and Southeast Asia are genetically unpromising," the authors wrote. In Latin America "the predominant character structure seems to be deficient in drive and this helps explain the lack of consistent progress in most of the area. Islam and Negro Africa are much clearer examples of cultural systems which create mentalities poorly adapted for successful functioning within the matrix of Western civilization." The problem is largely genetic, but partially environmental, and the latter fact offers a ray of hope. "If a free enterprise economy is allowed to be introduced into Latin America," predict Weyl and Possony, "dynamism toward the physical environment will tend to supplant the exercise of power toward individuals and, in the process, the traditional character structure of the Latin Americans will inevitably be modified."

The chief threat to the future of Western Civilization, or so Weyl and Possony believe, lies in the fact that democracy, communism, and false concepts of equality have led nations to pursue policies which are basically dysgenic. The "application of pseudo-egalitarian ideology to political, social and economic life" downgrades excellence and exalts mediocrity, and the population explosion of recent years is the result of "rampant reproduction" among "mentally incompetent" groups. To neutralize these threats, Weyl and Possony urge the nations of the world to seek out and nurture their "elites," the creative minorities who sustain and advance civilization. "Genetic factors play a major role in the rise and fall of civilizations," they insist, and if mankind is to avoid a genetic crisis, eugenic policies must be formulated and consciously followed. "Perhaps the voluntary artificial insemination of women with the sperm of geniuses," they suggest, "will eventually arrest the genetic impoverishment of the human race."

But they foresee major obstacles to the adoption of such policies. International communism promotes "dysgenic deterioration and catastrophe" as a means of achieving world revolution. Everywhere, "science is distorted . . . by a nihilism of values, by the dogma of equality as applied to nations, races, peoples, histories, art forms and civilization." The civil rights movement threatens national cohesion by asserting the claim to equality of "an ethnic group which is deemed below the national standard." "Egalitarian levelers preach that all men are equal in talent and relentlessly propagandize for indiscriminate miscegenation." The result is "miscegenation of the suicidal sort," mating "based on whim or sexual desire, which breeds the best with the worst and thus produces the mediocre."

It would be easy to believe that Weyl and Possony are jesting, that they intended this volume to be a satire on racists and racism. Apparently this was not the case, however, for they write with a sense of gravity that is devoid of humor, and offered *The Geography of Intellect* as a serious work of science. But how can one take seriously a work which uses the results of the 1960 Olympic Games to demonstrate the musculature of racial and ethnic groups and the "apparent geographic and ethnic concentration of prowess in sports?"

The Geography of Intellect has apparently had no influence upon scientific racists. While Weyl's other work, *The Negro in American Civilization,* is distributed by the Citizens' Councils and often cited by racists, *The Geography of Intellect* is systematically ignored. It seems too much to say that it is so patently absurd that racists are undeceived by it. An anonymous reviewer in *Mankind Quarterly* described it as a "major contribution" of "catholic" scope and "provocative of much new thought," and added, as if to reassure himself, that it "must be treated seriously." [30] But such remarks were atypical.

Perhaps segregationists ignored *The Geography of Intellect* because of the slurs it inadvertently casts upon Southerners. "There is reason to believe that hot climates shape human evolution in ways which inhibit, or at the very least do not adequately stimulate, the growth of mental capacity," wrote Weyl and Possony. They referred here to the evolution of Negroes in the heat of Africa, but since they wrote in general terms, their statement might have been taken personally by Southerners. When Caucasians are exposed to heavy work in great heat, the authors continued, "little blood gets to the brain, which may be why it is difficult for some white men to do creative work in hot weather." Again, Southern whites might have taken this personally; they might have understood it to mean that Southerners are lazy and shiftless. "These facts may provide a clue to the observed differences between the mental performance of Negroes, on the one hand," declared Weyl and Possony, "and Caucasians and Mongolians, on the other." And to overly sensitive Southern whites these "facts" might also provide a clue to the "observed differences" between the mental performances of Northern and Southern whites, such as Horace Mann Bond gleaned from the studies used by Audrey Shuey in *The Testing of Negro Intelligence*.[31]

Carleton Putnam, James Jackson Kilpatrick, and Nathaniel Weyl are perhaps the most influential popularizers of scientific racism. Each wrote an important summary of scientific racist ideas, and apparently each was widely read by segregationists across the South. But if the ideas of scientific racism were to achieve maximum acceptance among segregationists, the task of dissemination could not be left to chance. Nor was it. The Citizens' Councils of America, with headquarters in Jackson, Mississippi, assumed a major part of that task, and in recent years has been the most active agency disseminating scientific racism among segregationists in the South. *The Citizen* and its predecessor as official journal of the Councils, *The Citizens' Council*, contain numerous articles

[30] Unsigned review of *The Geography of Intellect*, *Mankind Quarterly*, IV (April–June, 1964), 223–24.

[31] See above, Chapter IV, Tables I and II, pp. 80 and 81.

by and about scientific racists. The Councils also distribute many items in the literature of scientific racism, and statements by Council spokesmen indicate they consider scientific arguments a major facet of their defense of segregation.

Perhaps the best illustration of the latter fact is the attention Council leaders give science when addressing audiences outside the South. One of the Councils' leading spokesmen is W. J. Simmons, editor of *The Citizen*. In the last several years Simmons has traveled throughout the nation spreading the Councils' racial views, and often devoted a part of his addresses to scientific racism. An address to the students of Carleton College, Northfield, Minnesota, on May 15, 1962, was typical. Among the subjects Simmons discussed on that occasion was "the equalitarian dogma" which, he told the students, "originated with the Boas school of social anthropologists." To refute this dogma, he cited the works of several of the more important scientific racists and several scientists who are not racists but who have pointed out the existence of significant differences between races. "The objective and carefully worded statements" of these scientists, Simmons declared, "confirm the experience of 34 million white people in the South, who have lived with the [race] problem all their lives." [32]

Simmons made more systematic use of scientific racism in "Race in America: The Conservative Stand," an article he wrote for Huston Smith's symposium, *The Search for America* (1959). Here he sought, among other things, to disprove the "claim that is being made today: that 'science' has shown that there are no significant differences among the races." By phrasing the "claim" in this manner, Simmons misrepresented it, but in doing so he sought, perhaps, to enhance the plausibility of his own position. He cited the works of R. Ruggles Gates, Pitirim Sorokin, Henry E. Garrett, Frank McGurk, and Audrey Shuey to prove that racial differences do exist, but added in a moment of candor that "the question of race differences and their significance is far from having been settled in the research laboratories." By this admission he hoped perhaps to make his readers forget that the only real justification

[32] W. J. Simmons, "The Race Problem Moves North," distributed by the Citizens' Councils of Jackson, Mississippi. Simmons repeated the same ideas in an address to the organizational meeting of the greater Los Angeles Citizens' Council, Los Angeles, California, June 30, 1964; also available from the Citizens' Councils of Jackson.

for segregation is the conviction that "the question of race differences and their significance" *has* been settled, and in the manner
described by scientific racists. To concede that the issue is still un-
settled is to admit that innate racial differences have not been
scientifically demonstrated.

Simmons' admission was a tactical device sometimes used by
racists to disarm an unfriendly audience by saying in effect, "We
segregationists make no dogmatic claims about Negro inferiority;
we only dispute the dogmatic claims of equalitarians." Among
segregationist audiences, however, this mask of open-mindedness
was dropped; in fact, it *had* to be dropped. Imagine a spokesman for the Citizens' Council telling an audience of Mississippi
segregationists that the issue of Negro inferiority "is far from having
been settled in the research laboratories!"

Despite his attention to scientific racism, Simmons seems not to
have taken science too seriously. Like Kilpatrick, he went through
the ritual of discussing scientific racism—just as Putnam had ad-
monished segregationists to do—but he clearly felt the basic issue
lay elsewhere. "Even if science were to prove the races to be absolutely equal in potential—which we must emphasize it has not—
such a finding would in no way affect the practical aspects of race
relations," Simmons wrote, "for these are rooted in social attitudes
which are totally unrelated to any kind of scientific premise whatsoever. Social attitudes arise from the everyday experiences of
generations which crystallize in time into customs and folkways.
It is these rather than the abstractions of the scientist that guide
men's actions. . . . The fact is that these [folkways] motivate
people and direct their actions, even if, being 'of the spirit,' they
cannot be measured in test tubes or by slide rules. Society is a living
organism, not a formula." Simmons, however, ignored his own advice. Society is indeed "a living organism" and, like everything
else about it, the folkways of segregation are not immune to change.

In their efforts to spread the ideas of scientific racism, segregationists have received little assistance from national news media.
Among national news magazines only *U.S. News and World Report*
has given them any support. Though its editors also print articles
by equalitarians and integrationists, *U.S. News and World Report*
has on a number of occasions included articles which incorporate
the views of scientific racists. The magazine pays scientific racists

the considerable compliment of treating their ideas as a point of view as worthy of serious consideration as that of equalitarians, and by so doing enhances the plausibility and attractiveness of those ideas among segregationists. This fact is especially significant because *U.S. News and World Report* is the only national news magazine which has any sympathy for southern segregationists on the issue of racial integration.

This should not be misunderstood. There is no explicit racism in *U.S. News and World Report*. It is the pattern of its treatment of Negroes, segregationists, and racial controversies that is significant. This magazine, edited by one of the nation's leading conservatives, David Lawrence, printed Frank McGurk's article purporting to prove that Negroes are innately inferior to whites in intelligence; reprinted Henry E. Garrett's "The Equalitarian Dogma"; interviewed Garrett on the consequences of racial intermarriage; and presented each of these as the views of responsible scientists.[33] It has also printed a number of articles comparing intelligence test scores of whites and Negroes in segregated school systems in the South. Each of these articles showed Negroes scoring much lower than whites, but in none of them did the author explain the complexities of this subject or discuss the influence of environment upon the test results. Nor did they explain the attitudes of psychologists toward racial intelligence. As a result the articles left the impression that Negroes do poorly on IQ tests because they are innately inferior to whites, and that widespread integration in the schools will inevitably lower educational standards and "hold back" the progress of whites.[34]

Taken together, the discussions of Negroes, civil rights, and school integration which have appeared in the last dozen years in *U.S. News and World Report* give a distinctly distorted view of those subjects, and the distortions do a disservice to Negroes. Civil rights advocates are often presented in an unfavorable light, while segregationists are treated sympathetically. One who reads nothing but this magazine is likely to believe that Negroes are

[33] McGurk, "A Scientist's Report on Race Differences"; Garrett, "One Psychologist's View of 'Equality of the Races,'" and Garrett, "Racial Mixing Could Be Catastrophic."

[34] See for example W. T. White, "What Dallas School Tests Show," *U.S. News and World Report*, September 21, 1956, p. 98; "Achievement Tests," *ibid.*, August 31, 1956, p. 8; and "Do Mixed Schools Lower Classroom Standards," *ibid.*, February 3, 1956, pp. 38–40.

unready for integration because of the criminality, immorality, and illiteracy or marginal literacy among the race; that Southern whites know best how to handle race relations in the South; that there is a bona fide debate among reputable scientists over questions of racial equality; that the South's position in civil rights disputes is more constitutionally correct than that of integrationists; that many civil rights leaders are potentially, if not actually, dangerous radicals, while most Southern white political leaders are responsible statesmen dedicated to constitutional government and orderly progress for both races.

Among national journals of opinion only *National Review,* edited by William F. Buckley, Jr., has opened its pages to scientific racists. Again, there is no explicit racism, only an occasional statement of views which segregationists find appealing. Editorially both the *Review* and its editor condemn segregation, racism, and white supremacy, but they also publish—and apparently take seriously—such articles as "Intelligence or Prejudice?" [35] in which Ernest van den Haag makes thinly veiled pleas for school segregation.

As one would expect of a writer in Mr. Buckey's journal, van den Haag is more sophisticated than other scientific racists, more elusive, more circumspect. The most prominent sociologist who has identified himself with segregationists and scientific racists, van den Haag was born in The Hague and educated in Europe and the United States, receiving a Ph.D. from New York University. He is a practicing psychoanalyst, a professor of social philosophy at his alma mater, and a lecturer in the New School of Social Research. In 1960 he published a critique of Kenneth Clark's testimony in the Brown cases, which he described as "pseudo-scientific" and "misleading," and accused Clark of deliberately misrepresenting his own research. Denying that he was himself a segregationist, van den Haag declared instead that he accepted the "common-sense view that Negroes are humiliated and frustrated by segregation." However, he found much to criticize in the Brown decision as well as in Clark's testimony. "It is mainly the compulsory feature that makes me uneasy," he wrote of the decision. "Though the end be laudable, the means do not suit it . . . compulsory congregation is objectionable and not the proper remedy for the at least equally

[35] Ernest van den Haag, "Intelligence or Prejudice?" *National Review,* December 1, 1964, pp. 1059–63.

objectionable compulsory segregation its [sic] replaces." He explained further, "The imposition of congregation by the Court in Washington will hardly make the local white children compelled to go to school with Negro children (or their families which influence them) receptive to the ideals to be fostered, nor will the circumstances help them perceive the actual individual Negro as distinguished from the stereotype, or generate the open mind and warmth the new school mates want." [36]

In "Intelligence or Prejudice?", which appeared in *National Review* in 1964, van den Haag's purpose was to dispute the booklet, *Race and Intelligence, A Scientific Evaluation* (1963), in which sociologists Melvin Tumin and Ralph H. Turner, anthropologist Sherwood L. Washburn, psychologist Silvan S. Tomkins, and testing authority Henry C. Dyer had criticized the works of Garrett, Shuey, and other scientific racists. Should the public schools be integrated? he asked himself. "Mixed education now would impair the education of Negro and of white children," he answered. "The white children obviously require for optimum education maximum utilization of their present performance abilities," while Negro children "require whatever can be done to increase their performance in view of the deficient environment of the past." This means, "at least for the time being, [that] the needs of Negro children would be met best—i.e., to their advantage and without disadvantage to others—by separate education geared to meet the obstacles presented by lack of opportunity and unfavorable environment." Van den Haag is "in favor of improving the quality of

---

36 Van den Haag's criticisms of the Brown decision are themselves open to challenge. They are inconsistent with much of the research on the effects of integration in newly integrated high schools. See for example Robert Coles, *The Desegregation of Southern Schools: A Psychiatric Study* (New York and Atlanta, 1963). They ignore the dynamic factor in the integration process; racial attitudes, in other words, are not static. They also place the Brown decision on the same moral level with laws and customs by which Southern whites enforce segregation. They do, however, permit van den Haag to have things both ways. They enable him to endorse racial integration and at the same time castigate the Brown decision as no better than the racist policies of segregationists. Van den Haag's views on racial segregation seem to reflect a profound misunderstanding of the nature of segregation in the South. In *Education as an Industry* (1956), for example, he suggested that the ideal solution to the problem of segregated education would be to provide three school systems which would afford all students a free choice between all-white, all-Negro, and integrated schools. The efficacy of such a system in the deep South would of course be problematical.

education for all," but "this can be done only if pupils are separated according to ability. . . . And this means very largely according to race."

There remains, however, the troublesome fact of racial overlap. Logically it might be argued that if van den Haag's interest is really intelligence and quality education rather than racial policy, he would favor a system which segregated students according to ability instead of race, or perhaps a system which would permit Negro children of exceptional ability to attend otherwise all-white schools. But he opposes both these systems. "I think this could demoralize the remaining Negro children and could be hard also on the transferred child," he said of the latter. "Nonetheless, if both the white and Negro children (and/or parents) desire it, this objection would be greatly weakened." He concluded that "Negroes and whites should be educated separately, unless there is evidence in specific cases that the learning of neither group suffers from congregation and that neither group objects. Instruction in schools for Negroes should attempt to remedy the disadvantages suffered by students coming from a culturally deprived home environment." But this, he added, "cannot be done except by separate education." Van den Haag thus inverted the rationale and logic behind the Brown decision and the school integration movement. He assumed that segregation, not integration, is the natural state of race relations, and shifted the burden of proof from segregationists to integrationists.

Van den Haag's discussion of school integration in *National Review* is even more revealing when compared to editor Buckley's criticisms of New York Congressman Adam Clayton Powell and others whom Buckley described as "racists" during his abortive campaign for mayor of New York City in 1965. "Racists are those who treat people primarily as members of a race," wrote Buckley in November 1965. [37] Only nine months earlier van den Haag had written the following in Buckley's journal: "mixed [i.e., integrated] education now would impair the education of Negro and white children"; "segregation by color . . . is educationally rational"; and "it would be cruel to sacrifice children to egalitarian ideolo-

[37] William F. Buckley, Jr., "Harlem is in New York City," *National Review*, November 2, 1965, p. 979.

gies." [38] By Buckley's own definition, van den Haag would seem to be a racist, and one who used Buckley's journal to disseminate his racism.

Through such individuals as Carleton Putnam, James Jackson Kilpatrick, and Nathaniel Weyl, such organizations as the Citizens' Councils, and such magazines as *U.S. News and World Report* the ideas of scientific racists filter down to the American public. In the process of being adapted to the uses of some of the more emotional segregationists, those ideas are sometimes grossly distorted and oversimplified. Often, however, the difference between the ideas developed by academic social scientists and the implications drawn from them by segregationists and white supremacists is a matter of degree and emphasis, rather than kind. More often than not the academic social scientists seek no more than a plausible defense for the status quo in race relations, and specifically disassociate themselves from the violence and intimidation by which Ku Klux Klansmen and other extremists preserve segregation. But the matter is not so simple. The social scientists cannot by a simple disclaimer completely disassociate themselves from the uses to which their ideas are put by extremists, especially when the uses are clearly implied in the ideas themselves. Extremists who quote the social scientists are often doing no more than carrying the social scientists' ideas to a logical and natural conclusion.

In 1957 the Citizens' Councils prepared "A Manual for Southerners," which they hoped would be used in the elementary schools of Mississippi. Among the portions written for fifth and sixth graders were the following scientific justifications for segregation:[39]

First of all, let's see how we know so much about the races being different. Many famous scientists have studied the races of man for hundreds of years. These scientists have ways they can weigh and measure the skeletons and brains of the different races. And all of these men agree that the black, yellow, red, and white men are very different from each other. Scientists have studied the habits of the different races. They find that men's habits can be grouped by races. The white man has certain habits

[38] The last three statements are in van den Haag's follow-up to the original article. See "Intelligence or Prejudice? Some Letters and a Reply," *ibid.,* February 9, 1965, pp. 101–02.

[39] *The Citizens' Council,* II (June, 1957), 3; *ibid.,* (July, 1957), 3.

that are very different from the black man's. Some of these habits that scientists study are:

1. The way a race worships its God
2. The kind of laws a race makes for itself
3. The kind of music a race likes
4. The kind of art that a race makes
5. The things a race thinks are right and wrong.

. . . The white man is very civilized, while the pure Negro in Africa is still living as a savage. . . .

. . . Negro children [in Washington, D.C.] were way behind white children in their school work. This is because white children can learn faster than Negroes can. So the children could not do the same work in the same grade. This made them feel unhappy.

The students were tested to see how fast they could learn school work. These tests showed that the white children can go much faster in their learning and work. When the races are mixed in school, the white children do not get as much education as they usually get. The whites have to wait for the Negroes to catch up.

Sustained exposure to such ideas, even when expressed less categorically, has conditioned the American people to accept the arguments of scientific racists and made their descriptions of Negroes more plausible. In fact, one of the chief advantages enjoyed by racists in their efforts to spread scientific racism is the fact that white Americans have been predisposed by their racial experiences to believe that Negroes are in fact inferior to white men. The attitudes of white Americans toward Negroes (and those of Negro Americans toward whites as well) have always reflected the relative status of the two races in this country. When Negroes were slaves whites assumed that slavery was the natural condition of the race. When segregation replaced slavery, that, too, became in the eyes of whites the natural condition of Negroes. Today, in most areas of the country, but especially in the South where the ideas of scientific racism are most popular, Negroes still occupy the most inferior places in life. Of the large ethnic groups in America, they are still the most poverty stricken, ignorant, and backward, and conform less to the social mores and moral code of the American middle class. The social, economic, educational, and political status of the race seems, at first glance to confirm what scientific racists were saying all along. It is this fact which makes white Americans, especially Southerners, susceptible to the preachments of scientific racists, and it seems logical to conclude that the susceptibility will disappear only when Negroes achieve equality and full integration into American life.

8

EFFORTS TO REVERSE THE BROWN DECISION

Segregationists were interested in science for practical rather than ideological or even scientific reasons. They were attracted to science, or rather to scientific racism, not because they felt it necessary to prove Negroes inferior to whites or that segregation is the best racial policy—they believed these things already. What they sought from science was a basis for telling the American people that there are valid, rational grounds for racial separation, especially in areas of social relations affecting courtship and marriage.

But these were general objectives, and segregationists were slow to understand that science could be useful to them in more concrete ways. Not until the early 1960's did they realize, and then rather suddenly it seems, that through science they might accomplish the most illusory of all their hopes, reversal of the Brown decision. By that time they had abandoned all expectation of reversing the decision on legal or constitutional grounds. Given the makeup of the Supreme Court, there was no possibility that the decision would be reversed on those grounds. A new strategy was called for, and segregationists who took a second look at the Brown ruling remembered earlier charges that it rested not upon law and constitutional precedent but upon works and theories of a few social scientists. Urged on by Carleton Putnam and others, they became convinced that social science was the Achilles heel of the Brown ruling. A challenge based upon science, they decided, might succeed where those using states' rights and constitutional literalism had failed. Thus the two elements in the story of scientific racism converged. Academic social scientists joined segregationists in a concerted effort to overturn the Brown decision. The shift of emphasis from legalism to science, however, was a change in tactics only; the ultimate goal—to destroy the legal basis of the civil rights movement—remained the same.

Perhaps the most striking fact about the shift was the grounds upon which it rested. When the Brown decision was announced in 1954, segregationists were unanimous in denouncing the Supreme Court for accepting nonlegal testimony and citing in footnote eleven social science authorities, some of whom were not discussed in the lower courts. Senator Richard B. Russell, of Georgia, complained that "the Court admittedly substituted psychology for law" and subjected the rights of the states and the liberties of the people "to findings of amateur psychology." Senator James O. Eastland, of Mississippi, was even more outspoken, denouncing not only the Court's use of "the unprecedented, unsound, and irrelevant authority of a group of recent partisan books on sociology and psychology" but also its use of authorities who were "left-wingers of the first order," "Communists or near-Communists." [1]

The latter charge by Eastland became a major theme among segregationists, who sought to discredit the social science by "exposing" the political views of the social scientists. On May 26,

[1] *Congressional Record*, 83rd Cong., 2nd Sess., C, Pt. 6 (May 27, 1954), 7252; and *ibid.*, Pt. 9 (July 23, 1954), 11522, 11525.

1955, Eastland, who was chairman of the Senate Judiciary Committee and its Subcommittee on Internal Security, delivered a lengthy speech in the Senate detailing his criticisms of the Court and urging a sweeping investigation of communist influences behind the Brown decision. The Senate and the American people, read a resolution which he urged his colleagues to adopt, "are now entitled to know beyond doubt and peradventure the complete extent and degree of Communist and Communist-front activity and influence in the preparation of the pseudo 'modern scientific authority' which was the sole and only basis for the decision of the Supreme Court." Accordingly, the resolution would order an inquiry into "the extent and degree of participation by individuals and groups identified with the Communist conspiracy, Communist-front organizations, and alien ideologies, in the formulation of the 'modern scientific authority' upon which the Supreme Court relied in the school integration cases." [2] In offering his resolution, Eastland told the Senate that the Supreme Court had been "indoctrinated and brainwashed by leftwing pressure groups." The Court had attempted "to graft into the organic law of the land the teachings, preachments, and social doctrines" of Karl Marx, he charged, and the effort was "part and parcel of the conspiracy to divide and destroy this Government through internal controversy." Only once before in the Western world had courts of law "resorted to textbooks and the works of agitators to sustain [their] decision[s]," Eastland continued, " . . . when the courts of Nazi Germany accepted 'Hitler's racist laws.' "

Despite the emotionalism and irrelevancy of much of the segregationist criticism, the Brown decision did raise fundamental questions concerning the use of expert nonlegal testimony in the courts, and it provoked a controversy on this issue among lawyers and legal theorists. The ruling offered lawyers (and social scientists) a rare opportunity to study the use of expert social science testimony in the courts, and debate such complex items as relevancy and admissibility of evidence, personal bias among social scientists, and the fact that social science opinion sometimes changes even on the most important subjects. The Brown decision itself pointedly illustrated the changes in social science opinion in the two

2 The resolution is printed in *Congressional Record*, 84th Cong., 1st Sess., CI, Pt. 6 (May 26, 1955) , 7120.

generations since the Court issued the Plessy ruling in 1896. In that year the separate-but-equal concept conformed to the racial views which predominated among social scientists but by 1954 the concept seemed hopelessly racist and unscientific. Then, too, the lawyers and social scientists encountered such difficult questions as the relative weight to be given expert testimony which disputed clearly established judicial interpretations. Did not the use of social science in the Brown decision introduce an undesirable, even dangerous, relativism into the law and violate the principle of *stare decisis*? Did not the decision introduce instability and uncertainty and threaten the principle of the rule of law as opposed to the rule of man? Might not the decision, by its own logic, be overturned should a majority of the Supreme Court at some time in the future personally favor segregation? Finally, and here scientific racists came in, might not the expert opinion which the Court accepted in the Brown decision be disputed, perhaps even refuted, by experts equally competent to those who testified in the lower courts and/or were cited in footnote eleven? Such questions are important ones, and their discussion in the law quarterlies is another measure of the impact of the Brown decision and of the intellectual crosscurrents it aroused.

Several distinguished legal theorists, among them Edmond Cahn of New York University and Charles L. Black, Jr., of Yale, both professors of jurisprudence, dismissed the social science testimony and the authorities cited in footnote eleven as of no influence upon the Court and no significance in the decision. Both Cahn and Black endorsed the decision itself and supported the principle of racial integration, but they considered the social science evidence presented by Clark and others too weak to be a satisfactory basis for so important a decision and so vital a principle. A sturdier basis was needed, which they found in legal and constitutional precedents. They argued impressively that the decision was fully consistent with constitutional guarantees of the Fourteenth Amendment and a long list of judicial decisions.[3]

Since Cahn was a staunch integrationist, his vigorous criticism of the social science testimony was especially appealing to scientific

[3] Edmond Cahn, "Jurisprudence," *New York University Law Review*, XXX (January, 1955), 150–69; and Charles L. Black, Jr., "The Lawfulness of the Segregation Decision," *Yale Law Journal*, LXIX (January, 1960), 421–30.

racists, and they quoted him frequently. "I would not have the constitutional rights of Negroes—or of other Americans—rest on such flimsy foundation as some of the scientific demonstrations in [the Brown testimony]," Cahn wrote. The social scientists who presented the evidence "are fine, intelligent, dedicated scholars," he continued, "yet one can honor them as they deserve without swallowing their claims." Their evidence simply did not prove their conclusions, though their conclusions were, in Cahn's judgment, plain common sense. Common sense and everyday observation manifest the harmful effects of segregation upon Negroes to anyone with an open mind, but neither doll and drawing tests nor any other social science experiment had ever objectively demonstrated the nature or scope of those effects. The testimony in the Brown cases had thus been superfluous, no more than a painstakingly elaborate ritual. The Court had not been "taken in" by the social scientists, as segregationists charged. On the contrary the Court had relegated the so-called experts to a footnote, and the footnote itself was merely a sop to those who had testified.

Legal experts who were also segregationists agreed with Cahn and Black that the social science evidence in the Brown cases was inadequate and misleading. They were unconvinced, however, by Cahn and Black's assertions that there was sufficient legal and constitutional authority for the Brown decision. Lawyers such as Eugene Cook, attorney general of Georgia, and William I. Potter of Missouri, thus attacked the decision as legally and constitutionally incorrect as well as scientifically unsound. The Brown decision did not hold that the separate-but-equal doctrine was bad law, they wrote in the *American Bar Association Journal*,[4] it held instead that the doctrine was bad sociology. The decision rested solely on social science, or more accurately on "pseudo-socioscience" which the Court accepted in disregard of the facts of the cases. Like Cahn and Black, Cook and Potter thought the social science testimony was an insufficient basis for overturning the hoary separate-but-equal principle and destroying the legal basis for race relations in a quarter of the nation. They, too, thought the social sciences too young, too imprecise, too changeable to be safely

4 Eugene Cook and William I. Potter, "The School Segregation Cases: Opposing the Opinion of the Supreme Court," *American Bar Association Journal*, XLII (April, 1956), 313–17.

used for such purposes. "Should our fundamental rights rise, fall or change along with the latest fashions of psychological literature?" they asked. "How are we to know that in the future social scientists may not present us with a collection of notions similar to those of Adolf Hitler and label them as modern science?"

The whole affair was troubling to Cook and Potter, who saw in it a grave threat to the orderly processes of law. "Under elementary and elemental law," they wrote, "a court may not consider treatises in a field other than law, unless the treatises themselves are the very subject of inquiry. The doctrine of judicial notice extends only to those things of common knowledge that lie without the realm of science." This narrow view of the judicial process served Cook and Potter as a basis for their defense of racial discrimination and a focus for their attack upon the Court.

> What has become of the accepted tests of constitutionality of statutes?
> What of the rule that a distinction in legislation is not arbitrary and not violative of the equal protection of the Fourteenth Amendment if any state of facts reasonably can be conceived that would sustain it? . . .
> What of the rule that 'legislative determinations express or implied are entitled to greater weight,' and that validity must be shown 'by things which will be judicially noticed, or by facts established by evidence,' and that 'the burden is on the attacking party to establish the invalidating facts'; that 'being a legislative judgment, it is presumed to be supported by the facts known to the legislature unless facts judicially known, or proved, preclude that possibility'? [5]

The position of Cook and Potter was substantially that taken by Southern segregationists and political leaders in their fight against the Brown decision and public school integration. It had the distinct advantages of being defensible upon the high ground of principle, including the principle that this is a government of law and not of man, and of showing respect for the certainty and continuity of law.

It had, however, gotten segregationists nowhere, for the Supreme Court disagreed with them concerning the admissibility of social science evidence in integration cases. Accordingly, they began to shift their ground, admitted the relevancy of social science, and resolved to beat integrationists at their own game. They would seek out their own social scientists, amass their own evidence, and built a scientific defense for segregation. In so doing, however, they

[5] *Ibid.*

compromised their principles and, in effect, accepted the contention of the NAACP that scientific knowledge has an important contribution to make in illuminating constitutional issues. But, characteristically, they let their zeal overcome their reason, and carried the idea too far. They then adopted a course which placed no limitation on the use of science in court and would in fact make science the master of law. Thus, their position was not the same as that of the NAACP in the Brown cases. "The Constitution should not be wedded to any social science any more than to a school of economics," Jack Greenberg, who later succeeded Thurgood Marshall as chief counsel for the NAACP, had written in defense of the Brown decision. "On the other hand, constitutional interpretation should consider all relevant knowledge. The Constitution turned on a moral judgment; but moral judgments are generated by an awareness of facts." [6] This view would circumscribe the role of social science and make it an auxiliary of law. Greenberg would have social science serve, not dominate, the law.

But segregationists, having convinced themselves that social science could be made to serve their ends, proposed to give it a much larger role. In cases in which they used social science to argue for a reversal of the Brown decision, the most important of which were *Stell v. Savannah-Chatham County Board of Education* and *Evers v. Jackson Municipal Separate School District*,[7] they based their arguments exclusively upon social science, and demanded that the Constitution be interpreted to suit their science. Accepting the tenets of scientific racism as completely valid, they insisted that "science" has proven Negroes inferior to whites in critical areas of intelligence and educational capacity, and insisted that public policy incorporate that fact. They demanded that constitutional interpretation conform to scientific facts, at least as they understood those facts.

Their position has important and fascinating implications. Apparently, segregationists, or at least those who handled the Stell

[6] Jack Greenberg, "Social Scientists Take the Stand: A Review and Appraisal of their Testimony in Litigation," *Michigan Law Review*, LIV (May, 1956), 953–70.

[7] Civil Action No. 1316, U.S. District Court for Southern District of Georgia; Civil Action No. 3379, U.S. District Court for Southern District of Mississippi.

and Evers cases, would make the meaning of the Constitution dependent upon science, and this without reservation. They would, in effect, make the constitutional guarantees of American citizenship dependent upon the latest findings of science. Carried to its logical conclusion this would reserve the rights of citizenship to those who can demonstrate scientifically that they belong to a racially—and why not ethnically?—superior group. If segregationists can "prove" that Negroes are racially inferior and thereby justify denying them the rights and privileges of citizenship, why cannot someone else do likewise for other minorities? Why cannot Anglo-Americans in the Southwest segregate Mexican-Americans and deprive them of the right to vote, and New Yorkers do likewise for their Puerto Rican minority? The implications in this for all non-Caucasians in America are manifest—their civil rights are at the mercy of anyone who "proves" them inferior to North Europeans. In their efforts to overturn the Brown decision, segregationists and scientific racists resorted to an expediency which, if followed to a logical conclusion, would make mockeries of the Constitution and American citizenship. But they did not expect to take their views so far. All they wanted was a return to the status quo before 1954, that is to the days before Earl Warren became chief justice of the Supreme Court and the federal government began meddling seriously in the racial affairs of the South.

Perhaps the real significance of the use of social science in the Stell and Evers cases was due to the willingness of segregationists to take from public officials, and thus the American people themselves, the chief role in interpreting the Constitution and defining the rights of citizenship. This role they would reserve for scientists, a fact which is especially remarkable since they placed no limitations on science, or, at least, on their own science. They accepted at face value the evidence and conclusions of scientific racists, and thought it axiomatic that an "inferior" race was not entitled to equality in American life. In view of the fact that the overwhelming weight of scientific evidence and opinion was against them, this position was, for their own self-interest, extremely shortsighted. Scientific racists cannot match in number or prestige the scientists and social scientists who endorse the equalitarian-environmentalist point of view, nor can they match in quantity or quality the amount of scientific evidence and opinion which disputes racist claims. In a fair contest before an impartial court, scientific racists are bound to lose, and their willingness to challenge integrationists on scientific grounds was a measure of their political and legal myopia and their desperation as well.

An equally striking fact about the use of science in the Stell and Evers cases was the violence segregationists did to their professed constitutionalism. Elsewhere they assumed the stance of unwavering political conservatives and professed to believe in strict interpretation of the Constitution. They attacked the Brown decision as court-made law which ignored a long line of legal precedents, and they never tired of reminding the Court that Congress had passed no law (before 1964) requiring integration of the public schools. In Stell and Evers, however, they turned completely around and urged the court to read into the law another principle which Congress had never passed—that the meaning of the Constitution depends upon scientific knowledge. Certainly Congress has never made the rights of the citizen dependent upon intelligence, brain size, or evolutionary development. The Fourteenth Amendment does not say specifically that racial segregation is unconstitutional, but it does state that all citizens are entitled to equal protection of the laws, and the Supreme Court has responsibility for interpreting that general principle in specific cases. It would seem farfetched indeed to argue that the principle includes, either implicitly or explicitly, a test of intelligence, brain size, or evolutionary development. It would seem even more farfetched for such an argument to come from strict constitutionalists.

The use of science in the federal courts was an expediency on the part of segregationists which destroyed whatever effectiveness they might otherwise have derived from posturing as men of principle. They talked solemnly and endlessly about freedom, individual rights, and self-government, but they would deprive Negroes of all these things, and for reasons beyond the power of the race to control. They would promote freedom, liberty, and individualism by depriving Negroes of constitutional rights and liberties already enjoyed by other Americans, and by denying the federal government the power to intercede for the race. It would be easy to believe that their primary concern was not liberty, individual rights, or constitutional government, but racial segregation and white supremacy. Despite their libertarian rhetoric, what they really sought was legal and constitutional justification for racial discrimination. They were fond of saying that Negroes have no "civil right" to integrated schools. The question remains, however, where did whites get their "civil right" to segregated schools?

The decision to use science to challenge the Brown decision in the federal courts was a result of the urgings of such men as Carleton Putnam, Henry E. Garrett, and R. Carter Pittman, the last a prominent Georgia attorney who is an articulate defender of segregation and a prominent spokesman for the Citizens' Councils.[8] On several occasions Putnam urged segregationists to challenge the Brown ruling on scientific grounds, promising them full cooperation from scientific racists. "I think I could assure you now that if a serious attempt were planned to reverse the Brown decision," he told the annual state Attorney General's Conference for District Attorneys in Louisiana in February, 1962, "I could name you a score of scientists who would be willing to testify— men who would come from abroad as well as Americans." [9] In October he broached the subject again in his open letter to President Kennedy in the aftermath of the crisis which followed James Meredith's enrollment in the University of Mississippi. "The cause of our trouble lies in the incomplete and partisan nature of the evidence on which the Supreme Court decision of 1954 was based," he told Kennedy. "Since 1954 much has become apparent concerning that evidence," and "much new evidence has also come to light." The best summary of this new evidence, he added, is George's *The Biology of the Race Problem.* "I would ask that you personally read the [George] report," he wrote the President, "and do what you can to clear the way to the Supreme Court for a new case based upon it, as well as upon voluminous other evidence now being assembled in various cases soon to be initiated in the lower courts." [10]

The cases to which Putnam referred included the Stell and Evers cases, *Brown v. School District 20 of Charleston County,*[11] and *Armstrong v. The Board of Education of the City of Bir-*

8 See for example R. Carter Pittman, "Equality Versus Liberty: The Eternal Conflict," *American Bar Association Journal,* XLVI (August, 1960) , 837– 80. Pittman was a member of the Honorary Advisory Board of *The Citizen.*

9 Putnam, "The Road to Reversal," 24.

10 Putnam to President Kennedy, printed in New York *Times,* October 3, 1962, p. 33.

11 For a summary of this case see *Southern School News,* September 1963, p. 22.

mingham,[12] in each of which social scientists or educators testified that segregated schools are preferable to integrated schools on both scientific and educational grounds. The Stell case was by far the most significant of these cases, for in it segregationists made their most concerted effort to refute the social science testimony in the Brown cases and to present, comprehensively and systematically, their own scientific evidence against integrated schools.

In its origins, the Stell case was not unlike dozens of other cases brought by Negroes to speed school integration in the South. For years after 1954 the school board of Savannah and Chatham County, Georgia, had done nothing to implement the Brown decision; on the contrary, members of the board used every tactic imaginable to thwart the decision, and ignored persistent pleas of Negroes for integrated schools. After repeated rebuffs from the board, a group of Negro parents went into the federal district court in Savannah in 1962 and asked Judge Frank M. Scarlett to enjoin the board from continuing to segregate the schools by race. Their complaints were typical. They charged that Negro schools in Savannah and Chatham County were inferior to white schools, especially in variety and quality of educational experiences offered students. By segregating children by race, they also charged, the school board was violating the Brown decision and depriving Negroes of rights guaranteed by the Fourteenth Amendment. The board routinely denied the charges, contending instead that a recent building program had equalized Negro schools and recently implemented pupil placement policies had ended the policy of racial segregation in the schools.

This pupil placement policy was the cornerstone of the board's defense. In the early 1960's, as the Supreme Court began methodically striking down all laws, ordinances, and administrative procedures which made distinctions based on race, the states and school districts in the South officially abolished those laws, ordinances, and procedures, and in their stead adopted pupil placement policies designated to perpetuate segregation without mentioning race. Such policies were transparently discriminatory, at least in the way they were applied, but they were accepted, if only in principle, by the Supreme Court, and soon became the chief means of preserving school segregation in the South. Accord-

12 Civil Action No. 9678, U.S. District Court for Northern District of Alabama.

ing to the policy then in effect in Savannah, the school board assigned each pupil to a particular school not on the basis of race
but on an elaborate set of educational, psychological, and sociological guidelines which included the following: "The scholastic aptitude and relative intelligence or mental energy or ability of the
pupil; the psychological qualification of the pupil for the type of
teaching and associations involved; the effect of admission of the
pupil upon prevailing academic standards at a particular school;
the psychological effect upon the pupil of attendance at a particular
school; . . . the home environment of the pupil; the maintenance
or severance of established social and psychological relationships
with other pupils and with teachers; . . . the ability to accept or
conform to new and different educational environment; [and] the
morals, conduct, health and personal standards of the pupil." [13]
The expressed purpose of these guidelines was to drop race as the
basis for pupil placement, but as interpreted by the Savannah-
Chatham County school board they resulted in assignment of *all*
Negroes and *all* whites to racially separate schools. The board insisted that this was coincidence, not design, and Judge Scarlett,
who heard the case, was unperturbed by the claim.

After Negro plaintiffs filed their action, a group of white parents
petitioned to intervene in the case, alleging that the school board
did not adequately represent the interests of their school-age children. It was the intervenors who transformed the Stell case into
an instrument for challenging the Brown decision on scientific
grounds. Their attorneys were R. Carter Pittman, Charles J.
Bloch, of Macon, Georgia, a prominent constitutional lawyer and
outspoken segregationist,[14] and George S. Leonard, of Washington,
D.C. Pittman and Bloch had both criticized the Supreme Court
for using expert, nonlegal testimony in the Brown decision, and
were vocal champions of states' rights and strict constitutionalism.
Now, however, they joined scientific racists in an effort to interpret
the Constitution by expert, nonlegal testimony of their own, and
for their purposes the Stell case was ideal. The most systematic,
recent study of comparative racial intelligence was Robert T. Osborne's report on the public schools of Savannah, and his conclusions were all Bloch and Pittman could ask.[15]

[13] Quoted in Savannah *Evening Press,* July 1, 1963.
[14] See Charles J. Bloch, *States Rights: The Law of the Land* (Atlanta, 1958).
[15] See above, pp. 83–87.

According to their petition to enter the Stell case, the intervenors were "Whites, sharing a common biological origin, cultural
heritage and consciousness of kind," who objected to their children
being "forcibly compelled to associate with plaintiffs and others of
their ethnic group in the common schools" of Savannah and
Chatham County.[16] Their petition, plus the briefs and arguments
they presented to the Court, are together the best exposition of
the ideas of scientific racism this author has seen. The briefs reflect
a substantial knowledge of the literature and ideas of scientific
racism, and their use of science is far more effective than that in
most segregationist writings. The emotionalism and invective which
mar so much of the literature of scientific racism are notably absent.
Authors of the briefs made a conscientious effort to discuss all
major points of disagreement between scientific racists and equalitarians, and though they were far from successful in proving their
case, their presentation was systematic and thoughtful. They sought
to reopen all the issues the Brown decision had ostensibly settled,
and their effort was clearly a serious one. They hoped—and expected—to take their case all the way to the Supreme Court and
make it a *cause celebre* in the struggle against school integration.

Their petition to the Court was a resume of racist arguments
against integrated schools, and emphasized the relevance of those
arguments to the public schools of Savannah. They first pointed to
Osborne's study, which they used as authority for contending that
the intelligence and educational achievement of white and Negro
children in Savannah are so disparate that "extensive racial integration will seriously impair . . . academic standards and educational opportunities" in white schools. Next, they noted the high
rate of immorality among Negroes, which, they insisted, made
widespread integration unthinkable. "Existing group differences in
socio-moral and behavioral standards in Savannah and Chatham
County are of such a magnitude that extensive racial integration
will seriously impair prevailing socio-moral standards in the now
all-White schools," they declared. "The rates of emotional instability, behavioral delinquency, illegitimacy and venereal diseases
among Negro children and their parents are vastly greater than

16 Record on Appeal from the U.S. District Court for the Southern District
of Georgia (Savannah Division) to the U.S. Court of Appeals for the Fifth
Circuit, *Stell v. Savannah-Chatham County Board of Education*, Civil Action
No. 1316, Pleas and Answer of Intervenors.

among White children and their parents." Finally, intervenors insisted that white-Negro differences are organic in nature. "Racial
differences in physical mental, psychical, and behavioral traits between plaintiffs and petitioners are, to a large extent, genetically
determined and are a natural result of the biological processes of
race formation," they wrote, emphasizing the debt of scientific
racists to darwinism. "The origin and formation of the various
races of mankind . . . resulted from differential and adaptive selection of hereditary variations (arising from mutations and genetic
drift), in reproductively isolated populations." The differences
thus begun were "perpetuated and stabilized through continued
isolation and inbreeding of the major races over long periods of
time," and are manifested today in the "anatomical, psychological,
and bio-chemical traits" of each race. As a result, there are "significant differences in cerebral morphology and physical constitution which are structurally related to racial differences in mental,
psychical and behavioral traits," and which "constitute a rational
basis for segregation of races in schools, particularly among the
young and immature."

To demonstrate this "rational basis" for segregation, intervenors
summarized the teachings of "modern social science," emphasizing
their implications for racial and educational policy. The ultimate
justification for school segregation, they told the Court, is a deeply
embedded "consciousness of kind" which instinctively leads individuals to prefer associating with members of their own race. "Selective associational or racial preference is a universal human
trait, which manifests itself in a variety of cultures and at a very
early age," intervenors declared, and it "may have a genetic basis,
arising out of the biological processes of race formation." It is
natural and healthy to prefer association with one's own race,
especially during the formative years of childhood and adolescence,
for only in this way can "optimal personality development and
social maturity" be achieved. Such association produces "a more
stable self-concept, fulfills in-group identity needs, and provides
an atmosphere more conducive to optimum social growth and maturity." To force children of widely differing racial groups into
integrated schools impairs the personality development and self-
image of individuals of both groups, and at critical points in their
physical and emotional growth.

By making "consciousness of kind" into an instinctive trait, the intervenors created for themselves the same problems that had plagued other racists on this point. It is difficult to understand why "a universal human trait" which "may have a genetic basis" needs reinforcing by environmental controls such as mandatory racial segregation in the public schools. If there is in fact an instinctive preference for one's own race, it is difficult to understand why Negroes go to such lengths to integrate the schools and why so many whites endorse their efforts. Moreover, if the desire to associate with one's own kind is instinctive, it seems paradoxical that school integration would produce the problems intervenors foresaw: "serious sex problems due to the lower moral standards of Negroes," "interracial social intercourse, interracial dating, [and] interracial dancing." Apparently the instinctive consciousness of kind did not preclude such problems. The intervenors seemed to say that Negroes have an unnatural sexual affinity for whites, and whites in turn, or at least those of public school age, are unable or unwilling to resist the Negroes' advances.

Another logical inconsistency was implicit in the intervenors' description of Negro schools. They repeatedly assured the Court that Negro schools in Savannah and Chatham County were equal to white schools. Yet one of their basic arguments against integration was that educational standards in white schools would deteriorate if significant numbers of Negro pupils were admitted. They warned that Negro pupils would bring with them "a severe increase in disciplinary problems resulting from the more prevalent use of violence, vile profanity, lascivious sexual behavior, thefts, vandalism, cheating, lying, and other anti-social conduct." Now if these are in fact the behavioral traits of Negro pupils, it would be difficult to imagine how Negro schools could be equal to white schools. The same argument applies to the assertion that Negro pupils are significantly below whites in educational achievement. If this is indeed the case, the educational level of Negro schools is necessarily below that of white schools, and the educational opportunities they offer must be proportionally lower.

In discussing Negro schools, intervenors came perilously close to suggesting that ignorant, unintelligent, antisocial, and criminally inclined students be shunted off into segregated schools where society can forget them. It seems not to have bothered them that social, sexual, disciplinary, and academic problems existed in Negro schools. Their concern was to keep those problems out of white schools. Conditions in Negro schools, they seemed to say, are a problem for Negroes, not for society at large. They said in effect that if Negroes are unintelligent and antisocial, so be it. Society can do nothing about problems which are genetically determined; it can merely recognize those problems and refuse to exacerbate them through unnatural schemes such as racially integrated schools. It follows from this that there is little hope that Negroes will improve their lot, but intervenors felt that what hope there is comes from segregated schools. There, Negroes can fraternize with members of their own race, develop "more substantial self-concepts and a lesser rejection of their own race . . . suffer less frustration and repressed hostility," and, hopefully, "exhibit greater race pride and solidarity." It seems ironic that such benefits will come from associating with other Negroes, a group which are, in intervenors' words, prone to "violence, vile profanity, lascivious sexual behavior, thefts, vandalism, cheating, lying, and other anti-social conduct." If associating with such a race will adversely affect white pupils, it seems illogical to say it will have the opposite effect upon Negroes themselves.

Technically, the effort to overturn the Brown decision rested upon the contention that the decision constituted a finding of fact rather than a ruling of law. In layman's terms this means that the decision enunciated no new interpretation of the Fourteenth Amendment to the effect that racial segregation is per se a violation of the equal protection clause. Instead, the Court merely found that the individual Negro plaintiffs in the Brown cases had been denied equal protection of the laws by certain specific actions of their local school boards. The Brown decision, in other words, had no general applicability; it applied only to individuals and school boards involved in the Brown cases. It enunciated the law in those cases, not the law of the land. Every case involving racial segregation must therefore be decided on its own merits and according to facts presented in testimony in the case itself. A Negro seeking admittance to a white school must first prove in court that his attendance in an all-Negro school deprives him, specifically and individually, of equal protection of the laws, and the court must decide his case on the merits of the evidence he himself presents. A case in 1963 could not be decided on the basis of evidence available in 1954, any more than the Brown cases were decided by evidence available in 1896. In 1963 intervenors in the Stell case demanded a "new appraisal of the facts" just as the NAACP had in 1954.

To accomplish their purpose, they had to prove, first, that the Brown decision rested upon factual error and, second, that the facts presented in the Stell case dictated a new finding which would in effect set aside the Brown ruling. The Brown testimony was full of "subjective value judgments" which were "unrelated to any objective findings," they told the Court, singling out the testimony of Robert Redfield and Kenneth Clark as especially weak and deceptive. As for the appendix to appellants' brief, it was a statement "signed but not sworn to, by 32 so-called 'Social Scientists' . . . none of whom had any first-hand knowledge of the problems discussed" in the Brown cases. "In 1963 there is serious academic and intellectual dissatisfaction with the sociological materials underlying the Brown decision," they declared. The "modern authority" in that decision was "obviously written in order to establish 'favorable social and economic theories' and to create a climate which would make possible the decision that was finally reached in Brown." In other words, equalitarians had conspired to produce a body of social science literature endorsing racial integration, and having done so they went to court demanding that public school segregation be abolished, citing their own works in justifying the demand.

A major portion of intervenors' brief was a list of scientific works supporting their views. Those works, the most substantial of which they included as exhibits in their brief, included items by Ernest van den Haag, Robert T. Osborne, Henry E. Garrett, Audrey M. Shuey, Frank C. J. McGurk, Nathaniel Weyl, E. Raymond Hall, Cyril Burt, R. Ruggles Gates, J. C. Carothers, and others.[17] As these names indicate, the brief was a distillation of

[17] The exhibits included van den Haag, "Social Science Testimony in the Desegregation Cases—A Reply to Professor Kenneth Clark"; Osborne, "Racial Differences in Mental Growth and School Achievement: A Longitudinal Study"; Osborne, "School Achievement of White and Negro Children of the Same Mental and Chronological Ages"; Osborne, "Racial Difference in School Achievement"; Garrett, "Klineberg's Chapter on Race and Psychology: A Review"; Garrett, "The Equalitarian Dogma"; Garrett, *Great Experiments in Psychology* (New York, 1951); Shuey, *The Testing of Negro Intelligence;* McGurk, "Psychological Test Score Differences and the Cultural Hypothesis"; McGurk, "A Scientist's Report on Race Differences"; Weyl, *The Negro in American Civilization;* Hall, "The Zoological Subspecies of Man"; Burt, "The Inheritance of Mental Ability"; Gates, *Human Genetics;* Carothers, *The African Mind in*

the scientific racism of recent years, and the Stell case is best understood as a culmination of that racism. It was an attempt to use the men and works already discussed in this study to reverse the Brown decision and thereby reinterpret the Constitution. Had the intervenors been successful, the Stell case would have done for segregationists what the Dred Scott decision did for slaveholders in 1857. It would have read segregation and white supremacy into the law of the land and deprived Negroes of many rights enjoyed by other Americans.

On the basis of the authorities listed in their brief, intervenors concluded that *"the bulk of available scientific evidence and modern authority in 1963 support the view that race is a valid unit of classification for educational purposes and that the operation of separate schools on the basis of race and color is a reasonable decision."* [18] In truth, however, "the bulk of available scientific evidence and modern authority" was not summarized by intervenors. In no sense was their brief a survey of the "available scientific evidence and modern authority" on the subject of race. It was instead a discussion of carefully selected authorities who directly or indirectly agreed with them concerning school segregation. The authorities were not representative of scientific opinion in the relevant disciplines, and to the extent that their data were valid, they did no more than prove that races differ physically and Negroes have inferior schools.

Like other racists, intervenors inevitably encountered the troublesome problem of overlap. In every characteristic, from intelli-

---

Health and Disease; David C. Rife, *Heredity and Human Nature* (New York, 1959) ; and Carleton Coon, *The Origin of Races* (New York, 1962) . In addition the exhibits included several articles which purported to prove that the average Negro brain is inferior to the average white brain. These were Raymond Pearl, "The Weight of the Negro Brain," *Science,* November 9, 1934, pp. 431–34; H. L. Gordon, "Amentia in the East African," *Eugenics Review,* XXV (January, 1934) , 223–35; F. W. Vint, "The Brain of the Kenya Native," *Journal of Anatomy,* LXVIII (January, 1934) , 216–23; and James H. Sequeira, "The Brain of the East African Native," *British Medical Journal,* I (March 26, 1932) , 581.

[18] Record on Appeal from the U.S. District Court for the Southern District of Georgia (Savannah Division) to the U.S. Court of Appeals for the Fifth Circuit, *Stell v. Savannah-Chatham County Board of Education,* Civil Action No. 1316, Supplemental Brief and Argument in Support of Motion to Intervene and for other Relief in Behalf of the Petitioners Named in the Original Motion. Emphasis in original.

gence to illegitimacy, from emotional stability to venereal disease, they found significant statistical overlapping. In their view, school segregation by ability grouping would be "reasonable if the *only* difference between the two ethnic groups were an overlapping statistical distribution of a *single* trait subject to precise measurement—such as IQ scores—and if the role of observable physical differences in social progress were ignored." Whites and Negroes differ in many psychological and behavioral traits, they pointed out, and "it is the *totality* of such differences, not any *one single* difference, that must be carefully considered in any evaluation of school segregation by parents and school officials. This is the same principle of frequency probabilities which underlies insurance rate classifications. . . . Race is the most convenient and rational classification for the operation of separate schools, since the race, not the individual, is the unit of inheritance and evolutionary change."

To clinch their argument for segregated schools, intervenors resorted to an analogy often used by racists. "An 'unintellectual' farm boy 'knows' that if you train breeds of rabbit dogs with breeds of bird dogs, pen them together, hunt them together and bring them up in the same environment, none of them will be worth killing either as rabbit dogs, bird dogs, or coon dogs," they wrote. "The knowledge that one may not send different breeds of dogs to the same school is simple for the farm boy but it becomes 'difficult and complicated' for many of those sheltered from realities." Such false analogies abound in racist literature. Intervenors are apparently saying that whites and Negroes are to be educated for different purposes, just as rabbit dogs and bird dogs are trained for different tasks, and they should therefore be educated separately. The fact is, however, that they are not educated for different tasks. The public schools of America attempt to stimulate their students intellectually, to prepare them for college and professional or vocational training, to impart to them an understanding of and appreciation for the moral, political, and economic principles of society, and to help them become better citizens. Nowhere do they attempt to train Negroes into whatever is the human equivalent of rabbit dogs and whites into the equivalent of bird dogs. The two races do not have separate roles in American society, though segregationists sometimes assume that they do. In their analogy with bird dogs and rabbit dogs, intervenors illustrated, perhaps inadvertently, their real feelings about the Negro's place in American society. They assumed that the Negro's role is separate and distinct from the white man's, and the function of the public schools is to prepare them for their separate roles.

The highlight of the Stell case was the testimony of Robert T. Osborne, Henry E. Garrett, Clairette P. Armstrong, Wesley C. George, and Ernest van den Haag. Their testimony naturally invites comparison with that in the Brown cases. Witnesses in the two cases touched upon many of the same topics, but the Stell testimony was broader in scope, shallower in content, and notably less convincing. The chief empirical data introduced in the case were from Osborne's study of intelligence and educational achievement in Savannah schools, which, according to Osborne himself, proved that segregation was necessary for quality education. Each of the witnesses discussed his own views of race and race relations, and in the process summarized the major ideas of scientific racism and assured the Court that those ideas are scientifically valid.

Garrett's testimony was the most wide ranging. He warned that school integration was evil, for the Negro's intelligence was vastly inferior to the white man's. "The differences between the negro [sic] and white are mostly within the realm of what you'd call abstract intelligence," he testified, "that is, the ability to deal with numbers, pictures, diagrams, blueprints, words, things of that sort, those things which made European Civilization and never have made a civilization in Africa in five thousand years. That, I call abstract intelligence and that is where the negro falls down." [19] He divided intelligence into three categories: abstract or scholastic, social ("the ability to get along with people"), and mechanical-motor ("the ability to deal with things with your hands"). "Could you approximate for me the differences between the two [races] so far as your experience goes in those three [categories]?" he was asked by an attorney for intervenors. "Well, I think the great difference comes in the abstract and the verbal side," he replied. "In social adaptability I don't know of any specific studies but my guess, maybe it's educated, I don't know, would be there isn't any great difference. In the mechanical-motor, I just don't know. I have read a lot of stories about how Africans fail to put oil in the motors and ruin them and all that kind of thing. I don't know how much that means." In the transcript of proceedings,

[19] *Ibid.*, Transcript of proceedings, 127–65.

there is no indication that the attorney, or the Court either, found anything extraordinary in this candid admission of ignorance by an "expert" witness.

Garrett's most important contribution to the intervenors' case was to relate the ideas of scientific racism to educational policy. The following exchange indicates his usefulness to segregationists (and, incidentally, the calibre of the Stell testimony) :

Q. Would the differences in these three types of ability you have discussed, Dr. Garrett, indicate to you the desirability of any different educational treatment in negro schools as against white schools?

A. Well, I am not an educator and I can't say. I think I know what I might do if I had a free hand, but I would prefer to let somebody, who is an educator, testify on that. I will say that if you should integrate massively that you ruin the white schools. . . .

Q. Well, in what way would it ruin them?

A. It would pull the achievement level down one to three grades through the elementary school and it would do so in the high school.

Q. In other words, your congregated schools would be pulled back from one to three grades on the average?

A. And neither group would be happy. One group would be challenged above its ability level and the other group would not be challenged enough.

Q. In psychology is there any normal reaction to that type of congregation, where you have two socially coherent groups mixed together?

A. It's frustration, of course, and frustration leads to aggression and aggression leads to broken windows and muggings and crime.

Q. And this effectively is the result of bringing the groups together?

A. Right.

Q. Under classroom conditions?

A. Right. . . .

Q. And adversely affect the education of both groups?

A. Yes. And I would like to say, too, that I am a friend of the colored man. I have never said that he was inferior. I say that he doesn't do some things as well as the white man. . . .

Q. Tell me, Dr. Garrett, what evidence is there that segregation per se causes injury to the negro students?

A. There is no evidence.

Nor, he added for good measure, is there "any possibility" that environmental factors account for the racial differences which Osborne reported in his study of Savannah schools.

Intervenors' third witness, Dr. Clairette P. Armstrong, was even more outspoken. She testified that school integration is "very detrimental" to Negro children because of racial differences in intelligence. In her study of truancy in New York City, *660 Runaway Boys* (1932), she found that 37 percent of Negro truants blamed their truancy on "the school situation," a fact which she took to mean that school integration increases frustration in Negro pupils who learn less rapidly than their white classmates. Racial differences in intelligence, she told the Court, are "organic" and "innate," and indicate that Negroes are inferior to whites. "Do you think that negroes are innately inferior to whites, is that your testimony?" she was asked. "There is a spread, of course, from the lowest to highest," she answered, "but the averages, on the average, the means are different, so that from my own experience I would say that it is an inferiority." [20] Under cross examination, she disputed statements that the poor performance of Negro pupils in Savannah could be caused by inferior schools. "A child, a bright child," she averred, "can teach itself to read, irrespective of anybody or anything." Intelligent children of either race can and do attain high levels of educational achievement regardless of the quality of their schools or educational experiences. The problem of Negro children, she stated, is not poor schools but lack of innate ability. If her argument is valid for Negroes, however, it should be equally valid for whites, in which case the alleged antisocial behavior of Negro pupils will not interfere with the education of whites in integrated schools.

Dr. Wesley C. George testified next, and his testimony was a summary of *The Biology of the Race Problem.* The only biological scientist to testify for intervenors, he was asked to describe the physiological and morphological differences between whites and Negroes and explain their practical significance. The most important difference, he testified, is the disparity in average brain weight of Negroes and whites. "Brain weight in large groups of people is indicative of the relative capacity of those races of people for learning in the higher mental processes," he explained. Intelligence is determined by brain weight, and brain weight, like skin color, is inherited. The relevance of this for educational policy is obvious:

Q. Now, Doctor [George], I will ask you to state whether or not, in your

20 *Ibid.,* 176–86.

opinion, differences between whites and negroes in intelligence and in ability to absorb an education are due to genetic factors?

A. That is my belief.

Q. Doctor, in your opinion would the placing of negroes in an environment created by white children and white teachers or, in other words, mixing them in the schools, would that eliminate innate differences in intelligence and in behavioral traits?

A. Not in the hereditary traits. The hereditary traits are the basis of our behavior. . . .

Q. Where two distinct races of mankind are unalterably different, as you say they are, is there any way . . . by mixing the groups together, that those differences can be changed to the benefit of both groups?

A. None has ever been demonstrated and I don't think that any exists.

Such was the social science testimony in the Stell case. Perhaps its chief weakness resulted from the tendency of witnesses to read more into their data than was actually there. They acted on the premise that regardless of the specific limitations of their evidence, its totality made it reasonable to assume that racial differences are genetic in origin. Thus, they concluded, it is reasonable to assume that Negroes are racially inferior to whites in intelligence and educability, and to insist that social and educational policies incorporate that assumption. Witnesses in the Brown cases, on the other hand, felt that since Negro inferiority had not been demonstrated, it could not be assumed, and that in any case the rights of citizenship are not dependent upon intelligence, brain size, or evolutionary development.

Attorneys for the NAACP made no effort to refute the Stell testimony. Mrs. Constance Baker Motley, who directed the plaintiffs' case, called no witnesses to dispute those who testified for intervenors. In brief cross examinations, she pointed out that the witnesses represented a tiny minority of social scientists, and their so-called scientific evidence was only a subterfuge for discrimination and white supremacy. She objected repeatedly to the introduction of social science testimony in the case, but her objections were invariably overridden by Judge Scarlett. Mrs. Motley took the position, which resembled that of segregationists in the Brown cases, that social science testimony was specious and irrelevant since the Supreme Court had already decided the constitutional issues involved in the case. The issue was clear-cut, she felt; the district court and the Savannah-Chatham County school board are both bound by the Brown decision. Confident that her position was constitutionally as well as scientifically correct and would be affirmed by higher federal courts, she told Judge Scarlett that he had no alternative but to order the school board to integrate the schools of Savannah forthwith.

Judge Scarlett, who had a long record of using his court to nullify the Brown decision and harass the civil rights movement, disagreed with Mrs. Motley. Throughout the case he cooperated fully with intervenors. He accepted at face value the testimony of their witnesses, and used it as the basis for his ruling.[21] In the course of his ruling, he cited Osborne, Miss Shuey, Garrett, McGurk, Miss Armstrong, van den Haag, H. A. Tanser, R. Ruggles Gates, Robert Bennett Bean, George A. Lundberg, Carleton Coon, and others, and summarized the arguments used by intervenors and their witnesses. There is no indication in his ruling that he asked himself whether the evidence presented by intervenors did in fact represent "the teachings of modern social science." His ruling gives the impression there are *no* valid scientific data and opinion contrary to that offered by intervenors.

As a judge, Scarlett felt it imperative to offer a legal rationalization for using the intervenors' evidence to declare the Brown decision inapplicable to the schools of Savannah. He turned, therefore, to the segregationists' contention that the Brown decision rested upon a finding of fact rather than a conclusion of law. "The existence or non-existence of injury to white or black children from integrated or segregated schooling is a matter of fact for judicial inquiry and was so treated in Brown," Scarlett ruled. "The factual nature of the finding of injury through segregation in Brown opened the door to the proof which intervenors have made in this case." He found then, as a fact, that racially segregated schools in Savannah and Chatham County were not discriminatory and did not deprive Negroes of the constitutional guarantee of equal protection of the laws. "All the evidence before the Court was to the effect that the differences in test results between the white and negro students is attributable in large part to hereditary factors, predictability resulting from a difference in the physiological and psychological characteristics of the two races," he continued. "The

[21] *Ibid.*, Opinion and Judgment. The Opinion and Judgment in the case is circulated in pamphlet form by the National Putnam Letters Committee. It is also printed in *Race Relations Law Reporter*, VIII (Summer, 1963), 514–28.

evidence establishes and the Court so finds that of the twenty-point difference in maturity test results between negro and white students in Savannah-Chatham County a negligible portion can be attributed to environmental factors. Further no evidence whatsoever was offered to this Court to show that racial integration of the schools could reduce these differences. Substantially all the differences between [white and Negro] children is inherent in the individual and must be dealt with by the [school board] as an unchangeable factor in programming the schools for the best educational results."

Scarlett also found that the results of school integration would be as intervenors had described. "The congregation of two substantial and identifiable student groups in a single classroom, under circumstances of distinct group identification and varying abilities would lead to conflict impairing the educational process," he declared. "It is essential for an individual to identify himself with a reference group for healthy personality development. Physical and psychological differences are the common basis of group identification, indeed they compel such self-identification. To increase this divisive tendency, it has been established without contradiction, that selective association is a universal human trait; that physically observable racial differences form the basis for preferential association and that patterns of racial preference are formed and firmly established at a pre-school age."

Scarlett felt the chief sufferers from integration would be Negro pupils. "Failure to attain the existing white standards," he wrote, "would create serious psychological problems of frustration on the part of the negro child, which would require compensation by attention-creating antisocial behavior." Later he added that "whatever psychological injury may be sustained by a negro child out of his sense of rejection by white children is increased rather than abated by forced intermixture, and this increase is in direct proportion to the number and extent of his contacts with white children." Nor could this difficulty be eliminated by integrating only the brightest Negro children into otherwise all-white schools. Bright Negroes transferred into white classrooms "would not only lose their right of achievement in their own group but would move to a class where they would be inescapably conscious of total social rejection by the dominant group." There they would be torn between the desire to associate with white classmates and the rejection they could regularly expect from them. The effects of such a policy would be "even more injurious" to children left in all-Negro schools, who would lose the benefits of associating with the best members of their race. "The Court finds," wrote Scarlett, "that selective integration would cause substantial and irremovable psychological injury both to the individual transferee and to other negro children."

Scarlett's ruling was welcomed by segregationists and scientific racists. *The Citizen* hailed it as "a good first step on the road to reversal" of the Brown decision. "Judge Scarlett's decision," read an editorial in the official journal of the Citizens' Council, "could go far toward replacing with reason and sanity the madness which has afflicted race relations in this country under the baneful policy of pro-Negro racism adopted by the Eisenhower and Kennedy administrations." [22] Judges on the Fifth Circuit Court of Appeals were less impressed. They peremptorily reversed Scarlett's decision and reprimanded him for "a clear abuse" of his discretionary powers as a judge. They directed him to grant forthwith the relief asked by Negro plaintiffs by directing the school board to integrate the public schools of Savannah and Chatham County. Scarlett did as ordered; the board obeyed his order and the schools of Savannah were integrated, at least tokenly, without serious incident.

The Stell case had been for naught.

Segregationists soon made another effort to use social science evidence to reverse the Brown decision, this time in *Evers v. Jackson Municipal Separate School District,* a case involving an effort to integrate the schools of Jackson, Mississippi. The evidence in this case, named, interestingly, for Darrell Kenyatta Evers, daughter of murdered NAACP leader Medgar Evers, was less systematic and inclusive than that in Stell, but it covered substantially the same ground and need not be repeated here.[23] In the Evers case Federal District Judge Sidney C. Mize heard testimony from several social scientists, among them Frank McGurk, and from several educators and nonscientists whose testimony was intended to supplement that of the social scientists. Mississippi Congressman John Bell Williams, a member of the 1957 House subcommittee which

[22] "A Good First Step on the Road to Reversal," *The Citizen,* VII (May, 1963) , 2, 25.
[23] It is summarized in *Southern School News,* June 1964, p. 14.

"exposed" the alleged evil effects of school integration in Washington, D.C., predicted similar conditions in Jackson if the schools there were integrated. Kirby Walker, superintendent of Jackson public schools, testified that integration would produce massive educational problems because of racial differences in learning ability and educational achievement. James Gooden, a Negro, who was assistant superintendent for Negro schools in Jackson, testified that segregated schools are in the "best interest" of both races.

The late Judge Mize used his "Opinion" in the Evers case to summarize the ideas of scientific racism and to plead for a reversal of the Brown decision. "There is no known scientific study showing the existence of injury resulting to Negro children through separate education," Mize wrote. On the contrary, "separate classes with teachers of the same race are academically superior[,] . . . maintain a better disciplinary status," and "substantially diminish the number of delinquents and drop-outs in the schools." He concluded that "integration—not segregation—injures the Negro school child."

But having accepted the arguments of scientific racists, Mize faced a legal problem. "It is conclusive that the existing assignment of children in the schools of Jackson constitutes a reasonable classification," he declared, and to change to integrated schools "would substantially destroy the present levels of academic achievement in the school district and deny to [whites] the equality of educational opportunity, which they are entitled to have." But having so found, he could go no further. The Fifth Circuit Court of Appeals had already rejected Scarlett's ruling in the Stell case, and for Mize to disregard the Brown decision in deciding the Evers case would be both futile and foolish, and earn for him a reprimand from the Court of Appeals. He understood this. He would have to uphold the Brown decision, but not before denouncing it thoroughly. That decision, he declared, rested "upon the determination of . . . a fact, as distinguished from the declaration of a rule of law" and legally it did not apply to the schools of Jackson. Neither the school board nor the school children of Jackson had been represented in the Brown cases, and according to the doctrines of *res judicata* and *stare decisis* are not bound by the Brown decision. The due process clause of the Fourteenth Amendment requires that the school board and school children of Jackson have the same opportunity to be heard in court as those school boards and children involved in the Brown cases.

But having said this, Mize refused to declare the Brown decision inapplicable to Jackson. The Appeals Court ruling in the Stell case, he declared, was "contrary to the facts and the law applicable thereto," but because of it he felt compelled to order the schools of Jackson to integrate. In so doing, however, he vented his despair over the Brown decision and the domination of the federal courts by integrationists. "In the opinion of this Court," he wrote, "the facts in this case point up a most serious situation, and, indeed, 'cry out' for a reappraisal and complete reconsideration of the findings and conclusions of the United States Supreme Court in the *Brown* decision. . . . Accordingly, this Court respectfully urges a complete reconsideration of the decision in the *Brown* case." Until that is accomplished, however, the schools of Jackson must integrate. The effort to reverse the Brown decision on scientific grounds had failed.[24]

24 U.S. District Court, Southern District of Mississippi, Jackson Division, Civil Action No. 3379, *Evers v. Jackson Municipal Separate School District,* Opinion.

9

SINCE THE STELL CASE

The Stell case was the high-water mark of scientific racism, and its outcome left the movement in a state of suspension and indecision. Racists had expected the case to go to the Supreme Court and become a *cause celebre* in their controversy with integrationists. Their expectation, however, was never realized, and Judge Mize's disposition of the Evers case reflected their disappointment and frustration too. They understood at last that the federal courts offered them no hope, and many of them apparently concluded that the whole excursion into scientific racism had been worthless.

213

Suddenly, however, their prospects brightened. Nineteen sixty-four was a presidential election year, and in the early months of the campaign the outlook for segregationists seemed to take on new hope. A "white backlash" against Negroes and the civil rights movement appeared as if from nowhere, gaining strength from race riots in Philadelphia, Rochester, and Harlem. Governor George Wallace of Alabama entered the Democratic presidential primaries in Wisconsin, Indiana, and Maryland and polled a significant minority vote in each state. Most important of all, segregationists saw, or thought they saw, in the presidential candidacy of Barry Goldwater an opportunity to blunt the civil rights movement, especially after he voted against the Civil Rights Act of 1964.

The hopes, however, were illusory. Goldwater conservatives and arch-segregationists suffered stunning political defeats everywhere except the deep South. Instead of slowing the process of integration, Goldwater's candidacy was in many respects a blessing in disguise for Negroes and the civil rights movement. The Senator unwittingly contributed to the defeat of many conservatives, and his own defeat not only demoralized the Republican party but demonstrated the potency of Negro voting and the political short-sightedness of his failure to disassociate himself completely from segregationists. Because their hopes were so high during the campaign, scientific racists were dejected by its outcome, which followed fast upon their defeats in the Stell and Evers cases. So widespread was their dejection that since the fall of 1964 they have undertaken no new offensive against integration or the Brown decision and published no new major works.

This does not mean that the dangers represented by the revival of scientific racism in the last decade have disappeared, or that segregationists have lost interest in science. On the contrary, the dangers are still quite real and segregationists remain interested in science. In October, 1965, Henry E. Garrett repeated the salient ideas of scientific racism in *The Citizen,* describing anew the ill effects he foresaw from school integration. Three months later, he addressed the annual leadership conference of the Citizens' Councils, which met to explore methods of circumventing school integration, including establishment of private schools under Council sponsorship.[1]

[1] See Henry E. Garrett, "How Classroom Desegregation Will Work," *The*

Today scientific racism remains potentially dangerous not because it offers a likely basis for reversing the Brown decision or
convincing national leaders that races are unequal and segregation should be the law of the land. The danger lies instead in
several factors which lend credibility to the ideas of scientific
racism and enhance their appeal among white Americans. Given
the proper catalyst, these factors might again at some future time
induce the nation to make "science" the basis of its racial policies.
Lest this be misunderstood, let it be repeated: today scientific
racism is only a potential danger, but potential dangers sometimes
become real.

Among the factors which account for this, several are especially
significant. The attitude of many white Americans toward Negroes
is still permeated with racism; segregation frequently prevents
meaningful contact between the races and thereby perpetuates
racial stereotypes; many respected and influential nonracists sometimes express anti-Negro views; ultraconservative groups provide
scientific racists with powerful political allies; and the low status
of Negroes in American life continues to provide ostensibly objective evidence to support the racist characterization of Negroes.

In 1965 public opinion analyst Louis Harris posed the following
question to a cross-section of white Americans: "I want to read off
a list of things about coming into contact with Negroes. . . . I wish
you would tell me if you personally would or would not object to
[the items in the list]." The figures below are percentages of those
who objected to various forms of contact with Negroes:[2]

	Nation	North	South
Working next to a Negro on the job	10%	7%	24%
Sitting next to a Negro on a bus	13	8	24
Sitting next to a Negro at a lunch counter	17	11	47
Sitting next to a Negro in a movie theater	20	14	50
Own children going to school with Negroes	20	13	53

Citizen, X (October, 1965), 4–17; and Medford Evans, "The Leaders of the
Leaders," *ibid.*, (November, 1965), 8–9. For the most recent detailed criticism
of the social science authorities cited in the Brown decision, see Peter A.
Carmichael, *The South and Segregation* (Washington, 1965), 108–75. The
Court's "presumption that 'modern authority' has established new grounds
giving new meaning to equal protection of the laws proves illusory," wrote
Carmichael, who is a philosophy professor at Louisiana State University.

2 Los Angeles *Times*, October 18, 1965, p. 4.

	Nation	North	South
Using same restroom as Negroes	25	18	58
Trying on the same suit or dress that a Negro has tried on in a clothing store	31	24	64
Having a Negro family as your next-door neighbor	37	30	71
Close friend or relative marrying a Negro	85	82	98
Your own teen-age daughter dating a Negro	92	90	100

As these figures demonstrate, white Americans, Northerners as well as Southerners, have deeply embedded prejudices against close contact with Negroes. It is to these prejudices that scientific racists appeal when they speak of "consciousness of kind" and instinctive preferences for one's own ethnic group, and when they insist that school integration is bound to cause "trouble" and Negroes are better off in schools of their own.

The strength of this white prejudice against close contact with Negroes is due in part to the fact that many, maybe even most, white Americans lead lives which for practical purposes are completely segregated. Many, perhaps most, white, middle-class Americans have no contact with Negroes except Negroes who are menials, servants, or in similar low-status occupations. They have no social contact with middle-class Negroes; they rarely work with members of the race, at least not as equals; nor do they worship with them. They rarely see Negroes in movies or on television in situations in which race is not important; and when they read about them in the newspaper, the Negroes are likely as not protesting something—picketing, sitting-in, or otherwise behaving in a manner that the middle class regards with suspicion or alarm.

The result is that whites do not know Negroes. They have few occasions to question their stereotyped views of the race, and those views persist even today, as the Harris survey pointedly revealed. "I want to read some things that have been said about Negroes," Harris also asked his cross-section of white Americans. "For each, tell me if you tend to agree more or disagree more with each statement." The results, expressed in percentages of those who agreed more, were as revealing as the replies to his first question:

	Nation	North	South
Negroes tend to have less ambition	58%	54%	80%
Negroes smell different	54	48	86

	Nation	North	South
Negroes have looser morals	53	48	77
Negroes laugh a lot	50	44	79
Negroes have less native intelligence	41	36	65
Negroes keep untidy houses	36	33	53
Negroes breed crime	33	30	50
Negroes care less about the family	32	29	46

Two years earlier, in 1963, Harris found that 41 percent of white Americans and 61 percent of white Southerners believed "Negroes want to live off the handout"; while 31 and 51 percent respectively believed "Negroes are inferior to whites." [3]

The characteristics in this list are the same as those ascribed to Negroes by scientific racists. Harris' survey, though it cannot be taken at face value because the interviewees were not asked whether the conditions are racial in nature, is nevertheless a striking illustration of the extent to which anti-Negro ideas permeate American thought.

Another reason for the potential dangers of scientific racism stems from the fact that anti-Negro ideas are found in the works of many notable authors (who usually wrote before 1954) who are not racists and make no plea for anti-Negro racial policies. This fact is significant since it enables racists to quote a variety of authors who are untainted with conscious racism, for example, Albert Schweitzer and Arnold Toynbee.[4] Similarly, they find such a standard reference work as *Encyclopedia Britannica* helpful to their cause. Under the entry "Races of Mankind," the 1964 edition of

[3] See William Brink and Louis Harris, *The Negro Revolution in America* (New York, 1964), 140–41.

[4] In relating his African experiences, Schweitzer often expressed views not unlike those which once inspired Victorian imperialists to shoulder the white man's burden. "The negro, then, under certain circumstances works well, but— only so long as circumstances require it," he wrote in *On the Edge of the Forest Primeval* (New York, 1922). "The negro is a child, and with children nothing can be done without use of authority. We must, therefore, so arrange the circumstances of daily life that my natural authority can find expression. With regard to the negroes, then, I have coined the formula: 'I am your brother, it is true, but your elder brother.' " *ibid.,* 83, 95. In his monumental *Study of History,* Toynbee, whom most Americans probably consider the greatest historian of this generation, wrote as follows: "It will be seen that, when we classify mankind by colour, the only one of the primary races, given by this classification, which has not made a creative contribution to any of our twenty-one civilizations is the Black Race." Toynbee, *Study of History* (London, 1934), I, 233.

the *Britannica* discusses Negroes in language somewhat akin to that of racists.[5] "In addition to woolly hair all these people have the following characters in common: dark skin sometimes almost black, broad noses, usually a small brain in relation to their size," the entry read. "In the skeleton there is a smoothness of contour which even in adults often recalls the bony form of a child, and among some members of the group the forehead has that prominent and smooth form which is so characteristic of the infant of our race." Though this appeared in the 1964 edition of *Britannica,* it was written about 1930 and reflects the racial views popular in the first quarter of the twentieth century. Of the dozen authorities listed in the bibliography, the most recent was published in 1928 and the oldest, William Z. Ripley's completely antiquated *Races of Europe,* was published in 1899. The author, L. H. Dudley Buxton, treated race solely as a means of dividing mankind according to physical features, and nothing in the article indicates scientists have learned anything about race in the last generation. Editor-in-chief of the 1964 *Britannica* was Harry L. Ashmore, a well-known liberal champion of civil rights and racial integration now with the Center for the Study of Democratic Institutions in Santa Barbara, California. Scientific racists could and did use Ashmore's name to enhance the authority and respectability of ideas expressed in "Races of Mankind."

Among scientists who are not racists there are a handful whose works directly serve the needs and interests of scientific racists. Racists often cite nonracist scientists to buttress their racism, but their use of authorities such as Wilder Penfield, Garrett Hardin, and Curt Stern is a bald deception which is obvious to anyone familiar with the works of those men. The same, however, cannot be said of their use of works by Carleton S. Coon, one of the nation's most eminent anthropologists, a past president of the American Association of Physical Anthropologists and formerly Curator of Ethnology and Professor of Anthropology at the University (of Pennsylvania) Museum in Philadelphia. Author of several major works of anthropology and ethnology, Coon is not a racist as that term is used here. He has repeatedly criticized racists and segregationists and emphasized his belief in the innate equality of races. "Neither in the field of hereditary potentialities concerning the

5 "Races of Mankind," *Encyclopedia Britannica,* (1964 ed.) , XVIII, 864A.

over-all intelligence and the capacity for cultural development, nor in that of physical traits, is there any justification for the concept of 'inferior' and 'superior' races," read a 1965 statement on race signed by Coon and several other scientists of international reputation. "The biological data (given in the report) stand in open contradiction to the tenets of racism. Racist theories can in no way pretend to have any scientific foundation." [6] Despite his endorsement of these views, Coon had three years earlier, in *The Origin of Races* (1962), published an hypothesis ideally suited to the needs of scientific racists.

To substantiate their ideas of racial inequality and Negro inferiority, scientific racists rely heavily upon the theory of evolution or some variation thereof. According to that theory, racial differences represent adaptations to the physical environment in which each race evolved. This theory, however, is not entirely satisfactory to racists, even with their own interpretation of it. It assumes that mankind was originally one, that races and ethnic groups have a common biological heritage, and racial differences, although not exactly superficial, are only part of the story of race. It is thus possible to accept both the evolutionary hypothesis and the unity of mankind, and on the basis thereof to defend the brotherhood of man and challenge the idea that race mixing is biologically harmful. What racists needed was a "scientific" theory disputing the biological unity of mankind from which to argue against both race mixing and the brotherhood of man.

Coon supplied such a theory. Not intentionally, to be sure; but the conclusions racists drew from his theory were logically drawn and did no violence to his hypothesis. Coon theorized that all mankind descended from a common ancestral species, *Homo erectus,* which evolved into *Homo sapiens* not once but five times and into five separate races. These races are Caucasoid, Mongoloid, Congoid (most African Negroes), Capoid (Bushmen and Hottentots), and Australoid (Australian aborigines), and the prototypes of each emerged before the evolution to the *sapiens* state. Not only did each race enter the *sapiens* state separately, according to Coon's theory, but just as important for racists, each did so at a different time. Using evidence provided by fossils, fire remains, and primitive human tools, Coon theorized that Caucasoids

---

[6] Los Angeles *Times,* October 2, 1964, p. 4.

220 Challenge to the Court

reached the *sapiens* state approximately 250,000 years ago, or perhaps 200,000 years ahead of the Congoids, from which American Negroes descended. The significance of this difference was obvious to racists, just as it was to Coon, who spelled it out in detail. "It is a fair inference . . . that the subspecies which crossed the evolutionary threshold into the category of *Homo sapiens* the earliest have evolved the most," he wrote, "and that the obvious correlation between the length of time a subspecies had been in the *sapiens* state and the levels of civilization attained by some of its populations may be related phenomena." [7]

Had Coon set out consciously to formulate a theory to fit the needs of scientific racists, he could hardly have done better. "Caucasoids and Mongoloids who live in their homelands and in recently colonized regions, such as North America, did not rise to their present population levels by accident," he wrote. "They achieved all this because their ancestors occupied the most favorable of the earth's zoological regions."

Racists have widely praised and just as widely exploited Coon's theory. Virtually every major work of scientific racism published in the last few years endorses the theory and uses it as evidence for racial inequality and Negro inferiority. Carleton Putnam wrote an article for *The Citizen* lauding *The Origin of Races* as definitive proof of Negro inferiority. Nathaniel Weyl reviewed it for *National Review* and praised its "massive evidence," "dispassionate scholarship," and "challenging conclusions." Coon had, according to Weyl's review, demonstrated "the reality of race." [8]

Despite the enthusiasm of racists, Coon's theory "has not been widely accepted" by American scientists. This at least is the conclusion of a survey made by *Science News Letter*. Anthropologist Frederick S. Hulse of the University of Arizona characterized Coon's theory as an "extreme opinion" with "no evidence of any nature to support it." Theodosius Dobzhansky thought the possibility that mankind had evolved from *Homo erectus* to *Homo sapiens* on five separate occasions "vanishingly small"; and Ashley Montagu dismissed Coon's theory as "far-fetched" and "quite out of harmony with the biological facts." [9]

[7] Carleton S. Coon, *The Origin of Races* (New York, 1962), ix–x.
[8] Carleton Putnam, "Evolution and Race: New Evidence," *The Citizen*, VI (July–August, 1962), 7–10; and Nathaniel Weyl, "The Reality of Race," *National Review*, January 15, 1963, pp. 33–35.
[9] "Theory on Negro Origin," *Science News Letter*, November 3, 1962, p.

Coon's theory, like the views of Schweitzer and Toynbee quoted above, contributes to the authority of and potential danger from scientific racism. Of even greater significance in this respect is a number of well-organized and well-financed pressure groups which espouse, in varying degrees of intensity and effectiveness, views which parallel those advocated by scientific racists. These are political or "educational" groups which inhabit the extreme right wing of American politics. Among them are a few significant groups such as the Citizens' Councils and John Birch Society, several less significant ones such as the Ku Klux Klan and National States Rights party, and a flock of others such as the Liberty Lobby, Dan Smoot's followers, and the National Eugenics party. These groups do not always agree with each other or with scientific racists, and each has its own ax to grind, but they do share certain philosophical assumptions about politics, society, and mankind which have significance for racial policy. The policies they endorse do not in the final analysis differ significantly from those advocated by scientific racists and white supremacists.

The relationship between scientific racism and ultraconservatism, however, is not always as obvious as this statement perhaps suggests. Individuals and groups on the right-wing fringe of American politics are not necessarily racists; in fact many of them have no—or very little—interest in race and race relations and rarely if ever discuss racial topics. Others, however, are racists and are preoccupied with race relations, and they look upon ultraconservatism as an instrumentality for preserving segregation. The confluence of ultraconservatism and scientific racism results from the common political and economic views they share, views which if translated into public policy would have the effect of perpetuating segregation, white supremacy, and the second-class status of Negroes in America. This is often true whether individual ultraconservatives are overt racists or not. Spokesmen for the John Birch Society, for example,

---

285; Theodosius Dobzhansky, "Possibility that Homo Sapiens Evolved Independently 5 Times Is Vanishingly Small," *Current Anthropology,* IV (October, 1963), 360, 364–66; and Ashley Montagu (ed.), *The Concept of Race* (New York, 1964), 229. Coon has summarized his views in "New Findings on the Origin of Races," *Harper's Magazine,* CCXXV (December, 1962), 66–74; and "What is Race?" *Atlantic Monthly,* CC (October, 1957), 103–08. His theory would seem to be completely superseded by the fossil remains recently discovered by anthropologist L. S. B. Leakey and others in southern Africa. See, for example, Robert Ardrey, *African Genesis* (New York, 1961).

insist that the Society is not racist, that it in fact advocates equal rights and opportunities for all Americans. The fact remains, however, that the Society urges policies which, if adopted, would destroy the civil rights movement and close the avenues of protest which have been most efficacious for Negroes. Spokesmen for the Society have advocated reversing the Brown decision, rescinding most of the civil rights legislation passed in recent years, revoking most of the executive orders and administrative policies through which the federal government seeks to eliminate racial discrimination, "restoring" public schools to local control, and impeaching Earl Warren. They object, they insist, only to the tactics of the civil rights movement, only to unconstitutional actions by the federal government, unconstitutional civil rights laws, infringement upon the property rights and personal liberties of white Americans, and "communist infiltration" of the civil rights movement.

But they cannot disassociate themselves from the obvious consequences of policies they advocate, policies which would effectually destroy the civil rights movement and preserve the racial status quo. In the view of spokesmen for the Birch Society, every effective tactic utilized by Negroes in the civil rights movement is "unconstitutional," "socialistically inspired," or part of a "communist conspiracy." Wrote John Rousselot, public relations director of the Society, "The overwhelming proportion of 'civil rights' agitation is manipulated from behind the scenes by Communists, Communist sympathizers, or fellow travellers." [10] If Rousselot is correct, if most civil rights "agitation" is in fact communist controlled, then communists are responsible for much of the success of the civil rights movement, for the "agitation" led directly to the successes. The Birmingham riots produced the Civil Rights Act of 1964, the Selma march, the Voting Rights Act of the following year. For Rousselot to give communists credit for achievements as popular as these are among Negroes would seem to be, from his own standpoint, extremely shortsighted. But his shortsightedness is not intentional; it is instead a result of his effort to oppose the civil rights movement on ostensibly nonracist grounds. Racists would destroy the effectiveness of the civil rights movement by shouting "Negro inferiority" and "equalitarian conspiracy"; Rous-

[10] John Rousselot, "Civil Rights, Communist Betrayal of a Good Cause," *American Opinion*, VII (February, 1964), 10.

selot and other ultraconservatives would accomplish essentially the same end by shouting "unconstitutional" and "communist domination."

The convergence of scientific racism and ultraconservatism is more than a coincidence of economic and political ideas, more than guilt by association. On numerous occasions in recent years ultraconservatives have directly and indirectly endorsed the ideas of scientific racists; and though they assiduously avoid saying that Negroes are racially inferior to whites, that is the clear and logical inference of what they do say. Dr. Revilo P. Oliver, formerly an associate editor of *American Opinion,* the magazine of the John Birch Society, and a prominent spokesman for the Society, endorsed the IAAEE Reprint Series, and it is reasonable to assume that he accepts the racism which is the chief ingredient of those reprints.[11] Medford Evans, a frequent contributor to *The Citizen* and a leading spokesman for the Citizens' Councils, is a contributing editor of *American Opinion.* In a recent typical installment of his column, "From the South," a regular feature in *American Opinion,* Evans denounced the Brown decision and lauded the establishment of private schools as a device for thwarting school integration in the South. The Brown decision, he wrote, is "perhaps the most racist ruling since the fall of the Third Reich," for it held that Negro schools are per se inferior to white schools.[12]

Some of the most characteristic ideas of scientific racism often appear in Birch Society literature. Earl Lively, Jr.'s *The Invasion of Mississippi* (1963), an account of the crisis which followed James Meredith's enrollment in the University of Mississippi, repeats many of those ideas. So also does Rosalie M. Gordon's *Nine Men Against America* (1958), an attack upon the United States Supreme Court and part of the evidence the Birch Society uses in its campaign to impeach Chief Justice Earl Warren. These works are items in the American Opinion Reprint Series and circulate widely in ultraconservative circles. The social science incorporated in the Brown decision, wrote Lively, "is rank opinion and conjecture and should not be given the dignity of consideration as 'scientific' thought. . . . The psychological and sociological opin-

[11] Revilo P. Oliver, "Brainwashing," *American Opinion,* VII (November, 1964), 32n.

[12] Medford Evans, "From the South," *American Opinion,* VIII (November, 1965), 67.

ions put forth in this case by the Court and its 'authority' are a far cry from anything 'scientific' " There is "some reason to doubt," he added later, "that the individuals referred to by the Court were selected for their abilities in their pseudo-scientific fields. Rather, examination of their works and the records of their personal conduct indicates that their interest in the case at hand was more political than academic." The contributors to Myrdal's study, for example, "represent a cross section of the leadership of the Communist movement that uses the Negro question as an issue for promoting revolution. They are Communists, fronters, ultra-liberal do-gooders, and professional agitators. Many are Negroes." Essentially the same views have been expressed by Robert Welch, founder and president of the Birch Society. In *The Politician* Welch credited unnamed communist conspirators with "forcing through the anti-segregation decision of the Supreme Court, which [they] certainly planned as far back as when [they] had Gunnar Myrdal brought over here to write his mammoth book." By that decision the communists made "it practically impossible for the coalition of conservative southern Democrats and conservative Republicans ever to be reestablished with the same strength again." [13]

The most illuminating example of ultraconservative "science" in Birch Society literature is an article which appeared in *American Opinion,* December, 1964, in which Revilo P. Oliver applied the principles of genetics, as he understood them, to history and some of the problems facing mankind today.[14] Like scientific racists, Oliver believes the study of genetics is inhibited by "liberal intellectuals" who allegedly find it necessary to suppress genetic truth. The truth they suppress, or so Oliver believes, demonstrates beyond dispute that heredity is the predominant influence in life,

[13] Earl Lively, Jr., *The Invasion of Mississippi* (Belmont, Mass., 1963), 41–43; Rosalie M. Gordon, *Nine Men Against America* (Belmont, Mass., 1961), 39–46; Robert Welch, *The Politician* (Belmont, Mass., 1964), 65, cxx; and Welch, "A Letter to the South on Segregation," (no imprint). For typical discussions of the civil rights movement in Birch Society literature see Medford Evans, "Mississippi, the Long Hot Summer," *American Opinion,* VII (November, 1964), 7–18; Scott Stanley, Jr., "Revolution, the Assault on Selma," *ibid.,* VIII (May, 1965), 1–10; and Alan Stang, *It's Very Simple: The True Story of Civil Rights* (Belmont, Mass., 1965).

[14] Revilo P. Oliver, "Biology, History and the Historians," *American Opinion,* VII (December, 1964), 63–83.

and he thinks this truth is vitally important for national survival. "All of the evidence thus far available," he wrote, "indicates that intelligence is as completely and unalterably determined by genetic inheritance as [are] physical traits," which are themselves "genetically determined beyond possibility of modification or alteration except by physical injury or chemical damage." Behavioral traits are thus innate and transmitted by heredity. There is "evidence", for example, "that makes it seem extremely probable that criminal instincts are inherited." Individual differences are products of "differences in genetic strains," and he declared, "All men are born unequal."

Individual differences add up to group differences, and these in turn produce cultural differences. Accepting this basic idea of scientific racism, Oliver concluded that cultural differences are genetically determined. "Historians who try to account for the rise and fall of civilizations by describing political, economic, philosophic, and religious changes without reference to genetic changes in the population are simply excluding what *must* have been a very important factor," he declared. "The continuity of a culture depends on a more or less instinctive acceptance of the common values of that culture," and instincts are inherited. This means, as scientific racists have repeatedly emphasized, that behavior is genetically, not culturally, determined and that every civilization reflects the genetic composition of the people who created it. Oliver avoided any mention of race, or at least any mention that could be literally construed to mean that races, as opposed to groups, of men are unequal.

He went to great lengths to explain "the scope of genetic forces in the continuity of a civilization," basing much of his explanation upon Lothrop Stoddard's *Revolt Against Civilization* (1922). Stoddard's volume, which the Freeland Products Company of New Orleans had recently reprinted in a paperback edition, was one of a number of similar works published around World War I. It combined racism, nativism, and popular notions about genetics in a manner designed to alarm "old Americans" with scare stories about an allegedly imminent "genetic crisis" in the world, a crisis supposedly caused by "race suicide" (that is, low birth rates) among genetically fit groups and promiscuous and uncontrolled breeding among the unfit. Stoddard feared that inferior racial and ethnic groups—"undermen" he called them—working through bolshevism and other dysgenic philosophies were destroying civilization, which he equated with the world supremacy of North Europeans.

After praising Stoddard's analysis as cogent, illuminating, and still timely, Oliver offered another authority on the same subject, Elmer Pendell's *The Next Civilization* (1960). Professor Pendell, of Jacksonville State College in Jacksonville, Alabama, offered a thesis similar to Stoddard's, but he treated it even more simplistically and with more abandon. (For example, he advocated organizing voluntary eugenic associations and "heredity corporations" and using artificial insemination to overcome the threat of eugenic catastrophy.) The real obstacle to eugenic reform, said Oliver in substantial agreement with Pendell, is the leftist-dominated government of the United States, which is consciously pursuing dysgenic policies. "The United States is now engaged in an insane, but terribly effective, effort to destroy the American people and Western civilization by subsidizing, both at home and abroad, the breeding of the intellectually, physically, and morally unfit," wrote Oliver, "while at the same time inhibiting, by taxation, and in many other ways, the reproduction of the valuable parts of the population—those with the stamina and the will to bear the burden of high civilization." These policies are threatening national survival and the future of civilization, and unless they are reversed in the near future it will be too late. "The reproduction of the superior stock" must be encouraged, and "the multiplication of the inferior" checked, but this can be achieved only by extreme measures. "We must use at least the taxing power of government, if not its power of physical coercion," Oliver declared, "to induce or compel the superior to have children and to prevent the inferior from proliferating." But even these measures, he conceded despairingly, offer little hope for the United States. Even if the leftist-dominated government in Washington could be induced to adopt eugenic policies, the decisions concerning who would and would not have children would be made by "a Senator Fulbright, a Walt Rostow, an Adam Yarmolinsky, a Lyndon Johnson, or a Jack the Ripper."

The real solution to genetic problems, he added, does not lie where most geneticists think it lies—in selective breeding of individuals of high IQ. A high IQ is important but is not sufficient by itself; it is only one of the qualities necessary for the advancement of civilization. Many so-called geniuses, for example, Einstein and the poet Shelley, are "in their judgement of social and political problems, virtually morons." Oliver labeled such persons "mattoids," a term he applied to anyone gifted in one area but feebleminded in other qualities equally important to the advancement of civilization. Many geniuses, he declared, suffer from "moral insanity," and are greater threats to civilization than the masses with low intelligence. The danger is not that "civilization is going to collapse from sheer lack of brains to carry it on"; the fact is that civilization "is now collapsing faster and harder from a superabundance of brains of the wrong kind." The danger is diabolical geniuses such as Stalin and Mao Tse-Tung, not a deficiency of brainpower in the masses.

Oliver ended his lamentation on a pessimistic note, which only emphasized the cataclysmic nature of his forebodings. Americans will "soon be drowned in the flood" caused by "the terrible multiplication of the populations of Asia and Africa," he warned in the manner of a latter-day Jeremiah. "The minority of the earth's inhabitants that is capable of creating and continuing (as distinct from aping) a high civilization" faces the distinct possibility of being exterminated.

Dan Smoot, editor of the *Dan Smoot Report,* is another ultra-conservative whose views parallel those of scientific racists. The Brown decision, Smoot wrote on one occasion, is based upon "the opinions of modern sociologists and psychologists, the chief of which [sic] was Gunnar Myrdal, a Swedish socialist with a communist front record, who, in a book called *An American Dilemma,* had proclaimed his utter contempt for the Constitution of the United States." The decision is one of a series in which Earl Warren has endeavored "to stretch the meaning of the Fourteenth Amendment, because the communists and socialists whom he cites as modern authorities think this should be done." On another occasion, Smoot cited Audrey Shuey's *The Testing of Negro Intelligence,* and Garrett's introduction to it, as proof that equalitarian and integrationist ideas do not coincide with the "findings of scientific" research. "It is obvious that Western civilization was produced by whites," he wrote in citing Garrett and Miss Shuey; but like Oliver he refused to say flatly that Negroes are inferior to whites. "For primitive living under harsh physical conditions, the black man is obviously better adapted than whites," he wrote, "but for living in the white man's civilization, whites are obviously better adapted than negroes [sic]." In other words, Negroes are not absolutely inferior; they are not inferior in everything, only in things that count.[15]

The community of interest between racists and ultraconservatives is a two-way street. Ultraconservatives accept many of the ideas of racists, and racists in turn accept many of the views of ultraconservatives. The social and political views expressed in Nathaniel Weyl and Stefan Possony's *The Geography of Intellect* and Carleton Putnam's *Race and Reason* to mention two notable examples, are the same as those expressed in the literature of ultraconservatism. This aspect of the relationship between racism and ultraconservatism is illustrated in an address which William J. Simmons delivered to the organizational meeting of the Greater Los Angeles Citizens' Council in the summer of 1964.[16] Amid the racism which constituted the larger part of his address, Simmons, who is editor of *The Citizen*, sprinkled his reactionary political views. The Citizens' Councils, he began, are concerned about two things—racial integration and the growth of "an all powerful Federal government [which] is taking us down the road to tyranny, with the resulting loss of our personal freedom." Both are threatening the future well-being of America and both result from essentially the same thing—"the wave of equalitarianism which started in our educational system, especially teachers' colleges like Columbia, before World War I." This wave spread slowly at first, "until the shock of the great depression and the advent of the New Deal provided a fertile ground for its proliferation." To Simmons, the New Deal was the instrumentality through which liberals, equalitarians, and intellectuals had conducted their assault upon traditional American ideals and institutions. Since Franklin Roosevelt's presidency, he remarked, "the nation has been managed from Harvard, with occasional ideological assists from Columbia."

New Dealers and their intellectual and political heirs, Sim-

15 See *Dan Smoot Report*, January 30, 1961, p. 35; and July 13, 1963, p. 222. For the most detailed ultraconservative indictment of social science as a tool of socialist-communist conspirators see *The Great Deceit: Social Pseudo-Sciences* (1964) , a Veritas Foundation study published under the supervision of Archibald B. Roosevelt and Zygmund Dobbs.

16 William J. Simmons, address to the Organizational Meeting of the Greater Los Angeles Citizens' Council, June 30, 1964, available from the Citizens' Councils of Jackson, Mississippi.

mons continued, served the interests of America's enemies, both foreign and domestic, in a variety of ways. They "saved Stalin from internal collapse by extending diplomatic recognition and thereby helped him obtain loans which tided him over"; and their aid to international communism continues even yet, its most recent expression being the limited nuclear test ban treaty of 1963. They are also responsible for the systematic attacks upon American business and industry which are part of a larger effort to undermine faith in free-enterprise capitalism. "The concept became ingrained in several generations of college students that profit was evil," Simmons declared. Business is "taxed unmercifully" to finance a burgeoning federal government and "stifled by regulations as the insatiable thirst for power of those in control in Washington [grows] apace." Labor unions have been coddled until their leaders have become political as well as economic tyrants.

In Simmons' view the most sinister of all New Deal policies, one which latter-day liberals have expanded far beyond the original designs of New Dealers, was the attack upon "the race which had developed the most advanced and most highly industrialized country in the world." This was, he felt, an integral part of the liberal assault upon free enterprise, states' rights, the Constitution, and the moral, religious, and social ethic of the middle class. The effectiveness of the attack was due in part to deception, to managed science as well as managed news, and in part to seductive slogans such as "peace," "equality," and "civil rights." The real nature of the attack, however, is indicated by the fact that "peace" and "civil rights" are today "the two top priority objectives of the Communist Party." The American government, Simmons said in peroration,

is today controlled by liberals or collectivists, or welfare staters, or whatever. Now why is this group able to maintain itself in power? Because primarily of the fact [sic] that the white conservatives are divided into conflicting political and sectional groups and the white liberals hold the balance of power through the leverage of the negro bloc vote. This is obvious in the heavy voting Northern states, and it is coming to be more of a factor in the Southern states. It was the negro vote in the South as well as in the North, for instance, that elected the present Democratic Administration. Hence the combined drive by the Administration and the negro pressure groups to force Southern states to register hundreds of thousands of unqualified negroes.

To get this bloc vote, the liberals promise more and more special privileges for negroes in the form of 'civil rights' bills, which not only would give them social and political preference, but economic as well.

The only way in which politicians have ever held the negro bloc vote is through an ever ascending rate of taxing whites and spending on negroes. Of all aspects of the welfare state, this is one of the most immoral, for it subsidizes laziness and waste at the expense of industry. Such brazen redistribution of the wealth amounts to no less than stealing.

It is not within the purview of this study to detail the views of "equalitarian" or "environmentalist" scientists. It seems appropriate, however, to comment in general terms upon certain of their major objections to scientific racism.

The basic error of racists is their misunderstanding of the concept of race. In their view, "race" is a fixed, permanent entity from which the individual inherits not only certain identifiable physical features, but equally identifiable mental, moral, and behavioral traits as well. There exist, then, or so racists believe, such things as "Negro intelligence," "Negro morality," and "Negro personality," and these are in large part racially and genetically determined. "Psychic" traits, in other words, are produced by evolution and transmitted in the genes in the same manner as skin color, hair texture, and facial configuration. From these assumptions racists reason that each race can be measured—and judged—by the culture it produces, the society it creates, the morality and intellectual achievement its members display. This means, among other things, that the improvement of Negroes in crucial areas such as IQ test scores and social behavior is largely beyond the power of Negroes themselves, or whites either, to accomplish. Improvement must await the long, slow processes of evolution. Eventually, perhaps, Negroes will reach the levels already achieved by whites, though even here the logic of racists is discouraging, for as Negroes evolve upward whites will presumably do likewise. The prospects of Negroes ever catching up would appear to be hopeless.

To equalitarians "race" is not nearly so powerful or static a force. It is instead a "process, a series of temporary genetic conditions always in process of change," and races are best defined as "populations which differ in the relative commonness of some of their genes," or as "genetically isolated mating groups with distinctive gene frequencies." [17] According to these definitions, races differ rela-

17 Ashley Montagu, *Man in Process* (New York, 1961), 91–92; L. C. Dunn and Theodosius Dobzhansky, *Heredity, Race and Society* (New York, 1946), 108; and Pettigrew, *A Profile of the Negro American*, 59.

tively, not absolutely, and the difference is in the frequency of certain genes. Genes (and the chromosomes which contain them) are the mechanism through which heredity operates, but they are not racial in nature. "Negro genes" do not differ in kind from "white genes." An individual Negro does not inherit a set of "Negro genes" which, by racist logic, would give him "Negro intelligence," "Negro morality," and "Negro personality." Though intelligence, morality, and personality are each influenced to some unknown but considerable degree by heredity, the influence operates on an individual, not a racial, basis. In every race there is a vast reservoir of genes, but an individual inherits only a minute number of those in his racial gene pool. Every individual (except identical twins), regardless of race, has a unique combination of genes and is a unique human being with distinctive characteristics and potentialities. His traits and abilities are his as an individual, not as a member of a race. There is a complete overlap of personality and morality types, as well as range of mental ability, among the basic racial groups.

Nor is the genetic composition of a race static. In the case of American Negroes there has always been a steady infusion of "Caucasian genes" so that perhaps one-fourth of the Negro's gene pool today consists of "alien genes." This has immense significance for the claims of racists, and their failure to take it sufficiently into account is a notable weakness in their ideology. It pointedly illustrates the difference between biological and social definitions of race. Natural selection, mutation, and genetic drift also operate to alter the genetic composition of racial groups, and thereby contribute decisively to the dynamic of race, to the constant reshuffling and recombination of genes, to the "process" mentioned above.[18]

Besides misconstruing the nature of race and inheritance, racists also misunderstand intelligence, which is vastly more complicated—and fascinating—than they believe. They look upon intelligence, as upon race, as fixed and static, and in large measure racially determined. But the evidence is massive and wholly convincing [19] that intelligence is individual and plastic. "Intelligence is not merely an inherited capacity, genetically fixed and destined to

[18] This subject is explained in layman's terms in Theodosius Dobzhansky, *The Biological Basis of Human Freedom* (New York, 1958); Dobzhansky, *Mankind Evolving* (New Haven, 1962) ; and Ashley Montagu (ed.) , *The Concept of Race* (New York, 1964) .

[19] See for example Pettigrew, *A Profile of the Negro American,* 100–35.

unfold in a biologically predetermined manner," wrote Harvard psychologist Thomas F. Pettigrew. "It is a dynamic, on-going set of processes that within wide hereditary limits is subject to innumerable experiential factors." [20]

The racists' approach to intelligence, like their approach to race in general, is curiously fatalistic. They have an almost blind faith in IQ test scores, and in interpreting those scores they invariably assume that IQ is static and innate intelligence will develop regardless of environment. Here also they ignore a vast amount of evidence which indicates, convincingly, that this is not the case. In the famous Demonstration Guidance Project in Junior High School 43 in New York City, to cite one example, striking improvements in IQ test scores and scholastic performance were achieved by a massive guidance and remedial program. When the project began in 1956 only 26 percent of the students in Junior High 43 had IQ test scores of 110 or better, a distinctly below-average group. Three years later this percentage was 58. In 1956 2.5 percent of the students had IQ scores of 140 or over; six years later 12 percent achieved that level.[21] Similar though less spectacular results have been achieved in the Higher Horizons project, also in New York City, the "Banneker Group" in St. Louis, and the integrated schools of Washington, D.C.[22]

Washington, D.C., provided the most rigorous test yet made of the effects of massive integration in the public schools. The schools in the nation's capital were integrated immediately following the Brown decision, and psychological and achievement tests in the first year of integration revealed an appalling situation. The average scores of students were far below national averages in every category tested, a fact which racists took as proof that Negroes are intellectually inferior and that integration inevitably lowers educational standards. A flood of newspaper and magazine articles "exposed" the situation; a congressional subcommittee dominated by Southern racists "investigated" Washington schools and recommended that "racially separate public schools be reestablished."

[20] Pettigrew, *A Profile of the Negro American,* 107.

[21] See the testimony of Dr. John Theobald, New York City School Superintendent, in U.S. House of Representatives, Committee on Education and Labor. *Hearings on Integration in Public Education Programs.* 87th Cong., 2nd Sess., March 1–April 16, 1962, 288–89.

[22] See the discussion in Pettigrew, *A Profile of the Negro American,* 125–29; and Charles E. Silberman, *Crisis in Black and White* (New York, 1964), 255–307.

The disparity in achievement between white and Negro students, the subcommittee declared, is too great for integrated schools to be effective. Integration, they found, creates discipline and sex problems which interfere with the learning process and produces morale problems for both teachers and students.[23]

The District Superintendent of Schools, Dr. Carl F. Hansen, however, was not dissuaded from the facts of the case. Integration had not lowered standards in District schools, he felt, it had merely revealed the stark inferiority of Negro schools. To him, the solution was not resegregation but improvement of school services and standards so as to raise the performance of all pupils, Negro as well as white. And this he accomplished. After 1955, when the schools were first integrated, there was steady improvement in the performance of Washington students on standardized aptitude and achievement tests; by 1960 their performance approached national averages in most areas tested. The significance of this is underscored by the fact that it occurred while the percentage of Negroes in the schools was steadily increasing, and in spite of the fact that the student population in Washington is decidedly atypical. Not only is the percentage of Negroes unusually large (81.5 percent in 1961) but a majority of the students are from the central city and a disproportionately small minority from affluent suburbs. "A brief summary of the [achievement test] results will show, where comparative data are available, a general upgrading of achievement levels since 1955," reported Dr. Hansen in 1960. "This has occurred during a period of steady increase in the percentage of Negro pupils, testifying to the capacity of the Negro pupil to respond to educational opportunity." [24]

It is obvious, then, that Negroes are as educable as whites and that integration does not itself lower educational standards, though it does reveal the inferiority of Negro schools. This, again, is an all-important point which racists invariably ignore. Negro schools *are* inferior, and grossly so, whether in the rural South or the

[23] U.S. House of Representatives, Committee on the District of Columbia. *Report of the Subcommittee to Investigate Public School Standards and Conditions and Juvenile Delinquency in the District of Columbia* (Washington, 1957) , 47.

[24] Carl F. Hansen, *Addendum: A Five-Year Report on Desegregation in the Washington, D.C., Schools* (New York, 1960) , 19. There is a detailed report on the improvement in test results in U.S. House of Representatives, Committee on Education and Labor. *Hearings on Integration in Public Education Programs.* 87th Cong., 2nd Sess., March 1—April 16, 1962, pp. 382–402.

ghettoized North and West. A few years ago, to cite one example, James B. Conant found that the total appropriations per pupil in Chicago averaged 21 percent less in all-Negro schools than in all-white schools.[25] The inferiority of Negro (and slum) schools, however, is not due solely to money expended; other factors not statistically measureable are also involved. The total school environment is more significant than expenditure per pupil. Negro (and slum) schools seem generally to have poorer and less experienced teachers than white suburban schools, or the teachers in Negro and slum schools rarely make the same demands upon their students. White suburban schools are oriented toward preparing students for college, and they accordingly insist upon respectable levels of achievement. In slum and Negro areas, the community, the parents, the school board, the teachers all expect little of students, and the students soon come to expect little of themselves. As Kenneth Clark has said repeatedly, Negro children do not learn because they are not taught, and they are not taught because no one expects them to learn.[26] A vicious cycle exists, and as a result the prophecy that Negro and slum children have low intelligence and little educability is self-fulfilling.

The principal weakness of scientific racism, however, is not its scientific deficiencies, though these are serious enough to discredit it; the principal weakness is the logical fallacy inherent in the idea that civil rights and race relations are genetic problems which are best approached through an understanding of the Negro's genetic inheritance and evolutionary development. Racial policies are first and foremost social policies and must be treated as such if they are to be solved. The American Negro is what he is today because of social, not genetic, reasons. He makes lower IQ scores than whites, earns less money, is more likely to commit certain crimes and deviate from middle class standards of morality and personal conduct. But these are products of racial discrimination and class differences and are irrelevant to the composition of his gene pool. Scientific racists refuse to recognize this fact, and as a result are unable to understand the real nature of the race problem. In fact, they are themselves an important element in that problem.

25 Cited in Silberman, *Crisis in Black and White*, 263.
26 See Clark, *Dark Ghetto* for a discussion of this aspect of the problem.

COMMENTARIES

A. James Gregor

On Learned Ignorance:
A Brief Inquiry into I. A. Newby's
Challenge to the Court

> "There's glory for you!"
>
> "I don't know what you mean by 'glory,'" Alice said.
>
> Humpty Dumpty smiled contemptuously. "Of course you don't—till I tell you. I meant 'there's a nice knock down argument for you!'"
>
> "But 'glory' doesn't mean 'a nice knock down argument,'" Alice objected.
>
> "When I use a word," Humpty Dumpty said in a rather scornful tone, "it means just what I choose it to mean—neither more nor less."
>
> "The question is," said Alice, "whether you can make words mean so many different things."
>
> "The question is," said Humpty Dumpty, "which is to be master—that's all."

Humpty Dumpty's abuse of the language is the object of urbane amusement and perhaps polite disdain. His arrogance and stupidities are so transparent, and he faults the language with such abandon, that he recommends himself as an object lesson to small children and all those who suffer linguistic handicap. Fortunately, or unfortunately as the case may be, our world abounds in individuals prepared to serve, with little or no provocation, in the same capacity. Amid that goodly number I. A. Newby has recently taken his place.

Newby's book, *Challenge to the Court: Social Scientists and the*

Defense of Segregation, 1954–1966, constitutes not only a catalogue of harrowing intellectual and academic abuses—including the purveyance of falsehoods and half-truths calculated to defame, misinterpretations and misjudgments that impugn the integrity and competence of his colleagues, innuendoes and asides that expose the objects of his attention to public odium, all beaded together on a string of feckless and indifferent logic—but it also manages to so systematically violate the canons of correct linguistic usage that it stands as a monument to Lewis Carroll's fictional hero.

These are hard judgments to make of a colleague. Only the decision by my attorneys and the attorneys of the Louisiana State University Press that Newby's libels are not legally "actionable" have driven me to put them into print. In itself, his work is beneath contempt. His characterization of me and his caricature of my work, however, place him outside the range of those men who have the right to expect the proprieties of academic treatment. Newby's book does not merit serious concern as an *academic* performance. It is a silly book so freighted with errors of fact and so perverse in logic that it contributes nothing to serious discussion on matters of vital importance to our nation and its people. But since a proper and easily comprehensible regard for my own professional and moral reputation demands that Newby's inanities be exposed for what they are, I am compelled to begrudge some time to this assessment.

First and foremost, Mr. Newby introduces his book with a clear statement of intent: he will concern himself with the ideas of a host of social scientists, ideas which will be "systematically analyzed and subjected unemotionally to tests of logic, reason, history, and science" (p. viii). He will "analyze and evaluate" the relevant literature, he will "challenge its premises, logic, and data, and point out its real nature . . ." (p. ix). Surely such an undertaking, presuming Newby to be equipped to discharge it, must deliver a notable and significant achievement.

Who are the objects of this ambitious enterprise? They are "racists," agents of "racism." Mr. Newby promises to subject to analysis, to submit "unemotionally to tests of logic, reason, history, and science" the ideas of American "racists."

Since Newby comes so formidably equipped with logic and reason, one might reasonably expect him to have a clearly defined class of individuals in mind, those "racists" with whose ideas he will treat. One might legitimately expect him to deploy the words "racist" and "racism" with at least minimal regard for the logic of their use. The words "racist" and "racism" must surely mean something specific for Mr. Newby—for that is what his book is supposed to be, in fact, about. Let us consider how well he defines the range of application of these critical terms.

Newby's Definition of "Racist" and "Racism"

Newby is quick to offer a definition of "racism":

Scientific racism, the chief concern of this study, rests largely upon several . . . assumptions or value judgments—that human nature is fixed by heredity and immune to environment, that behavior characteristics (morality, criminality, ethics) as well as intelligence are genetically determined and directly related to race, that racial differences are relevant to the formulation of public policy, that race, in short, is the basic reality of life (p. xi).

Further:

As I have used it here, "racism" suggests a belief in innate racial inequality, including the corollaries of Negro inferiority and white superiority. However, most of the individuals discussed in this study insist they are not racists, that they believe only in racial *differences*, not racial *inequality*. I have therefore applied the term "racists" to anyone who advocates racial policies such as segregation, civil disabilities against Negroes, and prohibition of racial intermarriage—policies which are meaningful only if the races are inherently unequal. A "racist" is anyone who believes in racial inequality and/or advocates the above racial policies, and a 'scientific racist" is one whose racism rests chiefly upon science or pseudoscience (p. xii).

Elsewhere in the text we are informed:

Racists categorize people as members of a race, and define their civil rights and social status in racial terms (pp. 70f.).

And further:

. . . racists [accept] the plot theory of history (p. 97; cf. p. 153).

And further:

Racists usually recognize certain activities as appropriate for Negroes and acknowledge—and applaud—their accomplishments in those areas (p. 101).

And further:

. . . racists . . . readily [make] the transition from scientist to social
critic (p. 115).

And further:

. . . racists sometimes [use] contradictory arguments . . . (p. 132).

And further:

The convergence of scientific racism and ultraconservatism is more than
a coincidence of economic and political ideas, more than guilt by association (p. 223).

If we attempt to provide a synoptic and seriatim list of the
criterial attributes which admit one to membership in the class of
"racists," agents of "racism," we find that (granted the reasonably
well-understood rules of grammatical transformation covering the
change of a substantive into an adjective) a "racist" is one who
harbors (or Newby "suggests" harbors) the following assumptions
or value judgments:

(1) that human nature is fixed by heredity and immune to
environment;

(2) that behavior characteristics (morality, criminality, ethics) as
well as intelligence are genetically determined and directly related
to race;

(3) that racial differences are relevant to the formulation of public
policy;

(4) that race is the basic reality of life;

(5) that there is an innate racial inequality—which entails as
"corollaries" that the Negro is inferior and the white superior;

(6) that racial policies such as segregation, civil disabilities against
Negroes, and prohibition of racial intermarriage are to be pursued
—"policies which are meaningful only if the races are inherently
unequal";

(7) that "racism" rests on the evidence of science or pseudoscience;

(8) that people are to be categorized as members of a race, and
that their civil rights and social status are to be defined in racial
terms;

(9) that history is the result of conspiracy;

(10) that certain activities are appropriate for Negroes;

(11) that a transition from scientist to social critic is legitimate
(or at least that "racists" are disposed to make such transits);

(12) that recourse to contradiction is to be countenanced (or at least that "racists" are disposed to countenance contradiction); and finally

(13) that scientific racism, in some loose sense, entails ultraconservatism.

This clearly will not do. If we scrutinize the list, there are evidently some assumptions which cannot qualify as independent criterial attributes. Number 7 is circular. It refers to "racism," the term which is to be defined. It would hardly be fruitful to characterize a "racist" as one committed to "racism." What Mr. Newby obviously intends is that once we identify a "racist" we can characterize a *scientific* "racist"—as one whose "racism" purportedly rests upon scientific or pseudoscientific evidence. Numbers 3, 6, and 8 are in large part redundant. If racial differences are conceived relevant to the formation of public policy, then public policies such as segregation, imposed civil disabilities, the prohibition of racial intermarriage, and the ascriptive determination of social status merely provide instantiation of that conviction. If numbers 1 and 2 are held conjointly, then number 10 follows. It says nothing more than is implicit in its antecedents. (But if Newby is disposed to indulge his reader, such an exercise in the obvious need not detain us.) Number 11 simply can not stand as an independent criterial attribute of a "racist." Newby (whether or not he qualifies as a scientist is not particularly relevant at this juncture) is disposed to be a social critic—so are the "integrationists" he cites. Scientists who make the ready transit from science to social criticism are not all "racists." Similarly, human fallibility being what it is, we all lapse into contradiction, so that the occurrence of contradiction in argument is not an independently defining trait of "racists." Mr. Newby's work is fat with contradictions. Mr. Newby is not a "racist" (I think). That disposes of number 12. Number 6 is obviously intended as a tendency statement. "Racists" tend to conceive events in history as the result of some sort of conspiracy. But since there are any number of people who countenance such a view of history, the disposition to so conceive history hardly qualifies as an independent defining trait of "racism" or "racists."

All of which leaves us with a more manageable list of independent critical attributes.

A "racist" for Newby is someone for whom

(1) human nature is *fixed* by heredity and *immune* to environment;

(2) behavior characteristics (morality, criminality, ethics) as well as intelligence are genetically determined and directly related to race;

(3) racial differences are relevant to the formation of public policy (which includes segregation, civil disabilities, the proscription of racial intermarriage, and status ascription);

(4) race is the basic reality of life;

(5) there is an innate racial inequality, with Negroes indentified as inferior and whites superior;

(6) scientific racism, in some sense, entails ultraconservatism.

That Newby thinks this collection of criterial attributes is adequate to define his class of subjects is evidenced by the facility with which he identifies "racists" and "non-racists." Mr. Newby *knows*, for example, that Carleton Coon is *not* a racist (p. 218). So secure is Mr. Newby's analytic insight that even a "cursory reading" of scientific material tells him that some social scientists "are not so obviously racists" as others (p. 134n15). He *knows*, with the same confidence and with even less than "cursory reading," that I am not only the youngest, but "in many respects the most distinctive of the prominent scientific racists" (p. 121). "Perhaps," he goes on to add sententiously, "it is accurate to say that Gregor is unique among them."

All of this with the same calm assurance, and with the same sense of responsibility, as a sleepwalker.

What Newby has proposed is what is referred to in the technical literature as a "range" or "criterial" definition.[1] Such a definition is given in terms of a set of overlapping criteria by virtue of which members of the class are identified. Such definitions are sharply distinguished from specific definitions that provide necessary and sufficient conditions for the denotation of a term. Specific definitions alone provide for applications that are sharply delineated; the necessary and sufficient criteria for application provide a conclusive test for admission into the membership class. Thus a thing is properly identified as a parallelogram if, and only if, that thing is

[1] Cf. M. Black, *Problems of Analysis: Philosophical Essays* (Ithaca, 1954), 24–37; M. Scriven, "Definitions, Explanations and Theories," in H. Feigl, M. Scriven, and G. Maxwell, *Minnesota Studies in the Philosophy of Science II* (*Minneapolis,* 1958), 105f.

a quadrilateral figure and also has parallel sides. Only the use of such a definition produces a sharply delineated class; everything that exists must be either wholly within the class or wholly outside it. Only if Mr. Newby had such a definition available would it be logically possible for him to make distinctions between "racists" and "non-racists" with assurance within his domain of inquiry. Newby, however, has no such definition. His class of "racists" is an ill-defined class, each member minimally possessing at least one of the logically independent criteria for admission, but the possession of no one of the criteria is individually necessary. Only in "paradigm" cases would a member possess all the criterial attributes. But while no one member need possess all the attributes, the possession of at least one is a logical necessity—and then inclusion in the class will rest on a responsible decision as to whether the one specific trait is sufficiently well defined to license entry into the class. A range or criterial definition of a term represents the complexity and continuous variability of the subject matter to which the expression refers.

Since the terms "racist" and "racism" are charged with such negative emotional force, and the implications of identifying someone as a member of the class are so serious, ascriptions should be made with due regard not only for right reason, appropriate academic proprieties, but moral responsibility as well.

So innocent is Mr. Newby of analytic sophistication, so devoid is he of moral responsibility, that he not only identifies me as a "racist" without seriously considering these matters, but numbers me among the most prominent. Which suggests I am a paradigm case. Let us briefly consider the facts.

A "racist," for Mr. Newby, is one for whom "human nature" is *fixed* by heredity and *immune* to the environment.

I claim a modest degree of expertise in matters concerned with human heredity. I have delivered communications before meetings of professional geneticists and have published my findings on the heritability ratios for various mental factors in standard professional journals.[2] If we restrict ourselves to my work published within the

2 A. J. Gregor, "The Heritability of Visualization, Perceptual Speed and Spatial Orientation," *Perceptual and Motors Skills*, XXIII (1966), 379–90, "Heritability of Numerical Facility," *Ibid.*, XXIV (1967), 659–66, "Heritability of Factor V: Verbal Comprehension," *Ibid.*, XXVI (1968), 191–202, "Hereditary Factors in the Performance of Visual Perceptual Tasks," Communications before the International Symposium on the Methodology of the Social Sciences (Rome, March 13–15,

period in which Newby claims competence (1954–66) we find (1) not only do I caution against ready judgments concerning the "innate potential" of entire classes of people,[3] but (2) in a study published in 1966 I specifically stated that psychogenetics, the "study of [the genetic] determinants governing human behavior" is "complicated by the very multiplicity of *ecological* and *inherited* factors and their *complex interrelationship*" (my emphasis), and further that hereditary mechanisms are . . . complex and *environmental factors influence the occurrence and intensity of [phenotypic] manifestation*" (my emphasis). I went on to specifically insist that "the difficulties which attend . . . attempts to assess the proportional contributions of *genotype* and *environment* as *codeterminants* of [phenotype] are well known" (my emphasis). I concluded with the admonition that studies in behavior genetics should be supplemented by research which "would indicate the general direction in which one should look for significant *environmental* variables" (my emphasis) and "genetic factors, as such, are excluded as *sole* determinants. As a consequence the developmental psychologist is interested in determining what *environmental* factors might contribute to variability" (my emphasis).[4]

My communication before the 1965 Rome symposium on methodology in social science indicated that various mental factors were inherited with a wide range of variance attributable to hereditary factors, ranging from an estimate of 89 per cent for some and as low as 15 per cent for others.[5] If I am to qualify as a "racist" it must be on other grounds than that I conceive "human nature" (whatever that means in Mr. Newby's lexicon of simplisms) "fixed" by heredity and "immune" to the environment.

To suggest that I hold such a quaint view by identifying me as a "racist" is to impugn my professional competence. Newby makes such imputations without the least regard for factual accuracy and responsible assessment.

1966), printed in the *Revue Internationale de Sociologie,* N.S. 2, II, 3 (1966), 274–82.

[3] A. J. Gregor, "Sociology and the Assimilation of Non-Industrial Peoples," *La sociologia y las sociedades en desarrollo industrial,* II (Cordoba, Argentina: University of Cordoba, 1963, pp. 337f., and "Sociology and the Mental Testing of Non-Industrial People," *Ibid.,* V. pp. 185f.

[4] Gregor, "The Heritability of Visualization," 379, 381, 387.

[5] Gregor, "Heritability Factors in the Performance of Visual Perceptual Tasks," 278f.

The second criterial attribute by which Newby identifies "racists" with such assurance is that which characterizes them as holding the conviction that manifest traits (morality, criminality, ethics, and intelligence) are genetically determined and directly related to race. Such a claim is so manifestly absurd that coherent rebuttal is all but impossible. Newby talks of "ethics" as a "behavior characteristic." Ethics is simply *not* a "behavior characteristic." Ethics, as it is normally understood, is a linguistic enterprise, the systematic study of the vindications governing significant choice. How he imagines, or conceives anyone else imagining, that ethics could be inherited is a complete mystery to me. I publicly defy him to identify *one* social scientist from any time and place in world history, who has maintained that "ethics" is "genetically determined."

But perhaps we are pressing Newby too hard. One can hardly demand more than his loosely framed and loosely jointed propositions can deliver. What he obviously intends is that a "racist" is convinced that a disposition to antisocial acts is "genetically determined."

In a monograph published in 1964, in a discussion devoted to the acculturation of the Australian Aborigines, I indicated that under the environmental stresses in which the Aborigine found himself one would expect "serious frustrations" to breed a "disposition to aggressive acts." I maintained explicitly that "the crime and delinquency rate among the Aborigines can be expected to exceed that of the white population at least during the initial acculturation period. Whether the crime rate stabilizes finally at the average [level of the community] will be determined by a number of considerations." [6] Nowhere did I suggest that the high crime rate prevalent among Australian Aborigines was "genetically determined."

In 1965 my communication, given before Medical Correctional Association Symposium on Violence in April, 1964, was published. I addressed myself specifically to the high crime rate prevalent in the American Negro community. The paper attempted "to describe in broad outline some of the *social factors* which dispose Negroes, as an identifiable class, to aggressive attitudes . . . attitudes [which] tend to discharge themselves in acts of violence or conduce to de-

[6] A. J. Gregor, "The Assimilation of a Peripheral People: The Australian Aborigines, *Mankind Monographs* (1964), 10, 14.

fensive response." (my emphasis) . I identified some of those factors as the "adaptive adjustments" which increasing urbanization demands, "competitive disadvantage in the search for urban employment," the high unemployment rate, economic insecurity, job frustration, female dominance, family instability, discrimination, and prejudice.[7] Nowhere did I suggest that the high crime rate prevalent among American Negroes was "genetically determined."

If I am to qualify as a "racist" it must be on other grounds than that I conceive criminality to be "genetically determined." Perhaps I might qualify as a "racist" by virtue of the fact that I believe "intelligence" to be "genetically determined." Once again I fail to qualify. I rarely talk of an omnibus "intelligence" as though "intelligence" had some discrete, determinate, and mensurable entity as its referent. In my published work I have clearly indicated that general intelligence, as it is popularly conceived, is a function of complex interaction of environment and mental factors, at least 60 of which refer to specific constituent mental abilities. Factor analysts have postulated over 120 such unitary mental factors. In my published accounts I attempt to provide responsible estimates of hereditary influence governing the behavioral manifestation of these factors. As I have indicated above, the heritability indices vary from factor to factor. Nowhere do I suggest that "intelligence" is "genetically determined." In fact, in my review (published in 1964) of N. Weyl and S. Possony's *Geography of Intellect* (a book to which Mr. Newby devotes some space without indicating that he is at all aware of the existence of my review [pp. 173–76] I argued: "Intelligence tests do not, in their turn, offer undisputed proof of either individual or group differentials in native (more accurately, genetic) potential. . . . So many factors enter into the determination of adult intelligence and temperament that any definitive judgments about their innateness are somewhat hazardous." [8]

The third criterial attribute which Newby suggests identifies "racists" is the conviction that racial differences are relevant to the formation of public policy and that policy includes "segregation" and "civil disabilities against Negroes," as well as the "prohibition of racial intermarriage." Analysis of this attribute is particularly difficult to deal with in summary fashion because, once again, his

---

[7] A. J. Gregor, "Race Relations, Frustration and Aggression," *Revue Internationale de Sociologie*, N.S. 2, II, 2 (March, 1965), 91–93.

[8] A. J. Gregor, "Heredity and Intellect," *National Review*, April 7, 1964, p. 288.

argument is framed in such a simplistic, vague, and impoverished form that there is barely a toehold for meaningful discussion. He has presumed, in fact, what he is obliged to prove.

It appears obvious that not *only* "racists" think that racial differences are relevant to the formation of public policy. The entire program of affirmative integration (the busing of schoolchildren *solely* on the basis of skin color in order to maintain "racial balance") is predicated on such a conviction. Apparently to qualify as a "racist" one must presumably advocate a public policy which *negatively* affects Negroes. I am not sure if Mr. Newby would characterize Dr. C. P. Oberndorf, former president of the American Psychopathological Association, as a "racist" because he asserted that "certain groups to which we belong, being biologically determined, never change," and included among such groups "color groupings," and then went on to suggest that Negro psychotics be treated in hospitals in which an "all-Negro staff of psychiatrists and nurses administers treatment to an all-Negro patient population" to serve the Negroes' needs more "efficiently." [9] If Dr. Oberndorf is to be characterized as a "racist," one has a right to know why. If not, why not? If an argument were to be offered which maintained that Negro children, within a specific or specifiable age range and under relatively specific circumstances, benefited from educational activities conducted in a racially insulated environment where their specific race-related needs could be more adequately met, would such an argument identify its proponent as a "racist"? If so, why? Similarly, if one were to argue against the advisability of racial intermarriage, as has Rabbi Albert Gordon, would that be enough to characterize him as a "racist?" Rabbi Gordon maintains: "Parents, I think, to the very best of their ability, ought to dissuade their children from intermarrying." Moreover, he argues that they should dissuade their children from the "close personal relationship encouraged by interdating" which "encourages intermarriage." He concluded, "I believe that intermarriage is . . . a threat to the children of such a marriage, in that it may tend to make them marginal in their relationships to parents, their faiths or their races." [10] Are these "racist" sentiments? Can such advice be predi-

[9] C. P. Oberndorf, "Selectivity and Option for Psychiatry," *American Journal of Psychiatry*, CX (April, 1954), 754–58.

[10] A. I. Gordon, *Intermarriage: Interfaith, Interracial, Interethnic* (Boston, 1964), 352, 355, 370.

cated *only* (as Mr. Newby insists) on the covert assumption of innate racial inferiority?

Perhaps what Mr. Newby intends is that such advice is "racist" only when it is conjoined with the commitment that such policies take the form of public law. If such is the case then neither I, Dr. Oberndorf, or Rabbi Gordon would qualify as "racists." What we have suggested is that for specific purposes, for specific periods of time, under specific circumstances, and for specific classes of people, policies which Newby disapproves of are recommended by what we feel to be substantial evidence. The issue of the advisability of racial congregation or racial homogeneity in the schools will be taken up in more detail below. The purpose of this brief inquiry, here, is to indicate that I have never advocated a public policy of negative segregation, civil disabilities for Negroes, nor prohibition of interracial marriage, and do not merit, on such grounds, membership in the increasingly select group of people who qualify as Newby's "racists."

The point here is simply that Newby's statements are so cavalier, so devoid of precision and specificity that one is at a loss to know when and where they apply.

Newby's fourth criterial attribute of a "racist" escapes any sensible appraisal. How does one know when an individual is convinced that "race is the basic reality of life?" How can one put into operation such a strange notion? What evidence would warrant the ascription of such a disposition to a social scientist? I have published two books, four monographs, and over fifty articles in professional journals. In my *Survey of Marxism* race is not mentioned once.[11] In my *Contemporary Radical Ideologies*[12] race is referred to only when it is relevant to the ideology which is the object of assessment—and my conclusion is to dismiss race as a serious foundation of any viable contemporary ideology.[13] The vast bulk of my published work makes no reference whatever to race. Surely this should constitute substantive counterevidence to any claim that I might hold race to be the "basic reality of life." If I am to qualify as a racist it must be on other grounds.

11 A. J. Gregor, *A Survey of Marxism: Problems in Philosophy and the Theory of History* (New York, 1965).

12 A. J. Gregor, *Contemporary Radical Ideologies: Totalitarian Thought in the Twentieth Century* (New York, 1968).

13 *Ibid.*, 335f.

The fifth criterial attribute of a "racist" is particularly significant because this is what lay opinion conceives to be the necessary and sufficient criteria for the identification of a "racist," and it is via this attribute that Newby musters me to class membership. A "racist" is one who entertains the conviction that there exists an "innate racial inequality" as well as its "corollaries" of "Negro inferiority and white superiority." Here Newby is no longer simply vague or silly—he is positively vicious. He insists that "Gregor believes" most Negro children "simply do not have the mental capacity to compete with whites," that I believe that "Negroes are in fact inferior" (p. 128).

At this point I insist that Newby no longer take refuge in fugitive statements, vague innuendo, bizarre logic, and compounded stupidity and simply quote one statement, out of all my published work (unpublished work or private correspondence—all of which is open to him—and has always been open to him had he had the simple decency and sense of responsibility to research his subject with minimal competence), which could in any sense warrant such an imputation. The fact is that I explicitly opted *against* such a conviction in one of the few articles of mine that Mr. Newby pretends to have read. In "On the Nature of Prejudice" (which Mr. Newby cites on page 123), in a discussion devoted to prejudice, I argued that "in every instance of European-Negro racial contact the Negroes or Negroid people have been forced into a subordinate slave or caste relationship. The universality of this fact leaves one the choice of but two alternative explanations: (1) the Negro is biologically inferior and succumbs in direct competition with Europeans, or—*as seems to be more likely*—(2) the non-White is discriminated against systematically (covertly or overtly) by a dominant group consciously or unconsciously motivated by a preference for its own kind" (emphasis supplied).[14]

Newby is obviously afflicted with a grievous case of selective perception. In one of the few articles of mine which he did read (and as I shall indicate below did not read very well), I specifically rejected the thesis he attributes to me and by virtue of which he elevates me to the undeserved status of a "prominent scientific racist." It is an honor I would rather not have thrust upon me. His pathetic attempts to identify me as a "racist" have forced him

14 A. J. Gregor, "On the Nature of Prejudice," *Eugenics Review*, LII January, 1961), 221.

to assume postures which would be an embarrassment to any responsible intellectual historian. Not only has he not read the bulk of my published work which was easily accessible to him, but he attributes ideas to me which are clearly at variance with my explicit statements in one of the few works published by me that he did take the trouble to read.

More specific are my statements in the review of *The Geography of Intellect*, published in 1964. The relevant material is too long to quote here, but in that review I argued (1) that mental characteristics are the *combined* consequence of heredity and environment; (2) that the effects of the environment on psychic traits is quantitatively, if not qualitatively, different from ecological influences on physical traits; (3) that the evidence of differential brain mass, structure, and cerebral cytoarchitecture "do *not* provide compelling evidence for the contention that individual and group variations are essentially hereditary and/or indices of differential psychic potential . . ."; (4) that there "does not seem to be any undisputed mental correlate to the 'primitive' features of Negroid and Capoid brains. We simply do not know enough about the function of the human brain to be able to argue with complete confidence from differential statistical frequencies of brain mass and structure between groups . . . to differential intellectual potential" and, finally, (5):

More interesting . . . is the suggestion made by the authors that social institutions can effect an "immense transformation" in individual or group behavior traits. . . . The authors are apparently prepared to admit that such personality transformations can be effected. If such is the case, one can legitimately wonder what the effect of living in a society with which he cannot identify might be upon the developing intellect and personality of the Negro child. . . . Even if some significant index of material equivalency is offered, can it be said with any assurance in the administration of intelligence or personality tests that the "environment" of the white child and the Negro child is the same in any exhaustive sense? Would a pervasive sense of one's own inferiority not militate against initiative, against emotional and psychological adjustment? [15]

Even someone as intellectually obtuse as Mr. Newby must understand such simple assertions. Where in any of my writings have I asserted or implied that I was convinced that "most Negro children . . . simply do not have the mental capacity to compete with whites" or that "Negroes are in fact inferior"? In 1965, in the conclusion

[15] Gregor, "Heredity and Intellect," 287f.

of my survey of social factors conducing to Negro intra- and extra-punitive aggressiveness and their disposition to abandon formal schooling I argued:

meaningful academic integration of the Negro minority . . . [requires] a preparatory educative program which would reduce [Negro] impairment. When Negro performance approximates the norms of the majority community, the increased incidence of nonwhite enrollment in the schools can no longer be interpreted as a threat to school standards so important to the status and goal aspirations of the average American. Under such circumstances the Negro child will not be identified with a low-performance group. Under such circumstances there will be less disposition on the part of the Negro student to abandon the challenge of higher education.[16]

Since 1961, throughout the period with which Newby pretends to deal, I have consistently denied the theses that he imputes to me. Mr. Newby has flagrantly and willfully misrepresented my views to serve some obscure motives known only to himself.

The sixth defining attribute of a "racist"—that "racists" are, in some vague sense, ultraconservative simply cannot be employed to identify me as a "racist." Although Newby quite characteristically offers no definition of "ultraconservative," leaving it to the intuitive insights of the reader to determine what this particular pejorative means, I am convinced he can find nothing in my writings that might so characterize them. I defy him to try.

In effect, I do not meet the minimum logical requirement for entrance into the class of "racists"—even as Mr. Newby has loosely defined this much-abused term. He attempts to force my entrance into the class by (1) falsifying my views, (2) misrepresenting my writings, (3) making gratuitous conjectures of facts not in evidence, (4) neglecting my relevant published writings which, in the public domain, were easily accessible to him and which it was his professional obligation to read objectively and with care. Newby has succeeded in violating every fiduciary obligation to which his intellectual responsibility commits him. He has taken it upon himself to impugn my professional competence as a behavioral scientist and my moral integrity as an academic and a citizen. But this is only the beginning.

Newby's "Interpretation" of My Work

If Mr. Newby has difficulty identifying the membership of the

[16] Gregor, "Race Relations, Frustration and Aggression," 106.

class he pretends to be studying, his interpretation of the work of those he misidentifies simply leaves one boggled.

On pages 123 and 124 Newby provides his innocent reader with a stenographic and interpretive account of my "racial views." The "primary ingredient" of my "view" is that "race prejudice" is a "deep-rooted, *instinctive* preference for one's own kind" (my emphasis). This "instinctive" explanation of race prejudice he informs us I "never bother to articulate." I thus "elevate" my bigotry to the "more satisfying one of human instinct." He then goes on to indicate that I insist that "*physical differences* set races and ethnic groups apart" (my emphasis), and further that "racial prejudices (or preferences) are . . . *instinctive,* and are *immune* to environmental influences . . ." (my emphasis).

All of this is arrant nonsense and a gross distortion of anything I have ever written.

Newby maintains (p. 122) that I am "perhaps more knowledgeable in the literature of scientific racism than any other social scientist . . . discussed in [his] study," and yet he insists that I have lapsed into the most simplistic of counterfeit explanations: the tautological "explanation" of manifest behavior by postulating a causal "instinct." In my article, published in 1962, entitled "The Dynamics of Prejudice," I maintained: "At the turn of the century, when Franklin Giddings articulated the concept of in-group amity as 'consciousness of kind,' the tendency was to treat the behavior associated with this aspect of ethnocentrism as 'instinctive,' a term seemingly justified by the universality of the trait complex. . . . But to call man's intergroup responses 'instinctive' does not convey much cognitive information." I then went on to indicate: "The disposition to identify with a group of select membership characterizes man as a social animal; *the specific object choice for such identification will be determined by the circumstances in which he is nurtured.*" [17] Nowhere in the article ("On the Nature of Prejudice") which Newby claims to have read do I maintain that racial prejudice is "instinctive" and in an article published at approximately the same time I specifically deny it. Furthermore I specifically denied not only that "racial prejudices" are "instinctive," but I specifically denied that such prejudices are "immune" to environmental influences. In the article Newby pretends to have

17 A. J. Gregor, "The Dynamics of Prejudice," *Mankind Quarterly,* III (October–December, 1962), 80.

read I stated flatly: "Among men [ethnocentric] behavior manifests itself as tribal, class, caste, national or racial exclusiveness, *the explicit form of preference being determined largely by the historic, social and political circumstances in which the particular human group finds itself.*" [18]

It is equally evident in the above quotation that I nowhere maintained that it was exclusively "physical differences" which "set races and ethnic groups apart." Once again, in the article Mr. Newby read in his own inimitable style, I said: "Among primitives . . . exclusiveness is tribal [with] distinctions . . . drawn along *cultural lines.* Human communities . . . distinguish themselves by *physical disparity, different territorial origins, varying speech, diverse political, moral and religious allegiances* as well as *different economic functions, modes of dress* and *adornment.*" And further, "These differences . . . reside, as we have seen, in *attitudes, religious opinions, speech, aesthetic judgments, technical achievements* or *observable physical differences.*" And further: "As we have indicated, group identification can be made on the basis of *language, dress, mannerisms, religious* or *political affiliation.*" [19]

How much more simply or how much more frequently would I have to assert such eminently clear propositions to defend myself against Newby's perverse misrepresentation? Or perhaps the more significant question might be: How biased and how stupid must a reader be who sees in this an "instinct" theory of "race prejudice" (when what I was clearly articulating was a *descriptive* and not an *explanatory* exposition of *ethnocentric* behavior which constitutes the psychosocial basis for "race prejudice"), in which such "instinctive" behavior is "immune to environmental influences"? How does one reply to someone who insists that an author is issuing a predictive claim that "physical differences" will "always" set races and ethnic groups apart whenever they meet (p. 123) when that author has just finished issuing the qualified assertion:

We can generalize (bearing in mind exceptions which can conceivably result from singular sociopolitical circumstances) that where two peoples, marked by gross physical dissimilarities, make contact, the attempt at assimilation is invariably met with tensions and disharmonies which it is almost beyond the power of men to resolve. . . . Only a sensitive awareness of the complexity of the problems which face our world in the in-

18 A. J. Gregor, "On the Nature of Prejudice," 217.
19 *Ibid.,* 218f.

creasingly frequent contact of races and cultures can assist us in avoiding the tragedy that has attended such contacts in the past. That men are capable of meeting those problems and resolving them equitably is admittedly something of an article of faith—an article of faith, however, supported by some compelling instances of contemporary racial accommodation. But it is an article of faith we must entertain if we are not disposed supinely to submit ourselves to tragedy.

My work in this area is recognized in the professional literature as a contribution to the analysis of *ethnocentrism*.[20] Racial prejudice refers to only a *subset* of *ethnocentric* responses. Racial preferences and racial prejudices, like the entire syndrome of manifest ethnocentric responses, is a function of interaction of disposition and environmental circumstances. Man is disposed to speak, just as he is disposed to identify with reference groups of limited compass, but the language he speaks and the group with which he identifies will be the consequence of a multiplicity of determinate environmental influences. In an article published in 1962, "The Biosocial Nature of Prejudice," I indicated that "the study of the *psychological mechanisms* which foster group isolation . . . has only begun" (my emphasis). I went on to discuss some of the studies relevant to a consideration of the "formation of preferences" which was considered to be the "result of primary socialization," a *conditioning process* which takes place at determinate and critical periods in the child's development.[21]

That Mr. Newby maintains I never "bothered" to articulate my ideas is a consequence of the fact that Mr. Newby has troubled himself to read only very little of what I have written. That Mr. Newby misinterprets and misconstrues what he purports to *have* read can be most charitably explained by the supposition that Mr. Newby simply doesn't know how to read reasonably simple English prose. But to be candid, perhaps the most responsible interpretation of Mr. Newby's grotesque performance is that he has convinced himself that I am a "racist." Since I am a "racist" I must believe that "race is the basic reality of life," I must believe that "human nature is fixed and immune to the environment," and so on down the sorry list of characteristics he attributes to "racists." It would do Newby some credit—even after his disastrous essay into contempo-

20 D. T. Campbell and R. A. LeVine, *Propositions about Ethnocentrism from Social Science Theories* (Northwestern University, March, 1965, Mimeo), 79, 173.
21 A. J. Gregor, "The Biosocial Nature of Prejudice," *Genus*, XVIII (1962), 3–15.

rary intellectual history—to admit that I simply do not qualify as a "racist"—and he might try to read my published works with some small measure of objectivity and comprehension. But then he might have to surrender his conspiratorial view of contemporary American social history. He might even have to admit that he is painfully ignorant of the material to which he addresses himself, that he is innocent of analytic skills, that he has faulted the historian's craft, done violence to logic, and abused the language.

But Mr. Newby is far from finished. He provides a performance that must be among the most singular since the "McCarthy Era" and its characteristic sweeping vilifications, its guilt by association, its innuendoes and snide asides. Newby, by dint of his own original and characteristically systematic research, has discovered that I am not only America's most prominent "racist," I am part of an international Nazi-Fascist conspiracy. Let us follow Mr. Newby through the looking glass.

Newby's Assessment of My "Nazi-Fascist" Kinships

On page 125 Newby informs his reader that "the most striking fact about Gregor's racism is its admitted kinship with some of the ideas of fascist race theorists." It is not clear who "admitted" this kinship. Mr. Newby asserts simply that it is "admitted." Then he informs the reader darkly that the kinship is with "some" of the ideas of fascist race theories. Surely the charge is far too serious to leave half-articulated in the confusion of Mr. Newby's prose.

He tells his reader that in 1958 I published an article in *The European*, then adds gratuitously that *The European* is "the journal of British fascist leader Sir Oswald Mosley." That aside might appear to be of some obscure significance to Mr. Newby. He nowhere else mentions the editor of a journal to which I have contributed. Surely Mr. Newby is too honorable a man, too well versed in academic proprieties to want to insinuate that I, as an author, could be held responsible for the political views of the editor of a journal in which an article of mine appears! Surely such a tactic would be abhorrent to any person who has a sense of academic responsibility. Surely such a reference was a thoughtless slip on the part of the liberal and honorable Mr. Newby. But since he has inadvertently supplied this information, the record should be kept straight. I not only published *one* article in a journal edited by a self-identified fascist, I published *four*. But since Mr. Newby has made this an issue (and Mr. Newby is an honorable man), let me supply further damaging information. I have published *three* articles in *Studies on the Left,* the now defunct organ of the "New Left" (shades of Joe McCarthy!).[22] Moreover, I published *two* articles in *Science and Society* which identifies itself as an "independent" Marxist journal, but which knowledgeable people inform me is part of the "apparatus" of the Communist conspiracy.[23] I should think that Mr. Newby (who is an honorable man) would want to include this pertinent information in his objective account —which conforms, he tells us, to the canons of logic, right reason, history, and science. With this new information Mr. Newby can now compute that I am four parts Nazi-Fascist and five parts Communist. Now we have a *real* conspiracy going.

Unfortunately, it is not at all as romantic as that. I have long entertained the perverse conviction that in social criticism "radical" opinion performs a singularly salutary function. I have always felt, and somehow I vaguely impute the notion to John Stuart Mill, that the expression of radical and dissident opinion forces us to scrutinize our own commitments with fastidious care—and provides us with the occasion to test our convictions in the fire of controversy. And so I must admit that I have foolishly contributed to radical and dissident journals of both the "right" and the "left" in roughly equal measure. While I was acting as an "assistant editor" (in name more than in fact) for the notorious "racist" journal *Mankind Quarterly,* I was also an "editorial associate" of *Studies on the Left,* and on the book review staff of *Science and Society.* I even worked on the executive committee of that notorious "racist" organization that Mr. Newby has so shrewdly analyzed, while I was, at the same time, Regional Secretary for the Society for the Philosophical Study of Dialectical Materialism.

I am sure that Mr. Newby finds my views and my actions hopelessly antiquated. They rest upon notions now largely forsaken by the Mr. Newbys of this world. My actions evidence a quixotic conviction that social criticism flourishes only in an atmosphere which permits all views to be heard, however reprehensible we

22 A. J. Gregor, "Philosophy and the Young Karl Marx," *Studies on the Left,* II, 3 (1962), Gregor, "Erich Fromm and the Young Karl Marx," *Ibid.,* III, 1 (1962), Gregor, "Lenin on the Nature of Sensation," *Ibid.,* III, 2 (1963).

23 A. J. Gregor, "Black Nationalism: A Preliminary Assessment of Negro Radicalism," *Science and Society,* XXVII (Fall, 1963), 415–32; Gregor "Marx, Feuerbach and the Reform of the Hegelian Dialectic," *Ibid.,* XXIX (Winter, 1965), 66–80.

may personally find them to be. I might even venture to say something like, "I may find what they say abhorrent, but I will defend their right to say it," but I'm sure that Mr. Newby would find this tedious.

But there is something more in Newby's discovery of my part in the "international fascist plot." I did, as a matter of fact, address myself to the evolution of racial theories in National Socialist Germany. And I did indicate that within Germany, during the National Socialist period, theorists (whether they were "Nazi theorists" or not I do not, and I'm sure Mr. Newby does not, know—I referred to them without the adjectival qualifier which is evidently so important to him) developed racial conceptions at variance with official National Socialist policy. I cited the theorists involved. They included Egon von Eickstedt and Hans Weinert. Both had, by that time, been cleared by the Allied occupation forces and the German "de-Nazification" tribunals. They had, in fact, during the Hitler period, developed a more humane and intellectually satisfying conception of race (and their views *did* influence some party theoreticians). None of these men attempted to justify the German National Socialist policy of mass extermination. Mr. Newby (who is an honorable man), however, felt that he had to specifically remind me in a footnote that during this period "the Nazis liquidated millions of Jews and Eastern Europeans in the process of implementing their racial views." He must think I didn't know this obscure fact. In doing this he insinuated that my discussion of theoretical developments in Hitler's Germany was a justification of "Nazi race theory" and "Nazi race theory" was a vindication for the mass extermination of innocents: *ergo,* Gregor is seeking to justify the mass immolation of innocents. No wonder Mr. Newby ventures on the curious judgment that I am "immune to emotion or humaneness" (p. 122). One wonders how Mr. Newby can remain so urbane in the face of my evident bestiality. Perhaps it is because Mr. Newby (who is an honorable man) renders these stupidities and slanders with something of a bad conscience. That is, of course, only a speculative possibility. Anyone who can so distort, misinterpret, and misrepresent the thought of an academic colleague is a rare creature indeed, a creature that, in himself, constitutes a unit class to which no known psychological regularities apply.

If Newby wished to familiarize himself with my views on National Socialism he could have solicited a typescript copy of my book, *Contemporary Radical Ideologies,* which, while it was not yet in print, would have been made available to him while he was doing his "research" into my social and political thought.

But we are not finished with Mr. Newby's discoveries. On page 126 he quotes *in extenso* from an article published by me in 1958, and he informs his reader that "the similarity between [Gregor's] own views and those he previously attributed to the Nazis is remarkable." The quote reads:

"Race" in any significant natural sense can only signify a given breeding community (a mendelian population) which displays a difference of relative frequency for specific variables. . . . Historic continuity for such a race can be established only tentatively by demonstrating the temporal persistence of an empirically ascertained genetic balance. This must always be qualified by the knowledge that balanced polymorphism is a dynamic constant, that relative frequencies can be altered by a differential birth rate, an accelerated mutation rate, successive changes in breeding practices . . . eugenic or dysgenic practices in the environment.

At this point I ask the reader to turn to page 230 where Newby characterizes how the "equalitarians" conceive "race": "To equalitarians 'race' is not nearly so powerful or static a force. It is instead a 'process, a series of temporary genetic conditions always in process of change,' and races are best defined as 'populations which differ in the relative commonness of some of their genes,' or as 'genetically isolated mating groups with distinctive gene frequencies.'" What I suggest to the reader is that there obtains a "remarkable similarity" between my views on what constitutes a "race" and those of "equalitarians." Mr. Newby has found me out. I am a crypto-equalitarian. I am a prominent "racist" who is four parts "Nazi-Fascist," five parts "Communist," and who harbors "equalitarian" views. But more important still, Mr. Newby has discovered that my views share a "remarkable similarity" with those of "Nazis" and it is evident that my views share an equally "remarkable similarity" with those of "equalitarians." We can, therefore, employing the crippled logic Mr. Newby recommends, conclude that "Nazi-Fascist" views are "remarkably similar" to "equalitarian" views!

Surely the reader will recognize that something is wrong here. What is wrong is Mr. Newby. In the course of exposition he employs every conceivable informal logical fallacy: faulty, hasty, and unrepresentative generalization; the material fallacies of composition and division; indiscriminate use of nonexclusive classifications as though they were exclusive; the exploitation of emotive and ritual language, *ad populum* appeals, personal attacks, special pleading, wishful thinking, and bias. Only rarely does he attain the level of formal fallacy. Mr. Newby is too unsophisticated for even that.

His entire discussion concerning the "remarkable similarity" between my "views" and those of "Nazis" turns on the fallacy of division: that is to say he assumes that what might be attributable to a complex whole taken together is necessarily true of its constituent parts taken separately. Thus we are all prepared to grant that National Socialism is "bad," but does that entail that *every* idea entertained by National Socialists is equally "bad"? If "Nazi" theorists employed statistics in research and I use statistics in mine —does this establish a "remarkable similarity" between us?

The concept of race which Newby finds in my discussion of racial theory as it developed in National Socialist Germany, which he finds "remarkably similar" to my own, and which is evidently "remarkably similar" to that entertained by "equalitarians," is recognized, by anyone even minimally apprized of what is going on in the study of population genetics, as the "populationist" conception of race. It was this "populationist" conception of race which von Eickstedt and Weinert began to insist upon even during the period of National Socialist dominance. This conception of race was then largely, and is now generally, accepted by the international scientific community as more adequate to the purposes of analysis and theory construction in population genetics. Only if one suffers gross intellectual impairments and is possessed of invincible ignorance can such a conception be conceived a "Nazi" product any more than the principles which govern our space research (largely developed in Hitler's Germany) are "Nazi" products. The "populationist" conception of race was developed by scientists in a variety of political environments. What all this means is that scientific conceptions must be judged on their intrinsic merits and not because some fragments of these ideas may or may not appear in complex and often confused ideas trumpeted by political ideologists. Only commitment to the informal fallacy of division permits Newby to discover in my work a "kinship" with "Nazi" ideas. But responsible people attempt to avoid fallacy, for fallacy lends itself to specious argument only by exacting a terrible toll. It drives one's argument from one absurdity to another—and makes one the object of public ridicule.

Newby's paranoid preoccupation with conspiracies leads him to find "connections" between "racism," "fascism," "segregation," and "ultraconservatism." He finds such "connections" readily since he

makes no meaningful nor consistent distinctions anywhere. Where
no distinctions are made, all things are one. Where all things are
one, not much can be said. Newby does not understand this. So he
talks on and on for 234 pages saying nothing of substance. He is
truly a remarkable man. Were he intelligent, he would be dangerous.

Newby's Assessment of My Work as "Segregationist"

If Newby's interpretation of my work is grotesque, and his
slanders gratuitous and uncivil, his assessment of my published
writings on the circumstances which surround Negro education in
our troubled land is particularly vicious. No simple treatment of
his sustained stupidities is sufficient to dispel the suggestion of
malevolence he attributes to me. The term "segregation" is so emotionally charged—like all the terms he employs with such irresponsibility—that to so identify an academician is to seriously impair his
credibility. And this is pernicious. For our society demands a free
and frank discussion of the issues that today divide it. The dismissal of complex arguments by identifying them as "racist" and
"segregationist" is of sufficient disservice to our community to
justify its condemnation. To conceal the nakedness of such a dismissal with the fig-leaf of counterfeit argument is reprehensible.
In order to offset the impact of Newby's caricature of my argued
convictions I have herewith appended an Appendix that provides a
contemporary restatement of the convictions I first presented to my
academic colleagues five years ago. I leave it to the reader to judge
whether such convictions qualify me as a "racist" and a "segregationist." I leave it to the reader to judge whether Newby's searching
criticisms have defeated my contentions—my reasoned plea that
current policy may well do serious disservice to Negro youth, youth
upon whom so much of the Negro's future depends.

Since 1963 I have argued my case before professional audiences
either in communications to assemblies of my peers or in professional journals of acknowledged international reputation. In 1964
I published a communication upon the issue of school integration
in the professional journal *Psychiatry*.[24] Six months later Dr.
Florence N. Holland published counterarguments.[25] This year the
editor of *Pediatrics Digest* solicited an article from me on the same

[24] C. P. Armstrong and A. J. Gregor, "Integrated Schools and Negro Character
Development," *Psychiatry*, XXVII (February, 1964), 69–72.

[25] F. N. Holland, "A Comment on the Segregated Learning Situation as an In-
sulating Device for the Negro Child," *Psychiatry*, XXVII (August, 1964).

subject. The fact is that there is some evidence that the strength of my argument (for which I am only in part responsible) is being more and more frequently and independently recognized.

Newby makes no mention of my article published in *Psychiatry,* a journal whose internal editorial board includes some of the nation's foremost psychiatrists. This is not unusual. His research scholarship is singularly deficient. It appears that Newby, a professional historian, simply does not know how to conduct a literature search.

Be that as it may, there is something singularly presumptuous about Newby's "criticism" of my work. For one thing he has discovered in my work some singular "errors." They include, for example, the fact that I simply do not understand that the Negro "child almost certainly comes from an environment in which *de facto* segregation and race discrimination are the rule, not the exception," and that "the effects of this environment cannot be put on and taken off like a cloak when the child enters or leaves an 'integrated' classroom." Furthermore, I have failed to understand that "the school is not isolated from society; on the contrary, it reflects the society it serves" (p. 127).

Newby has discovered that I simply do not know (1) that a Negro child comes from an environment in which *de facto* segregation and race discrimination are the rule, not the exception; (2) that the effects of this environment cannot be put on and taken off like a cloak (I must have said somewhere that "the effects of this environment, which I do not recognize, can be put on and taken off like a cloak." I just don't recall having said it.); (3) that the school is not isolated from society, but rather "reflects" it.

This is truly devastating criticism. How stupid I am. And how incompetent. How pleased I am that there is a Newby to inform me concerning these obscure and complex matters. I must confess that I really don't know how these things escaped me. But there is one consolation. All the professional psychiatrists and pediatricians and child psychologists who had to pass on the merits of my argument before they afforded it space in some of the nation's foremost professional journals failed to see the error of my account. Fortunately there was Newby.

I am now in the process of revising my article for *Pediatrics Digest* —which the internal editorial board characterized as "excellent" —to better accord with Newby's devastating criticisms. I will add several sentences which will read: "Negro children certainly come from environments which are *de facto* segregated and in which race discrimination is the rule and not the exception." "The effects of this environment cannot be taken off like a cloak." "The school is not isolated from society—rather it reflects it." This will certainly elevate the intellectual quality and analytic and substantive merit of my work. If only Newby would publish in professional social science journals—how much light he would shed.

Newby must have conducted a great deal of original research to discover these facts. One day he must teach me something about research design, data collection, processing, and interpretation. We have among us, the Newton of the social sciences.

But Newby favors me with more of such criticisms. He sheds considerable light on my humble efforts. He tells his reader that "Gregor did not merely dispute the testimony in the Brown cases; he *asserted positively* that the available data indicate that Negro children are psychologically better off in segregated schools" (my emphasis). After attributing to me this *positive assertion,* he somewhat dulls the edge of his analysis by *quoting* my relatively precise statement: ". . . where social science material is available, it *tends* to support racial separation in the schools, at least through adolescence . . ." (p. 127).

Now I must admit to being a trifle confused. Do I "assert positively" or do I offer a *tendency* statement qualified by a recognition of the paucity of probative evidence? It would seem that two different truth claims are being advanced. One Newby *attributes* to me. That one is a *positive assertion.* The evidence condition for such a claim is demanding. Then he *quotes* me as making a *tendency statement,* qualified by an admission of a lack of probative evidence. The evidence for such a claim is relatively modest. My arguments were directed toward professional audiences. My assumption was that qualified, responsible men would read them. I had no idea Newby would read them. Had I anticipated that contingency I would have added a footnote to the effect that "A tendency statement is *not* a positive assertion and Newby should *not* so construe it—for to do so would make him appear foolish, particularly if he is going to quote my tendency statement immediately after he has attributed to me the issuance of a positive assertion."

I suggest Mr. Newby pen in that footnote in the copy of my article which he presumably has.

But this is not all. He makes one final discovery which should net him some special award. He has discovered "Gregor's real view" about American race relations. What "Gregor" is *really* arguing is that Negroes should "accept their assigned place in American society and halt their efforts 'to identify with the upper caste'. . . ." This, he sagely informs his innocent reader, is Gregor's "real solution to the integration dispute" (p. 129).

Surely this is a discovery that is almost as monumental as his devastating criticism of my substantive work. Newby has discovered my "real view." It escaped the attention of an archcritic whose work Newby (who is an authority on "close reasoning") tells us was "closely reasoned." No one who has criticized my argument noticed my "real view." No one else has charged me with such views. Only Newby, with his critical intelligence, teased them out.

The reader is advised (1) to search out and read my original article and (2) read my restatement in the Appendix to this inquiry. In my original article I was arguing that "it is difficult to assess with scientific precision the weight of each of the multitude of variables which negatively affect the personality" and then I went on to indicate that among the Guatemalan Indians the same variables that negatively affect the Negro personality apparently have on the Indians no similar deleterious result. From that I then concluded that "race relations involve . . . ill-defined variables, each apparently of substantially different, but as yet undetermined weight." [26] My reference to the differential effects among the Guatemalan Indians of the variables alluded to was made in order to indicate that we have no clear evidence that would assign specific causal efficacy to any one or any combination of them. The initial conditions surrounding the impact of such ill-defined variables have obvious determinate influence on their effects. If we are to speak of the effects of any one or combination of them we need far more probative evidence. How Newby came to interpret this to mean that what I was advocating was that Negroes should "keep their place" is completely mystifying. But since we know something of the caliber of Newby's mind by this time, it would perhaps be more generous to let the reader provide his own explanation for this outrageous imputation.

One final thing provides the last bit of evidence of Newby's

[26] A. J. Gregor, "The Law, Social Science, and School Segregation: An Assessment," *Western Reserve Law Review*, XIV (September, 1963), 634f.

tendentious malice. His parting shot, appended as a footnote on page 129, informs his reader that Ovid Lewis' criticism of my article of 1963 maintained that I had "quoted [authorities] out of context." Mr. Newby tells his audience that this is "most damaging." What he does *not* communicate to his readers is that I replied to Lewis' charges and, I think, effectively refuted them.[27]

Newby has done his best to misrepresent my work, caricature my analyses, falsify my explicit statements, reflect upon my competence, impute moral frailty and conspiratorial intent to me, identify me as inhumane, a calculating deceiver, an oppressor of Negroes, an advocate of genocide, and the heir of all the human vices and some that Newby has himself invented.

But to have said that Mr. Newby has done his best at anything is, itself, to do violence to the language. Newby is so ignorant of the facts (for example, he says that I am the only "prominent scientific racist" born after 1914 and that Robert Kuttner, another "prominent racist," was born between 1888 and 1914 [p. 122]. Professor Kuttner's mother will be much surprised to hear that—because she was eight years old in 1914. And Professor Kuttner is much disturbed—because he has been, erroneously apparently, celebrating his birthday as March 10, 1927, for so many years.)—so ignorant of the very language of behavioral science (for example, in order to charge Professor R. T. Osborne with "racist" convictions, Mr. Newby insists that Professor Osborne's Savannah study, since it was entitled a "genetic longitudinal approach" implies that Professor Osborne was studying "genetics" [p. 86]. Any first-year student in psychology could have informed Mr. Newby that "genetic" so employed means "developmental" and not "hereditary.")—so selective in his citations (he never cites any material that might in any way mitigate his malicious and slanderous judgments)—and so bizarre in his treatment of men and ideas, that to apply a term of approbation to anything that issued from the troubled bog of Newby's mind is to do more than considerable violence to the common language.

The limitations of space preclude a detailed treatment of the remainder of Newby's catalogue of abuses. His arguments are model instances of impaired reasoning. But something should be said of Newby's general disservice to the community which has so long suffered him. His arguments are signal instances of counterfeit and vexed reasoning. He tells us, for instance, on page 7 that there

[27] A. J. Gregor, "The Law and Social Science: A Reply to O. C. Lewis," *Western Reserve Law Review*, XV (December, 1963).

"seems to have been no instance" of a segregationist scientist or an equalitarian scientist ever changing his views as a consequence of research in the area of human relations, human biology and human social and individual psychology. Having made this pontification he immediately proceeds to defeat it with counterinstances. On page 77 he tells us that Carl C. Brigham, who had come to "racist" conclusions on the basis of his study of tests administered to Army inductees in World War I, "had second thoughts about the matter and repudiated his earlier findings. . . ." Was Brigham's change the result of further inquiry or a reassessment of his earlier analysis —or perhaps the result of a lobotomy—or perhaps his change from "racist" to "equalitarian" persuasion was suborned? But we really don't know what Mr. Newby intends by half the things he says. Which, of course, still gives us considerable advantage over Mr. Newby. He *never* seems to know what he intends to say.

Has Mr. Newby thoroughly canvassed the relevant literature (and just imagine what kind of scholarship *that* would entail—we know the kind upon which he trafficks) for evidence that would warrant that judgment? If such a judgment is true, what does it imply? Does it mean that systematic and careful research can neither influence our judgments nor help us to resolve human problems? If so, to what must we have recourse? Violence perhaps? Or the issuance of bromides? Declamations of pious intentions? Emotional appeals? Propaganda? Mr. Newby, in fact, informs us that the world is divided into "scientific racists" and their "critics." Their differences, he tells us, are not subject to factual resolution. They are differences in "rival value systems." Newby has thus made a discovery regularly made by college freshmen. Like them he is systematically anti-intellectualist and incorrigibly obscurantist. Facts can't conceivably assist in the resolution of issues. What we need is "democracy, justice, and human decency" (p. xi). If there is a dispute between two authorities and one suggests that racial congregation in the schools, now and with respect to children within a reasonably determinate age range, may have negative personality effects on Negro children, and the other disagrees—the only way to resolve their differences is to appeal to "democracy, justice and human decency." How very profound! How curious of men never to have hit upon that solution before. Not only does Newby reveal himself as the Newton of social science, he is a master of metaethics, the Cagliostro of problem resolution, the Rasputin of race relations.

What Newby has done is to have reduced the discussion to so

puerile a level, to have so impoverished the factual and moral dimensions of the issues that face our nation, that one can only weep.

His book continues in this fashion for 234 doleful pages. That he found an academic publisher to publish this collection of half-truths, tortured reasonings, tormented logic, brazen falsehoods, unrelieved stupidities, and gross and malicious slanders, is astonishing. The book is a calculated affront to the academic community, a masochistic display of one man's lack of professional competence and integrity. That the living and working research workers, scholars and academicians so grievously and maliciously maligned by Mr. Newby were not given the opportunity of reviewing his work *before* publication has rendered this embittered reply a necessity. For the necessity of this reply—for its exacerbated tone—for the very existence of Mr. Newby's book—the Louisiana State University Press must bear ultimate responsibility.

Appendix

Social Science Research
and the Education of the Minority-Group Child *

A. JAMES GREGOR

Now that the demand by Negro parents that their children be accorded an education suitable to their aptitudes and special circumstances has descended to the level of riot, there has been some searching reappraisal of the *facts* determining optimum conditions for the education of the minority-group child on the part of the social science community—and it has become evident that that community has been at least partially remiss in its obligations, not only to the disciplines which constitute the foci of its concerns, but to those minority-group children its efforts had been mobilized to succor. Moral profusions are no substitute for a competent assessment of relevant facts. Knowledge claims tendered by social scientists from a variety of disciplines have played a critical role in strategic policy decisions which have significantly influenced the course of race relations in our country. Here our attention will be restricted to an assessment of the influence of social science findings in the formulation of educational policies directly affecting the conditions surrounding the instruction of minority-group children.

Obviously any discussion which attempts to confine itself to the prescribed length of this appendix must necessarily be schematic. Almost all of its constituent propositions would have to be qualified in significant ways, but an author is faced, more likely than not, with the option of restricting his discourse to propositions which are true (in a rigorous sense of truth) or asserting statements which are relevant to broad and vexedly ill-defined but nonetheless urgent

* The term "minority-group child" can be understood throughout to refer to Negro children. The more generic term is employed simply because some of the evidence reported includes results obtained from assessments which included other nonwhite minority groups. Since Negroes constitute over 92 per cent of America's nonwhite population, the results obtained for nonwhite minority groups have as their essential reference the Negro minority. In effect, "minority-group child" can be read as "Negro child" throughout without seriously impairing the truth status of any proposition which has "minority-group child" as its subject.

human problems. Happy are the circumstances in which an author can restrict himself to the utterance of truths which meet both the rigorous tests of validity and the criterion of relevance to broad issues as well.

With such considerations in mind, it will be here suggested that in the past a host of social science propositions subsequently employed in policy-making deliberations meet *neither* the test of rigorous truth *nor* the criterion of relevance with respect to the issues to which they were putatively addressed. The consequence might well be the impairment of the life circumstances and future prospects of American Negroes. No appeal to emotive and persuasive terms like "justice," "freedom," and "equality" can substitute for a substantive inquiry into possible effects.

The most signal illustrative instance of the use of social science testimony in policy making as well as the seeming issuance of knowledge claims purportedly true which were, in fact, neither true in any rigorous sense of the word, nor relevant to the issue at hand, is that exemplified in the deliberations which preceded the Supreme Court decision in the school segregation cases of May, 1954, which inaugurated what is now termed the "revolution in civil rights" in the United States.[1] Some jurists have argued that the Court's decision at that time was based specifically on "the findings of modern authority," and that that "modern authority" was social science. Philip Kurland has argued that the Court's decision to declare the maintenance of separate but equal educational facilities for white and Negro children unconstitutional was based upon the "factual propositions" of contemporary social science—propositions which were "irrefutable" and conclusively relevant to the issue at hand.[2]

Somehow in the lengthy proceedings which were antecedent upon the Court's decision, the impression was conveyed to the Justices and to the interested public that either the written appendix to the appellants' brief, signed by a number of eminent

[1] It is to be clearly understood that the subsequent discussion does not address itself to the constitutional issues involved in *Brown vs. the Board of Education*. The decision may have been made exclusively on the grounds of constitutionality or unconstitutionality of the suspect legislation. (This would be the judgment of jurists of repute like E. Cahn [cf. his "Jurisprudence," *New York University Law Review*, XXX (1955)]). It seems impossible at this point in history to determine the specific grounds employed by the Court for the reversal of the "separate but equal" legislation.

[2] Cf. P. Kurland, "The Legal Background of the School Segregation Cases," in K. B. Clark, *Prejudice and Your Child* (2nd ed.; Boston, 1963), 143–55.

social scientists,[3] or the oral testimony of Kenneth Clark,[4] certified the truth of the proposition: "Segregation of white and colored children in public school has a detrimental effect upon the colored children." Responsibility understood this proposition means that colored children taken as a determinate population (defined presumably by the possession of certain criterial attributes) within a specified or specifiable age range suffer some kind of determinate or determinable physical or psychical injury *solely* as a consequence of being housed in separate facilities during instruction.

It is sometimes suggested that one cannot distinguish the issue of racial separation in the schools from the total and complex pattern of social segregation and discrimination. As a factual and interpretive matter this is perfectly true. But right reason demands that in recognizing this factual and interpretive matter one does not commit a counterpart fallacy. To recognize that "segregation," understood to refer to an entire class of complicated interpersonal and institutional patterns, has negative impact on the personality and performance of Negroes does not warrant the conviction that every instance of interpersonal and institutional behavior (under all and every circumstance), which makes up the complex, incompletely specified, and tangled collection of behaviors and institutions that make up "segregation," is all equally counterproductive. If the Court addressed itself to the issue of whether separate schooling, *per se,* might negatively affect the hearts and minds of Negro children the Court was obliged to concern itself specifically with that issue and not escape into the general recognition that segregation, prejudice, and discrimination are "bad."

The fact is that at the time of the Court's decision there was no probative evidence and little presumptive evidence to support the contention that separate schooling, maintained in fact or by law, in and of itself produced determinate or determinable injury to minority-group children. Furthermore, the social scientists directly involved in the proceedings recognized this to have been the case.

The logic of the case before the Supreme Court in 1954 required, as Robert Redfield early appreciated, that "segregated education" (understood to mean the provision of separate but equal educational

3 Appendix to Appellants' briefs, *Brown vs. Board of Education of Topeka,* 347 U.S. 483 (1954).

4 Cf. J. L. Fletcher, *The Segregation Case and the Supreme Court* (Boston, 1958), 54–58.

facilities for groups of children individually characterized as "white" or "colored") constituted, in fact, *unequal treatment resulting in injury.*" Such treatment (the occupancy of separate but equal facilities during their hours of instruction) must be understood to result in "injuries to the personality, which like injuries to the body, are recognized in science and medicine as definite and serious." [5]

In effect, what was required for truth and relevance was hard evidence that one variable, "school segregation," out of a complex tangle of variables, effected a serious and determinate deleterious influence upon the "personality" of the minority-group child.[6] In fact little, if any, evidence was available at that time, and hardly more is available now that would lend substantive support to such a claim. Kenneth Clark, one of the principal witnesses for the appellants in *Brown v. the Board* had maintained, even before the Court's decision, that "unfortunately for scientific accuracy and adequacy, thoroughly satisfactory methods of determining the effects of prejudice and discrimination on health of personality have not yet been devised." [7] More specifically, when the attorneys for the appellants realized what was required and approached Clark for more explicit judgments, i.e., "to present evidence showing that public school segregation, in itself, damaged the personalities of Negro children," Clark "pointed out to them that the available studies had so far not isolated this single variable from the total social complexity of racial prejudice, discrimination, and segregation. It was therefore not possible to testify on the psychologically damaging effects of segregated schools alone." [8] Whatever the expert testimony in *Brown v. the Board* accomplished, it did not establish with any credibility the claim that attendance in segregated schools, *per se,* was injurious to minority-group children.

That this was somehow conveyed to the Court is indicated, it would seem, by the fact that the Court's judgment was couched in

[5] R. Redfield, *The Papers of Robert Redfield,* ed. H. P. Redfield, II (Chicago, 1963), 165, 167.

[6] The Court expressed this in the following fashion: "To separate them [the colored children] from others of similar age and qualifications solely because of their race generates a feeling of inferiority as to their status in the community that may affect their hearts and minds in a way unlikely ever to be undone."

[7] K. B. Clark, "Effect of Prejudice and Discrimination on Personality Development," in H. L. Witmer and R. Kotinsky (eds.), *Personality in the Making* (New York, 1952), 139.

[8] Clark, *Prejudice and Your Child,* 193.

the form of a hypothetical: school segregation, *per se, may* "affect the hearts and minds" of minority-group children in such a way "unlikely ever to be undone."

But whatever the circumstances governing the now historic decision of the Court—we are now required by common humanity and a concern for our fellow man to determine whether separate schooling for minority-group children does, *in fact* and *in itself,* produce negative personality and performance results. This question is of crucial significance in our own time. Some people have interpreted the Court's ruling as interdicting *any* discrimination solely on the basis of racial criteria.[9] And yet programs of affirmative integration are predicated on such discrimination. The distinction which urges itself upon us is the distinction between *beneficial* and *detrimental* results that attend school assignment determined by racial criteria. The rationale supporting affirmative school integration can only be warranted by *factual evidence* that Negro and/ or white children *benefit* by attending schools with a racially heterogeneous population. The proscription against all-Negro schools can only be warranted by *factual evidence* that the personality and performance of Negro children are *impaired* by attendance in such an institution.

Current desegregation policies are based on the assumption that the proposition, "School segregation, in and of itself, negatively affects the personality development of minority-group children," is certified fact. The policy of affirmative integration is based on an illicit inference drawn from the above which tenders a claim of the following sort: "The housing of minority-group children in educational institutions in which the incidence of white children does not fall below a critical if variable level, produces positive results in the personality development and performance of minority-group children."

Such an inference is obviously faulty. Even if it were the case that segregated instruction, in and of itself, was detrimental to the personality development and performance of minority-group children, it would not necessarily follow that "integration" (understood to refer only to the numerical ratio of Negroes to whites in any given school situation) would prove less detrimental or benign, much less beneficial. Nothing follows from the contention that

[9] Cf. A. Rose, *De Facto School Segregation* (New York, 1964), 5, 56n2.

segregated schooling, *per se,* is injurious to the minority-group child except that segregated schooling, *per se,* is injurious to the minority-group child. Should one wish to argue that integrated schooling is not injurious or that it is, in fact, beneficial, a number of auxiliary premises would have to be introduced which would have to independently meet tests of consistency and truth.

However, no conclusive answer to the first question has been forthcoming. In the effort to provide convincing answers social scientists have implicitly or explicitly introduced auxiliary premises to the effect that a measure of the psychic injury suffered by minority-group children in segregated learning situations is given in the degree of academic deficiencies that all but universally characterize their performance. In effect, it is argued that the "detrimental effect" and/or "injury" referred to in the discussions preceding the decision by the Supreme Court in 1954, and which remain current in our own time, obliquely refers to reduced academic proficiency. Segregated schooling is understood to exercise a depressing effect on the aspirations and academic performance of minority-group children. Impaired academic efficiency is generally understood to provide a measure of the injury suffered by minority-group children as a consequence of segregated instruction. The entire discussion thus ultimately addresses itself to the fact, universally acknowledged, that the magnitude of Negro intellectual performance deficiency throughout the United States, irrespective of geographic locale, measures approximately fifteen points on standardized IQ tests (such test results serve as effective predictors for academic achievement). The issue then becomes: Can the fact of Negro performance deficiencies on standardized tests of intellectual potential and academic accomplishment be attributed exclusively or in part to the retarding effect of instruction in a racially homogeneous environment?

The effort to identify specific factors in the life circumstances of minority-group children which might be reasonably conceived as having retarding effect on school performance and the learning rate has produced an abundant literature. Pasamanick, Knobloch, and their associates, for example, have related cumulative performance deficits to depressing effects of avitaminosis and nutritional deficiencies that characterized the pre- and perinatal circumstances of minority-group children.[10] Other authors have found positive cor-

10 B. Pasamanick, "A Comparative Study of the Behavioral Development of Negro Infants," *Journal of Genetic Psychology,* LXIX (1946), 3–44; B. Pasa-

relations between group deficiencies and the lack of family intactness, deprived home environment, and the number of siblings.[11] These are disabilities and features which attend low socioeconomic status in the United States but they are singularly more emphatic in the case of the Negro. The nonwhite family median income in the United States is approximately 53 per cent that of white income, with the bulk of the minority-group children attending public schools coming from families enjoying only marginal economic viability. Furthermore, only a minority of Negro children who reach eighteen years of age have lived all their lives with both parents. In the lowest economic class 43.9 per cent of Negro children come from homes from which the father is absent (compared to 15.4 per cent for white children from the same socio-economic class).[12] In effect, Deutsch suggests, when we record deficient academic performance for Negro children "what we might be tapping is the cumulative effect of fatherless years." [13]

The average minority-group child is lodged in a network of pathogenic influences. One of every four live births, for example, among Negroes in the United States is illegitimate. Since 1930 the Negro unemployment rate has remained consistently twice that for whites. The majority of Negro children today receive public assistance under community social security and benefits program (56 per cent of nonwhite children received some such assistance at one time or another as against 8 per cent of white children). Forty-four per cent of Negro families are matriarchal, in effect lacking an adult male model requisite to effective primary socialization of children. The Negro home characteristically offers less cultural stimuli, is less disposed to provide an adequate diet for its members, is more frequently without a male head, is more overcrowded, is

---

manick and H. Knobloch, "Further Observations on the Behavioral Development of Negro Children," *Journal of Genetic Psychology,* LXXXIII (1953), 137–57; I. N. Kugelmass, L. E. Poull, and E. L. Samuel, "Nutritional Improvement in Child Mentality," *New York State Journal of Medicine,* XLIV (1944), 2604–05.

[11] M. Deutsch, "Minority Group and Class Status as Related to Social and Personality Factors in Scholastic Achievement," II, *Society for Applied Anthropology Monographs* (1960).

[12] D. P. Moynihan, "The Negro Family: The Case for National Action," in L. Rainwater and W. L. Yancey, *The Moynihan Report and the Politics of Controversy* (Cambridge, Mass., 1967), 82.

[13] M. Deutsch and B. Brown, "Social Influences in Negro-White Intelligence Differences," *Social Issues* (April, 1964), 31. This is disputed by A. B. Wilson, *Educational Consequences of Segregation in a California Community* (University of California, Berkeley: Survey Research Center, December, 1966, mimeo.).

economically less viable, and is more regularly open to pervasive criminal and morally injurious influences than its white family counterpart.

Should this partial list of factors be conceived as part of the explanation of Negro academic deficiencies one major fact becomes manifestly evident. These factors are totally unrelated to the instructional situation. They obtain whether the minority-group child attends an all-Negro or an integrated institution. The very logic of this kind of account would lead one to conclude that the minority-group child would display emphatic academic deficiencies in *either* a racially homogeneous *or* a racially heterogeneous school situation. It is an acknowledged fact that minority-group children, unless they are arduously selected on the basis of those attributes to be tested, never perform at the academic level of white children irrespective of the racial or class composition of the schools they attend.[14] There is a tendency for the mean performance level on tests of verbal and nonverbal abilities to decrease (all things being equal) in direct proportion to the increased incidence of non-whites in any given school. The inverse relationship between overall poor performance in any particular school area and the high incidence of minority-group children in that area remains constant irrespective of geographic locale, irrespective of segregated or congregated school circumstances, appearing in almost the same magnitude in the Mideast, the Northeast as well as the Southeast and the Southwest.[15]

Within the context of more adequate assessments made throughout the nation, the reported improvement of Negro performance in desegregated facilities can most responsibly be attributed to compensatory education, improved teaching, enriched curriculae, and more adequate instructional plant. There has been an historic tendency for schools occupied by minority-group children and lower class white children to enjoy lower per pupil expenditures, to be staffed by qualitatively and quantitatively inferior teaching staffs, and to be characterized by deficient plant. A significant measure of the incremental improvement in the performance of the minor-

14 Cf. O. Klineberg, "Negro-White Differences in Intelligence Test Performance: A New Look at an Old Problem," *American Psychologist*, XVIII (April, 1963), 200f.

15 G. R. Burket, *Project Talent: Identification, Development and Utilization of Human Talents. Selected Pupil and School Characteristics in Relation to Percentage of Negroes in School Enrollment.* (Washington, D.C., 1963), 4.

ity-group child attributed to racial congregation in the schools can be responsibly ascribed to the amelioration of these deficiencies which, in our own time and for all intents and purposes according to the Coleman report of the U.S. Office of Education, no longer exist. Some increment might be the consequence, of course, of the nonwhite child's association with white peers possessed of more sophisticated verbal skills and higher motivation brought from enriched home environments.

Other than such peripheral influences, however, there is little substantive evidence[16] that the mere congregation of white and nonwhite children in the same institutional environment (once controls have been effectively employed to account for equality of plant and instructional staff) conduces, in general, to a significant increment in academic performance on the part of minority-group children. Experiments calculated to isolate the specific impact of segregated (*de jure* or *de facto*) as distinct from congregated education have been conducted since at least 1932. M. R. Crowley in 1932, M. D. Gregg in 1938, and R. W. Pugh in 1943 conducted inquiries which attempted to provide probative data in this regard. Pugh summarized the results with the following conclusions: "There is no statistically significant difference in the academic achievements of Negro students in the two types of schools [segregated and congregated]" once extraneous variables were at least partially controlled.[17] In 1954 Ferguson and Plaut reported results from eleven biracial schools in northern and western states that reveal essentially the same performance deficiencies for minority-group children found in all-Negro southern schools.[18] In 1963 the

16 Any qualitative verbal response of teachers and administrators reporting "significant gains" for both white and nonwhite children through congregation is obviously suspect. One would hardly expect a teacher or an administrator to impugn his own efforts by indicating that, no matter what the circumstances, he was unable to bring enrichment to the lives of his charges. For this reason, little serious attention is here paid to survey reports like H. W. Wey's "Desegregation—It Works," *Phi Delta Kappan*, May, 1964, and H. W. Wey and J. Corey, *Action Patterns in School Desegregation* (Bloomington, 1959).

17 R. W. Pugh, "A Comparative Study of the Adjustment of Negro Students in Mixed and Separate High Schools," *Journal of Negro Education*, XII (Fall, 1943), 608. Cf. M. R. Crowley, "Cincinnati's Experiment in Negro Education: A Comparative Study of the Segregated and Mixed School," *Journal of Negro Education*, I (April, 1932), 25–33; H. D. Gregg, "Non-Academic and Academic Interests of Negro High School Students in Mixed and Separate Schools," *Journal of Negro Education*, VII (January, 1938), 41–47.

18 H. A. Ferguson and R. L. Plaut, "Talent: To Develop or to Lose," *Educational Record*, XXXV (April, 1954), 137–40.

results obtained by testing sixth-grade students in (1) white, (2) congregated and (3) all-Negro schools in Chicago indicated that the overall performance of the children in congregated schools was, for all intents and purposes, the mean of the combined scores of white children and minority-group children. The mean performance of children in the integrated school was, in fact, slightly lower than the mean of the combined scores of minority-group and white children undergoing instruction separately. If congregating the two groups had accomplished anything, it had somewhat lowered the expected overall performance level.[19] In instances where congregation was reported to have had initial beneficial or benign effects (as in Washington, D.C.[20]) the subsequent flight of whites from the core city has resegregated the public schools[21] and made confirmation of the reported improvements impossible.

Whatever evidence is available indicates that a biracial school environment, in and of itself, cannot be expected to significantly alter the learning rate and performance level of minority-group children. Negro children throughout the United States continue to perform significantly below national norms, irrespective of the racial composition of the schools they attend. Anyone moderately apprized of the complexity of problems that beset the nonwhite child could hardly have expected anything else. The factors most generally accorded causal significance, economic deprivation, impaired motivation, family instability, and the attendant negative self-image these are calculated to engender, exercise their influence outside the school. Marked deficiencies in performance skills and motivation have been reported, in fact, among Negro children

19 P. M. Hauser, *Report to the Board of Education, City of Chicago, by the Advisory Panel on Integration of the Public Schools,* March 31, 1964 (mimeo).

20 Cf. C. F. Hansen, *Miracle of Social Adjustment: Desegregation in the Washington, D.C. Schools* (New York, 1957); Hansen, *Addendum: A Five-Year Report on Desegregation in the Washington, D.C., Schools* (New York, 1957); Hansen, "The Scholastic Performances of Negro and White Pupils in the Integrated Public Schools of the District of Columbia," *Harvard Educational Review,* XXX (Summer, 1960), 216–36.

21 Cf. J. Alsop, "No More Nonsense About Ghetto Education!" *The New Republic,* July 22, 1967. We are not concerned here with the all but universal phenomenon of white flight in the face of a markedly increased incidence of nonwhite occupancy of the schools. It has long been recognized that white parents are critically sensitive to any threat to school standards. Concern for declining educational standards has been the precipitating cause of white flight in any number of interracial contact areas. Cf. S. Fauman, "Housing Discrimination, Changing Neighborhoods and Public Schools," *Journal of Social Issues,* XIII, No. 4 (1957), 21–30.

entering school for the first time. Those factors which negatively influence the performance of minority-group children and are school related have nothing to do with the racial composition of the school. They include at least pupil/teacher ratio, per pupil expenditure, the nature of instructional programming, the qualifications of teaching personnel, the adequacy of plant and teaching materials, and the availability of special staff to service poor performers. Of all these combined school related and unrelated factors, Cramer, Campbell and Bowerman have indicated that population per household, the nature of family employment, and per pupil expenditures in the school provide a maximum of predictive power in accounting for variations in academic performance levels.[22]

It is obvious that no single set of predictors, construed as independent variables, constitutes an exhaustive explanation of performance variance. Performance is the result of an interaction of a complex and indeterminate set of interdependent biological and ecological factors. What can be said with considerable assurance is that the racial composition of the school attended can hardly be expected to significantly influence the performance level of the minority-group child. The educational benefits to be derived for minority-group children from racial congregation are most frequently the consequence of exposure to more competent teaching personnel and enriched instructional programs.

There is little direct evidence that racial segregation in the schools, in and of itself, has any detrimental effect on the academic achievements and motivation of the minority-group child. There is as little direct evidence that racial congregation in the schools, in and of itself, has any beneficial effect. There is, in fact, some presumptive and some substantive evidence that racial congregation in the schools may deleteriously effect the minority-group child. If the performance norms of white schools are higher and make demands that minority-group children cannot be reasonably expected to meet, the presumptive result would be stress for the minority-

[22] Cf. M. R. Cramer, E. Q. Campbell, and C. E. Bowerman, *Social Factors in Educational Achievement and Aspirations among Negro Adolescents* (Chapel Hill, 1966) Chapter VI. In this regard Jensen indicates: "At most some 10 to 20 percent of the [total] variability in educational attainment is associated with [all] school variables. . . . [The] truly causal environmental influences on educability . . . are now thought to lie in more subtle psychological aspects of intra-family and inter-personal interactions during the child's development." A. R. Jensen, "Social Class, Race, and Genetics: Implications for Education," *American Educational Research Journal,* V (January, 1968), 2, 19.

group child, a decrease in motivation, withdrawal, and a decrement in performance. Just such an assessment has been advanced by Arthur Jensen and Irwin Katz.[23] Surprisingly little effort has been made to date to corroborate or infirm such a contention.[24] Whatever indirect evidence is available, however, lends it support. Experiments conducted among Negro college students indicate that when work teams are composed of Negro and white students of similar intellectual capacity the Negroes tend to be passively compliant, to rate their own performance as inferior and express less satisfaction with the team experience than do their white peers.[25] Thus even in a situation in which a Negro young adult is placed in a peer group containing whites with whom he is capable of effectively competing, he suffers stress and a diminution of motivation. How much more emphatic the impact of such a situation is upon minority-group children, particularly when they are faced with a group characterized by significantly different performance profiles, can only be conjectured. In Princeton, New Jersey, where voluntary desegregation was begun in 1948 most Negroes indicated that what they called "white attitudes, conscious and unconscious," had "a particularly important role in 'paralyzing' them, psychologically and academically, in their school work." [26] Yarrow's study of Negro children introduced into a biracial camp situation, administered by a staff highly motivated to make desegregation succeed, produced evidence of emphatic stress responses on the part of Negro children.[27] It appears to be the case that in biracial school situations Negro students tend to develop "feelings of intellectual inferiority which arise from an awareness of actual differences in racial achievement, or from irrational acceptance of the white group's stereotype of Negroes." [28]

The minority-group child, in a biracial situation in which Negro-

23 I. Katz, "Review of Evidence Relating to Effects of Desegregation on the Intellectual Performance of Negroes," *American Psychologist*, XIX (September, 1964), 383f.; Jensen, "Social Class, Race, and Genetics," 3; *How Much Can We Boost IQ and Scholastic Achievement?* (University of California, Berkeley: Institute of Human Learning, 1968).

24 Cf. J. B. Conant, *Slums and Suburbs* (New York, 1961), 38.

25 Katz, "Review of Evidence Relating to Effects of Desegregation," 396.

26 P. Streit, "Princeton's Lesson: School Integration is Not Enough," *New York Times Magazine*, June 21, 1964.

27 M. K. Yarrow, "Interpersonal Dynamics in a Desegregation Process," *Journal of Social Issues*, XIV (1958).

28 Katz, "Review of Evidence Relating to Effects of Desegregation," 386f.

white performance can frequently be plotted in a bimodal distribution, can hardly help assessing the group with which he is inevitably identified by traits of high social visibility as one composed of low performers. (The "standard" Negro/white overlap is 15 to 20 per cent, which means that under normal circumstances approximately 80 percent of the Negroes involved in an interracial situation will perform below white norms. There are, however, frequent instances reported in the literature in which no white child's performance was as poor as that of the best Negro child's performance.) The only conceivable result under these circumstances would be a further impairment of the minority-group child's already fragile ego structure. Whatever evidence is available (and it is fragmentary at best) suggests that minority-group children in a biracial environment develop a more negative self-image than those in racially insulated circumstances. In the early studies conducted by Clark and Clark, they found that while over 70 per cent of the Negro children in biracial schools made a negative response to a colored doll ("looks bad"), only 50 per cent of those Negro children in an all-Negro school made a similar reaction. Only 20 per cent of the Negro children in interracial schools indicated brown skin color as their preference while 80 per cent of the Negro children from racially homogeneous schools evinced such an ego supportive preference.[29] Goodman found the same emphatic negative response to their own racial community on the part of minority-group children in biracial nurseries in New England.[30] Recently van den Haag, Armstrong and Gregor, and Silberman have called attention to the possible negative impact of biracial schooling (under ordinary circumstances and within a relatively specific age range) in just this regard.[31] The evidence provided by Gregor and McPherson further suggests that Negro children in a uniracial school environment evidence a more positive and more viable self-image

[29] K. B. Clark and M. P. Clark, "Racial Identification and Preference in Negro Children," in G. Swanson, T. Newcomb, and E. Hartley (eds.), *Readings in Social Psychology* (New York, 1952), 559; Clark, *Prejudice and Your Child*, 44.

[30] M. E. Goodman, *Race Awareness in Young Children* (Cambridge, Mass., 1952).

[31] E. van den Haag, "Social Science Testimony in the Desegregation Cases: A Reply to Professor Kenneth Clark," *Villanova Law Review*, VI (1960), 77; C. P. Armstrong and A. J. Gregor, "Integrated Schools and Negro Character Development," *Psychiatry*, XXVII (February, 1964), 69–72; C. E. Silberman, *Crisis in Black and White* (New York, 1964), 302.

than those from biracial school environments.[32] Hill had early reported similar conclusions, and Springer's study of Oriental children in Hawaii indicated that there was a significant difference in positive response to their own racial group made by Oriental children from a racially homogeneous school compared to those from a biracial school.[33]

If, in fact, protracted interracial contact in circumstances of high emotional salience succeeds in inducing or making more emphatic the minority-group child's negative response to his own racial community (with which he will forever be inevitably identified) we could reasonably predict impaired motivation, a decrement in manifest performance, and a subsequent disposition to withdraw from the stressful learning situation to ultimately obtain. In this regard Gottlieb has reported suggestive evidence to the effect that "a greater proportion of Negro students from Southern segregated schools indicate a desire for college than do Negro students from Northern schools. It is among the Negro students in the interracial school that fewest students with college-going intentions are found."[34] The survey of Clark and Plotkin reported, furthermore, that "students from southern high schools (for the most part segregated) on the average have higher academic grades in interracial colleges than students from high schools in New York, Pennsylvania and New Jersey which are presumably non-segregated."[35]

The minority-group child in a biracial situation must contend with a pervasive and apparently indefeasible Caucasian aesthetic preference as well as the demanding performance norms of the white majority. Any normally constituted aggregate of white children will find their own group traits more admirable and their collective performance superior to that of minority-group children. Any departure from these norms would be, at best, tolerated by

[32] A. J. Gregor and D. A. McPherson, "Racial Attitudes among White and Negro Children in a Deep South Standard Metropolitan Area," *Journal of Social Psychology*, LXVIII (1966).

[33] M. A. Hill, "A Comparative Study of Race Attitudes in the All-Negro Community in Oklahoma, *Phylon*, VII (1946), 260–68; D. V. Springer, "Awareness of Racial Differences by Preschool Children in Hawaii," *Genetic Psychology Monographs*, XLI (1950).

[34] D. Gottlieb, "Goal Aspirations and Goal Fulfillments; Differences Between Deprived and Affluent American Adolescents." Paper delivered before the Annual Meeting of the American Orthopsychiatric Association, March 19, 1964 (Mimeo.).

[35] K. B. Clark and L. Plotkin, *The Negro Student at Integrated Colleges* (New York, 1963).

the majority. Under such circumstances the minority-group child is "stigmatized." [36] Should the minority-group child assimilate prevailing majority assessments, he intensifies the negative self-image that characterizes the personality profile of an inordinate number of Negro children. We know that there is a strong tendency on the part of the minority-group children to adapt their judgments to better accord with those of the majority.[37] The introjection by minority-group children of Caucasian aesthetic preferences (Clark reports that Negro children attending an interracial school were more likely to prefer light skin color than children of the same age attending all-Negro schools[38] and Brenman reports that the Negro child's rejection of his race and consequently of himself is a function of early childhood experience integrated as a minority-group member of a white community[39]), and the recognition of their group's failure to meet white performance levels, are productive of an impaired sense of self. Such an impaired-self system could only reduce motivation, depress performance, and generate the entire syndrome of reactive response which take on the various forms of intra- and extrapunitive aggressiveness, withdrawal, and, in some cases, pathological extension in color denial, the refusal to accept identification with one's racial confraternity.

Furthermore, in a biracial situation the minority-group child, has reduced opportunities for identifying with authority figures who share with him the socioperceptual traits of his race. Because the Negro child derives so frequently from a fatherless home environment, such diminished opportunities would seem to be particularly disabling. Gottlieb reports that Negro students are more apt to see Negro as opposed to white teachers as understanding their goals and as being more sensitive to their life problems. Negro teachers, in turn, tend to evince more job satisfaction in teaching nonwhite children and more sympathy and understanding of problems which characteristically beset the minority-group child. "[We]

36 Cf. R. B. Ammons, "Reactions in a Projective Doll-Play Interview of White Males Two to Six Years of Age to Differences in Skin Color and Facial Features," *Journal of Genetic Psychology,* LXXVI (1950), 323–41.

37 B. Berenda, *The Influence of the Group on the Judgements of Children* (New York, 1950), 52.

38 Clark, *Prejudice and Your Child,* 48.

39 M. Brenman, "The Relationship Between Minority-Group Membership and Group Identification in a Group of Urban Middle Class Negro Girls," *Journal of Social Psychology,* XI (1940), 171, 195.

would," Gottlieb concludes, "take the position that Negro teachers tend to be less critical in their perceptions as a result of their deeper identification with these children. The backgrounds of the Negro teachers would, we maintain, add to the less critical tone of their student evaluations. Finally, we would suggest that Negro teachers are less pessimistic in their evaluations of students because many of the teachers themselves have come from backgrounds similar to that of their students yet managed to overcome social barriers and attain positions of responsibility and status." [40]

The available evidence indicates that school integration, *per se*, is hardly calculated to produce the results popularly imagined. There is no probative evidence and little presumptive evidence to suggest that introducing minority-group children into a biracial school environment is benign much less beneficial. While there is some evidence that a pupil's academic performance is related to the socioeconomic and educational background and aspiration levels of other students in his instructional situation and that minority children could be thus conceived as benefiting in interracial contact situations,[41] Gottlieb reports that a greater proportion of Negro students from racially homogeneous schools have higher aspiration levels, are more academically serious, and are more likely to match expectations with aspirations than those from biracial schools.[42] Moreover there is some substantive evidence that in specific instances minority-group children introduced into biracial school environments suffered a performance decrement of statistically significant proportions.[43]

In the recent past an impressive number of Negro parents have become increasingly insistent upon the education of their children in all-Negro schools where their special, and race-related needs, can be more effectively met. The sanguine assumption, so long a part of the "liberal's" armory of conjectures (the consequence in no small part the vague and unqualified assessments tendered by the

40 D. Gottlieb, *Teaching and Students: The Views of Negro and White Teachers* (East Lansing, Mich.: Michigan State University, 1963, mimeo.).

41 *Equality of Educational Opportunity* (U.S. Department of Health, Education and Welfare. Washington, D.C., 1966), 22; T. Pettigrew, "Race and Equal Educational Opportunity," *Symposium on Implications of the Coleman Report on Equality of Educational Opportunity* (Cambridge, Mass.: Harvard University, 1967, mimeo.).

42 Gottlieb, "Goal Aspirations and Goal Fulfillments."

43 H. Kurz, "Official Testing Shows Ill Effects of Shifting Pupils," *New York World Telegram,* Febr. 23, 1965.

social science establishment concerning school segregation and congregation[44]), that racial congregation in the schools would do anything to ameliorate the personality and performance deficits of the minority-group child, must be re-evaluated. Social action programs justified by promises of positive outcomes, that in fact produce nothing or further impair the life chances of those they were instituted to assist, generate only increased social tension and constitute a grievous imposition on the forebearance of Negro Americans.

That such an assessment should be conceived of as "racism" and a brief for "segregation" is a sad commentary on the state of free and responsible discussion concerning vital issues in our society in our own time.

[44] K. Clark's *Prejudice and Your Child* is one of those books designed to impart the impression that the racial integration of minority children would significantly enhance their academic performance and ameliorate their personality deficits. Cf. my review of this book: A. J. Gregor, "Science and Social Change: A Review of K. B. Clark's *Prejudice and Your Child*," *Mankind Quarterly*, III (April, 1963), 229–37.

Frank C. J. McGurk

An Answer to Newby

The usual scientific approach to any problem involves, first, a statement of the problem (the hypothesis), which must be formed in such a way that an answer to the hypothesis can be obtained. Next, information pertinent to the hypothesis must be collected in some objective fashion (the experiment). Third, the hypothesis is considered in terms of the data collected, and fourth, the hypothesis is either rejected or not rejected. Rejecting a hypothesis or failing to reject a hypothesis takes place on the basis of some mathematical probability that the information obtained about the hypothesis could have occurred by chance. This involves no "interpretation"; it is a statement of probability which is completely independent of anyone's wishes, hopes, fears, dreams of social justice, or ideas of democracy.

Newby's Attitude Toward Scientific Procedure

After discussing the assumptions upon which "scientific racism" rests, Newby states (p. xi): "Most social scientists . . . who are not racists, and who reject the major ideas and value judgments of racism, believe those assumptions are false, or largely false, and they, too, base their position on what they accept as the "teachings of modern scientific authority." Scientific authority is a poor substitute for knowledge, and at best, the statements of authorities in science become the hypotheses which other scientists test. In traditional science, there is no authority except evidence, and this is implicit in H. J. Seligman's comments. Seligman is no "scientific racist," yet his approach to the race problem is this:

With full realization that by proper choice of "experts" and "authorities" it is possible to prove almost any point of view in this war-swept field [of race differences], one may nonetheless approach the entire subject in a spirit of inquiry, or willingness to receive and consider whatever facts may be available. If as a guide in proceeding through a wilderness of fact . . . it may be necessary to set forth a basic attitude, one may without imputation of narrow bias confess to the belief, until the contrary be proved, as it has not yet been proved, that mankind is one species. . . .[1]

Newby continues (p. xi), saying that, while the differences between the "scientific racists" and others are the result of different value systems, and that the data, therefore, may be interpreted in favor of racial inequality ". . . there are other data which seem clearly to indicate that races are equal, or potentially equal." This is hardly a matter of the interpretation of data; it is a duality of data, and Newby is saying that some of the available data support the inequality of races while other data support the doctrine of equalitarianism. There is a difference between interpreting one set of evidence in two ways, and two sets of evidence, each of which points to a different conclusion. If it were a matter of interpreting one set of data in two different ways, different value systems would be of prime importance; if there were two sets, each with its own meaning, there seems to be no reason for raising the question of value systems. Moreover, if there were other data that support

1 Seligman, H. J., *Race Against Man* (New York, 1939), 41.

equalitarianism, value systems would be unnecessary; the evidence, itself, would suffice. So far, no one has presented such data, although many have talked of them. What seems to be the major concern of the social scientist is not the existence of objective evidence that there are race differences in psychological test performance—these can be "interpreted" to mean something else; the real concern is that such objective data will be disseminated to the public, after which the public will understand the objectivity of race differences. This latter is considered bad.

In still another place (p. 25), Newby reveals this approach to scientific procedure: "The value of Clark's findings is due not to the fact that they substantiate the conclusion quoted above—this they do not do in any conclusive, objective way—but to the fact that they corroborate what common sense suggests and experience makes manifest: that the practice of racial segregation in this county is demeaning to Negroes, and an organized means of exploiting and suppressing the race. And as a practical matter, this is what Clark concluded." Clark's conclusions, to which Newby referred, were those which Clark had drawn from his much-disputed doll test: " 'On the surface [quoted Newby, p. 24] these findings might suggest that northern Negro children suffer more personality damage from racial prejudice and discrimination than southern Negro children. However, this interpretation would seem to be not only superficial, but incorrect. The apparent emotional stability of the southern Negro child may be indicative only of the fact that through rigid racial segregation and isolation he has accepted as normal the fact of his inferior social status. Such acceptance is not symptomatic of a healthy personality.' " Thus, Clark's data are "interpreted" to suit Clark's purpose, and of this, Newby approves. The evidence that Clark had collected showed that the southern Negro child was a better adjusted child according to Clark's doll test, but this could not be made public. Moreover, it did not suit Clark's purpose—which was to influence the Supreme Court. In addition, Newby also points approvingly (p. 30) to Clark's use of Deutscher and Chein's survey of opinions about the effects of segregation, which opinions were completely unsupported by evidence.

It is unquestionably true that the majority of social scientists look on segregation as having harmful effects on the personality of Negro children, but these social scientists feel no necessity to support their convictions with evidence. On the contrary, some social scientists feel that creating distorted evidence is morally proper if it leads to what they, the social scientists, consider to be a betterment of the Negro. Thus, Weyl comments about Herskovits that "his aim was to endow the Negro '. . . with the confidence in his own position in this country and in the world which he must have.' " [2] Clyde Kluckhohn, a social anthropologist who was highly regarded as a classics scholar, was perfectly willing to create a complex civilization for the Negro at Timbuktu: "The twelfth-century Negro university at Timbuktu compared favorably with contemporary European universities—as did the general level of civilization in the three great Negro kingdoms of that time. The iron working which is so important a base of our technology, may be a Negro creation." [3] Weyl's comment about Kluckhohn's statement is to the point: "The only one of these statements which is true is that iron working is important to modern technology." Weyl then demolishes Kluckhohn's statements in order.[4]

The unreliability of the writings of some of the social scientists may be seen in this incident. Newby tells us that Juan Comas, a cultural anthropologist associated with the University of Mexico, denounced as racist the journal *Mankind Quarterly*. Comas attempted to substantiate his accusations against *Mankind Quarterly* in *Contemporary Anthropology*, a journal more friendly to his point of view. Newby (p. 142) notes that Comas' article was a "systematic critique" of Garrett, who, in *Mankind Quarterly,* had criticized Klineberg's ideas of race and psychology. Comas' article was published in *Contemporary Anthropology* in October, 1961.

On February 14, 1961, The editor of *Current Anthropology* invited me to submit comments on the Comas article (entitled, coincidentally perhaps. " 'Scientific' Racism Again?") referred to by Newby. Along with the invitation, I received a galley proof of Comas' article. Normally, articles get into galley proof only when they have been checked carefully and approved by the editor responsible for their publication. On this assumption, I prepared my comments.

I noted Comas' propensity to quote arguments instead of facts. Further, I pointed out that Comas mentioned forty authors in his

2 Weyl, Nathaniel, *The Negro in American Civilization* (Washington, D.C.: Public Affairs Press, 1960), 139.

3 Kluckhohn, Clyde, *Mirror for Man* (New York: McGraw, Hill, 1949), 126.

4 Weyl, *The Negro in American Civilization,* 139–41.

article who were not included in his "References Cited," and, more surprising, he included sixty other authorities in "References Cited" which appeared nowhere in his article. In addition, there were approximately twenty other names included under the UNESCO series of articles included in "References Cited" which also were not mentioned elsewhere in his article. This impressed me as unscientific padding of a bibliography.

I noted further that Comas quoted others without checking the quotation or the source carefully. Thus, in the "systematic critique," whereby Newby holds (p. 142) that Comas sought to discredit Garrett and the *Quarterly* by demonstrating the racism of both, Comas quoted Klineberg. A search of the Klineberg reference given by Comas revealed no such statement as Comas claimed that Klineberg had made.[5] The quotation that Comas had laid on Klineberg's shoulders was a gross misrepresentation of the author's attitude toward race differences.

On March 24, 1961, my comments were submitted to the editor of *Contemporary Anthropology.* On April 4, 1961, the editor returned them with the explanation that Comas' article was a translation from Spanish, and that the translator ". . . omitted some passages, rendered others incorrectly, and took a number of unwarranted liberties with the text." [6] (McGurk, 1961). It was explained further that these errors were discovered only after the original text had been set in galley form. The translator, for example, changed Comas' original "Bibliography" to "References Cited" and had omitted certain sections of Comas' original text. That accounted for the inclusion of names in "References Cited" which could not be found in the text. My criticism of the appearance of references in the text which were not listed in "References Cited" was accepted by the editor as valid.

It was explained that the translator inserted the incorrect quotation from Klineberg; Comas' original reference was to a 1956 publication by Klineberg.

Also on April 4, 1961, I was asked to make the needed changes in my original comments. I declined. This is the "systematic critique" which Newby (p. 142) lauds as Comas' denunciation of Garrett.

5 Klineberg, Otto, "Mental Testing of Racial and National Groups," in H. S. Jennings (ed.), *Scientific Aspects of the Race Problem* (Washington, D.C.: Catholic University Press, 1941).

6 McGurk, Frank C. J., personal communication.

Some Personal Matters

There is some personal history to be set straight. I did not receive my undergraduate training at Catholic University of America, as Newby states on page 65. My bachelor's degree (in economics) and my master's degree (in psychology) came from the University of Pennsylvania. My doctorate came from Catholic University.

In discussing my doctoral dissertation, Newby shows some confusion of facts. I administered one test, not tests, as Newby writes. This test contained 75 questions—not 184. In the test, there were thirty-seven pairs of questions wherein one question of each pair was rated as cultural, and the other question of the pair was rated as noncultural. One of the seventy-five questions was a placebo: it was not scored. Questions were rated cultural or noncultural on the basis of judgments of a panel composed of school teachers, sociologists, and psychologists. Questions were also rated for degree of difficulty by a pilot study on high school seniors (not included in the experimental sample). When a noncultural question was paired with a cultural question, both were equivalent in degree of difficulty.[7]

Newby's comment (p. 66) that I "administered tests consisting of 103 'least cultural' and 81 'most cultural' questions . . ." indicates that he not only errs in reporting, but that he completely misunderstands the critical necessity for pairing the cultural and noncultural questions for difficulty.

I have carefully avoided use of the word "intelligence" in all of my publications because I do not like the implication that such a relatively simple psychological test can measure a complicated mental activity. Newby indicates that he has read my attitude toward "intelligence,"[8] yet he comments (p. 71*n*16) that I matched my subjects for specific socioeconomic characteristics and that "[I] believed that [I] was enabled thereby to eliminate or neutralize environmental factors and thus, measure intelligence." I must repeat, psychological tests are something-less-than-perfect predictors of school achievement, but I most emphatically do not regard them as measures of intelligence.

[7] McGurk, Frank C. J., "The Performance of Negro and White High School Seniors on Cultural and Noncultural Test Questions" (Washington, D.C.: Catholic University Press, 1951, [microcard].

[8] McGurk, Frank C. J., "Negro vs. White Intelligence: An Answer," *Harvard Educational Review*, XXIX (Winter, 1959), 54–62.

Newby's very succinct summary of another article is not quite complete.[9] In preparing my doctoral dissertation, after having tested some four thousand high school seniors in fourteen different schools, I had collected complete data on 213 Negro children. On the basis of each Negro child's score on a measure of socioeconomic status (a modification of the Sims Record Card) a white child was found who matched the Negro child as perfectly as possible. There were fourteen matching factors involved in this process, and whenever an exact match could not be effected, a white child was selected who was never superior in socioeconomic status to the Negro with whom he was matched. Thus, when it is said that there were 213 matched pairs of subjects (one a Negro and one a white), it means that the subjects were matched on the basis of the fourteen socioeconomic matching factors. All of the Negro children who were tested were included in the 213 pairs, but not all of the white children; only those whites were included whose socioeconomic factors would permit them to be paired with the Negro children. The 213 pairs of subjects were ranked according to the Sims Card score of the Negro member of the pair, and since a white subject was paired permanently with every Negro subject, the white subjects were in an equivalent rank order by Sims score also. The fifty-three Negroes with the highest Sims scores (and the fifty-three white subjects who were paired with them) were designated the High Socioeconomic Group; the fifty-three Negroes whose Sims scores were the lowest (and the whites who were matched to them) were designated the Low Socioeconomic Group. Thus, four groups were formed: the High Negro Socioeconomic Group, the High White Socioeconomic Group, the Low Negro Socioeconomic Group, and the Low White Socioeconomic Group. The High Negro Socioeconomic Group included the highest 25 per cent of all of the Negro subjects, in terms of socioeconomic status, but the whites included in the High White Socioeconomic Group did not include the highest 25 per cent of all of the white subjects; the latter group included only those whites whose socioeconomic status matched the Negroes in the High Negro Socioeconomic Group. In like manner, the Low Negro Socioeconomic Group included the lowest 25 per cent of the Negroes (by Sims score), and it is very probable that the Low White Socioeconomic

9 McGurk, Frank C. J., "On White and Negro Test Performance and Socioeconomic Factors," *Journal of Abnormal and Social Psychology,* XLVIII (July, 1953), 448–50.

Group included the lowest 25 per cent of the whites—by Sims score. The relative meaning of high socioeconomic groups and low socioeconomic groups is not made clear by Newby (p. 66) when he discusses my work. "High Status," when applied to Negro subjects means the very best 25 per cent of the Negro subjects by socioeconomic level. When applied to whites, "high status" does not mean the very best 25 per cent of the white subjects by socioeconomic level; it means those fifty-three white subjects whose socioeconomic status matched the fifty-three high status Negro subjects. In the case of the "low status" subjects, it is likely that it means the very poorest 25 per cent of both racial groups.

In commenting on my finding that culturally loaded test questions do not penalize the Negro subject, Newby (p. 66) says: "[The Negro subjects] did better on the 'most cultural' than on the 'least cultural' items, a fact which McGurk took as additional evidence that the low scores of Negroes cannot be explained by environment." As I pointed out, in 1951, a very common explanation of the test inferiority of Negroes is that Negroes obtain little experience with, or knowlege of, verbal material, and since most psychological tests are made up at least partly of verbal material, the Negro is thereby penalized. What remained, then, was to test the hypothesis that verbally loaded psychological test questions did penalize the Negro in his psychological test performance. That verbally loaded questions *enhance* the test performance of Negroes was clearly shown,[10] and the hypothesis held by the majority of the social scientists who are experts in this field, had to be rejected—not merely because of lack of evidence—but because the direction of the available evidence was opposite to that hypothesized by social science. Because of the frequent appeals of social scientists to authorities, this is an important matter.

Some Matters of Fact

Commenting on my 1956 article, Newby sketches the main outline, noting that I had compared each of several race studies done between 1935 and 1950 with the performance of Negroes and whites upon the Army tests during World War I. Then Newby says (p. 67): "McGurk reasoned that the socioeconomic status of Negroes had

[10] McGurk, "On White and Negro Test Performance,"; McGurk, Frank C. J., "Socioeconomic Status and Cultural Weighted Test Scores of Negro Subjects," *Journal of Applied Psychology*, XXXVII (1953), 276–77.

improved markedly since World War I, and, if the environmental hypothesis were valid, Negroes should score significantly higher in 1935–50 than they had in 1917–18. The first of these assumptions is no doubt valid, but to transpose it into the conclusion that Negroes should therefore score higher on psychological tests is fallacious."

Here, Newby is objecting not only to one of the prime requirements of scientific research, but to what is held by the most prominent of the social scientists.

At the beginning of this article, I noted that scientists perform their function by setting up hypotheses, and then collecting data. According to the data collected, the hypotheses are either rejected or not rejected. F. J. McGuigan puts it this way: "On the basis of that hypothesis, he is able to predict an outcome of his experiment; he sets up the experiment to determine whether the outcome is, indeed, that predicted by his hypothesis." [11] A little later, McGuigan notes: "Put another way, the hypothesis says that *if* such, and such is the case, (the antecedent conditions of the hypothesis), *then* such and such should happen (the consequent conditions of the hypothesis)." [12]

Newby confuses his own words. What he initially calls "the environmental hypothesis" is, in the next sentence, called a conclusion. It would, indeed, be fallacious if one transposed one's hypothesis into a conclusion, as Newby accuses me of doing, but this was obviously not done. If any transposition took place, it was with the data which I collected; they did not support the hypothesis that, as environment improves, Negro-white test score differences decrease.

If my reasoning be erroneous, as Newby says it is (p. 67), every social scientist who supports the Culture Hypothesis is erroneous also. (What Newby calls the environmental hypothesis is, in the social sciences, also known as the Culture Hypothesis.) Klineberg states the Culture Hypothesis this way: "If the environment has an effect, there should be a rise in intelligence at least roughly proportionate to the length of residence in New York." [13] The above was in reference to his famous New York study. Later, Klineberg says this: "We have a right to say that the results obtained by the

11 McGuigan, F. J., *Experimental Psychology* (Englewood Cliffs, N.J.: Prentice Hall, 1968), 61.
12 *Ibid.*, 63.
13 Klineberg, Otto, *Negro Intelligence and Selective Migration* (New York: Columbia University Press, 1935), 24.

use of intelligence tests have not proved the existence of racial and national differences in innate mental capacity; and also that as the social and economic environments of the two ethnic groups [Negroes and whites] become more alike, so do their test scores tend to approximate each other." [14] And, still again, Klineberg says: "There is . . . definite evidence that exposure to a superior environment effects an unmistakable rise in the test scores [of Negroes], and that this rise is, in general, proportionate to the length of exposure to such a superior environment." [15]

Ashley Montagu states the Culture Hypothesis somewhat differently,[16] but exactly as it is set forth by "a group of distinguished social scientists . . .": "Wherever it has been possible to make allowances for differences in environmental opportunities, the tests have shown essential similarity in mental characters among all human groups. In short, given similar degrees of cultural opportunity to realize their potentialities, the average achievement of members of each ethnic group is about the same." [17] On the flysheet of the above reference, Ashley Montagu calls his book: "An extended discussion in plain language of the UNESCO statement by experts on race problems." Oddly enough, neither the UNESCO publication nor Ashley Montagu's article contains a speck of evidence for its statements.

If Newby objects to my statement of the Culture Hypothesis, he must also object to Klineberg, to whom he refers on page 57 as one of the thirty-five leading social scientists, and on pages 58 and 74 as having produced evidence contrary to the racist point of view. If Newby objects to me because I transposed an assumption into a conclusion, he must also object to Ashley Montagu whose comments he uses (p. 220) to deny Coon's theory of evolution of the races of man. In short, Newby apparently does not realize that he praises Klineberg and Ashley Montagu for saying the thing which he called fallacious when said by me.

It might be worth adding here that neither Klineberg, Ashley Montagu, nor the "group of distinguished social scientists meeting

[14] Klineberg, "Mental Testing of Racial and National Groups," 284.

[15] Klineberg, Otto, "Tests of Negro Intelligence," in Otto Klineberg (ed.), *Characteristics of the American Negro* (New York: Harper and Bros., 1944), 46.

[16] Montagu, Ashley, *Statement on Race* (New York: Schuman, 1951), 14.

[17] UNESCO "Statement on Race" (Lake Success, N.Y., July 18, 1950); "Does Race Really Make a Difference in Intelligence?" *U.S. News and World Report*, October 26, 1956, pp. 74–76.

in UNESCO House in Paris" spelled out the factors of the environment about which they were talking—an omission which I, also, had made, according to Newby (p. 67): ". . . McGurk also failed to specify the environmental improvements among Negroes which he thought should improve their relative test scores." I had made clear that I had equated my racial groups for fourteen specified factors.[18]

Newby raises some question (pp. 67–68) about whether the socioeconomic status of the Negroes had improved between 1918 and 1950: "In a thousand subtle and unsubtle ways they were still made to feel inferior and despised. Despite such factors as these, McGurk found that the Negroes' performance had not significantly changed between 1917–18 and 1935–50, and their overlap of white averages was only 20 to 30 percent in each period. The significant improvement in socioeconomic status, he concluded, had not materially affected their performance on psychological tests." Less than half a page before this, Newby had admitted (p. 67) that the Negroes' environment had improved in that time period: "The first of these assumptions [my assumption that the socioeconomic status of the Negro had improved since World War I] is no doubt valid. . . ." Thus, Newby accepts my statement that the socioeconomic position of the Negro had improved by 1950 over what it was in 1918. In the above quotation, however, Newby misstates my findings. What I found was not that the Negro's performance had not changed in that time period, but that, as far as psychological test performance was concerned, the Negro test scores in 1950 bore the same relationship to white test scores in 1950 (overlap was about 25 per cent) as Negro test scores in 1918 bore to white test scores in 1918 (overlap about 27 per cent).[19]

It appears to mean much to Newby (p. 67) that eighteen social scientists and UNESCO rejected my 1956 publication. Of the eighteen social scientists cited by Newby only one had ever done any empirical work in the field of psychological race differences, and this one had never attempted to test the Culture Hypothesis. In their article, they reiterated the opinions which they had given elsewhere. The reader should note that these eighteen social scientists (Klineberg was among them) presented absolutely no evidence

18 McGurk, "The Performance of Negro and White High School Seniors."
19 McGurk, Frank C. J., "A Scientist's Report on Race Differences," *U.S. News and World Report,* September 21, 1956, pp. 92–96.

for their contentions, and it is questionable whether the presentation of unsupported opinion would be accepted as fact in any science except social science. Similar comment may be made of the 1950 UNESCO statement on race, on which these distinguished social scientists relied. Unquestionably, the UNESCO report is the official statement on race by UNESCO, but there is considerable doubt now about how many of the world's "experts" agree with it. Regardless of that, however, it must be regarded as factually unsupported. But this does not deter Newby from saying (p. 69): "In more specific terms they rejected McGurk's claim that he (or anyone else) had adequately controlled or neutralized environmental factors which affect the results of psychological tests." That this was an unfortunate statement for Newby to make is apparent by the use of the word "adequate." In addition, Newby shows again his confusion about the testing of hypotheses; I was testing the Culture Hypothesis, using the same unspecified environmental factors, perhaps, that Klineberg and Ashley Montagu referred to when they used the Culture Hypothesis. What I had shown was that, regarding performance on psychological tests, the position of the Negro had not changed, relative to the white, in the period between World War I and 1950—and this in spite of the improvement in the Negro's socioeconomic status (which Newby agrees had happened). This makes no claim about controlling or neutralizing the environment. Actually, I took great pains to state that I did not regard the socioeconomic conditions to be equal for Negroes and whites: "Even though there was not true equality between the social and economic status of Negroes and whites, any approach to such equality should be reflected in a decrease in the difference between their [Negro and white] average test scores." [20] And again I wrote:

In order to test the culture hypothesis, it must be shown that, under a given set of socioeconomic factors, an observed racial test score difference changes when the socioeconomic factors change. In terms of the culture hypothesis as so stated, one must demonstrate that the Negro-white test score difference, observed under an unfavorable set of socioeconomic factors, decreases as the socioeconomic factors become more favorable for the Negro. This is what Klineberg means when he states that differences between Negro and white mean test scores tend to disappear when the socioeconomic differences between Negroes and whites become less and less (7). One must, therefore, begin with a clearly specified Negro-white test score difference obtained under socioeconomic factors that are unfavorable

20 *Ibid.*, 93.

for the Negroes, and end with a Negro-white test score difference when the socioeconomic factors are more favorable for the Negro than they were previously. The socioeconomic factors under which the Negroes live at the end do not have to be identical with the socioeconomic factors under which the whites live at the end. If the culture hypothesis has any meaning, it is necessary only to show that, at the end, the socioeconomic condition of the Negroes and the whites was more alike than the socioeconomic condition of these two groups were at the beginning, and that, accompanying this decrease in the difference between socioeconomic factors for Negroes and whites, there was a decrease in the difference between the mean test scores of Negroes and whites.[21]

Newby errs further when he writes (p. 70) that I claimed to have constructed what he calls "a valid 'noncultural' test." He shows confusion when he states: "As two of his critics point out, the indices of socioeconomic status which McGurk used in formulating "noncultural" tests were designed to measure the difference between social *classes,* but the difference between social *castes* cannot be reduced to a neat index." This statement, too, is unfortunate—not only for Newby to have made, but for the critics to have pointed out. In a previous section of this paper, I discussed Newby's very same confusion concerning my original research in 1951. I did not construct noncultural tests; I selected noncultural questions. Moreover, I did not select the noncultural or the cultural questions by a ratio, index, or any other mathematical device. There were no "indices of socioeconomic status" used in the selection of my questions. As I said before, the noncultural and the cultural questions were selected by submitting certain psychological test questions to a panel of judges. What the panel judged to be a noncultural question *was* a noncultural question. What the panel judged to be a cultural question *was* a cultural question.[22] In what sense does this involve an index of socioeconomic status? Newby has no way of knowing that I considered not worth answering the comments of those authors whom he regards as critical of my methodology.[23] Newby could easily have verified the statements of Dreger and Miller by checking my dissertation; Dreger and Miller could have checked their charge before they published it.

Out of his unfortunate citation of a confused article, Newby

21 McGurk, "Negro vs. White Intelligence," 55, 56.
22 McGurk, "The Performance of Negro and White High School Seniors."
23 Dreger, R. M. and Kent S. Miller, "Comparative Psychological Studies of Negroes and Whites in the United States," *Psychological Bulletin,* LVII (1960), 361–402.

deduces a number of things. He charges me with unscientific methodology because Dreger and Miller said so. The unscientific methodology stems from Newby's failure to verify Dreger and Miller's charge before he used it. My methodology was not unscientific; evidently Dreger and Miller did not understand it. Newby charges me with reading too much into my data and then chides me for not reading more into the data; he holds that I ignored a direct relationship between test scores and environmental factors. I had no evidence for concluding that environment was the responsible factor because subjects of high socioeconomic status obtained higher test scores than subjects of low socioeconomic status. I explained before that social scientists created the Culture Hypothesis; I was only testing it. I was testing the power of the environment to reduce racial test score differences as Klineberg and Ashley Montagu hold. I found, and emphasized, that Negroes of low socioeconomic status obtained *higher* scores on the *cultural* questions than did the whites who were paired with them, but that the Negro subjects of high socioeconomic status obtained lower cultural scores than did the associated white subjects. On the basis of the Culture Hypothesis, this is hardly expected; here, the most culturally-deprived Negro group behaves more like the associated white subjects than the most advantaged Negro group resembles the white subjects with which it was matched. This does not ignore environment; it simply shows that the differences in environment between the low socioeconomic group of Negroes and the high socioeconomic group of Negroes did not improve the test performance of the high socioeconomic Negroes.[24]

Moreover, when the same comparison was made using the least culturally weighted (the noncultural) questions, similar behavior was shown. Between Negroes and whites of low socioeconomic status, the average difference, for the same type of question, was 4.32 points. There is no evidence here that improving the environment of the Negroes improves their test performance relative to the associated white subjects.[25] It might be worth noting that only 2.22 points separated the mean nonculture scores of Negroes of high socioeconomic status and Negroes of low socioeconomic status. Only 1.21 points separated the mean cultural scores of the same two groups of subjects. If the Culture Hypothesis were operative,

24 McGurk, "On White and Negro Test Performance."
25 *Ibid.*

one could expect a significantly greater difference between Negroes of high socioeconomic status and Negroes of low socioeconomic status on the cultural questions than on the noncultural questions. Actually, the difference in socioeconomic status of the Negro subjects was associated with a larger, but statistically insignificant, difference on noncultural questions.[26] Newby does not mention that these findings are a complete rejection of the Culture Hypothesis. Newby does not mention this latter article at all.

In a footnote on page 71, Newby cites what he calls evidence which shows that "IQ test scores are closely related to environmental factors." He credits McCord and Demerath with this information.[27] It is interesting that Newby does not tell his readers I answered McCord and Demerath (1959).[28] I pointed out that the finding that they and Newby think is a contradiction of my data actually confirms my earlier findings that, at low socioeconomic levels, Negroes and whites tend to obtain equal mean test scores[29] (McGurk, 1953a). McCord and Demerath used ten-year old urban northern boys from integrated schools, and from "lower class or the lower-middle class."[30]

Newby (p. 72) makes much of the comment that differences within races are greater than differences between races. Just to document other social scientists who have made this same statement would fill a page. The statement is true, and it is completely irrelevant to those who understand statistics. Differences within races are raw score differences. Their significance depends on the standard deviation (SD) of the scores, and their limits, generally, are set at plus and minus 5 SD. Differences between races are differences between means. Their chance distribution centers around zero, and they may range in a plus and minus direction according to 5 times the standard error of the mean (SE). Since the SE is the ratio of the SD to the square root of the number of subjects, SE is always smaller than SD. Thus, the range of mean differences (differences between races) must always be smaller than the range of scores (differences within races). The significance of mean differ-

26 McGurk, "Socioeconomic Status and Cultural Weighted Test Scores."
27 McCord, W. M. and N. J. Demerath III, "Negro versus White Intelligence: A Continuing Controversy," *Harvard Educational Review*, XXVII (Spring, 1958), 120–35.
28 McGurk, "Negro vs. White Intelligence."
29 McGurk, "On White and Negro Test Performance."
30 McCord and Demerath, "Negro versus White Intelligence," 125.

ences depends on the random distribution of such differences between samples chosen and paired at random. The significance between scores depends on the SD. It is impossible for differences to be any other way; differences within racial groups will always be larger than differences between racial groups, and this will always be irrelevant to the comparison of mean differences.

Instead of comparing Negro-white psychological test performance in terms of differences between means or overlapping, Newby suggests that the range of scores (the difference between the highest and lowest scores) be used. He comments (p. 72): "Perhaps a more meaningful way to express test results to laymen is to point out the range of scores made by each racial group." The range of scores emphasizes the fact that differences within the races are more important than differences between the races, and this is the impression that Newby wishes the layman to have. In addition to what I have just said, it is unfortunate for Newby that the range is the most untrustworthy of statistics, and even the novice in statistics is warned to avoid it whenever possible.

In this latter suggestion, as in many of his other suggestions, Newby seems more concerned with the impression made on the public than with scientific accuracy. It is true that emphasizing the differences within distributions, or pointing out the range of scores will, for the average person, obscure the real nature of the obtained data. However, this is not the purpose of the traditional scientist.

Summary

Newby constantly forgets that I was interested in testing the Culture Hypothesis. This hypothesis holds that psychological test score differences between Negroes and whites are the result of differences in cultural factors. Those who created the Culture Hypothesis—the social scientists—have not presented a shred of evidence to support their own creation, and Newby has not made the situation any better.

It is one thing to believe, on moral grounds, that there are no race differences. This I can easily understand. It is another thing, however, to insist that the available evidence demonstrates the factuality of this belief.[31] Whatever objective evidence exists is

31 Green, Arnold W., "Science or Dogma," *National Review*, February 13, 1968, pp. 148–49.

completely out of keeping with the claim of racial equality in psychological test performance.

I think that this is worth repeating: the social scientists who created the Culture Hypothesis failed to test it. Everyone who has ever done any scientific work in the field of race differences in psychological test score has found the same thing. There are racial differences in psychological test performance, and there is absolutely no evidence that they will go away simply because social scientists hope they will.

BIBLIOGRAPHY

"Does Race Really Make a Difference in Intelligence?" *U.S. News and World Report,* October 26, 1956, pp. 74–76.

Dreger, R. M. and Kent S. Miller, "Comparative Psychological Studies of Negroes and Whites in the United States, *"Psychological Bulletin,* LVII (1960), 361–402.

Green, Arnold, W. "Science or Dogma," *National Review,* February 13, 1968, pp. 148–49.

Klineberg, Otto. "Mental Testing of Racial and National Groups," in H. S. Jennings (ed.), *Scientific Aspects of the Race Problem* (Washington, D.C.: Catholic University Press, 1941).

––––––. *Negro Intelligence and Selective Migration* (New York: Columbia University Press, 1935).

––––––. "Tests of Negro Intelligence," in Otto Klineberg (ed.), *Characteristics of the American Negro* (New York: Harper and Bros., 1944).

Kluckhohn, Clyde. *Mirror for Man* (New York: McGraw, Hill, 1949).

McCord, W. M. and N. J. Demerath III, "Negro versus White Intelligence: A Continuing Controversy," *Harvard Educational Review,* XXVIII (Spring, 1958), 120–35.

McGuigan, F. J. *Experimental Psychology* (Englewood Cliffs, N.J.: Prentice Hall, 1968).

McGurk, F. C. J. *"The Performance of Negro and White High School Seniors on Cultural and Noncultural Test Questions"* (Washington, D.C.: Catholic University Press, 1951, [microcard]).

––––––. "On White and Negro Test Performance and Socioeconomic Factors," *Journal of Abnormal and Social Psychology,* XLVIII (July, 1953), 448–50.

––––––. "Socioeconomic Status and Cultural Weighted Test Scores of Negro Subjects," *Journal of Applied Psychology,* XXXVII (1953), 276–77.

————. "A Scientist's Report on Race Differences," *U.S. News and World Report,* September 21, 1956, pp. 92–96.

————. " 'Negro vs. White Intelligence': An Answer," *Harvard Educational Review,* XXIX (Winter, 1959), 54–62.

————. Private communication, 1961.

Montagu, Ashley. *Statement on Race* (New York: Schuman, 1951).

Newby, I. A. *Challenge to the Court: Social Scientists and the Defense of Segregation, 1954–1966* (Baton Rouge: Louisiana State University Press, 1967).

Seligman, H. J. *Race Against Man* (New York: Putnam, 1939).

UNESCO "Statement on Race." (Lake Success, N.Y., July 18, 1950).

Weyl, Nathaniel. *The Negro in American Civilization* (Washington, D.C.: Public Affairs Press, 1960).

R. T. Osborne

Challenge to the Court: A Reply

In the preface of *Challenge to the Court* Newby says (p. xi) the chief concern of his study is "scientific racism," an ambivalent term coined by him to describe those who "look to science for guidance in formulating public policy." I believe that Newby would demand that we look to science for help in formulating public policy concerning agriculture, food, drugs, commerce, transportation, and communication, but when it is suggested that the method of science be applied to racial problems he yells foul and invokes human decency, justice, and democracy. Since the Negro riots began in 1965, several prominent scientists (William Shockley, Arthur R.

Jensen, Dwight Ingle, Robert Kuttner) have had the courage to call for a serious scientific effort to research the distribution of hereditary potential for intelligence among our black citizens. Even by Newby's standards these men could not be called racists. They are true scientists who have the "courage to doubt in the face of the desire to believe." [1]

My reply to Newby will concern only those portions of *Challenge to the Court* which refer to my work. Others who were cited in the text may or may not elect to reply to the offer of "equal time."

It is obvious from the citation on page 83 that Newby had either misread or interpreted carelessly the two references he quotes when he says: "In his [Osborne's] opinion the fact that Negro pupils did relatively better in arithmetic than in reading corroborated 'the careful work of McGurk. . . .' " In this sentence there are three errors. In the first place, Negro pupils do not perform relatively better in arithmetic than in reading; in the second place, if they had, my work would not have corroborated McGurk's; and in the third place, the footnote reference is incorrect. What I actually said was:

It is in the area of arithmetic achievement that the Negro child seems to be most deficient (Figure 6). Negro children of mental age grade placement equal to that of white children are unable to learn mathematical skills at the same rate as their white experimental partners. The Negro children, a majority of whom were selected from the top fourth of their group in terms of mental age grade placement, are unable to keep pace with the group of white children, most of whom were drawn from the lowest fourth of their class. Over the six-year period of the study the rate of learning new arithmetical skills for Negro children was about 50 per cent that of the standard norm rate and about 68 per cent that of the rate of the equated white experimental group. [2]

In Newby's second reference I say:

The present writer, in an earlier study, also found the American Negro to be handicapped on performance-type mental tests rather than in the language-verbal areas. McGurk's well known and carefully documented study concludes that "There is no evidence here that culturally weighted test material discriminates against the Negro. There is no evidence that as the socio-economic status of the Negro increases, racial test score dif-

[1] William Shockley, "Proposed Research to Reduce Racial Aspects of the Environment-Heredity Uncertainty." Paper read at the National Academy of Sciences, Washington, D.C., April, 1968.

[2] R. T. Osborne, "Racial Difference in School Achievement," *Mankind Monographs*, III (November, 1962), 13.

ferences decrease." It is, however, Professor Heuse, writing in *Revue de Psychologie des Peuples,* who perhaps offers the most crushing argument against Klineberg's egalitarian position. Dr. Heuse finds "The Black American or African shows no ability (for reasons evidently neuro-genetic and psycho-genetic in nature) for mathematics. The capacity for manipulation for mathematical symbolisms which is closely linked to the capacity for abstraction is so minimal that we can call it, if we compare their capacity to that of the whites, apherasthenic." [3]

In a recent monograph Gerald Lesser has shown that the Negro deficit in numerical ability relative to verbal ability is constant across socioeconomic strata within the Negro population. In his study of four ethnic groups, Chinese, Jews, Negroes, and Puerto Ricans (each ethnic group having a middle and lower socioeconomic group), he found that, whereas social class affects only the absolute level of ability, ethnic group membership produces "significant differences in both the absolute level of each mental ability and the patterns among these abilities." [4]

Elsewhere (p. 85) Newby states that the validity of my conclusions "rests almost entirely upon the implicit though unstated assumption that Negro schools in Savannah are equal to white schools. . . ." As I pointed out earlier, in terms of teacher qualifications, salary, recency of training, and number of advanced degrees the Negro teachers were significantly ahead of the white teachers in the same school system.

Of the other categories of measurement which Newby claims to be relevant, the authoritative Coleman Report has shown that: "Per pupil expenditure, books in the library, and a host of other facilities and curricular measures show virtually no relation to achievement if the 'social environment of the school—the educational backgrounds of other students and teachers—is held constant.' " [5]

Newby later (p. 86) states that my "failure to give weight to environmental factors suggests that he [Osborne] believed the results of his tests were genetically determined." My belief that test results are largely genetically determined is not based upon any *a priori* assumption, but rather on the basis of careful consideration

[3] R. T. Osborne, "Cultural Bias of Psychological Test Items," *The Mankind Quarterly,* IV (January–March, 1964), 134–35.

[4] Gerald S. Lesser, "Mental Abilities of Children from Different Social-Class and Cultural Groups," *Monographs of the Society for Research in Child Development,* XXX, No. 4 (1965), 82.

[5] J. S. Coleman, "Equal Schools or Equal Students," *Public Interest,* No. 4 (Summer, 1966), 73.

TABLE 1

CORRELATIONS BETWEEN MENTAL
AND SCHOLASTIC ASSESSMENTS [6]

	Identical twins reared together	Identical twins reared apart	Noniden- tical twins reared together	Siblings reared together	Siblings reared apart	Unrelated children reared together
Mental						
"Intelligence"						
Group Test	.944	.771	.542	.515	.441	.281
Individual Test	.921	.843	.526	.491	.463	.252
Final Assessment	.925	.876	.551	.538	.517	.269
Scholastic						
General Attainments	.898	.681	.831	.814	.526	.535
Reading and Spelling	.944	.647	.915	.853	.490	.548
Arithmetic	.862	.723	.748	.769	.563	.476

[6] Sir Cyril Burt, "The Inheritance of Mental Ability," *American Psychologist*, XIII (January 19, 1958), 6.

of twin research. The vast weight of evidence in this area has shown that heredity plays a significant part in determining scholastic ability. One relevant example of the findings of twin research is reproduced herewith.

Finally, Newby states (p. 86) that "his [Osborne's] endorsement of segregated schools indicates that to him racial differences are permanent and largely immune to environmental influences." I have never stated that racial differences are entirely immune to environmental change. However, I believe that heredity sets an upper limit on the amount that environment can influence achievement, and therefore the hereditary potential for intelligence is a highly relevant variable in determining a pupil's achievement and hence must be considered in pupil placement.

Wesley Critz George

A "Scientific Racist's" Rejoinder

Several of my friends and I, whom Professor Newby has referred to as the field marshals of scientific racism, have sought to bring about a critical consideration of the nature of the race problem and its resolution on the basis of the significance of racial differences rather than on the basis of an emotional denial of them.

As suggested in Newby's preface to the first edition of his *Challenge to the Court*, the thesis of the "scientific racists" is that there are fundamental differences between the races, that these differences have a structural basis ranging from gross anatomy to molecular structure, that they are genetic in origin and therefore transmissible

307

from generation to generation, and that these structural features underlie and in large measure determine the behavior, the accomplishments, and the limitations of the individuals whose bodies and personalities they form. And finally, we contend that different population groups, different races, are composed of individuals in whom different human characters, e.g., pigmentation, bone structure, brain structure, are distributed in different proportions. On this basis I accept the designation "scientific racist."

The Problem

It has also been our belief that a people and a government should examine the facts bearing on the problem of race *before* decisions for revolution are made and *before* laws are passed to bring about irreversible social and protoplasmic changes in our population. We have sought to encourage examination of the already recorded facts and an extension of research into fields where adequate facts may not exist or where asserted facts require confirmation.

But the molders of public opinion have whipped up such a lather of emotionalism in favor of "brotherhood" and integration that the hierarchies of government, of the church, of the universities and of organizations of scientists have summarily rejected examination of evidence and have committed themselves to action now.

Professor Newby, too, rejects the relevance of scientific data to our race problem and suggests that the basic issue is constitutional, not scientific. We assume that he refers to the constitution as interpreted by the Warren Court, not as written nor as interpreted by conservative constitutional lawyers or previous Supreme Courts. It seems that Newby is not too firmly convinced of his position regarding the relevance of constitutional interpretation versus scientific data, because he admits (p. 15) that law "must reflect scientific truth, for to deny such a principle is, presumably, to say that truth is irrelevant to law."

Regrettably, integrationists in general are unwilling to admit pertinent biological data but base their case on social science testimony, and they are unwilling to have this evidence subjected to critical examination. Persuasive assertion seems to be preferred to truth. "Scientific racists," on the other hand, ask for a critical examination of all pertinent evidence.

In lieu of weighing evidence, one of the favorite techniques of the integration phalanx is to create and publicize terms of special opprobrium and then apply those terms to those who oppose them. In addition to "racist," the words "prejudice" and "bigotry" have served quite effectively in lieu of sound argument. Attacks to discredit the opposition is also a common technique.

Polemics of Race

In his book, Newby devotes several pages to demeaning me and my attempted contribution to an understanding of the race problem, especially to my *Biology of the Race Problem*.[1] He speaks of the magnitude of my deception and uses various devices and charges for depreciating and nullifying the influence of my writings. It may be justifiable to take note of some of these. In a comment (p. 112) on my discussion of race and crime, he charges me with ignoring the literature opposed to my conclusions and he cites one publication that I should have considered. I shall not here review and evaluate the merit of that publication, but merely note that it was dated two years *after* my booklet was published. Failure to take cognizance of a publication that appeared two years later scarcely seems a culpable offense.

On page 108 he condemns me for not informing my readers of the "relative stature" of the scientists whose testimony I cited and whether or not they were racists. He seems to be under the delusion that validity of testimony may be determined by the popular distinction of the witness and his antiracist orthodoxy, rather than by the truth of the testimony.

As a matter of fact, all of the authors cited by me in support of racial differences are men of competence and merit, trained in their fields; men who investigated an important and difficult problem with the material and resources available to them. They have not discouraged further investigation with adequate resources.

I am well aware of the incompleteness and inadequacies of the evidence regarding physical differences in the structure of Negro and white brains, but the evidence is too strong and too important to be pushed aside as being of no consequence while fateful and irreversible compulsory programs are instituted on less meritorious foundations. Let's investigate the problem and resolve the doubts before the decisions are made and executed, not afterwards.

In some instances our author goes a bit beyond the bounds of

[1] W. C. George, *The Biology of the Race Problem* (National Putnam Letters Committee, 1962).

academic etiquette in trying to make a case against my arguments. In the beginning of my booklet I identified authors to be cited on special points of scientific fact and dissociated them from necessarily joining me in my position regarding school integration. Instead of accepting this at face value, Newby goes to some pains to give a malevolent interpretation to my statement and indicates that I cited them because I felt that their names would add luster to my work. Nonsense! I cited them as reputable scientists, not as window dressing or doctrinaire witnesses, on important points of scientific fact or judgment. Their testimony was relevant to points at issue. None of them has reneged, so far as I know, on the testimony cited. On the contrary, one of them, Halstead, has said publicly, "This is my view, and I am quoted correctly." But he does not wish to be considered a racist. Newby cites others who wish to stand from under any charge of racism. I cannot condemn them for that.

I have noticed, however, that those who have stood from under and condemned racism in published statements have offered no significant evidence to support equalitarianism or to disprove the evidence and argument I presented in *The Biology of the Race Problem* and elsewhere. They have merely condemned me and racism, sometimes emotionally. For example, Newby quotes Halstead as saying, "In my opinion, the ghost of racist dogma must be laid to rest before any comprehensive investigation of the important scientific problem posed by race can be undertaken." This is to say we must make and implement our decision in a predetermined way before we consider the facts. Unfortunately, this seems to be the prevalent attitude created by decades of massive emotional propaganda.

Newby, while trying to indict me for misrepresenting Curt Stern, states (p. 109) that Stern is in fact "an outspoken equalitarian." Then, a little further on, he charges me with "creating and then demolishing an equalitarian straw man." Now we have an equalitarian and now we don't. In an argument it is nice if you can have it both ways.

Regarding my citation of distinguished neurologists Penfield, Rasmussen, and Herrick, for points on general neurology, he suggests that my authorities did not support my thesis that the behavioral and personality traits of Negroes are explained by the morphology of the Negro brain. The fact is that I never cited them on this point. I doubt, however, that any one of them would disagree with the general proposition that there is a causal relation between brain structure and behavioral and personality traits. Herrick has made himself quite clear on this point, and I shall quote him later.

The equalitarians' unwillingness to admit for consideration any evidence that opposes their dogmas is illustrated by Newby's terminal statement (p. 117) in the pages devoted to me: "There is no evidence that Negroes are in any way racially inferior to whites." This is an extreme statement that calls for more than mere assertion. I wonder if the authors of that statement would be willing to say that there is no evidence that whites are in any way racially inferior to Negroes. I would not.

Behavior and Structure

Since Professor Newby sees fit to challenge me specifically on (1) the relation between behavior, personality, and structure, and (2) structural differences between Negro and white brains, I shall comment further on these two points.

Regarding the first, is there good evidence and informed judgment that behavior and personality traits have any important basis in hereditary morphological features? Since Penfield, Rasmussen, Halstead, and Herrick have been involved in this argument, let's see how one of them, Herrick, expressed himself:

Even in the exigencies of war combat, whether the soldier comes out of the battle strengthened and stabilized or irreparably shattered by war neurosis depends in large part upon personal qualities that were his own before he entered the army.

We are led to the general conclusion that every behavioral act is the resultant of the interplay between presently operating agencies and a structural organization with a pattern of action that has been elaborated during the previous experience of the individual and of his species in the long course of evolutionary change. It is also clear that during the progress of these changes "behavior evolves from within outward" (Yakovlev '48); that is, the primary determiners of the patterns of behavior reside within the organism, not in the environment. In all studies of behavior the focal point of interest is the behavior of the individual, for behavior is primarily personal and its effect upon the person is the crucial issue.

This statement does not carry the implication that any behavior is exclusively motivated by the internal factors, for environmental influences (immediate or previous experiences) are always present, and in some situations, particularly in the social relations, the external factors are clearly predominant. Yet an overall survey of the evolutionary and personal development shows that the intrinsic factors play the larger part in shaping the course of this development. How the organism adjusts to the environment depends primarily on the qualities of the organism itself.[2]

This is quite in conflict with the equalitarian, journalistic science expressed in *Time* for September 29, 1967: "It is well established that the controlling factors in human achievement are cultural and environmental."

Pursuing the matter of structure and function further, when one correlates the old gross and microscopic anatomy and physiology with the new electron microscopy and biochemical physiology, the conclusion is confirmed that every metabolic reaction and every physiological process has its basis in structure. It follows that where the structure is lacking so is the reaction.[3]

Relating our problem specifically to the nervous system, Sir John Eccles, neurophysiologist of Australia, in commenting upon the meeting of neurologists at the 1965 Rome meeting of the World Academy of Arts and Sciences, said: "It was agreed by all participants that every conscious experience—every perception, thought and memory—has as its material counterpart some specific spatio-temporal activity in the vast neuronal network of the cerebral cortex and subcortical nuclei, being woven of neuronal activity in space and time in the 'enchanted loom' so poetically described by Sherrington." [4]

To discover how data supports informed opinion, let us begin with the classical researches of G. E. Coghill.[5]

Coghill assumed that function is the operation of a mechanism and that the mechanism must be present before one can have function. In order to test this hypothesis, he devised means of making precise observations on developing salamander embryos. He found that the behavior pattern develops in a regular order of movements which is consistent with the order of development of the nervous system and its parts. He states that the neural mechanism is potentially the behavior insofar as the pattern is concerned. Although

2 C. J. Herrick, *The Evolution of Human Nature* (Austin: The University of Texas Press, 1956).

3 From a lecture by Irwin J. Kopin, NIH, at the University of North Carolina Medical School, October 28, 1967.

4 Sir John Eccles, "The Fundamental Importance of Brain Research," in S. Mudd (ed.), *Conflict Resolution and World Education* (The Hague: Dr. W. Junk, 1966).

5 G. E. Coghill, *Anatomy and the Problem of Behavior* (London: Cambridge University Press, 1929).

recognizing that the experience of the individual is a factor in determining the specificity of function of constituent neurones, his observation led him to the conclusion that behavior patterns are determined, insofar as our present knowledge goes, exclusively by the laws of growth within the organism—observations and conclusion that obviously have much bearing on the heredity versus environment issue.

Passing from salamander to man, Coghill noted that "while man's behavior pattern is still of the simplest order, long before birth, his mechanism that has to do with the most refined adjustments in life has already the major structural features that characterize it in the adult."

Although Coghill's research was done mostly on the lowly salamander, the principle that he established (that mechanism comes before function in nervous activity) may be assumed to apply to man. It seems impractical to confirm this assumption by duplicating on man the type of observations Coghill made on salamanders. However, there is considerable evidence derived from another approach that supports the conclusion that in man, too, nervous function in general and in detail is dependent upon the existence and the maturation of the nervous mechanism. I cite first the work of Dr. LeRoy Conel, of Boston University Medical School.[6]

As a result of a microscopic study of brains of many children of different ages and a correlation of their structure with observed behavior of children of corresponding ages, Dr. Conel reached the conclusion that in man, too, functional proficiency is dependent upon the existence and the maturation of the nervous mechanism.

He found, for example, that the sequence in the state of development of the cortex conforms to the degree of control in the voluntary use of muscles in the child. He found also a substantial increase in the thickness of the supragranular layers of the cortex of the frontal lobe of the six-year-old child as compared to four-year-olds—an increase corresponding to increase in intellectual understanding in the six-year-old as compared with the four-year-old. This is in harmony with the discoveries and concepts of Bolton to be discussed further on.

In case any one might wonder if this postnatal differentiation of the cortex was largely determined by environmental experience,

[6] LeRoy Conel, *The Postnatal Development of the Human Cerebral Cortex* (8 vols.; Cambridge: Harvard University Press, 1967). See especially Vol. VIII.

it would be instructive to know the course of events before birth. Fortunately, information has been provided by Th. Rabinowicz of the Laboratory of Neuropathology, Lausanne, Switzerland.[7] He found in the eight-month fetus that the general plan of cyto-architectonic structure of the cortex is already established but that there are differences in degree of development in different areas. He reports, for example, that the anterior areas of the frontal lobes, the chief centers for intellectual functioning, are less advanced in development than the cortex of the precentral gyrus, the area for discharge of voluntary motor impulses in the fetuses' prenatal movements. He states specifically that the primary motor and sensory areas are more matured than the association areas in all cerebral lobes. Confirming the work of others, he reports that the infragranular layers, believed to be especially concerned with the more instinctive functions, are matured earlier than the supra-granular layers, which are more especially concerned with the higher intellectual activities.

Pertinent also at this point is a report by S. Sarkisov of the Brain Institute, Moscow.[8] He points out that in two and a half- to three-month human fetuses autonomic action and reflexes involving the earliest maturing portions of the brain prevail. He states that "as the brain cortex matures, the character of the reactions changes." And after birth "the formation of higher nervous activity in children is determined by the degree of maturation of the brain."

All of this testimony leaves little grounds for doubt that behavior has its basis in structure in man as well as in Coghill's salamanders. It also adds further support to the belief that the supragranular layers of the cortex are especially concerned with intellectual capacities.

Comparative Morphology

We come next to a consideration of the second point upon which I was challenged by Professor Newby. I refer to the matter of comparative differences in the morphology of Negro and Caucasian brains. In this area Newby displays a propensity to dismiss as pseudoscience unwelcome testimony that he has inadequate testi-

---

7 Th. Rabinowicz, "The Cerebral Cortex of the Premature Infant of the Eighth Month," *Progress in Brain Research*, IV: 39–86.

8 S. Sarkisov, "The Evolutionary Aspect of the Integrative Function of the Cortex and Subcortex of the Brain," *Progress in Brain Research*, IV: 30–38.

mony to refute. This is a very crucial field and deserves our sincerest study. Some points call for further study while other points are so well established that perhaps no one familiar with the evidence would care to question them. One of these well established points is the average size of Negro and Caucasian brains. Several studies based on many brains, made throughout the world, show the average weight of the Negro brain to be about 10 per cent less than the white brain. The meaning of this is disputed.

Many, perhaps all, critical scholars who have considered the relation of brain size to intelligence seem in agreement that when considering the various animal groups in the vertebrate class, the comparative level of intelligence in the group is related to the average size of the brain. Equalitarians are unwilling to apply to man the general principle established in the vertebrate class. This rejection of the principle seems illogical. It is a point deserving of special effort at resolution.

Aside from weight, the comparative racial feature of the brain of greatest significance appears to be the comparative thickness of the horizontal layers of the cortex. This brings us to an evaluation of the work of Vint and its significance to the race problem.[9] Newby is ready to dismiss it as of "little scientific value" or as "pseudoscience." I do not know that Newby or his advisers are qualified to dismiss seemingly good research so peremptorily.

Vint appears to have been a competent scholar experienced in the field of anatomy. His research was based on a considerable number (100) of East African brains. The report of his research was published in one of the most reputable anatomical journals in the world. The report was not massive but it was adequate to give an account of his technique and a clear summary of his results. His technique of selecting brains, of handling them in preparation for study appears to have been good. So far as I know, no similar study has ever been made for comparison. This is urgently called for. Meanwhile, Vint's research can not be wisely nor justifiably dismissed and the opposite of his findings assumed to be true and taken as justification for fateful decisions in order to carry out revolutionary ideology.

Although there have been no parallel studies confirming (or discrediting) Vint's observations, there have been collateral intra-

[9] F. W. Vint, "The Brain of the Kenya Native," *Journal of Anatomy*, LXVIII: 216–23.

racial observations that tend to give validity to his work. I refer to measurements of the layers of the cortex at different stages of human development. Some of these have been referred to above. I have in mind also the work of Bolton and others during the early years of this century, work which the best neurologists of that time and since have considered to be of great significance. These studies dealt with the comparative thickness of the layers of the cortex in lower mammals and man, and their difference in thickness in human individuals of different levels of intelligence. In view of the importance of knowledge in this field to contemporary social and educational problems and procedures, it may be desirable briefly to review some of the findings and conclusions.

For preliminary clarification to those not acquainted with general structure of the cortex, I should say that it has been found that throughout most of the cortex there are six layers above the deeper white matter of fibers. The fourth or approximately middle of these layers, known as the granular layer, is primarily concerned with receiving and relaying incoming messages. Layers one, two, and three (above the fourth) are known as the supragranular layers; five and six (below it) are known as the infragranular layers. The infragranular layers have most of their connections with lower centers; the supragranular connections are mostly associative connections within the cortex. The infragranular layers are well developed in lower mammals as well as higher; the supragranular layers are not. The supragranular layers are the latest to arise in evolution and the latest to arise and mature in individual development in man. For some details concerning the thickness of layers in some low mammals see Watson[10] or for the rat see Krieg.[11]

On the basis of total evidence, neurologists have been led to the conclusion that the infragranular layers and the supragranular layers though cooperating in function, have different roles to perform. It is believed that the infragranular layers are primarily involved in the more primitive and more fundamental animal reactions, primarily of a motor character. The supragranular layers are believed to be primarily concerned with the higher, associative mental functions.

10 G. A. Watson, "The Mammalian Cerebral Cortex, with Special Reference to Its Comparative Histology," *Archives of Neurology*, III: 50–117.

11 W. J. S. Krieg, "Connections of the Cerebral Cortex," *Journal of Comparative Neurology*, LXXXIV: 277–323.

Joseph Shaw Bolton made extensive comparisons of these layers in animals and man.[12] He observed that there are notable individual differences in degree of development of the cortex of children of different ages, and he said: "This truth is the anatomical counterpart of the great individual differences in the degree of mental development of infants and young children." We have seen above that Bolton's findings in children have been confirmed by the recent work of Conel. On the basis of his study of mentally deficient individuals, Bolton reported that the thickness of the supragranular layers shows an almost exact correspondence with the degree of amentia or dementia that existed.

Marion Hines remarked: "If Bolton is anywhere near right, educability may inhere in the upper layers where the interpretation, correlation and discrimination of incoming proprioceptive sensibility seem to take place." [13] Certainly it emphasizes their importance to some human problems.

Superimpose on the above general knowledge of the layers of the cortex the findings of Vint that the Cortex of the Negro is about 14 per cent thinner, mostly in the supragranular layers, than that found in white Europeans, it should be obvious that we have here some biological facts that demand careful examination and consideration before we decide on a compulsory program of revolutionary changes in social and educational procedures.

The Power of Genes

Shall we dismiss the genes in considering human social problems? There is a doctrine that inherent contrasting characters and abilities can be equalized if from early life the environment is equalized artificially by government pressures and programs. It might be well therefore to examine the results on contrasting genetic characters of equalizing the environment from early life, from very early prenatal life. I cite the work of Beatrice Mintz, experimental embryologist with the Institute for Cancer Research, Philadelphia.[14]

The experimenter produced composite mice, hundreds of them,

[12] Joseph Shaw Bolton, "A Contribution to the Localization of Cerebral Function . . . ," *Brain*, XXXIII: 26–142; and Joseph Shaw Bolton, *The Brain in Health and Disease* (London: Edward Arnold, 1914).

[13] Marion Hines, "On Cerebral Localization," *Physiological Reviews*, IX: 462–574.

[14] Beatrice Mintz, "Gene Control of Mammalian Pigmentary Differentiation," *Proceedings of the National Academy of Science*, LVIII: 344–351.

through the process of fusing segmenting eggs from pregnant donor females. Each composite embryo was then reimplanted in a pseudo-pregnant host. For donor females the experimenter selected inbred strains of white mice and of colored mice. With continued cell division, cells of these two different genotypes intermingled in the composite embryos. In the course of future development melanoblasts were formed to give color to the embryos. For our purposes, the significant fact is that the two original genic types of melanoblasts developed in accordance with their separate genetic types in spite of having been intermingled in a common environment. For what it is worth, it seems desirable to note that in the mature mice there was not a blended gray color or a pepper and salt distribution of black and white melanoblasts but a regional segregation of black and white melanocytes.

If one be tempted to consider that genetic laws are pertinent to melanoblasts but not to neuroblasts and the whole nervous system, it seems worth recalling that melanoblasts are derived from the neural plate which gives rise to the nervous system. It would seem a bit biased, to say the least, to observe genetic control of melanoblasts and deny it for neuroblasts.

The above facts give no support to the equalitarian dogma that environment will overcome hereditary qualities in a population. The reality and the significance of race seem demonstrated. If there are still lingering doubts, our society should postpone radical programs and demand a thorough research of the doubtful points.

R. Gayre

A Reply to
Challenge to the Court

I am not concerned here with Professor Newby's general arguments except to say that, despite his qualification of his use of such words as "racialists" and "racists" in his preface, a part of a book which most readers ignore, the very use of such expressions is calculated to prejudice the reader against those whom he seeks to attack. It is as bad as if he had said that when he used the term "Nazi" he did not mean German Hitlerian Nazi. As far as the reader is concerned, the use of that term would, for all that, imply that the person attacked was a German Hitlerian Nazi in some form or another. I consider that such a usage discredits the objectivity of the author himself.

What I am concerned with, however, are the references made to *The Mankind Quarterly* and the present respondent, who is its editor.

Professor Newby is, according to the dust jacket, an historian, and so is not in any way an expert in the fields of ethnology and anthropology which are those with which we (the present writer and *The Mankind Quarterly*) are concerned. Nevertheless, this does not deter him from assessing the qualities of publications in fields in which it appears he is in no way qualified. However, the fair test is to see how far Professor Newby's findings can stand up to qualified analysis in the field of race. On page 138 he says: "*Mankind Quarterly,* a small journal with an imposing name, is the nearest thing scientific racists have to an official journal. Published in Edinburgh, Scotland, it has, since its first issue in 1960, played a major role in the promotion of scientific racism."

Any unbiased and discerning reader must realize that Newby is approaching the subject not as an impartial critic but as an advocate with a particular point of view—a point of view the opposite of "racism," which must be "a-racism" and must therefore be as propagandist as the alleged "racism" of which he accuses *The Mankind Quarterly.*

It will also be observed at the outset that Newby is not concerned to meet and destroy the scientific papers of scientists published in *The Mankind Quarterly,* but directs his arguments *ad personam,* to the denigration of the publication itself.

The Mankind Quarterly is a *small* journal—but so are the Gospels *small* books, although he would be a brave and equally foolish man who condemned them on that score. But it appears to this professor of history that the size of the publication is material, and knowing that size is important, as the size of their herd must have been to the Gadarene swine, he makes that point at the outset, not omitting to make the further point that it is the only journal of this outlook—which is in fact the classical exposition of anthropology as always understood in the past by the majority of its greatest exponents.

The fair-minded reader will not have failed to observe also Dr. Newby's use of the expression "a small journal with an imposing name." But is this name not appropriate for a journal which consistently since its first publication has been concerned with the races of mankind? However, I am certain that this learned professor of the history department of the California State College, Fullerton, is interested only in scoring a cheap and shoddy point of propaganda, on the score that his readers will be immediately conditioned, as were Pavlov's dogs, into reacting adversely to the juxtaposition of *The Mankind Quarterly* and "small journal," "imposing name," "nearest thing scientific racists have to an official journal," and so on.

How far should Professor Newby be taken as an historian at all in this field which he has chosen for his exercise in expert and subjective denigration? An historian is supposed to sift the facts and have evidence for the statements he makes. Newby states, without any apparent embarrassment whatsoever, that not only has *The Mankind Quarterly* played a major role in the promotion of what he calls "scientific racism" but "in many instances the same men direct the affairs of the *Quarterly* and the IAAEE."

Only one person directs *The Mankind Quarterly* and that is the editor and publisher, the present writer. Naturally, since Professor Henry E. Garrett, Professor Stanley D. Porteus, Professor Wesley C. George, and others he mentions are distinguished men in matters connected with the studies of race, they are associated with *The Mankind Quarterly* and with the IAAEE.[1] But this does not prove any common direction between these organizations and it is purely fortuitous that some persons happen to be associated with both. I was asked to join the IAAEE at its inception, but never once has my opinion been asked on any matter, never once have I been called to a meeting—nor, so far as I know, have I ever been asked to contribute a single paper for its publications. It is therefore untrue to suggest that there is a common direction of *The Mankind Quarterly* and the IAAEE.

Professor Newby states that I am editor, and that "R. Ruggles Gates, a British geneticist who generally endorsed the ideas of scientific racism, was, until his death in 1962, an honorary associate editor." Surely Newby should give all the relevant historical facts in his thesis? R. Ruggles Gates was a very distinguished professor of London University, a fellow of the Royal Society of London, a former president of the Royal Anthropological Institute, and the author of over four hundred papers and books on heredity and

[1] Professor Frank C. J. McGurk, Dr. Audrey M. Shuey, Dr. Charles C. Tansill, Professor Herbert Sanborn, Professor Clarence P. Oliver, Professor Harry Turney-High, Dr. Robert Kuttner, and Professor A. James Gregor.

related subjects—among which are large works on human heredity. Is the omission of those facts not a prime example of a lack of any impartiality?

Newby goes on to say that, while *The Mankind Quarterly* claims to be an international journal dealing with race and inheritance in various scientific fields, "in point of fact, however, it is little more than an outlet for disseminating the ideas of scientific racism. . . ." He alleges (p. 138) that this can be proved by the fact that it espouses "racial views which were fashionable among social scientists two generations ago but which have since largely disappeared from scientific circles."

This statement is no more accurate than many other generalizations in his book. *The Mankind Quarterly* certainly takes a stand which is based upon the classical views of anthropology and inheritance, and certainly the great pioneers in this field from Darwin to Mendel—and on to Sir Arthur Keith, Sir Elliot Grafton Smith, Sir William Turner, Beddoe, Denicker, Ripley, Professors Sergi, Dixon, Fischer, Hooton, Pittard, and Karl Pearson, and a host of others—would find themselves in agreement with its general bases of thought. Now the work of one generation of science does not destroy another's, for if it did, then there would be no scientific progress whatsoever. Science makes new discoveries based on the older, and one evolves from the other. It would therefore be a matter for great surprise if it were found that classical genetics and anthropology were destroyed by modern discoveries in these fields. Furthermore, that his statement is not true is self-evident when it is remembered that nearly all the scientists assailed by the Professor in his apologetic are living persons, and even Professor Ruggles Gates who died in 1962 was completely up to date in all his genetics at the time of his death. There are also other scientists holding university chairs in these subjects, who are not mentioned in his book, who subscribe to the view of heredity as a potent force in the development of man, and therefore believe in the importance of race. Indeed, although most geneticists and physical anthropologists would prefer to avoid the issue when they realize the denigration they are likely to suffer if they are forced to declare themselves, they would, if pressed, agree with expositions which reject the Lamarckian concepts on which so many sociological schools of thought are today based.

This brings us to consideration of Professor Newby's citation of present-day social scientists. We might very well ask what the majority of them have to do with the question of race and heredity at all. With few exceptions they are not scientists, they gravitate to the concepts of Lamarck (environmentalism), and although they dare not reject Mendelian genetics outright in favour of those obsolete views (because they know that to do so would make them a laughing stock even in the present climate of opinion), they nevertheless fail to appreciate or base their teaching upon heredity and scientific fact. Since they are largely moved by social and political concepts and do not make their expositions with regard to the known facts of heredity, their views in the vast majority of cases are entirely irrelevant to the issues with which *The Mankind Quarterly* is concerned.

It would be tedious to take all the numerous points which Newby seeks to make, as there are limits to what can be printed in this reply. But to suggest that the editors encourage papers which deal condescendingly with "natives" is entirely untrue. As a native of Scotland I have never had any difficulty in the proper use of this word, and since a significant number of articles, especially on the races and tribes of Africa, are written by me, I can say that I have never used the word in a condescending manner at any time.

Of course, numerous writers in *The Mankind Quarterly* attack environmentalism and Franz Boas, that appalling disaster to American social anthropology whose influence in the end has divorced the social studies of man from their scientific base in physical biology. But this is a duty which falls to anyone making an objective analysis of social thinking as it relates to anthropology today —and I have no doubt that Mendel will triumph over Lamarck and Boas in the end, and thereby justify *The Mankind Quarterly* for its refusal to be swept aside from objective into subjective scholarship. If in the course of this, some writers in *The Mankind Quarterly* have found it necessary to refer to the views and activities of so-called "liberals," "integrationists," and communists, they are justified in so doing as this is relevant, for Marxist thought is based upon the scientific heresies of Lamarck, and it is this political dogma which in a greater or lesser degree has come to infect many elements engaged in sociological propaganda of one kind or another. It is precisely because such people have made little or no attempt to accept scientific principles as a basis of their expositions that it has been necessary to protest against this invasion of what pretends to be science (although many of us would deny that sociology or social anthropology could qualify for such a designation) by unproved and, indeed, useless and unprovable dogmas of environmentalism.

One would imagine that Dr. Newby is joking when he accuses me of opening the pages of *The Mankind Quarterly* to racists, segregationists, political reactionaries, and some who are not scientists, for he himself, quite obviously, comes into a political propagandist category, and one fails to see why he should object to people of precisely his own kind but of opposite point of view making their ideas felt while he retains such rights for himself.

On page 139 Professor Newby says: "Each issue includes several book reviews, a surprisingly large number of which are of works that are not scientific and make no pretense to being scientific." These are reviews of books relating to social anthropology or racial history, or works dealing with persons concerned with applied anthropology or the administration of colonial peoples, which are all relevant subjects to a knowledge of mankind, although they are not scientific works, but they are nevertheless to be regarded as scholarly in the majority of cases. To review, for instance, *The Diaries of Lord Lugard,* or *Caste in Modern India,* or *Folk Tales of Pakistan,* is just as relevant to the subject as to deal with human genetics. In making the foregoing complaint Professor Newby clearly indicates his own ignorance of the nature of the subject.

Newby's impartiality and accuracy can clearly be assessed from his statement that each issue contains reviews of which a surprisingly large number are of works that are not scientific, most of which deal with civil rights and racial integration. In Volume I there were 93 reviews of which only three were concerned with those subjects, and in Volume III there were only 2 out of 79. In the first seven volumes (down to 1967) there are 395 reviews of which only 38 can be said to deal with books concerned with integration and the white-black problem. This is only about 9 per cent of the total. In view of the importance of this issue today this must be well below the average in many other journals.

On page 140 Professor Newby commits himself to a statement which is no less than suppression of facts. There he quotes a communication in *Man* from a Jugoslav anthropologist, the late Bozo Skerlj, to the effect that he had resigned from *The Mankind Quarterly* for its alleged racialism. Professor Newby follows up with other criticisms from *Man,* which is the journal of the Royal Anthropological Institute, London.

Does Professor Newby tell his readers what was the outcome of Bozo Skerlj's statement in *Man,* which was, according to him, the prelude to a series of attacks on *The Mankind Quarterly?* He does not. In fact, Bozo Skerlj, the editor of *Man* and the Royal Anthropological Institute were sued for libel by the editors of *The Mankind Quarterly,* and as a result the defendants had to withdraw the defamatory statement by Skerlj they had published, by printing their retraction of it in *Man;* they had to make restitution for the damage which the editors had suffered, and they had to pay the costs to which we had been put.

Newby has before him the volumes of *The Mankind Quarterly,* but he apparently deliberately distorts facts as to the number of reviews dealing with integration problems, and then he quotes an attack on *The Mankind Quarterly* without telling his readers that the substance of that attack was withdrawn before the High Court of Justice, in London, and that the publication in which it appeared, *Man,* had to make a retraction and pay the costs involved. This information is available to him in *Man,* which he cites when it suits him, and which in any case as an historian it is his duty to investigate.

I feel that the attempt to make the respondent a "racist" (pp. 143–44) can be ignored, as the judicious reader can form by now his own conclusions as to the value to be placed upon Professor Newby's assertions where *The Mankind Quarterly* and its editor are concerned.

Carleton Putnam

A Reply to
Challenge to the Court

Unfortunately, Professor Newby's volume crossed in the mail, so to speak, my latest book, *Race and Reality*, which appeared only slightly before *Challenge to the Court* and had not yet come to Newby's attention. *Race and Reality* answers so many of the questions, and I believe clarifies so much of the misunderstanding, in Newby's work that I would like at the outset to recommend it to any sincere student of our racial difficulties, particularly in view of the limitations of space available to me here.[1]

Obviously Newby and I approach the problem of race from op-

[1] *Race and Reality* is published in both hard cover and paperback by Public Affairs Press, Washington, D.C.

posite points of view. Newby takes the position that the preponderance of evidence is decisively on the side of the nonexistence of significant genetic differences in intelligence and temperament between the white and Negro races. I take the view that the balance is overwhelmingly on the other side. It so happens that the Council of the National Academy of Sciences, the most illustrious scientific group in the country and an official agency of the United States government, declared publicly on October 23, 1967, that "there is no scientific basis for a statement that there are *or that there are not* [emphasis mine] substantial hereditary differences in intelligence between Negro and white populations." In other words, it is the position of the Academy at the moment that Newby and I are both wrong.

Remember, however, that Newby's view has been the exclusive dogma presented to the Anglo-American public for more than a generation. Consider also that the Academy's statement occurred in a context which is nothing if not revealing. The Academy was responding to a plea by William Shockley, Nobel laureate and co-inventor of the transistor, that the Academy sponsor research on race differences. Shockley, one of the Academy's most distinguished members but a newcomer to the race debate, had been jolted by the discovery that what I and others had been saying about the suppression of research and the persecution of nonequalitarian scientists was true. His own investigation within the Academy had confirmed it.

Shockley perhaps imagined that all he would need to do would be to call this state of affairs to the attention of the Academy's Council and prompt action would follow. He may, indeed, have been startled by the sequel, but I was not. In fact, after ten years of involvement in this struggle, I believe I can assure any impartial investigator that the reason the Academy will not sponsor research on this most urgent question, concerning which they admit total ignorance, is that they fear the result. They know that they have condoned for thirty years a policy on the part of our educational establishment and our mass media of indoctrinating the public in a fantasy. They also know that whatever their definition of "scientific basis" may be, the overwhelming preponderance of the credible evidence is on the nonequalitarian side. More research, they realize, can only confirm it and thus place them in the position of participating in their own impeachment.

But before going further with this subject I would like to deal with a few introductory matters. It has long been the habit of equalitarians to present their case in such a way as to arouse anger rather than reason toward their opponents. When Newby uses the terms "racist" and "racism" throughout his book he must know that since the days of Hitler these words have implied a certain opprobrium. Newby in his preface defines "racist" in a way which, while not precisely a definition of my own position, cannot be considered objectionable. But such a preface does not erase the general effect of the term on the reader's emotions. If I were constantly to use the words "subversive" and "subversion" in regard to Newby's ideology, it might produce a similar effect, even though I were careful to say at the outset that by "subversion" I meant only the rewriting of our Constitution by judicial interpretation instead of by amendment. I would ignore the point were it not that the smear technique rather than genuine analysis seems to characterize much of Newby's writing—ridicule and innuendo are more noticeable than relevant facts. It is often Newby's habit to quote a nonequalitarian statement in a context of ridicule and then to assume it needs no further answer, whereas in fact it is his ridicule that is ridiculous, not the nonequalitarian statement. Specifically regarding the charge of "racism," I can only remark that if Dr. George, Dr. Garrett, or I are "racists," then Washington, Jefferson, and Lincoln were "racists," since our position is identical with theirs.

On the other hand, I can hardly condemn Newby's amusing error in stating that I do not have a science degree, but only the degree of "bachelor of science in history and politics." This is, of course, a little like remarking that a man has a degree of bachelor of arts in physics. Apparently Newby has been confused by the fact that in seeking as broad an undergraduate education as possible I took honors in the department of history and politics at Princeton while at the same time completing all of the courses for a regular science degree, which I received. Save for Newby's comment that Southern references to my science degree are intended to create "a false impression" this, too, would be irrelevant. In *Race and Reality* I concede quite frankly that "I have a science degree, as well as a law degree, but I have never pretended to be a professional scientist or a specialist in racial matters. What I have done is listen to both sides and read materials presented by both sides—at the same time noting the efforts by the scientific hierarchy to suppress and distort evidence and to persecute other scientists who offer material exploding the equalitarian dogma. Then I have tried to call the attention of the public to what is going on."

I would like next to examine Newby's use of the words "segregation" and "segregationist." While characterizing my work as "simplistic," Newby seems to me very simplistic here. At least as far as my personal views are concerned one gets the impression from Newby that separation everywhere and always is my aim. Yet I define my position clearly in *Race and Reality* in these words:

> I cannot over-emphasize the importance of the concept of variability in dealing with any racial problem. We have the variability of the genetic spectrum, of the population ratio, and finally of the community setting. Consider a small town in Montana which has two or three Negro families whose predominantly White genes show in blue eyes, straight hair, sharp noses, and relatively high I.Q., and whose Negro genes are only apparent in skin color; then compare this town with one in Alabama where the population is over fifty per cent Negro of pure or nearly pure blood, with prognathous jaws, kinky hair, flat noses, everted lips and relatively low I.Q. In the first situation it might be justifiable to have no segregation at all, while in the second some segregation might be essential. What could be more apt to invite community disruption than to try to control racial problems in those two towns by the same set of laws made by politicians sitting in Washington and hoping to win the Negro vote in New York—or by a Supreme Court which has heard only one side of the evidence on genetic racial differences?

I say elsewhere in my book that, if one must search for a general rule, a program of desegregation in nonsocial situations, and segregation in social situations, would be as close as I could come to it, defining "social situation" as one which has genetic implications. But even this would have to be modified by the paragraph just quoted.

Newby also leaves the impression that I would deny voting and other civil rights to Negroes although I would deny no civil rights to anyone, provided such rights are defined as originally written into our Constitution and not as reinterpreted by a Supreme Court noted for substituting its judgment for the amending process. The Constitution leaves voting requirements to the several states which, in this instance particularly, is exactly where it belongs. While the Constitution does not permit discrimination by race in these requirements, it does, thank God, permit discrimination by intelligence and other criteria.

It would undoubtedly be unreasonable to say that simply because a man is a Negro he cannot vote, but on the other hand it may be essential as a practical matter to establish a more rigorous procedure for selection of voters, both white and black, in communities with heavy Negro concentrations, since the consequences of a failure in, or evasion of, the procedure are more serious. Unfortunately we know from historical experience that Negroes as a race have never been able to maintain a stable, free society, and that government by a Negro majority has invariably ended in either anarchy or dictatorship. With large numbers of Negroes in a community, therefore, it is vital to be *sure* that the level of intelligence of the voting Negro is high, even if this means cutting out larger numbers of less intelligent whites than might be necessary in an all-white community.

I am quite aware of the danger implicit in Newby's point that if a majority of Negroes gain control of any given area by the exercise of their civil right to vote (as I have defined it) they could in that area force integration and other policies to suit themselves. If this occurred widely enough, we would no longer have the American Republic as we have known it, but a Negro republic. Those who contemplate such an eventuality should investigate other Negro "republics" throughout the world and throughout history. The problem deserves study in its relation to our immigration laws and other controls. The uproar in Britain today, where the issue is just arising, indicates a healthy instinct.

If Newby's view of segregation as a social device is simplistic, his legal approach to integration as a "civil right" is more so. There is no "right" to integration, either in our Constitution, our moral code, or our religious precepts. Segregation *for valid reasons* is an accepted social procedure. I cannot claim that I am denied "equal rights" or "civil rights" or "citizenship" as an American, or that I am made a second-class citizen, or that I am deprived of "human dignity," if I am refused the use of a ladies' restroom or if, having a contagious disease, I am placed in a segregated hospital. We need be concerned only with whether the reasons for segregating the Negro are valid, and here the question of the genetic versus the environmental source of his limitations becomes decisive. It is the most basic of all questions, and one which the Supreme Court answered on a record replete with misrepresentation and concealment.

Newby grows even more confused when he contemplates the relation between the individual and his race. He seems to feel that because individuals differ widely and it would be impossible to pick a single individual who was entirely average, therefore the whole concept of race should be discarded in the administration of our political affairs. When I point out that we discriminate against minors in voting, marrying, and driving cars, although certain minors are more intelligent than many adults, he replies: "But the discriminations against minors apply to all minors and are temporary." To which I must rejoin: So do the discriminations against Negroes apply to all Negroes, and if they are not temporary they are easier to evade in practice by moving to other jurisdictions than are the discriminations against minors. What Newby would say about state laws which discriminate against women by forbidding them to work overtime in factories, even though certain women are stronger than many men, I cannot guess. I give these illustrations not to compare hardships but to point out that the *principle* of discrimination by groups is an accepted one in our society. As I have said elsewhere, to damage a whole nation with torrents of injurious influences in order to accommodate the exceptional few is something new even to socialism.

In point of fact, the exceptional Negro has done very well in the United States. I cite here, as but one example, the case of S. B. Fuller which I mention in the footnote on pages 133–34 of *Race and Reality*. What Fuller has to say about the average Negro is noteworthy. And when Newby talks about "clean, God-fearing, hardworking, patriotic, intelligent, middle-class Negroes," I can only remark that if these Negroes were typical there would be no race problem in the world today. Percentages of overlap in IQ vary considerably with the groups chosen for study in different sections of the country and different classes of the population, but a rule-of-thumb across-the-board of 15 per cent for the Negro overlap of the White population as a whole would be generous. In other words 15 per cent of all Negroes surpass the *average* White.

I might add that these are the Negroes whom the liberals in our mass media and our government are always pushing forward on television, in the movies, in advertisements, and in the society columns as representative of the race. Whether these Negroes appreciate their function as ideological decoys, I do not know.

I return now to the essential question: Are there or are there not substantial genetic differences in intelligence and temperament between the white and Negro races? We have seen that the National Academy of Sciences has recently come round to the position that this question is open, although the stance of the scientific hierarchy as a whole for the past thirty years has been strongly on the equalitarian side. We have also noted that the Academy has refused to sponsor research to resolve the matter, giving as their excuse that "none of the current methods can produce unambiguous results" and that "collecting still more data that would be of uncertain meaning" would "invite misuse." I venture to remark that if such a justification had been accepted by scientists in the past, no scientist would ever have discovered anything, and I reiterate my view that the refusal of the Academy is transparently the result of fear of the facts—both the facts that have already been established (but withheld from the public) and such additional facts as new research would disclose.

As is the case with most equalitarians who have attacked my books, Newby makes much of the point that the hierarchy does not support my position, overlooking the main issue with which I deal and which is the whole theme to which *Race and Reality* is addressed, namely, the *reasons why* the hierarchy takes the stand it does. I do not have space here to repeat everything I have said on this point in Chapter II of that volume, but I invite the attention of interested readers to it. It is my contention that any reasonable mind, once it is alerted to all the circumstances and once it examines all the available data, can come to only one conclusion as to the evidence. It is overwhelmingly on the side of the existence of innate race differences, and it has been suppressed solely on account of the social and political bias, not the scientific judgment, of the hierarchy.

I would point out, further, that where public policy is concerned, society often must make its decisions on the basis of the *preponderance* of the evidence; it cannot wait in every case until every facet of every issue is supported by conclusive proof. While mathematical exactness is necessary and practical in the physical sciences, this is frequently not the case in the life sciences, and it is rarely true in the management of human societies. For example, our Anglo-American legal system requires simply a preponderance of the credible evidence in civil cases and proof "beyond *reasonable* doubt" [emphasis mine] in criminal cases. It would be manifestly impossible to function at all if absolute certainty were a prerequisite, either for every decision at law or for every public policy. And I would emphasize that in the current racial situation, not only is the preponderance of the evidence sufficient in my opinion to constitute proof beyond reasonable doubt, but that we are forming all our public policies, both foreign and domestic, on the assumption that the opposite of this evidence is true. Again I invite the reader's attention to *Race and Reality*, this time to Chapter III.

Newby seems oblivious to all of these matters. For instance, he makes much of Dwight Ingle's attack on W. C. George's *Biology of the Race Problem* in which Ingle depreciates Connolly's comparative studies of the structure of white and Negro brains. But George was not offering Connolly's material as final proof. He was offering it as one of many items of *evidence*. As to its admissibility as such evidence, I need only state that it was called to my own attention by Carleton S. Coon, whom Newby himself describes as "one of the nation's most eminent anthropologists, a past president of the American Association of Physical Anthropologists and formerly Curator of Ethnology and Professor of Anthropology at the University of Pennsylvania Museum in Philadelphia." I might add that it was likewise Coon who directed me to the statement of Garrett Hardin. (If Newby wonders why Coon signed the Moscow statement of 1964, let him examine the circumstances surrounding that event as I report them on page 37 of *Race and Reality*.)

Newby next revels in the fact that Wilder Penfield, Theodore Rasmussen, and Ward C. Halstead have disassociated themselves from George's *general* position, but Newby again forgets that George cited them only on *specific* items of evidence. What George did was to quote Penfield *et al.*, on the relation between the frontal lobes of the brain (regardless of race) and certain aspects of intelligence. He then cited other scientists on race differences in the frontal lobes. Penfield, Rasmussen, and Halstead had conducted no research on race differences, and they were not cited on race differences. Apparently it is Newby's view that if one wishes to support a proposition which requires evidence on both point A and point B, and if one uses one witness to testify on point A and a different witness on point B, the testimony of the first witness is valueless on point A because he differs with the second witness on point B. This is a form of reasoning which I find somewhat unusual. Yet it constitutes the main burden of Newby's attack on *The Biology of the*

Race Problem, not only as regards Penfield and his associates but other scientists as well.

Indeed one finds it difficult to pick and choose among the misconceptions and misunderstandings which sprinkle almost every page of *Challenge to the Court.* I will pause for only one further specific illustration. In his last chapter the author entangles himself in a discussion of IQ and overlap which must raise the eyebrows of all informed readers. Let me explain, first, that an IQ test, ideally administered, is intended to measure the *potential* of the mind, divorced as much as possible from environmental factors. Potential is one thing. Actual performance in a given situation may very well be quite different. Poor environment will undoubtedly inhibit an accurate IQ measurement, but good environment cannot increase an IQ beyond the individual's potential. Two individuals with very different potentials might conceivably be so depressed by a bad environment that they would perform equally poorly on an IQ test. The only significant question is: How would each perform in an environment which inhibited the IQ of neither?

Let us consider this point in relation to what Newby calls the "famous" Demonstration Guidance Project in Junior High School 43 in New York City. Here seven hundred Negro pupils were carefully selected for academic promise. From $80 to $250 more per pupil was expended on materials and extra tuition. The project proved one thing and one thing only, namely, that carefully selected Negroes, specially treated, show higher performance than average Negroes, something which no nonequalitarian would have questioned in the first place. The experiment revealed nothing as to the relative performance of whites and Negroes under similar conditions. And enough is now known on the latter question for us to say that had white pupils been included and given similar special advantages their improvement would have been greater still.

As to the Banneker study in St. Louis, the purpose there was to demonstrate that greater motivation would improve the performance of Negro pupils in twenty-three elementary schools which were 95 per cent Negro. In two years the number of Negro pupils entering Track I (the highest) increased from 7 to 16 per cent. The median IQ increased from 85 to 90. (Plus or minus 5 per cent is considered the allowable margin of error.) Over the same time the percentage of white pupils entering Track I increased from 26 to 39 per cent. Meanwhile 7 per cent of the Negroes were not promoted to the eighth grade, against two-tenths of one per cent of the whites. Obviously the withdrawal of low-grade children from regular classrooms in large and increasing numbers gave an artificial appearance of rising intelligence, such as it was, in the Negro group.

The Washington, D.C., schools add nothing to Newby's case. As of 1966, 93 per cent of these schools were Negro. Only one per cent of the ninth grade students were of college caliber while 41 per cent were retarded from three to seven grades. Let it again be emphasized that some improvement will always result from special effort and attention up to the point of the individual's, or the group's, potential. It cannot increase potential. The folly consists in assuming that potentials are equal, either as between individuals or races, and the greatest folly of all is to deceive the average Negro with the assumption that his capacity is equal to the average white's. Or perhaps I should say the next to the greatest folly—for the supreme stupidity consists in teaching the Negro that his condition nationally is the result not of his own limitations but of white injustice. Here is the root cause of the plundering, burning, and rioting.

For those who wish to explore the subject further I can recommend the speech delivered by Dr. Shockley before the National Academy of Sciences on April 24, 1968. He referred there to the recent study of Dr. Robert E. Kuttner who "has had the ingenuity to extract from the massive and expensive Coleman report the obvious, but previously overlooked, fact that American Indians overcome greater environmental disadvantages to outperform Negroes on achievement and ability tests." Shockley then discusses the researches of Nancy Bayley (1965), M. Harlow (1967), H. M. Skeels (1966), A. B. Wilson (1967), C. Higgins and C. H. Sivers (1958), G. S. Lesser, G. Fifer, and D. H. Clark (1965), M. M. M. P. de Lemos (1966) and other cases to indicate the preponderant power of heredity in overcoming environmental handicaps.

The important thing to recognize is that genetic potential is the controlling factor, and that the point of diminishing returns must be faced in the expenditure of money and effort on the improvement of Negro environment. The solution consists in training the average Negro along the lines of his particular aptitudes, not in assuming that these are identical to those of the average white. As Shockley appropriately points out—after noting that Albert Schweitzer once referred to himself as the Negro's brother, it is true, but his elder brother and that Carleton Coon has speculated that the Negro as a race may be as much as 200,000 years younger than the white man on the ladder of human evolution—"if these conjectures are true, than to demand that a younger brother perform beyond his basic inherent capacities is a most irresponsibly cruel form of brotherhood."

Since I am calling Dr. Shockley as my chief witness in this paper, not on the point of the existence of race differences but on what I have said was the main theme of *Race and Reality,* namely, the reason why it is necessary that the public question the official position of the Anglo-American scientific hierarchy and study the evidence for themselves, it is perhaps proper for me to stress once more his value in this controversy. Dr. Shockley is personally one of the most distinguished members of our scientific establishment. I would judge him also to be one of the most humanitarian of men. As a scholar of exemplary scientific training, yet as one who comes to the subject of race with a fresh viewpoint unbiased by the turmoil of past debate, his qualifications for testifying to what he finds are unique.

Not only did Shockley receive the Nobel Prize for his discovery of the transistor. He was awarded the Medal for Merit for his work as Director of Research of the Anti-submarine Warfare Operations Research Group of the United States Navy during World War II. He also holds the Holley medal of the American Society of Mechanical Engineers, the O. E. Buckley prize of the American Physics Society, the Comstock prize of the National Academy of Sciences and the Morris Liebmann prize of the Institute of Radio Engineers. He received his doctorate from the Massachusetts Institute of Technology. He became the Director of the Transistor Physics Department of the Bell Telephone Laboratories in 1953 and, in addition to this work, is presently Poniatoff Professor of Engineering Science at Stanford University.

Shockley, in other words, knows something about scientific method and has a broad acquaintance throughout the highest echelons of the National Academy. What he is finding and reporting in regard to the suppression of evidence and the persecution of nonequalitarian scientists is therefore of some importance. One such report is on the jacket of *Race and Reality.* Others will be found in his speech of April 24 before the Academy.

But Shockley also has something to say on the evidence itself. He has now been engaged for about two years in his investigation of our race problem. In his speech of April 24, he stated: "An objective examination of relevant data leads me inescapably to the opinion that the major deficit in Negro intellectual performance must be primarily of hereditary origin and thus relatively irremediable by practical improvements in environment." He notes that he calls this his "opinion" and not "proof" *less because he doubts its soundness* than because it "has not yet been subject to the test of objective, open-minded appraisal by a competent scientific tribunal." Here I would ask the question: Where is the competent scientific tribunal to be found? The National Academy has refused to act for what I believe to be the reasons already stated.

Shockley continues:

During the past two years of my part-time investigations I have come to accept as facts, not yet perhaps facts at the level of pure mathematics or physics, but nonetheless facts that I now consider so unassailable that I present them before fellow members of the National Academy of Sciences with a clear scientific conscience. The basic facts are these: Man is a mammal and subject to the same biological laws as other animals. All animals, including man, have inheritable behavioral traits. *The concept of complete environmental plasticity of human intelligence is a nonsensical, wishful-thinking illusion. . . .*

The most dangerous illusion . . . facing humanity today is the belief [which] most scientists lack the courage to doubt, at least for the record, typified by the expressions of our government through its Department of Labor and echoed by the Office of Education. I quote: "There is absolutely no question of any genetic differential: Intelligence potential is distributed among Negro infants in the same proportion and pattern as among Icelanders or Chinese or any other group." The only reason that I do not characterize this statement as a lie, and in my opinion as a damnably evil lie, is that I have no way to appraise the intellectual acumen of its authors. They may actually believe it.

I would find it difficult better to express my own judgment of the central thesis of *Challenge to the Court*. Frankly I remain unimpressed by the implication which runs through so much of Newby's book that those who agree with him are on the side of the angels while the rest of us are travelling the road to perdition. I believe quite the opposite to be the case. And although Newby delights in ridiculing the views of William Massey, I might well repeat one of them here. Referring to the ideologists of which Newby is so typical, Massey says:

This is not a campaign by men who love humanity, but by men obsessed with a vision. Their vision is of a united mankind marching toward a Utopian world. It is the stylized, inhuman vision they love, not man. They do not look at man dispassionately, or even with affection, to see his condition and help him. Instead they preach a mystic brotherhood of man that is both goal and means to the goal. This brotherhood is not reached by good will, understanding and tolerance. It is a fanatic's dream, a will-o'-the-wisp that gives them the self-righteousness to vent their hatreds with a clear conscience. Better an honest enemy than so strange a brother.

In my view, kindness and thoughtfulness of others is an ideal to which every man might well subscribe, but unlimited brotherhood is not. I believe that the man who loves all nations and all races as much as he loves his own is like the man who loves all women as much as he loves his wife. He merits suspicion. I believe the majority of our English-speaking stocks cherish the principles to which their forefathers dedicated their lives and for which they often died. These principles were enshrined in the American Republic which they inherited. They value these more than the thought processes which created the Congo, or Russia, or China, and while they are willing to share the fruits their forefathers bequeathed them, they are not willing to dilute them, nor to kill the tree that bore them, for the Negro or anyone else. I believe that what the blood in their veins earned for them, they are entitled to, and some control over how it is dispensed to those whose genes did not earn it. Charity is one thing. Plundering the provident and intelligent to buy the votes of the shiftless or unintelligent is another matter.

This is not to say that I do not favor or do not, indeed, urge, programs in the slums and elsewhere to determine Negro aptitudes and to place Negroes in employment suitable to those aptitudes. Such studies as are presently being conducted by Dr. Arthur Jensen at the Institute of Human Learning (University of California) in Berkeley, with results described by him to the American Educational Research Association in February, 1968, are worth a hundred inflammatory reports from a Presidential Commission on Civil Disorders.

As for the fruits of Newby's tree, I ask the reader to examine them as of the spring of 1968: racial tensions worse than ever before; a soaring crime rate; murder, rape, and robbery in our streets and stores; the sack of our national capital; cities from coast to coast put to the torch and looted; a welfare burden that proliferates hourly; a fiscal situation in disarray and bled by policies based upon the most disastrous scientific hoax of human history; defiance of properly constituted authority from our campuses to our homes; a weak and divided national leadership; and everywhere a general climate of the appeasement of evil. I venture to say that under the aegis of Newby's ideology there are few indices of a healthy civilization that have not declined.

Finally, I would maintain that if there be any hatred in the hearts of those for whom I believe I speak, it is not towards the Negro, but towards the white man who has deceived the average Negro about his innate capacities and has led him to think that white injustice rather than his own limitations is the primary cause of his status in our society. Undoubtedly the Negro has been done injustice, individually and collectively. So have many other individuals and races throughout history. But to give the impression, as our "liberals" constantly do, that the primary or principal blame for his condition is to be laid at the white man's door is a "damnably evil" lie.

The Negro, and the white man himself, have been saturated with the white-injustice hypothesis for more than a generation. Quite naturally this has produced a desire for revenge in the Negro and a false sense of guilt in the white man. It accounts not only for Negro rioting but for white appeasement and the indulgence of lawlessness. There is just one cure for the whole inexcusable situation: Tell the truth.

Clearly it is not the prerogative of Newby, nor of the National Academy of Sciences, nor of any other clique of intellectuals to dictate what the people in our republic are to be told about the scientific facts, whether it be a question of the preponderance of the evidence or of proof. The present situation is an arbitrary defiance of the democratic process. The people are entitled to know the facts, and when they do, we will begin to find solutions to our problems, both at home and abroad.

It is, I believe, obvious that nothing in this paper is intended to imply that Dr. Shockley either shares, or does not share, my views save as he is expressly cited or quoted.

Nathaniel Weyl

How Not to Write History

In the preface to his *Challenge to the Court,* Professor I. A. Newby proposes "to relate as straightforwardly as possible the major ideas of scientific racism, and to do so in a factual, objective manner." Had Dr. Newby adhered to this laudable purpose, he might have filled a gap in our knowledge and might even have produced a book of some scientific value. Unfortunately, he seems to have preferred the role of prosecutor to that of judge and to have been more interested in abusing his opponents than in understanding their thought. In the pages that follow, I shall not deal with Dr. Newby's tract as a whole, but almost exclusively with those parts of

340

it which misrepresent my opinions, my writings, and my qualifications.

The Charge of "Nativism"

In 1963, I collaborated with Professor Stefan T. Possony, Director of Political Studies at the Hoover Institution on War, Revolution and Peace, in writing *The Geography of Intellect*. On page 173 of his polemical work, Newby characterizes *Geography of Intellect* as "a collection of racist and nativist ideas. . . ." I shall defer consideration of the epithet "racist" until later; at the moment, I am concerned merely with the charge of "nativism." The word is defined in the *Random House Unabridged Dictionary* (1966) as "the policy of protecting the interests of native inhabitants against those of immigrants." American nativism, of which the Know-Nothing movement was perhaps the most notorious manifestation, was dedicated to opposing the immigration of people of other than Anglo-Saxon and North European stock on the theory that they were inferior, unassimilable, or both.

Does *The Geography of Intellect* oppose the entry of non-Anglo-Saxons or characterize them as inferior? On pages 93–99, Dr. Possony and I appraise China and Jewry as "the supreme instances of civilizations which set up elaborate and ingenious institutions to select men of exceptional mental ability and promote them into intellectual elite groups of more than average fertility." On page 183, we note "the astounding intellectual contributions of the Chinese in America in recent years in such fields as university teaching and research science, not to mention the Chinese Nobel Prize winners in physics. . . ." At pages 127–28 and 162–65, we present evidence of general Jewish superiority to all other groups in respect to musicality, psychometric intelligence, and quantitative contributions to the world's scientific and intellectual elites. In the light of these passages, it is difficult to see how any scholar of normal intelligence and integrity could have arrived at Dr. Newby's conclusion.

My 1966 book, *The Creative Elite in America*, discusses the pre-eminent Jewish role in the American creative minority and its historic causes in much greater detail than does *Geography*. At pages 73–75, it deals with Japan and China, concluding that "the Chinese and Japanese show up as outstanding elite groups in the American academic and professional world" and "seem to be rapidly emerging and advancing elements whose future contributions to the American creative minority will almost certainly be even greater than their present contributions."

Chapter XII of *The Creative Elite in America* is entitled "Some Implications for Immigration Policy." Since nativists are primarily concerned with immigration controls, one would have assumed that Dr. Newby would have given this chapter his close and careful attention. Had he done so, he would have discovered that I take sharp issue with such advocates of restrictive legislation as Professors Anthony Bouscaren and Joseph J. Spengler. He would have noted that I recommend a policy "directed toward admission of the intellectually gifted," and that I particularly urge liberalization of immigration policy toward those impoverished countries of Asia which lack the requisite domestic facilities for the training of viable intellectual elites.

Thus, Professor Newby's charge that either I or *The Geography of Intellect* is nativist is not only an unmitigated falsehood, but one that is clearly contradicted by my writings. On page 173, Newby refers to *The Geography of Intellect* and *The Creative Elite in America* and characterizes both of them. Under the circumstances, I should like to ask him this question: "If you have read these books, as you clearly imply on page 173, how do you reconcile your status as an historian with the misrepresentation of their contents?"

Attack on The Geography of Intellect

In appraising *The Geography of Intellect,* Newby (p. 175) suggests that Dr. Possony and I were "jesting" and that we intended the book "to be a satire on racists and racism." He even fantasizes that *Geography* was "so patently absurd" that "racists" may have seen through it and decided to ignore it. Now the review of *Geography* which Newby cites (p. 173) is a hatchet job by Martin Mayer in *Commentary*. Newby is foolish enough to quote the Mayer review as stating that *The Geography of Intellect* contains "a relatively complete list of what it is we shall overcome." Now if our book contains the evidence and theory that Mayer, Newby, and other equalitarians must refute, then it can hardly be "patently absurd."

Since *The Geography of Intellect* advanced hypotheses concerning the relation between history and civilization which are unpopular at the moment, its review coverage was generally adverse. Newby's statement that the book was "systematically ignored" is, however, a misstatement and a distortion of the facts. Psychologists, geneticists, and anthropologists, whose emotional commitment to the civil rights movement was sometimes just as strong as Newby's, took issue with us, but they neither ignored *Geography* nor descended to Newby's vituperative and sneering level. To give a few examples:

Professor Otto Klineberg of the University of Paris, who has pioneered in studies purporting to show that Negro-white differences in IQ are environmental in origin, devoted three pages of the *Harvard Education Review* to a critique. Klineberg took issue with us for such offenses as having asserted that the results of the Scottish IQ Survey were consistent with a secular decline in Scottish intelligence and for having overlooked a disclaimer in his own writings, observing finally that the book was "interesting and well-written and contains a large number of valuable references."[1]

Another critical review was that by Dr. L. C. Dunn, Professor of Zoology at Columbia University, an outstanding authority on genetics and co-author with Professor Theodosius Dobzhansky of *Heredity, Race and Society*. Writing in the *Political Science Quarterly,* Dunn found us over-dogmatic, but he noted that the section on name-frequency analysis was an "original contribution by Mr. Weyl" and took pains to summarize the method used and the conclusions reached by it.[2]

A third and final example is the review by Dr. Edward E. Hunt in the *American Journal of Physical Anthropology*. While Hunt found fault with an excessive "stress on genetics," he wrote: "Despite their fervent eugenic position, Weyl and Possony are Jeffersonians in maintaining that the intellectual vigor of a nation depends on abundant gene flow from the masses to the elite, and the maintenance of intellectual and moral vigor in the most responsible members of society.

"In a modest way, *The Geography of Intellect* is a worthy contribution to the literature of universal history, as exemplified by such luminaries as Spengler, Toynbee and Kroeber." [3]

1 Otto Klineberg, review of Weyl, Nathaniel and Stefan T. Possony, *The Geography of Intellect,* in *Harvard Educational Review,* XXXIV (Fall, 1964), 610.

2 L. C. Dunn, review of Weyl, Nathaniel and Stefan T. Possony, *The Geography of Intellect,* in *Political Science Quarterly,* LXXIX (June, 1964), 289.

3 Edward E. Hunt, review of Weyl, Nathaniel and Stefan T. Possony, *The Geography of Intellect,* in *American Journal of Physical Anthropology,* XXII (March, 1964), 121.

These passages will enable the reader to judge the truth of Newby's assertion (p. 175) that *The Geography of Intellect* was "systematically ignored" and may assist him in differentiating between intellectually responsible and reputable criticism and the sort of attack contined in Newby's volume.

Let me now consider the manner in which Dr. Newby reports and summarizes the ideas of those from whom he dissents.

Quoting *The Geography of Intellect*, Newby writes (p. 174): " 'The I.Q. distributions of Protestant nations,' the authors remark solemnly, 'tend to be markedly higher than those of Catholic nations.' " The adjective "solemnly" is injected to make the reader conclude that the observation is ridiculous. It is, I believe, of some interest that Newby should be so unfamiliar with the literature in the field which his book discusses that he does not recognize that the etiology of Catholic-Protestant IQ and achievement differences is an old problem. Hunt, in the review just cited, refers to the topic as "the allegedly dysgenic effects of clerical celibacy" and correctly observes: "This putative genetic mechanism has bemused a long line of scholars—notably Galton and Max Weber."

Newby (p. 175) sneers at Possony and me for referring to "the results of the 1960 Olympic Games to demonstrate the musculature of racial and ethnic groups and the 'apparent geographic and ethnic concentration of prowess in sports.' " He is presumably ignorant of the fact that Dr. J. M. Tanner launched an anthropological study of Olympic athletes in 1960, published as *The Physique of the Olympic Athlete,* and that a considerably broader inquiry into the genetic and biological factors favoring the development of athletic prowess was scheduled for the 1968 games under the leadership of Dr. Alfonso Leon de Garay, director of the genetics and radiobiology program of the National Nuclear Energy Commission.

Dr. Newby's summary of *The Geography of Intellect* is less than competent. He has failed to grasp the main threads of the argument or to present the position he attacks as a coherent whole. Thus, on page 174, he states that Possony and I infer "the inferiority of the [Negro] race" from the psychological findings of Dr. J. C. Carothers and his associates and from the views of such people as Jefferson, Montesquieu, and Hume. This, like so much of what Professor Newby writes, is a crass distortion of our views. The opinions of Jefferson, Montesquieu, Hume, and others were presented as part of a summary chapter on the history of ethnopsychology. They are relevant to the history of thought about race, but, like other pre-scientific judgments, have no validity in terms of an appraisal of the Negro's contemporary mental status.

The three books of mine which Professor Newby cites, and thus inferentially claims to have read, deal with such potential causal factors for the Negro's shortfall in psychometric intelligence as: dearth of mental stimulus and defective evolutionary selection for intelligence in tropical habitats, the competition between brain and heat-equilibrating mechanisms for blood supply in high temperatures, the influence of racial somatic differences, particularly in pelvic structure, on brain shape and size, etc. The evidence for genetically caused differences includes: racial differences in cortical size and in brain histology, ethnic differences in neonatal kinesthetic maturation rates, race differences in electroencephalographic patterns and their possible implications, the inferences which can be drawn from intelligence test scores under varying conditions of control, etc. I should not have expected Dr. Newby to summarize Possony's and my findings in these areas because, after looking at his book, I doubt he has the training to do so. However, I should have expected a conscientious historian to have informed his audience that this material is compiled, presented, and analyzed in *The Geography of Intellect* and constitutes the basic evidence upon which the book's conclusions rest.

The Charge of "Racism"

Rather than attempt a dispassionate presentation and analysis of my ideas and those of Professor Possony, Newby attempts to place us in Procrustean categories to which he attaches derogatory or abusive labels. With monotonous regularity, he refers to Possony and me as "racists" or "popularizers of scientific racism." Since the term "racism" suggests Nazi extermination camps, one would have supposed that a conscientious scholar would have taken great pains to avoid its indiscriminate use, particularly in the case of writers who have been consistently anti-Nazi and who have consistently advocated equality of opportunity under law for all races.

What does Professor Newby mean by "racism"? Since he is in the habit of calling his opponents "racists," a precise and unambiguous definition would seem indicated. If a man is accused of a crime, he should be told the nature of the offense. But Newby gives at least three definitions of "racism." These are vague, incompetent, and/or mutually inconsistent.

On page xi, Newby states that "scientific racism" rests on such assumptions as "that human nature is fixed by heredity and immune to environment." This definition suffers from the fatal disadvantage that nobody with scientific training could possibly believe that man's mind and character are "immune to environment." Hereditary and environmental factors continuously interact to create, shape, and transform human psychic qualities. There is disagreement as to the specific modes and processes of these interactions and as to the comparative importance of the two sets of factors in various situational contexts, but that is all. The all-or-nothing issue posed by Newby is merely another instance of his tendency to debase the intellectual coinage of his contemporaries.

On page xii, Newby makes a second attempt and informs us that racism "suggests a belief in innate racial inequality, including the corollaries of Negro inferiority and white superiority." This is clear enough. It places contemporary American "racists" in such congenial and distinguished company as that of Thomas Jefferson, James Madison, James Monroe, Abraham Lincoln, and William Howard Taft. (It is indicative of Newby's mental confusion that he assures his readers on page 217 that the late Dr. Albert Schweitzer was no racist and made no plea for "anti-Negro racial policies." Yet in the same breath, he quotes Schweitzer as stating: "The negro is a child, and with children nothing can be done without use of authority." Childhood in adults implies inferiority. Most of Newby's civil rights colleagues would consider that treating colored people as children was an "anti-Negro" policy. (Presumably, Professor Newby's difficulty in this area is that he would like a definition of "racism" which would include all those people he dislikes, but would exclude all those who are respected, if not venerated, by intelligent and educated Americans.)

Newby's third attempt at definition (also p. xii) reads: "I have therefore applied the term 'racist' to anyone who advocates racial policies such as segregation, civil disabilities against Negroes, and prohibition of racial intermarriage—policies which are meaningful only if the races are inherently unequal. A 'racist' is thus anyone who believes in racial inequality and/or advocates the above racial policies, and a 'scientific racist' is one whose racism rests chiefly on science or pseudoscience."

The reader will note that, in his first two attempts at definition, Newby made the criterion acceptance or rejection of certain statements of fact about races; in this third floundering attempt, he shifts his ground to advocacy of certain social or political policies as the touchstone. Now "racism" is *either* a matter of entertaining certain beliefs about the nature of ethnic groups *or* it is a matter of advocating certain political changes. It cannot simultaneously be both unless one necessarily follows logically from the other. There seems to be some dim awareness of this difficulty in Newby's mind, so he adds the statement that discriminatory policies are "meaningful only if the races are inherently unequal."

The trouble with this statement is that it is simply untrue. It is another instance of Professor Newby's tendency to oversimplify and distort any intellectual concept which he attempts to express. One can advocate segregation of Negroes without considering them to be genetically inferior. As I understand it, this is the officially proclaimed position of the Republic of South Africa. One can believe that two peoples may be equal, but that their mores, history, institutions, languages and civilizations are so mutually incongruent that they cannot possibly form a single nation and therefore should be kept apart and prohibited from interbreeding. One can favor segregation on aesthetic grounds; one can believe that the two races are equal, but that their hybrids are inferior; there are doubtless many other possibilities. In suggesting these options, I am not presenting views that I hold, but am merely illustrating the slipshod logic of Dr. Newby.

If to be a racist one must advocate segregation by law, civil disabilities based upon race, and the banning of interracial marriages, then I am not one. As I stated in *The Negro in American Civilization* and have since reiterated elsewhere: "The sensible solution would seem to be the separation of pupils, not on the basis of race, but on that of intelligence, aptitude and school achievement, providing separate classes, courses and, where possible, separate schools for the superior, average and retarded (pp. 318–19)." As for racial intermarriage, I wrote in the same book: "The right to marry the person of one's choice is more basic than the right to attend a mixed school (p. 248)."

Newby's confused attempts to define "racism" both in terms of factual judgments and value judgments proceed from his simplistic assumption that only one specific social policy can follow from a specific set of genetic premises (p. 12). This is quite untrue. If we conclude that the Negro population, as a whole, is markedly less gifted mentally than the Caucasian or Mongolian population and that this difference is partially of genetic origin, it does not necessarily follow that race segregation is a desirable social policy. We are not dealing here with typological absolutes, with discrete yes-or-no situations, but with the statistical characteristics of populations. We know, for instance, that only about 8 per cent of the Negroes taking the Armed Forces Qualification Test equalled or exceeded the median white score. Since these 1966 figures refer to a national sample of ten million men between the ages of eighteen and twenty-six, they are representative. We hypothesize that this Negro overlap might rise to 12 per cent, because of sex-differences in IQ frequency distributions between the two races, if women were included. We have some reason to believe that the Negro overlap is showing a declining secular trend, possibly because of a higher inverse correlation in the Negro than in the white population, between SES and fertility.[4] Even given this somewhat alarming picture, legislated school segregation by race would not effectively achieve the goal of grouping students in accordance with their learning ability, but would penalize the mentally normal and superior Negro minority and over-reward the mentally retarded white minority. Racial segregation cannot be justified as a means of grouping students by intellectual ability as long as more accurate and refined means (IQ tests, other psychological tests and academic records) are available. In broader terms, the fact that groups may differ in innate ability does not justify their segregation by law nor is this difference incompatible with the basic American political premises of representative government and equality under law.

Two Minor Derogatory Observations

On page 78, Newby applies another epithet to me—this time "ultraconservative." I suppose this connotes someone whose religious beliefs are orthodox or fundamentalist, who is a Puritan in sexual matters, who wants social security abolished, who repudiates deficit spending and Keynesian economics, who disapproves of foreign entanglements and international commitments, who wishes to return to untrammeled state rights and who dreams that the federal

[4] Arthur R. Jensen, "Social Class, Race, and Genetics: Implications for Education," *American Educational Research Journal*, V (January, 1968).

government will shrink to McKinley-era dimensions. If so, I hold none of these views. The fact that I do not hold them is evidenced by numerous articles and speeches I have written or delivered over the years. Under normal circumstances, Professor Newby would be under no compunction to be that familiar with my thoughts and utterance. When he tries to put me into one of his pigeonholes, however, he falls under a moral obligation to know what he is talking about.

On page 163, Newby makes the gratuitous observation that I am not a scientist, a comment calculated to persuade readers to ignore my writings as not based on adequate formal training. The facts are briefly these: After taking an undergraduate degree at Columbia University in economics and philosophy, I did two years of postgraduate work toward a Ph.D. at Columbia University and the London School of Economics in economic theory and international finance. I did not take my doctorate, preferring a position in the United States government as economist. I have served as chief of Latin American research for the Board of Governors, Federal Reserve System; worked as an expert in the reorganization of Latin American central banks; chaired the Interdepartmental Balance of Payments Committee—all positions which require professional competence in economics. I have written on international banking and international financial theory in such places as *Collier's Encyclopedia* and the *American Economic Review*. I am and/or have been a member of such professional societies as the American Economic Association, American Political Science Association, American Statistical Association and National Academy of Sciences, India, to name only a few. In the field of Latin American studies, my name is on at least one roster and bibliography of experts. As for anthropology and ethnology, I believe I am the only one of those whom Newby attacks in his book who is cited for original work in the text and footnotes of Carleton S. Coon's *The Living Races of Man* (1965). I do, however, plead guilty to not being an employee of a university or research institution. I do not find the salary either pays to be an inducement.

A Few Loose Ends

One of Professor Newby's less attractive devices is to denigrate his opponents by citing attacks against them in eminent periodicals and *per contra* defenses in obscure or far-right journals. Two instances will suffice:

In dealing with Carleton S. Coon's controversial and brilliant *The Origin of Races* (1962). Newby cites the hostile views of Theodosius Dobzhansky, one of the foremost living geneticists, and of Ashley Montagu, who is nationally known as a popularizer of anthropology and other subjects. *Per contra,* he juxtaposes an article by Carleton Putnam in some newspaper I have never heard of and my evaluation of Coon's book in *National Review,* an organ of conservative opinion, but not of science. The inference the reader will be inclined to draw is that the entire scientific community bore down on Coon's head like an avalanche for his temerity in proposing the thesis of prehominid raciation.

Professor Newby neglects to inform his readers that Dr. Coon's book was reviewed in *Science,* the outstanding scientific periodical in the United States, by Ernst Mayr, professor of zoology at Harvard, who called it "a milestone in the history of anthropology." As for Professor Mayr, his *Animal Species and Evolution* (1963) was praised by Dobzhansky and hailed by Sir Julian Huxley in *Nature* as "certainly the most important study of evolution that has appeared for many years—perhaps even since the publication of *The Origin of Species* in 1859."

Newby used the same ploy on Dr. Audrey Shuey's *The Testing of Negro Intelligence.* Newby cited a B'nai B'rith-sponsored questionnaire to four social scientists as representative of the critical reaction to the book. Since the B'nai B'rith is fervently committed to civil rights and its underlying ideology of Negro-white equality, four "experts" were found who dutifully reported that Dr. Shuey had failed to prove genetically-based Negro inferiority in intelligence. No doubt the governor of Mississippi could have found four equally qualified persons to report a contrary verdict. In any event, the question had practically nothing to do with the value of the book.

Professor Newby goes beyond this and tells us that social scientists were "almost invariably critical" of the Shuey book. Newby (p. 78) cites my characterization of the Shuey survey as "definitive" as the judgment of "a disseminator of ultraconservative and racist views," abusive characterizations the falsity of which I have already demonstrated. He neglects to inform his readers that the Shuey volume was highly praised by Professor Dwight J. Ingle of the University of Chicago in *Perspectives in Biology and Medicine* or that

Professor Arthur R. Jensen, of the Center for Advanced Studies in the Behavioural Sciences and the University of California, Berkeley, referred to it as presenting "all the evidence of Negro-white intellectual differences based on such tests. . . ." Let me add that I do not believe that nose counts, even of distinguished scientists, are a means of proving or disproving the truth of any proposition. I go into this matter merely because Professor Newby prefers marshalling authorities to a more reasoned approach and, since it is my tedious task to disclose his departures from objectivity, his misinterpretations, and his false statements, I am obligated to follow him into this dreary terrain.

The Case of Dr. Simon Biesheuvel

Finally, I should like to comment briefly on Newby's derogatory and distorted statement about Dr. Simon Biesheuvel. My reasons for doing so are that Newby has thrown so much more mud on other people that this reference is likely to pass unrefuted, particularly since its victim is a resident of South Africa. All that Newby says about Biesheuvel is that he "described Negroes in much the same language as Carothers, Stevens, and Galton" and that he did not offer "any empirical evidence to substantiate" his position.

At the risk of being repetitious, let me say that Newby is again distorting the facts. What Biesheuvel said, as quoted by George, was: "The effective intelligence of Africans, in terms of ability to reason, to make adjustments to the needs of Western technological society and to profit by higher education, is appreciably below the mean of European communities." Thus, his comment is not at all "much the same" as the characterizations of Negro emotional attitudes quoted from Carothers and Stevens. Is it comparable to Galton's assertion that the African native exemplifies the "incapacity of savages for civilization. . . ."?

Obviously, it is not. When Biesheuvel says *"effective* intelligence," he is referring to African intelligence, as it today is, without any reference to what it may in future become. Newby's complaint that Biesheuvel adduces no evidence in favor of his belief is silly on two grounds. First, it is hardly necessary to document the assertion that tribal Africans perform much more poorly than whites in reasoning, technology, and school work because the vast amount of data available is in agreement on this point. Second, when Professor Newby states that Dr. Biesheuvel has not presented any empirical evidence, he is displaying a degree of effrontery matched only by his ignorance. Dr. Biesheuvel has probably done as extensive, far-ranging and valuable investigations of the African native mind as any living person. I append as a footnote a listing of a few of Biesheuvel's papers.[5] A circumstance that makes Newby's slur on Dr. Biesheuvel ironic is that he is attacking a psychologist who is regarded in South Africa as perhaps the most outstanding scholarly liberal on the race issue, who has consistently combatted the view (which I personally hold) that the weight of the evidence points to genetically-caused Negro inferiority in respect to intelligence, and who has pioneered in relating defects of the African native mind to foetal, neonatal, or subsequent *kwashiorkor* [severe malnutrition].

I have found this task of refutation tedious because Professor Newby never rises to a level of intellectual competence at which discussion could be rewarding. As a history of a scientific controversy, *Challenge to the Court* is a bad book because its author is so ignorant of genetics, psychology and cognate disciplines that he makes such fundamental errors as trying to apply typological thinking to situations of population dynamics[6] and entering into con-

---

[5] *African Intelligence* (South African Institute of Race Relations, Johannesburg. 1943); "Psychological Tests and Their Application to Non-European Peoples," Chapter 4 in *The Yearbook of Education* (London: Evans Bros., 1949); "The Study of African Ability," Parts 1 and 2, *African Studies*, II (University of Witwatersrand, 1952); *Race, Culture and Personality* (Johannesburg: Institute of Race Relations, 1959); "Objectives and Methods of African Psychological Research," *Journal of Social Psychology*, XLVII (May, 1958) 161–68; *The Development of Personality in African Cultures* (London: Scientific Council for Africa, 1959); "The Effects of Cultural Factors on Intelligence-test Performance" (with R. Liddicoat), *Journal of the National Institute of Personnel Research* (1959); "The Measurement of Occupational Aptitudes in a Multi-Racial Society," *Occupational Psychology*, XXVIII (October, 1954); "The Influence of Social Circumstances on the Attitudes of Educated Africans," *South African Journal of Science*, LIII (July, 1957), 309–14; "Methodology in the Study of Attitudes of Africans," *Journal of Social Psychology*, XLVII (May, 1958) 169–84; *Entwicklungspolitik, Handbuch and Lexicon* (Stuttgart, 1966); "The Nation's Intelligence and Its Measurement," *South African Journal of Science*, XLIX (October–November, 1952); "Symposium on Current Problems in the Behavioural Sciences in South Africa: The Growth of Abilities and Character," *South African Journal of Science*, LIX (August, 1963); "Behavioural Adaptation to Hot Climates," *South African Journal of Science*, LXII (January, 1966); "The Development of African Abilities," speech to the University College of Rhodesia, October 3, 1966.

[6] Ernst Mayr, "Agassiz, Darwin and Evolution," *Harvard Library Bulletin*, XIII (Spring, 1959); Ernst Mayr, *Animal Species and Evolution* (Belknap Press of Harvard University Press: Cambridge, Mass., 1963); G. G. Simpson, "The Role of the Individual in Evolution," *Journal Washington Academy of Science*,

troversies that are obsolete.[7] I believe he has shown himself to be an equally bad historian because he cannot stand outside of his own prejudices. The historian should pursue the goal set by Leopold Ranke: *"Ich will bloss sagen wie es eigentlich gewesen ist."*

XXXI (1941), 1–20; Theodosius Dobzhansky, "Variation and Evolution," *Proceedings of the American Philosophical Society*, CIII (1959), 252–63.

[7] For instance, Newby's point that intelligence test scores cannot tell us directly to what extent I.Q. differences are due to genetic factors. This is universally conceded. There is, however, no discussion of such relevant factors in the study of the relationship of I.Q. to genetic differences in intelligence as: studies of orphanage children institutionalized from birth (same environment, diverse heredity); concordance rates of monozygotic and dizygotic twins for I.Q.; I.Q. scores of monozygotic twins reared apart (same heredity, diverse environment), and Galtonian regression to the mean in respect to I.Q. On this, see Jensen, "Social Class, Race and Genetics"; Loise Erlenmacher–Kimling and Lissy F. Jarvik, "Genetics and Intelligence: a Review," *Science*, CXLII, 1477–79 (December, 1963.)

tionists, to vote, but opposed prohibition or integration, could we infer that he would deny them the right to vote for either? Is the "right to vote" defined by Newby as "the right to vote my way only?" There is no evidence that Garrett so defines it. As though his idea were not silly enough, Newby then proceeds to blame "scientific racists" for not having satisfactorily resolved the "paradox" produced by his own defective reasoning (p. 98).[2]

II
Pro Domo Mea

"Racists," Newby writes (p. 79), "were not impressed" by Melvin Tumin's (ed.) *Race and Intelligence,* and he mentions me as the (only) unimpressed racist. He does not give my views.[3]

For good reason. Tumin's authors say that "the concept of native intelligence is essentially meaningless" because native intelligence cannot be measured. I pointed out that one does not follow from the other (nor does nonexistence follow); further, if genetic inheritance is standardized (as it is with monozygotic twins), differences in performance must be due to learning; this permits us to measure the contribution of learning, and thus of inheritance, to tested "intelligence." The same could be done also if learning opportunity were standardized; or if tests excluded learned material—which is more difficult but not impossible in principle. I also pointed out that H. G. Eysenck (a well-known English psychologist and no racist) concludes, as do many others, that "tests of mental ability" are "surprisingly successful" in measuring "innate factors," the evidence being "by now quite conclusive." Anyway, it is inconceivable to me that Albert Einstein became—well, Einstein—only because of a favorable environment; and I. A. Newby became—well, Newby—only because of an unfavorable one.

Innate differences among individuals indicate the possibility of innate differences of average intelligence among groups—e.g., Negroes and whites—but not the actuality. I went on to stress that we do not know to what extent the observed difference in average in-

---

[2] Incidentally, Newby, described as "Professor of History," asserts (p. 99) that Negro "voting strength" has brought about integration. That must be news to his colleagues.

[3] See my "Intelligence or Prejudice," *National Review,* Dec. 1, 1964, pp. 1059–63.

telligence is genetic or environmental. (Since I wrote, evidence for the genetic possibility has accumulated; I still do not think it conclusive, though it is certainly suggestive.) Nothing in Newby's comment here indicates why I was wrong to be unimpressed by Tumin's booklet which argued for opposite views. I now am unimpressed by Newby too.

Later Newby quotes me, correctly (p. 181–82), as concluding that improvement of education for all requires separation according to ability, which at present will largely amount to separation of whites and Negroes.[4] Newby points out—as though I hadn't—that "tracking" would place the more intelligent Negro with white students but adds that I oppose this (p. 182). I do not. I merely warn that there are psychological problems to be overcome, most easily if "neither group objects" (p. 182). Prejudice is exacerbated by compulsion, particularly since, as I point out, the poor whites (who are, to begin with, the most prejudiced) could not, while the rich could, attend segregated private schools. (Sizable numbers of Negroes now prefer separate education—as I expected they would—though the reasons given often do sound "racist.") Wherein is it proof of "racism" to disagree with the Supreme Court on whether people have a constitutional right to voluntary segregation or congregation, for the sake of whatsoever prejudice when—as I (but not the Court) think—it does not inflict damage? I also disagree with Mr. Newby on how to reduce prejudice. I may be wrong, but I am not shown to be by being called "racist." Mr. Newby offers no other argument—and does not reproduce mine.

* * *

Newby (p. 182) asserts gratuitously that I believe "that segregation, not integration, is the natural state of race relations." I don't. Nature never told me anything about race relations, which I believe are determined by social preferences, none of which is more "natural" than the other. My own preference is for (1) noncompulsiveness, (2) integration. I would not sacrifice (1) to (2)—which is my actual difference with Newby.

* * *

Newby believes oddly enough (p. 182) that, according to William Buckley's definition—"racists are those who treat people primarily

---

4 When the integrationist school board in Washington, D.C., noticed as much, it caused the pro-integration superintendent—who also favored ability "tracking" —to resign; a Federal court even prohibited "tracking" in Washington!

as members of a race" (a more intelligent and applicable definition than his own)—I am a racist, since I think that at times segregation by color "is educationally rational." Newby does not tell why this makes me guilty of treating people "primarily as members of a race." He must think that "primarily" means "ever" or "on any occasion." Whether his confusion is genetic, motivational, or due simply to insufficient command of the English language—which might be overcome by education—I do not know. But it seems "immune to the [collegiate] environment" in which Mr. Newby lives.

* * *

What Professor Newby does not quote from "Intelligence or Prejudice" is more significant than what he quotes, misunderstands, or distorts. As mentioned earlier, he accuses me of being a "racist" or "scientific racist," believing in "Negro inferiority and white superiority." Here is what I wrote on this point.

One may regard others as inferior to oneself, or to one's group, on the basis of any criterion, such as mating, eating, drinking or language habits, religious practices, or competence in sports, business, politics, art or finally, by preferring one's own type, quality or degree of intelligence, skin or hair color and so forth.

By selecting appropriate criteria each group can establish the inferiority of others, and its own superiority. This can be and is done by Texans, Democrats, workers, Yale alumni, Frenchmen, extremists, moderates, and Chinese. The selection of criteria for superiority or inferiority is arbitrary, of course. The judgment of inferiority applied to others thus remains a value judgment, even if the qualities judged to render people inferior are actual characteristics of the group so judged. I do not believe that intelligence is any more relevant to judgments of inferiority than, say, skin color is.

If Negroes on the average turn out to have a genetically lower learning ability than whites in some respects, e.g. the manipulation of abstract symbols, and if one chooses this ability as the ranking criterion, it would make Negroes on the average inferior to some whites and superior to others. Suppose four-fifths of Negroes fall into the lower half of intelligence distribution. Chances are that, say, one-third of the whites will too. Hence, if intelligence is the criterion, the four-fifths of the Negro group would be no more "inferior" than the one-third of the white group. (It seems clear that some such overlap would exist, regardless of what we will ever learn about native intelligence.)

Judgments of inferiority among whites are rarely based solely on intelligence. There certainly are many people who do not rank high on intelligence tests but are, nonetheless, preferable, and preferred, to others who do. I know of no one who selects his associates—let alone friends—purely in terms of intelligence. God knows, we certainly do not elect to political office those who are most intelligent. I would conclude that whatever we may find out about Negro intelligence would not entail any judgment about general inferiority. At present we do not know whether the average native intelligence of Negroes differs from that of whites with certainty any more than we know whether average native musical ability does. I cannot see why one should be of more importance for judgments of inferiority, superiority or equality than the other.

This is what Professor Newby read in my article "Intelligence or Prejudice." I am forced to conclude that he reads English no better than he writes it; or else he deliberately misleads his readers.

* * *

Reading comprehension is anyway not Newby's forte. Contrary to his statement (p. 180), I did not "accuse" Professor Kenneth Clark of "deliberately misrepresenting his own research." Instead I ended my controversy with him as follows: "From Professor Clark's experiments, his testimony and, finally, the essay to which I am replying, the best conclusion that can be drawn is that he did not know what he was doing; and the worst, that he did." [5]

The same alternative conclusions must be drawn from Professor Newby's book. However much inclined I am to believe that he was deliberate in misrepresenting my views, I have learned not to underestimate simple stupidity, particularly when abetted by fanaticism.

* * *

I originally objected to the Brown decision because it replaced legally compulsory separation (which I oppose) with legally compulsory togetherness (which I oppose as well).[6] I do not believe that compulsory congregation is constitutionally mandated, morally justifiable, or, finally, likely to reduce group hostilities. Newby insists on my "segregationist" views, even though his own quotations show that I oppose not congregation, but compulsion, and favor voluntary association or dissociation, i.e., freedom of association.[7] Newby argues (p. 181n) that "the efficacy of such a system [of free choice] in the deep South would of course be problematical." I guess that by "efficacy" Newby means effectiveness in achieving in-

[5] Ernest van den Haag, "Social Science Testimony in the Desegregation Cases— A Reply to Professor Kenneth Clark," *Villanova Law Review*, VI (Fall, 1960), 69–79.

[6] Ralph Ross and Ernest van den Haag, *The Fabric of Society* (New York: Harcourt, Brace, and World, 1957), 161–66.

[7] See also my "Negroes and Whites: Claims, Rights, and Prospects," in *Modern Age*, IX (Fall, 1965), 354–62, for a fuller statement on (and definition of) freedom of association, fair employment, etc.

tegration. In respect to freedom, welfare, education, and reduction of prejudice, I think my "system" has greater "efficacy" than the Court's. It's "efficacy" in achieving integration or, for that matter, the elimination of the boll weevil, is "problematical" indeed. A serious charge, had my "system" been intended as a means to achieve either.

*   *   *

Let me turn now to Newby's treatment of my controversy with Professor Kenneth Clark. Clark's experiments and his testimony in the lower courts "were utilized by the Supreme Court to provide a factual basis [for] its conclusion." [8] Because I believe that the Court—to an unspecifiable degree—was influenced by this "modern authority," and, that there is no other "factual" basis for the Brown decision, which requires us to believe as a fact that segregated schools are "inherently" unequal and harmful, I paid some attention to Clark's activities. I pointed out originally[9] that there was no scientific basis for Clark's conclusions. Clark replied [10] and I rejoined.[11] Even though he allegedly describes the views of those who offered a challenge to the Court, Newby gives Clark's side of the controversy (in a confused way) but makes no effort to give mine.

Newby tells us (p. 21) that in Clark's "brief, succinct report is (*sic*) found many of the basic ideas which social scientists later presented in testimony," and refers to "two ingenious tests, his famous doll test and a coloring test." He confuses two purposes which Clark rightly distinguishes: the testing of color discrimination *per se* and of racial awareness. Clark's results are described by Newby without indicating whether obtained in a segregated or mixed school, i.e., the point of the matter is left out. Newby (p. 22) adds that "to Clark 'prevailing social attitudes in his community' was (*sic*) the heart of the matter." Nonetheless, Newby also thinks that Clark believes his findings are specifically due to the "stultifying effects of segregation" (p. 22). We are not informed when or where Clark presented which of these interpretations; but we are told that Clark attributes harmful effects as well to the Negro

[8] Professor Philip Kurland in Kenneth B. Clark, *Prejudice and Your Child* (2nd ed.; Boston: Beacon Press, 1963). Clark enthusiastically agrees (*passim*).

[9] Ross and van den Haag, *The Fabric of Society*, 161–66.

[10] Kenneth B. Clark, "The Desegregation Cases: Criticism of the Social Scientist's Role," *Villanova Law Review*, V (Winter, 1960), 224–40.

[11] Van den Haag, "Social Science Testimony."

child's seeing "for himself that Negro schools are inferior to those reserved for whites" (p. 23).

Newby unfairly compounds Clark's own confusions. Unlike Newby, Clark knew that the question before the Court was not: Are "Negro schools (materially) inferior to those reserved for whites" and is this harmful? (This question was (a) *res iudicata* (b) excluded by stipulation.) Nor was it relevant to ask: Are prevailing "racial attitudes in his community" harmful to Negro children? The Court dealt *only* with the question: Is segregated education—when all material circumstances are equalized—still "inherently unequal" and (therefore?) harmful? Clark quite properly attempted to show that his experiments proved not that community prejudice is, nor that materially inferior schools are, harmful, but that segregation is. Newby is wrong—and Clark's testimony would have been entirely irrelevant were Newby right—when he says (p. 25): "[Clark's] tests were not designed to determine the specific effects of school segregation. . . ." (p. 25) They were presented for no other purpose, were undertaken with segregated and unsegregated children, and would have been irrelevant had they been considered merely "to show how Negro children are affected by life in [our] society . . ." (p. 25). The relevant question; to which I addressed myself, is, thus, quite simply: Did Clark show that segregation is harmful to Negro children?

The following verbatim extract from Clark's testimony in the Briggs case which I quoted indicates that Clark, unlike Newby, understood this point: (Newby points out [p. 32] that "the significance [of Briggs'] is apparent in the Brown decision.") ". . . my opinion is that a fundamental effect of segregation is basic confusion in the individuals and their concepts about themselves conflicting in their selfimages . . . this result was confirmed in Clarendon County . . . by the results of these 16 children [and is] . . . consistent with previous results which we have obtained in testing over 300 children."

I did, but Newby does not, make it clear that, deliberately or not, Clark misled the Court.[12] His Clarendon County testimony, indeed, all his testimony against segregation is totally inconsistent with his "results . . . in testing 300 children," contrary to his assertion. With these children, Clark found and honestly reported—before the Court cases—that more unsegregated and fewer segregated Negro

12 *Ibid.*

children prefer to play with the white doll, think that it is "nice" and identify with it, while regarding the black doll as "bad." [13] The "basic confusion," the "conflicting" which leads the children to be "definitely harmed in the development of their personalities" [14] as demonstrated by the preference for, and identification with the white doll happens to more unsegregated Negro children and to fewer (to a smaller proportion) of segregated Negro children. Yet, Clark misled the Courts into believing that the harm was produced by segregation, i.e., happened more frequently to segregated Negro children.

Somehow Newby never brings this out. He finds (p. 25) the space, however, to repeat over and over that Clark's work "represents the most advanced scholarship" (Heaven help us!), that Clark is a "preeminent authority" (p. 26), etc. Yet, Clark misled the courts, either deliberately, or because he does not understand the meaning of his "ingenious" experiments. His "preeminence" derives, paradoxically, from his race, not from his competence.

Newby uneasily attempts to play it safe by quoting Clark's later defense (p. 24) of his experiments—as groovy an instance of gobbleydegook as one can find. Clark is quoted (p. 24) to the effect —heads I win, tails you lose—that either, indeed any, outcome of his "experiment" shows that segregation is bad. In court he testified that segregation was bad, as shown by the harmful identification of segregated Negro children with the preferred white doll. But if his attention is drawn to the fact that he himself has reported— before his testimony—that a higher proportion of desegregated than of segregated Negro children do so identify, this *also* shows that segregation (not desegregation as would be logical) is bad: fewer segregated Negro children identify with the white doll only because they have "accepted as normal the fact of [their] inferior social status." [15] (Professor Clark neglected to acquaint the Court with this reasoning.) By his reasoning *either* outcome confirms Clark's hypothesis that segregation is bad; indeed, any conceivable outcome would. The "experiment," therefore, does not test

[13] Kenneth B. Clark and M. P. Clark, "Racial Identification in Negro Children," in Theodore M. Newcomb and Eugene L. Hartley (eds.), *Readings in Social Psychology* (New York: Henry Holt Company, 1947), 169–78.

[14] Clark testifying in Briggs. (He never attempted to *establish* harm, temporary or lasting, as distinguished from discomfort.)

[15] Why such an acceptance (whether or not morally deplorable) is a sign of pathology is not clear. It is not, unless all the lower classes and castes throughout history were sick.

the truth of this (or of any) hypothesis; it is irrelevant to any issue about segregation if interpreted as Clark interprets it. As originally interpreted to the Court, the experiment with three hundred children would show that segregation is better for Negro children than desegregation—although Clark affirmed the contrary.

Newby (p. 25) vaguely admits as much: "The value of Clark's findings is due not to the fact that they substantiate . . . but to the fact that they corroborate. . . ." Etymologically, "corroborate" means "strengthen." Dictionaries define "corroborate" to mean "make more certain," "confirm," or "establish." I thus find it hard to see how Clark's experiments do not "substantiate" but do "corroborate" what he wishes to prove. It is obvious that they do neither and have no value whatsoever, except to suggest lack of acquaintance with scientific method on the part of those who take them to "corroborate" anything, to be anything more than crude pseudo-scientific make-believe.[16]

There are additional reasons to question the experiment so curiously interpreted by Professors Clark and Newby. Clark nowhere validates the assumption that misidentification by a child indicates personality damage. Suppose teddy bears had been added to the dolls, and the children had preferred them and identified with them. Would we explain this by the higher status teddy bears enjoy in America or by the legal segregation of children from them? If not, why leap to this conclusion when Negro children identify with white dolls?

I wrote further:

Control tests—which unfortunately were not presented—might have established an alternative explanation for the identification of white with nice, and black with bad: in our own culture and in many others, including cultures where white people are unknown, black has traditionally been the color of evil, death, sorrow, and fear. People are called blackguards or black-hearted when considered evil; and children fear darkness. In these same cultures, white is the color of happiness, joy and innocence. We need not speculate on why this is so to assert that it is a fact and that it seems utterly unlikely that it originated with segregation (though it may have contributed to it). Professor Clark's findings then can be explained without any reference to injury by segregation or by prejudice. The "scientific" evidence for this injury is no more "scientific" than the evidence presented in favor of racial prejudice.[17]

16 Both before and after sounding his ineptly defensive note, Newby describes Clark's experiment as "ingenious."
17 Ross and van den Haag, *The Fabric of Society*, 165–66.

Newby's "factual objective manner" appears to have prevented him from informing his readers of my alternative explanation of Clark's results. My article in the *Villanova Law Review* (quoted in material which Newby excerpts) is ignored.[18] This brings my esteem for Professor Newby's objectivity as a reporter to the level of my esteem for Professor Clark's objectivity as a scientist.

*   *   *

Newby's inaccuracies, misrepresentations, confusions and misinterpretations are so many that I can do little more than illustrate. He does not understand the Brown decision or the legal and philosophical arguments urged against it by myself and others;[19] nor is he aware of the pseudoscientific nature of the evidence accepted by the Supreme Court and the grounds for my criticism of Professor Clark. He does not distinguish between segregationists, who want to impose segregation by law, and people who, while not favoring segregation, think that such laws are constitutional; or those who think such laws unconstitutional—as I do—and that the compulsory togetherness which the Supreme Court has mandated is no less so. Newby does not see a difference between those who —as I do—think that what is measured as intelligence is partly innate, and those who feel that behavior characteristics are immune to the environment. (How I could practice as a psychoanalyst if I believed that, beats me.) Neither does Newby distinguish between people who believe that there are genetic differences among individuals and groups, including, possibly, differences of intelligence, and those who believe in "Negro inferiority and white superiority." It seems pointless to comment further on the work of an author so indiscriminate. Let me give just two more instances of the tactics employed.

Professor Isidor Chein surveyed the attitudes of social scientists on segregation; they thought segregation bad. His survey is quoted several times, but Newby nowhere mentions that Chein himself wrote: "Facts are not established scientifically by holding a poll

18 As Newby knows, it was my criticism of Clark that involved me in the controversy. Newby ignores it, as he does the Stell opinion (which largely follows my testimony), etc. He concentrates on misrepresenting my *National Review* article—which has little to do with Brown, his subject.

19 Newby writes (p. 192) that in the Stell case, intervenor's witnesses "resorted to an expediency" (*sic*) which would "justify denying [Negroes] the rights and privileges of citizenship" because they are "racially inferior." This is untrue. Moreover, the only issue was whether segregation is educationally rational or harmful to Negro children.

among scientists." Considering what the outcome of such a poll a hundred years ago would have been, this seems reasonable. (What would a poll on heliocentrism have produced in Galileo's time?) Only a minority of the social scientists polled had ever worked in race relations. Had scholars in the humanities been polled, the result would have been the same—and for the same moral and political (not scientific) reasons.

Newby several times quotes the physiologist Dwight J. Ingle as an authority (which he is) critical of findings of differences between Negro and Caucasian brains. He is. But Newby neglected to mention that Professor Ingle believes (as I do) that "the hypothesis that some races differ significantly in genetic endowment basic to intelligence and other qualities of intellect is credible and supported by a considerable amount of indirect evidence" and "the conclusion that individuals of different races are on the average equally endowed with the genetic bases of intelligence. . . . does not meet any of the requirements for proof [of] science." [20]

An accurate and fair case for the Brown decision and against the views of dissenters can be made. Newby has not made it.

* * *

Any inquiry into "racial" differences is now regarded as intolerable blasphemy against the "liberal" dogma that races are genetically equal. As I am writing (May, 1968) W. Shockley, a Nobel Laureate in Physics, who earlier had been asked to address a symposium of scientists at Brooklyn Polytechnical Institute, was asked not to do so, because in his address he wished to propose systematic scientific inquiry into genetic differences among human groups. Shockley's courage has become more exceptional than the repression of his views, the rudeness, and the fanatic intolerance of "liberal" dogmatists.

A historian might have investigated what social forces and ideological developments have produced this medieval atmosphere even among scientists and in universities. Professor Newby instead has written a *Malleolus Maleficarum* in which "racists" take the place of witches. Jacob Sprenger would have been proud of Newby's definitions. Any day now Professor Newby might see me flying over the rooftops to meet my co-conspirators. I shall wave to him and wish him good luck in his academic career. His zeal certainly deserves my respect. In his book nothing else does.

[20] *Perspectives in Biology and Medicine,* VIII (Spring, 1965), 403–408. Ingle elaborated on his views in *Science,* CXLVI Oct. 16, 1964, pp. 375–79.

I. A. Newby

A Last Word

The author who writes of sensitive subjects must be thick-skinned indeed. Whatever his approach or treatment, his work is certain to invoke strong, even passionate, reactions. The more apparent he makes his own "prejudices" and the more forthright his interpretations, the more likely he is to antagonize those who disagree with him. Serious and strong-minded men who reject his "prejudices" will surely dispute his interpretations. When they are themselves the object of his discussion, their disapproval is virtually certain. This not only inhibits the study of crucially important subjects, but precludes open, candid discussion between men of widely differing opinions. As far as I can discern, no one who has seriously studied race, racial attitudes, and racial policy is completely "objective" about them. Indeed, I fear that the recent Nergo revolt (and the white man's response to it) has further diminished our ability to discuss race dispassionately.

This conclusion, reached slowly and reluctantly over the last few years, has been reinforced in a personal way by the reactions to my book, *Challenge to the Court*. Though the book received less notice than I hoped it would, the reviews and comments were revealing. As a social scientist might phrase it, there was a high correlation between racial attitudes and reactions to the book. With a few exceptions, men whose racial views are what I would call "equalitarian" reacted favorably and found in my discussion substantial though varying degrees of merit. Without exception, apparently, those whose views are what I would call "non-equalitarian" found the book wholly without merit, with some in fact labeling it a malevolent disservice to the study of race itself.

In reactions as disparate as these, it seems to me, the book itself is not the only factor involved. Consider the responses printed above. Not one of the respondents finds any merit in the book. On the contrary, their responses are a catalog of charges that I smeared them personally and falsified, distorted, or misrepresented their writings and racial attitudes. When I first read them, I had visions of replying in kind to each charge and allegation—with twice the fervor and thrice the detail. Later reflection has convinced me this would serve no useful purpose. In every controversy there comes a time when disputation must cease and judgments be made. That time has clearly been reached here. I therefore ask the reader's indulgence for only a few general comments.

The discussion above of *Challenge to the Court* has generated much heat, but little light; there has been no real discussion of issues. In pages vilifying me, the respondents accuse me of vilifying them. In passages denigrating my intelligence and character and good intentions, they accuse me of denigrating theirs. Charging that I distorted and misstated their views, they distort and misstate mine. In paragraphs liberally sprinkled with invective and name-calling, they denounce me for allegedly using invective and calling them names. In sentences saturated with smears and loaded terms, they profess outrage at my alleged use of the same tactics. Displaying the most obvious emotions and biases, they denounce me for making subjective judgments and intruding my prejudices into the discussion of race. Accusing me of omitting evidence which contradicts my own viewpoint, they omit everything which disputes theirs (or undertake to explain it away). The list might be extended indefinitely—and pointlessly. The reader was no doubt struck by the disparity between the standards of logic, objectivity, and scientific methodology the respondents professed and those they practiced. I invite him to judge my discussion and theirs by both standards.

The tone of the responses is more striking than the substance. The factual errors reported are surprisingly few and inconsequential. Misstating Robert Kuttner's birthdate, Frank McGurk's alma mater, and the number of questions in one of McGurk's experiments is indefensible, but of little significance. Confusing the results of the arithmetic and reading tests administered by Professor Osborne, however, is significant, and more indefensible. I offer no excuse for such errors, and welcome the corrections.

But if factual errors were surprisingly few and generally inconsequential, allegations of distortion and misrepresentation were numerous and serious. I am charged with distortion by omission, for not noting, for example, the suit brought against Bozo Skerlj by *Mankind Quarterly*. I am further charged with distortion by commission, for mentioning, for example, Sir Oswald Mosley's association with a journal in which some of A. James Gregor's writings appeared. The former did not strike me as especially germane to my discussion and the latter did. I am also charged with being overly selective in discussing the respondents' writings and racial ideas. Checking these charges against what I wrote and both against the facts of the matter as I see them, I find no more distortions than are inevitable in brief summaries of long, involved views. (There is an exception to this involving Professor Gregor, which I will note below.) Much of the criticism stems from the fact that the respondents and I have different standards of relevance. I was not so much concerned with detailing their social and racial philosophies as I was with summarizing those ideas, drawn from science and social science, which have been used since 1954 to defend racial segregation, attack the Negro rights movement, and/or criticize the Brown decision. By that criterion, the essentials of my summary and commentary still seem defensible and valid.

Yet on this point of distortion and misrepresentation, which is the heart of the charges against me, the respondents and I are chasms apart, and there seems no prospect of reconciling our differences.

They cannot, they insist, recognize their own ideas in my summaries and discussion; I certainly do not recognize my ideas in their presentation of them. The impasse, I suggest, is a manifestation of our inability to discuss our own views on race without emotion. Their criticisms boil down to a charge that I simply did not understand the writings I discussed. The problem, I think, is not stupidity or malevolence, either on my part or theirs. It is instead, in large part, language. "Race" is a word so fraught with emotion and value judgments that language itself often hinders communication. Words do not always mean the same thing to men of widely differing views. Witness, for example, how much attention the respondents devoted to the meaning of words.

The respondents objected most vehemently to my use of "racist," "racism," and "scientific racism." These terms *are* emotion-laden, and it was for this reason that I defined them in the preface. Despite my definitions (or sometimes, it seems, because of them), the respondents without exception object to the terms and criticize my using them. Such words, they say, are smear words, the use of which conjure up scenes of storm troopers, gas chambers, and genocide. My use of "racist"—and I thought this was clear from my definition—was in its American context, where "racism" typically manifests itself not in genocide but in varying kinds of discrimination against minorities, and in ideologies which justify or rationalize the discrimination. It also includes ideas which *have the effect of making invidious distinctions* between races and ethnic groups, whether they are inspired by intentional malice or not. By these criteria I adjudged it "racism" for Professor George to urge, on the basis of his study of white and Negro brains, that interracial marriage was undesirable; for Professor McGurk to use psychological test scores to make what seem to me invidious comparisons between the educability of whites and Negroes; for Professor Osborne to use his study of Savannah school children as a basis for endorsing school segregation; for Professor Gregor to write that "where social science material is available, *it tends to support racial separation in the schools, at least through adolescence under conditions approximating equality of plant and instructions*" (his italics); for Mr. Weyl to write that "Negro Africa, the Middle East, Latin America, and Southeast Asia are genetically unpromising"; for Professor van den Haag to join the effort of Southern segregationists to overturn the Brown decision.

But having said this, I must concede that the respondents are probably right on this point. As a practical matter, the definition of a word is what people understand the word to mean. In retrospect, it is clear that my use of the term was unwise. If it did nothing else, it made it easier for critics to cry "smear." Were I writing the book again, I would avoid it. From the outset, I had questions about the term, but I never found a suitable substitute. I considered "non-equalitarian," "hereditarian," and "segregationist," but rejected them. The first, I thought, was awkward and the others too one-dimensional.

The problem of language, however, is broader than my use of "smear terms." Many words and phrases simply do not communicate the same thoughts to the respondents and me. Professor van den Haag, for example, uses the term "non-compulsiveness" to characterize the racial policies he supports, policies which he believes are sensible, meaningful, and moderate alternatives to the compulsions inherent in integration and the Brown decision. To further his "non-compulsiveness," he joined the effort segregationists made in the Stell case to reverse the Brown decision. To me, these things are irreconcilable. One man's "non-compulsiveness," it seems to me, is another man's compulsion. Repealing the Brown decision will only replace its compulsions with those of segregationists. The choice is not between "compulsiveness" and "non-compulsiveness." It is between alternative compulsions, and the relevant question is which compulsions are socially more desirable and justifiable. As long as anyone objects to segregation or integration, both will involve a measure of compulsion. Where racial feelings are intense, the kind of freedon of choice van den Haag endorses is impossible, and to urge repeal of the Brown decision in the name of "non-compulsiveness" is grotesque. Or so it seems to me. In any case, van den Haag and I have no meeting of the minds on "non-compulsiveness," or on the nature and substance of his explanations of it.

I have the same difficulty understanding Putnam's characterization of racial equalitarianism. It is, he says, "a fanatic's dream" whose adherents find it attractive because it affords them "the self-righteousness to vent their hatreds." In contrast, he writes, non-equalitarianism and attendant policies of segregation, especially in social relations, are rooted in "kindness and thoughtfulness of others." Everything I know about the history and present state of race relations suggests that Putnam's language is fanciful. It does not say to me what it apparently says to him. To me it is a striking example of the "Newspeak" of Orwell's *1984.*

The problem of language involves tone as well as terminology. The reader was no doubt struck by the remarkable difference in tone between the two responses of Professor Gregor. The first is emotional and subjective, full of moral outrage, injured innocence, broadside invective. The second is ostentatiously neutral, even bland, in language and presentation of data. It is obviously intended as an unemotional, scientific treatment of a serious subject. But when read carefully and measured against a more representative spectrum of literature on "social science research and the education of the minority-group child," it is hardly less subjective and argumentative than the first. Gregor selected from the literature those parts of it which support his contention that "there is no probative evidence and little presumptive evidence to suggest that introducing minority-group children into a biracial school environment is benign, much less beneficial." The point of his article, as I read it, is that Negro children are likely to find segregated schools more efficacious than integrated ones, though the negative nature of the above statement makes its precise implications for educational policy comfortably vague. Yet Gregor insists that his article should not be "conceived of" as "a brief for 'segregation.'" I wonder, then, how educators or laymen seeking guidance from "social science research" should construe it. Interestingly, the above conclusion is far less positive than his earlier statement on the same point (made in 1963) that available social science material *"tends to support racial separation in the schools, at least through adolescence under conditions approximating equality of plant and instruction."* If these statements are not suggestions that separate-but-equal schools are better for Negroes than integrated schools, I miss their meaning entirely.

My difficulties with Gregor include other problems of language. The reader will recall the amount of attention he gave to the definition of words. He attributed an Alice-in-Wonderland quality to my language, alleging that I used terms to mean whatever I wanted them to mean. Whether this be true or not, the reader must judge for himself. Certainly Gregor himself sometimes draws curious meanings from his own language. He has, he tells us, "a quixotic conviction that social criticism flourishes only in an atmosphere which permits all views to be heard, however reprehensible we may personally find them to be." He adds, "I might even venture to say something like 'I may find what they say abhorrent, but I will defend their right to say it,' but I'm sure that Mr. Newby would find this tedious." Now, I do not find this tedious at all. I find it admirable. I do not recall ever having tried to inhibit Professor Gregor's freedom of expression on any subject. But I do believe that his attempt to have *Challenge to the Court* removed from circulation was a curious way of honoring a conviction that "all views [should] be heard, however reprehensible we may personally find them to be." I shudder to think what his reaction would have been had he not been so dedicated to freedom of speech and "social criticism."

A considerable portion of Gregor's first response is devoted to analyzing my definitions of "racist" and "racism," and proving their inapplicability to him. His task here would have been less lengthy had he not passed so lightly over the central statement: "I have therefore applied the term 'racist' to *anyone who advocates racial policies such as segregation* [italics mine], civil disabilities against Negroes, and prohibition of racial intermarriage—policies which are meaningful only if the races are inherently unequal." Gregor was included under the label because I took his 1963 statement, quoted above, to mean that he thought that "*racial separation in the schools, at least through adolescence under conditions approximating equality of plant and instruction*" was desirable, inasmuch as available social science material "*tends to support*" it. I pointedly distinguished between his ideas and those of the other men I discussed by stating that his "intellectual orientation" was "vastly different" from theirs, and that he was in fact perhaps "unique" among them. I attributed to him only a few of the ideas from which he disassociates himself with such passion and at such great length. The "charges" I made against him revolved around two questions: Do his ideas concerning "social science research and the education of the minority-group child" add up to a "brief" for or an endorsement of school segregation? Do they contain any suggestion of racial inequalitarianism? I answered these questions "yes." These are, in essence, the things I "charge" him with.

Most of the distortions Gregor accuses me of relate to the fact that I did not discuss his views in the detail he thinks they merit. But his role in my story was not large, as he himself insists. It was in fact peripheral. Yet in rereading his writings, especially the most recent ones, I discern in them a dimension which was not apparent to me before. It seems clear to me now that his ideas on race have undergone a rather distinct evolution away from the sentiments I

stressed in my discussion, and toward greater caution and circum-
spectness. As I read his writings today, he now seems less willing to
emphasize nonequalitarianism or take at face value the claims of
non-equalitarians. His association with non-equalitarians seems less
close than it once was, when he collaborated on an article with
Clairette P. Armstrong; stated at the outset of his critique of the
social science aspects of the Brown decision that Henry E. Garrett
and Miss Armstrong "acted as consultants and are in substantial
agreement with" his conclusions; published several articles in Sir
Oswald Mosley's journal; and was an assistant editor of *Mankind
Quarterly*. I should have made this evolution clear in my original
discussion. But granting this, Gregor's response is not always convincing. As I read them again and study their context, his discussion
of the German race theorists during World War II, his reference
to the Indians of Guatemala, and his treatment of social science
evidence concerning school segregation do not seem to me as innocent or disinterested as he insists they are. The reader must
judge for himself.

The respondents have varying degrees of interest in public policy.
With some of them this is the primary concern and they explicitly
endorse racial separation, at least in social relations. Others seem
more interested in other things—science, the constitution, states'
rights, "individual freedom," the genetic quality of the American
people. My concern was, and is, racial policy.

This fact is central to an appreciation of what I tried to do in
Challenge to the Court and is obscured by the tone and language of
the responses. I am a historian, not a social scientist, and I made
no claim then, and make none now, to expertise in the sciences or
social sciences relevant to the materials I discussed. I do, however,
profess to know something about racial attitudes. My intention,
clearly stated, was to summarize and present the major ideas of
science and social science which have been used in recent years in
the defense of segregation. "My primary objective," I wrote, "was
to illuminate the segregationist mind." It was not, I might add, to
present or evaluate, either systematically or exhaustively, the vast
body of scientific data relating to race, racial genetics, comparative
racial intelligence and brain morphology, or other related subjects.
My intention was to explain what segregationists believe is the
scientific truth about race, and to do this by examining the ideas of
scientists and social scientists who endorse segregation or whose

writings segregationists cite, endorse, and circulate. My critique of those writings was intended to indicate the nature of their logic, authority, and data, and set forth their implications for racial policy. I cited scientists and social scientists who have criticized those writings to show that the views expressed in them are generally rejected in scientific and scholarly circles. If the precise and limited nature of my objective is recognized, much of the respondents' criticism appears in an altered light.

I also made no attempt to hide my own "prejudices." On the contrary, I stated them explicitly. Since no one is entirely objective about race and racial attitudes, it is imperative that those who write on these subjects understand their own "prejudices" and face them squarely. In my own mind, I doubt if "objectivity" is altogether desirable, if it means ignoring the problems of race relations or setting aside the ideals of democracy and justice. These things may be scoffed at as irrelevant to "scientific" inquiry. But it seems no more "prejudiced" to me to include them than to exclude them, especially where the latter leads to segregation and perpetuates inequality. Certainly equalitarians are no more "prejudiced" than non-equalitarians (the responses prove this) though some of the respondents seem to think they are. Both, I suggest, are fundamentally subjective, and their rightness or wrongness must be judged by the desirability of the social and political policies each advocates. None of this means that race is insignificant, or a "myth." It does not mean that I endorse a kind of neo-Lamarckian environmentalism, as George suggests I do. Nor does it mean, as McGurk alleges, that I believe "the available evidence demonstrates" that "there are no race differences." It means that racial policies, like all other public policies in America, must result from the give and take of the democratic process and be consistent with basic constitutional guarantees.

One other point merits a brief remark. I have no desire to stifle research on race, comparative racial intelligence, the genetics of racial inheritance, or anything else. Nor would I, even if I could, inhibit public discussion of these subjects. Like Putnam, I deplore any action which limits or discourages scientific inquiry and public discussion. But I do not agree that non-equalitarians satisfy their responsibilities on this point when they denounce "equalitarian dominated" scientific groups for allegedly discouraging research and discussion. As Putnam, Gayre, and others insist, there *are* a number of scientists and social scientists who dispute the premises of equalitarianism and stress the significance of race, heredity, and racial differences. The talent necessary for racial research is available outside equalitarian circles, and judging by the affluence of many conservative organizations and political movements today, adequate financial resources are too.

Those who have read through this controversy must long ago have been appalled by it. The entire episode has about it an air of monumental irrelevance, not to say incredibility. Here we are at this late date, grown men in a society threatened by racial holocaust, white men in a largely white nation in a largely non-white and restive world, arguing whether "social science research" and psychological test scores indicate that schools should be segregated along racial lines; whether the frontal lobes of Negro brains are underdeveloped enough to make interracial marriage unwise; whether Negroes are capable of exercising the responsibilities of citizenship; whether racial equality is a hoax; whether, in effect, the winds of racial change can be halted by what amounts to repressive measures of white supremacy. The argument would have been much more appropriate seventy-five years ago, when Americans were institutionalizing those racial practices and ideologies which today constitute the heart of the racial problem. The episode, however, is not without meaning. Certainly it reminds us that racial attitudes are intensely held. Perhaps it also reminds us in its own small way that the President's Commission on Civil Disorders spoke knowingly when it suggested that racial attitudes of white men are a major element in our racial difficulties today.

INDEX   *The Commentaries are not indexed.*

377